# Applications for Judicial Review

## Law and Practice of the Crown Office

# Applications for Judicial Review

## Law and Practice of the Crown Office

Second Edition

**Grahame Aldous LLB**
Barrister

**John Alder LLB, BCL**
Professor of Law, Keele University

**Butterworths**
London, Dublin, Edinburgh
1993

| | |
|---|---|
| United Kingdom | Butterworth & Co (Publishers) Ltd, 88 Kingsway, LONDON WC2B 6AB and 4 Hill Street, EDINBURGH EH2 3JZ |
| Australia | Butterworths, SYDNEY, MELBOURNE, BRISBANE, ADELAIDE, PERTH, CANBERRA and HOBART |
| Belgium | Butterworth & Co (Publishers) Ltd, BRUSSELS |
| Canada | Butterworths Canada Ltd, TORONTO and VANCOUVER |
| Ireland | Butterworth (Ireland) Ltd, DUBLIN |
| Malaysia | Malayan Law Journal Sdn Bhd, KUALA LUMPUR |
| New Zealand | Butterworths of New Zealand Ltd, WELLINGTON and AUCKLAND |
| Puerto Rico | Equity de Puerto Rico, Inc, HATO REY |
| Singapore | Butterworths Asia, SINGAPORE |
| USA | Butterworth Legal Publishers, AUSTIN, Texas; BOSTON, Massachusetts; CLEARWATER, Florida (D & S Publishers); ORFORD, New Hampshire (Equity Publishing); ST PAUL, Minnesota; and SEATTLE, Washington |



A CIP Catalogue record for this book is available from the British Library.

ISBN 0 406 00576 1

Typeset by Phoenix Photosetting, Chatham, Kent
Printed and bound in Great Britain by
Mackays of Chatham PLC, Chatham, Kent

# Preface

In this, the second edition of *Applications for Judicial Review*, we have attempted once more to bring together the viewpoints of a practising barrister and an academic lawyer to shed light on the complex procedures and substantive rules of judicial review. On some matters our views differ, but that is hardly surprising given the diversity of judicial opinion that emerges from the reported cases. We hope, however, that the bringing together of our differing viewpoints is of benefit when endeavouring to explain the fragmented and diffuse body of concepts, doctrines and presumptions of statutory interpretation that make up the law of judicial review.

We have expanded the scope of the second edition by including habeas corpus, case stated, statutory rights of challenge and statutory appeals. We have also included a separate chapter on the basic framework of the Crown Office List and the way that it operates.

Since the first edition the House of Lords has delivered the landmark decision in the GCHQ case which has given rise to the 'Diplock categories' for judicial review. These categories have severe limitations if treated too rigidly but they are now so universally adopted as a shorthand for reference to the basic concepts of judicial review that we have accepted them as a framework for analysis in this edition.

The role of the theory of ultra vires in questions of jurisdiction and nullity in judicial review is in decline as the courts lose patience with its limitations. Increasingly the courts are approaching problems as a matter of discretion. Whilst this approach allows a simplicity and flexibility that may be welcomed, it makes life difficult for academic lawyers to state the law, practitioners and litigants to measure the prospects of success and, ultimately, judges who end up in a dilemma as to how to exercise their discretion if it becomes too wide. Thus, we make no apology for referring once again to the historical background of judicial review in this edition since it is a necessary part of understanding the present condition of judicial review and providing a framework within which discretion can be exercised.

We have attempted to state the law on the basis of materials to hand on 15 February 1993.

Once again we have others to thank for their help and encouragement. We are especially grateful to Vanessa Knapp, Jackie Greatbach and to Mrs Knapman and the staff of the Crown Office for their help and comments.

*Grahame Aldous*
*John Alder*

# Contents

# Table of statutes

# Table of cases

PAGE

## C

## D

## H

PAGE

## L

PAGE

## X



## Y

CHAPTER 1

# Judicial review: introduction

## THE BACKGROUND TO A MODERN PROCEDURE

The purpose of this book is to examine the law and practice relating to that part of the activities of the High Court which would formerly have been called Crown Practice. In Chapters 1 to 16 we consider the law and procedure of judicial review. The procedure for obtaining the High Court's leave to apply for judicial review and for making the application is to be found primarily in Ord 53 of the Rules of the Supreme Court.

Before 1977 the procedures provided by Ord 53 were anachronistic and cumbersome remembrances of past times. As judicial activism grew apace with governmental social and economic activity, greater burdens were thrown on the procedures of the old King's Bench which had been designed for gentler times. Order 53 provided then, as it does now, exclusive procedures for obtaining the prerogative orders of mandamus, certiorari and prohibition. It was not possible, however, to seek declarations, injunctions or damages in the same proceedings as applications for prerogative orders. This led to problems similar to those experienced by litigants generally before the Judicature Acts 1873–75. Thus if they discovered that they had applied for the wrong form of relief they would be denied a remedy and would have to start again. The consequence of this was not only that the inflexibility of the courts deterred applicants from seeking relief but also that unwarranted distinctions arose between the various forms of relief.

In 1977 the first of two major modern reforms of Ord 53 was undertaken. It had been prompted by a report of the Law Commission in the previous year.[1]

The main changes in 1977 (in force January 1978) were as follows:

1. a single form of application was introduced, known as an application for Judicial Review. Within the single application the Divisional Court could grant such of the prerogative remedies as they saw fit;
2. applicants were for the first time allowed to claim declarations, injunctions or damages in an application under Ord 53. Such relief could be claimed either with or without a claim for a prerogative order. The language of the new Order appeared to permit rather than oblige applicants to seek relief other than prerogative orders by Ord 53;[2]
3. provision was made for interlocutory relief including discovery and interrogatories to be available to applicants for any of the remedies;
4. a uniform preliminary test of locus standi at the leave stage was introduced. The court was not to grant leave unless it considered that the applicant had sufficient interest in the matter to which the application related;[3] and

1 Report on Remedies in Administrative Law 1976 (Law Com no 73 Cmnd 6407). A more wide-ranging working paper under the same title had been published by the Law Commission in 1971 (1971 no 40) and a Law Commission Consultation Paper (1993 no 126) on Judicial Review and Statutory Appeals was published in January 1993.

2 See ch 10, below.

3 For the effect of this see ch 9, below.

5. the court was given a discretion to refuse to grant either leave to make an application or the relief sought where there was undue delay, or in the case of certiorari three months' delay, if it would be likely to cause substantial hardship to, or substantially prejudice the rights of, any person or would be detrimental to good administration. Previously there had been a limit of six months in the case of certiorari only. The court had power to extend time but would only do so when a strong case for it was shown. In the 1980 rule changes the 'good administration' test was removed in favour of a three-month time limit which the court could extend where there was good reason to do so. The 'good administration' test was, however, reintroduced as an additional test by s 31(6) of the Supreme Court Act 1981.[4]

The changes in 1977 produced a more logical and flexible form of application but they did little to clear the practical delays which had built up through the sheer volume of work under a system where the principal criterion for distributing judicial manpower was whether the application was made during a Law Term or during Vacation. It was to such matters of judicial efficiency that the second major reforms of Ord 53 in 1980 were directed. Even before the 1980 reforms there had been moves towards a better use of judicial time. These changes owed a great deal to a passion for efficiency shared by two men in particular. The first was Lord Lane who was appointed Chief Justice in April of 1980. He brought with him considerable vigour in comparison with the stupor that had befallen the Divisional Court during the last years of his predecessor, Lord Widgery, whose illness had deprived the Court of much-needed leadership. The second was Donaldson LJ who in 1980 was given the task of reducing the backlog of cases then awaiting a hearing before the Divisional Court. It took him six months to remove a waiting list of over 600 cases which had been waiting in the Divisional Court's List for over two years. Shortly thereafter he was, of course, to repeat the performance in the Court of Appeal when appointed Master of the Rolls in succession to Lord Denning. In an effort to reduce the waiting list the customary constitution of the Divisional Court as a three-judge court presided over by the Lord Chief Justice was broken down. The constitution of the Divisional Court was in fact provided for by s 63(6) of the Supreme Court of Judicature (Consolidation) Act 1925 which predicated a two-judge court as the normal structure. From 1979 such two-judge courts became more frequent and on occasions single judges sat to hear applications for judicial review.[5] The pressure on the judicial workload is undoubtedly a background factor when the courts consider such questions as the threshold for entertaining applications for judicial review, the scope of the jurisdiction and the exercise of the discretion to refuse a remedy. Judicial review is still regarded as a remedy of last resort.[6]

The 1980 rule changes (in force from January 1981) divided the work of the Divisional Court under Ord 53 between applications in criminal causes or matters and applications in other (ie civil) causes or matters. This distinction had already been in use, for example, in determining the method of appeal from the Divisional Court. In essence the rule changes provided that criminal causes or matters would be dealt with by a Divisional Court consisting of two or more judges whilst applications in civil cases would normally be dealt with by a single judge. In every case, however, leave to make an application could be

4 See below, ch 12.
5 For an excellent account of this period of change see Louis Blom-Cooper QC 'The new face of judicial review: administrative changes in Order 53' [1982] PL 250.
6 See eg *Puhlhofer v Hillingdon London Borough Council* [1986] AC 484, [1986] 1 All ER 467, HL.

dealt with by a single judge and would, if desired, be dealt with without even the necessity for a hearing.

Finally when Parliament passed the Supreme Court Act 1981 it took the opportunity to put the new structure of judicial review on an express statutory footing thus quietening earlier murmurs that the rule changes had been ultra vires the Rules Committee.

There is now, therefore, within the Queen's Bench Division a procedure specifically designed for dealing with matters of administrative law. All applications under Ord 53 and any other suitable cases come before the High Court in what is known as the Crown Office List,[7] and the cases are heard by judges of the Queen's Bench Division specially assigned for the purpose and therefore developing a suitable expertise. The Crown Office List has been likened to the Commercial List[8] within the Queen's Bench Division and some, including Lord Denning,[9] have expressed the desire that it be called the Administrative List. The most important procedural features of judicial review are the requirement to obtain leave, the short time limits and the rules on locus standi. These features reflect the fact that judicial review extends to persons without legal rights in the ordinary sense and also the range of third parties potentially affected when government action is challenged.

Judicial review proceedings are sui generis. They are not strictly speaking 'civil proceedings' between parties[10] and the doctrine of res judicata does not apply to the prerogative orders.[11] However, the court can make a binding declaration of individual rights.

Discretion is the keynote of judicial review. The remedies themselves are discretionary and the substantive concepts are sufficiently flexible to allow the courts to impose different levels of review in different contexts depending both upon the nature of the decision that is being challenged and the ground of challenge. The English courts do not adopt a strict 'rule of law' or separation of powers approach which distances them from the executive. For example in *R v Lancashire County Council, ex p Huddleston*,[12] Sir John Donaldson MR referred to a 'partnership' between courts and government to ensure high standards of public administration. This partnership requires that a decision-maker should disclose in judicial review proceedings, as far as necessary but no more, the reasons for its decision so as to enable the court to decide whether the decision was reached by taking into account irrelevant considerations or failing to take relevant considerations into account.[13] This must not be confused with a general duty to give reasons and applies only once leave to apply for judicial review has been given. Fishing expeditions are frowned upon. It is also presumed that all relevant factors have been taken into account unless the

7 See ch 19.
8 Although the Commercial List has a statutory basis in s 6 of the Supreme Court Act 1981.
9 *O'Reilly v Mackman* [1983] 2 AC 237 at 258.
10 *R v Greenwich London Borough Council, ex p Lovelace (No 2)* [1992] 1 QB 155, [1992] 1 All ER 679, CA.
11 *R v Secretary of State for Education and Science, ex p Avon County Council* [1991] 1 All ER 282, 284–5, CA; *R v Secretary of State for the Environment ex p Hackney London Borough Council* [1983] 3 All ER 358, [1983] 1 WLR 524. An issue reopened without good cause, however, may be struck out as an abuse of process, see *Hunter v Chief Constable of West Midlands Police* [1982] AC 529, [1981] 3 All ER 727, HL (now discredited on its facts but remaining good law).
12 [1986] 2 All ER 941 at 945, CA.
13 *Lloyd v McMahon* [1987] AC 625, [1987] 1 All ER 1118, CA; *R v Immigration Appeal Tribunal, ex p Khan* [1983] QB 790, [1983] 2 All ER 420, CA; *R v Civil Service Appeal Board, ex p Cunningham* [1991] 4 All ER 310, CA.

applicant can show otherwise.[14] The legal burden of proof, but not necessarily the evidential burden, lies with the applicant.

In *R v Monopolies and Mergers Commission, ex p Argyle Group plc*[15] Lord Donaldson MR expanded on the notion of good public administration. The court will use its discretionary power to refuse a remedy in the interests of good public administration. The court prefers substance to form in applications for judicial review and will not interfere if the applicant has suffered no detriment or where the defect would not in the court's view have affected the outcome. Good administration also requires speed, finality, consideration of third party interests and of the public interest in the particular statutory context. The court may therefore refuse to interfere if there is another convenient remedy, if the decision in question has been relied upon or if quashing it would cause serious disruption. A wide range of factors is taken into account including matters of cost effectiveness.[16]

Judicial review has become a victim of its own success. Despite the procedural reforms of the 1980s there are now backlogs and delays of up to two years. The panel of specialist judges assigned to Crown Office work has expanded to 18 and the rate of applications is increasing at about 20 per cent per annum. Recent legislation, including the Environmental Protection Act 1990, several Education Acts, and the Children Act 1989, has created extensive governmental powers.[17] Planning, immigration, housing (despite the decision of the House of Lords in *Puhlhofer v Hillingdon London Borough Council*[18]) and magisterial law also generate considerable caseloads.

However, many applications appear to be pursued with little possibility of success perhaps because the scope of judicial review is overestimated by lawyers and their clients or the desire for a public airing of a complaint to bring political pressure to bear outweighs an objective assessment of the prospects of success. In 1990, out of 2129 applications for leave only 902 were successful.[19]

An applicant must specify which remedy he is seeking out of the prerogative orders of declarations, injunction and damages. Any or all can be applied for except that damages cannot be sought without other relief.[20] The court in its discretion can grant whatever combination of remedies is most appropriate regardless of what an applicant actually applies for.

The introduction of the application for judicial review procedure and its subsequent confirmation by statute did not directly affect the substantive law relating to the scope of the individual remedies. In the case of the prerogative orders the existing law was expressly confirmed by s 29 of the Supreme Court Act 1981. The position with regard to the declaration and injunction is not so clear. The Act and Ord 53 require that in making a declaration or granting an injunction the Court must have regard to the availability of the prerogative orders. Apart from that the position depends upon whether it would be 'just and convenient' in all the circumstances of the case to make a declaration or

14 See below p 19.
15 [1986] 2 All ER 257 at 266. See also *R v Secretary of State for Social Services, ex p Wellcome Foundation Ltd* [1987] 2 All ER 1025 at 1032, CA.
16 See *R v Secretary of State for Employment, ex p Equal Opportunities Commission* [1992] 1 All ER 545 at 557–8.
17 See Woolf, [1992] PL 221. Sunkin (1992) *Journal of Child Law*, p 109.
18 [1986] AC 484, [1986] 1 All ER 467, HL.
19 [1992] PL 221 at 223, and see Sunkin [1990] PL 490 for a review of the use made of judicial review.
20 RSC Ord 53, r 7.

grant an injunction as the case may be.[1] The relationship between the two groups of remedies is a pervasive problem which we shall discuss in particular contexts.

## THE SCOPE OF JUDICIAL REVIEW

The basis of the power of the High Court to review decisions of inferior courts, public bodies and tribunals is that it can make such bodies do their duty and stop them from doing things which they have no power to do. The High Court cannot determine whether decisions are right or wrong on their merits. The procedure under Ord 53 is thus not an avenue for appeal against decisions.

If a public body is under a *duty* to perform a certain act then the High Court can order that the act be done. By such relief the High Court may be able to confer a direct benefit on an applicant and help him achieve his desired purpose. Where the High Court is being asked to control the exercise of a *power* by a public body, however, its ability to aid an applicant is less direct. The High Court cannot require that a power be exercised in any particular way, it can only require that the discretion lying behind the decision to exercise a power be used lawfully. In *Padfield v Minister of Agriculture, Fisheries and Food*[2] the House of Lords held that a minister had failed to exercise his discretion properly when considering whether to use his power to refer a complaint about milk prices to a Committee of Investigation. The evidence suggested that he had refused to act in case he was politically embarrassed by a favourable report from the Committee. The Court was unable to interfere with the price structure directly or even to order that the complaint be investigated by such a Committee. All it could order was that the minister exercise his discretion properly. Once the minister made a proper and lawful decision it remained possible that he would nevertheless have decided not to refer the complaint for investigation. Notwithstanding this limitation the *Padfield* decision was regarded as a breakthrough in judicial control of ministerial discretion.

## GROUNDS FOR JUDICIAL REVIEW: 'THE DIPLOCK CATEGORIES'

The various grounds for judicial review have been expressed in different ways in different contexts. One of the main problems faced by practitioners in attempting to define the grounds for judicial review is the inconsistent terminology adopted by the courts. Judges reach decisions on a case by case basis without the need or desire to worry about establishing a unified body of law. In their need to find a shorthand definition of the grounds for judicial review, practitioners have seized upon the so-called 'Diplock Categories' from the speech of Lord Diplock in the GCHQ case, *Council of Civil Service Unions v Minister for the Civil Service*.[3] Lord Diplock categorised the grounds of judicial review under three broad heads. These heads are illegality, procedural impropriety and irrationality and Lord Diplock stated that further grounds may be added by future developments on a case by case basis.[4] They have

1 Supreme Court Act 1981, s 31(2).
2 [1968] AC 997, [1968] 1 All ER 694, HL.
3 [1985] AC 374, [1984] 3 All ER 935, HL.
4 Ibid at 950; he expressly mentioned the possible development of the European Community concept of 'proportionality' but to date the courts have been unenthusiastic about attempts at such development.

become widely accepted as the classic statement of grounds for review even though they are so broad as to be almost meaningless on their own. Illegality includes acting ultra vires the governing legislation, errors of law, failing to take relevant factors into account and taking irrelevant factors into account. Procedural impropriety includes violating procedural requirements imposed by the governing legislation and also acting 'unfairly'. The notion of acting 'unfairly' covers what used to be referred to as violating the common law rules of natural justice. Thus 'fairness' requires that the decision maker be impartial to the extent that circumstances permit[5] and that persons affected by a decision be given a fair hearing.[6] 'Fairness' may require that a person with a 'legitimate expectation' be given a hearing. The area of 'legitimate expectation' is one of the present growth areas of judicial review relating not only to a right to a hearing but also perhaps to substantive rights. Irrationality is also called 'Wednesbury' unreasonableness following Lord Greene's classic statement in *Associated Provincial Picture Houses Ltd v Wednesbury Corpn.*[7] Under this head the courts interfere with decisions only if they are so unreasonable that no reasonable authority properly directing its mind would have made them. The limitation on the use of this ground is intended to prevent the court from acting as an appellate body and substituting its own view for that of the decision maker. Nevertheless, in politically sensitive cases, the court may appear to tread close to the line of interfering with a decision on its merits. We consider the grounds for judicial review fully in the next chapter.

## PUBLIC AND PRIVATE LAW

The scope of Ord 53 has been limited to decisions of a 'public law' character. The distinction between public law and private law is alien to the English legal tradition and has caused considerable difficulty. There are two distinct but confused issues. Firstly, a public law *decision* falls within Ord 53. Secondly, a public law *right* falls *exclusively* within Ord 53. However, a private law right relating to a public law decision can but need not be asserted under Ord 53. We shall discuss this topic in Chapter 10.

5 Nemo judex in re sua.
6 Audi alteram partem.
7 [1948] 1 KB 223, [1947] 2 All ER 680, CA.

CHAPTER 2

# The grounds of judicial review

## INTRODUCTION—THE DIPLOCK CATEGORIES

The grounds on which the High Court will intervene to review the activities of inferior bodies have developed piecemeal and without any consistency in terminology. In the GCHQ case, *Council of Civil Service Unions v Minister for the Civil Service*,[1] Lord Diplock subsumed the grounds of judicial review under the three heads of 'illegality, irrationality and procedural impropriety'. This formula has become widely used as the conventional basis for structuring an argument and is supported by a great weight of authority.[2] However it is no more than a convenient umbrella and includes a cluster of specific grounds, some of which overlap and for which there is, unfortunately, no generally accepted taxonomy. Lord Diplock said that he did not intend the three categories to be exhaustive by which he appeared to mean that other heads of review might emerge in the future. The only context to date where the Diplock formula has been rejected appears to be that of voluntary regulatory bodies[3] and this has not involved the creation of new grounds of review.

1. Illegality. This includes acting ultra vires in the traditional sense of exceeding the limits of the power conferred by statute. As a result of *Anisminic Ltd v Foreign Compensation Commission*,[4] where the House of Lords reversed an uncharacteristically narrow judgment of Diplock LJ (as he was then), it appears that all errors of law by administrative bodies are reviewable under this head.[5] This remains controversial and arguably extends judicial review too far. 'Illegality' also includes the fettering of a discretion by a rigid rule or policy or because of an undertaking or agreement, failing to take relevant factors into account, acting for a purpose outside the scope of the governing legislation and acting in bad faith.[6]

2. 'Irrationality' is the concept of 'unreasonableness' derived from Lord Greene's well known judgment in *Associated Provincial Picture Houses Ltd v Wednesbury Corpn*.[7] Unreasonableness is the least clearly defined head of review. An unreasonable decision according to Lord Greene is 'one that no reasonable body could have come to. It is not what the court considers reasonable'. This

1 [1985] AC 374, [1984] 3 All ER 935.

2 Eg *Nottingham County Council v Secretary of State for the Environment* [1986] AC 240, [1986] 1 All ER 199, HL; *R v Secretary of State for the Environment, ex p Hammersmith and Fulham London Borough Council* [1991] 1 AC 521, sub nom *Hammersmith and Fulham London Borough Council v Secretary of State for the Environment* [1990] 3 All ER 589, HL; *R v Independent Television Commission, ex p TSW Broadcasting Ltd* (1992) Times, 30 March, HL; *R v Secretary of State for the Environment, ex p Brind* [1991] 1 AC 696, sub nom *Brind v Secretary of State for the Home Department* [1991] 1 All ER 720, HL; other formulations have become fashionable in particular contexts, eg *Seddon Properties v Secretary of State for the Environment* (1978) 42 P & CR 26n (planning).

3 *R v Panel on Take-overs and Mergers, ex p Guinness plc* [1990] 1 QB 146, [1989] 1 All ER 509, CA.

4 [1969] 2 AC 147, [1969] 1 All ER 208.

5 *O'Reilly v Mackman* [1982] 3 All ER 1124 at 1129 confirmed in *Page v Hull University Visitor* [1993] 1 All ER 97 (below p 40).

6 *Hammersmith and Fulham London Borough Council v Secretary of State for the Environment* [1990] 3 All ER 589 at 636–7.

7 [1948] 1 KB 223, [1947] 2 All ER 680, CA.

ground of review is sometimes called 'perversity' in order to emphasise that the court will interfere only in extreme cases, where there is no rational basis for the decision.

3. Procedural impropriety. This has two aspects. Procedural impropriety includes violating procedural requirements prescribed by the governing legislation and, second, the violation of standards of fair procedure developed by the courts themselves. 'Fairness' has replaced natural justice as a general label although the latter term is still in use. The two expressions are interchangeable although 'natural justice' may be associated particularly with courts and judicial bodies and perhaps with very serious defects.[8]

The discretionary element in judicial review must again be stressed. It is not enough to establish a technical defect. The court will also look broadly at the substance of the decision. For example a decision will not be quashed for unfairness or irrelevant considerations if the defect has not affected the outcome or caused injustice. This approach might cause disquiet because it blurs the distinction between legality and merits. On the other hand there are public policy arguments concerned with the efficient use of resources in favour of this approach. In the context of the right to a fair hearing it has been emphasised that the courts should be extremely reluctant to conclude that a hearing would have made no difference to the outcome.[9]

We shall discuss the specific grounds of review in this chapter.

## LEGITIMATE EXPECTATION

In the GCHQ case Lord Diplock said[10] that 'to qualify for judicial review the decision must affect other persons either by altering their private rights or by depriving them of a "legitimate expectation"'. This is too narrow in as much as it suggests that in the absence of these ingredients judicial review is not possible at all. For example neither private rights, nor legitimate expectations are a necessary condition for locus standi or a right to a hearing[11] although they may well be a sufficient condition for both.[12]

The concept of legitimate expectation has developed since the 1960s.[13] It is to be contrasted with legal right and the word 'legitimate' is equivalent, but preferred, to reasonable. Legitimate expectations can be regarded as an aspect of the fairness principle.[14] It is well established that a legitimate expectation can generate a right to be heard[15] but the concept also has a substantive dimension. It may require government to act consistently in the sense of being required to honour a previous agreement, promise, undertaking or announced

8 *R v Panel on Take-overs and Mergers, ex p Guinness plc* [1989] 1 All ER 509 at 539 per Woolf LJ.

9 See *John v Rees* [1970] Ch 345 at 42; *Malloch v Aberdeen Corpn* [1971] 2 All ER 1278, [1971] 1 WLR 1578; *R v Secretary of State for the Environment, ex p Brent London Borough Council* [1983] 3 All ER 321 at 357.

10 [1984] 3 All ER 935 at 949.

11 Below, ch 9; *R v Great Yarmouth Borough Council, ex p Botton Bros Arcades Ltd* [1988] JPL 18; *R v Secretary of State for Defence, ex p Sancto* (1992) Times, 19 September.

12 *O'Reilly v Mackman* [1982] 3 All ER 1124 at 1129 (Lord Diplock).

13 *Schmidt v Secretary of State for Home Affairs* [1969] 1 All ER 904 at 949; *A-G of Hong Kong v Ng Yuen Shiu* [1983] 2 All ER 346 at 350. Cf *McInnes v Onslow Fane* [1978] 3 All ER 211 (a private law context).

14 *A-G of Hong Kong v Ng Yuen Shiu* (loc cit, above); *Council of Civil Service Unions v Minister for the Civil Service* [1984] 3 All ER 935 at 949.

15 See cases cited below in nn 1–5, pp 9–10.

policy. In this sense a legitimate expectation is akin to an estoppel, although, as we shall see, the analogy should not be applied too strictly.

Legitimate expectations have been unsuccessfully evoked in many cases. This is because the concept is sometimes abused as an umbrella term for any claim to judicial review and sometimes because the courts have taken an increasingly strict approach to the factual basis of a legitimate expectation.

## The meaning of legitimate expectation

Lord Fraser's speech in the GCHQ case has frequently been relied upon.[16] His Lordship said that a legitimate expectation may arise either from an express promise given by a public authority or from the existence of a regular practice which the claimant can reasonably expect to continue. In *GCHQ* there had been a previous practice of consulting the unions concerned before introducing new employment conditions. In the *Shui* case[17] the applicants had been told that their applications to remain in Hong Kong would be considered on their merits, thus implying a hearing. Legitimate expectations are not confined to express promises or practices. A legitimate expectation might also arise where the applicant has been given some benefit in the past which is now being withdrawn.[18] General policy statements as well as individual undertakings may generate a legitimate expectation.

There is an analogy with estoppel although it is unlikely that a legitimate expectation could bind a public authority absolutely. In *GCHQ* the legitimate expectation to be consulted was overridden by national security considerations. In *Re Findlay*[19] the government's policy relating to parole was changed to the disadvantage of prisoners who had been expecting to be considered for parole on the basis of the previous policy. The House of Lords held that the statutory objectives of parole were not compatible with the prisoners' expectation. The prisoners' only legitimate expectation was that the policies of the day would be applied fairly to them. This makes the concept superfluous. In *Re Preston*[20] it was emphasised by the House of Lords that interference with a legitimate expectation was an aspect of the wider principle of abuse of power and cannot conflict with a statutory duty.

In the context of statements or undertakings the factual ingredients of a legitimate expectation are as follows:

(i) The authority's statement or undertaking must be clear and unambiguous and not merely tentative or provisional.[1]

(ii) It must be reasonable for the applicant to have relied upon the expectation raised by the authority. Subjective belief on the part of either applicant or authority will not suffice.[2]

(iii) Except where the authority gives a formal undertaking the applicant

16 [1984] 3 All ER 935 at 944. Bingham LJ's judgment in *R v Board of Inland Revenue, ex p MFK Underwriting Agencies Ltd* [1990] 1 All ER 91 is also much cited.

17 Above n 14. See also *Preston v IRC* (below); *HTV Ltd v Price Commission* [1976] ICR 170, CA; *R v Liverpool Corpn, ex p Liverpool Taxi Fleet Operators' Association* [1972] 2 QB 299.

18 *Council of Civil Service Unions v Minister for the Civil Service* [1984] 3 All ER 935 at 949 (Lord Diplock); *McInnes v Onslow Fane* [1978] 3 All ER 211; *Breen v Amalgamated Engineering Union* [1971] 2 QB 175, [1971] 1 All ER 1148—confirmation of election to union office.

19 [1985] AC 318, [1984] 3 All ER 801. See also *Hughes v Department of Health and Social Security* [1985] AC 776, HL. *R v Immigration Appeal Tribunal, ex p Patel* [1987] Imm AR 164 at 172.

20 [1985] AC 835, sub nom *Preston v IRC* [1985] 2 All ER 327.

1 *Preston v IRC* [1985] 2 All ER 327 at 341; *R v Board of Revenue, ex p MFK Underwriting Agencies Ltd* [1990] 1 All ER 91; *R v Secretary of State for the Environment, ex p British Telecommunications plc* [1991] RA 307.

2 *R v Swale Borough Council, ex p Royal Society for the Protection of Birds* [1991] JPL 39.

must make full disclosure to the authority of all relevant information. 'Fairness is not a one way street' and a 'cards on the table' principle applies.[3]

(iv) The applicant must perhaps have suffered some detriment in reliance upon the statement of the authority.[4] The position is unclear. Arguably there is a distinction between specific promises or representations and cases where general policies or practices are in issue, detrimental reliance being required only in the latter.[5] Otherwise why should one citizen be advantaged over another?

The content of a legitimate expectation depends upon how the expectation arises and what is stated. In the case of statements, practices or policies the expectation might be solely one of a hearing or consultation. There is no need for any independent interest or claim. An undertaking to give a hearing may itself generate a legitimate expectation.[6] Where the expectation arises out of a benefit previously enjoyed then the continuation of the benefit is the content of the expectation. A statement or practice or policy may also create an expectation that the applicant will secure some specific benefit or that the policy will not be changed. This might be protected only by a right to a hearing or to the giving of reasons but substantive protection is also possible (below).

## The effect of a legitimate expectation

In *Lloyd v McMahon*[7] Lord Templeman warned against extravagant use of the concept of legitimate expectation. 'This extravagant language does not tempt me to elevate a catch phrase into a principle. The basic principle is that (a decision maker) must act fairly.'

A legitimate expectation can give procedural protection in the form of a right to be heard before a benefit is withdrawn or a statement overridden. In *R v Secretary of State for the Home Department, ex p Ruddock*[8] the Court of Appeal held it could also give substantive protection in the sense of requiring the authority to stick to a previous statement in relation to the applicant. The case concerned the question whether published Home Office guidelines on telephone tapping had been adhered to. No question of a hearing could in the circumstances arise. It was held that the guidelines had been followed but the court held that it could have interfered had they been departed from. On the other hand we have already seen that in *Findlay*[9] the Home Office was entitled to change its policy to the detriment of prisoners who had relied on a previous published policy. Similarly in *R v Secretary of State for Health, ex p United States Tobacco International Inc*[10] the Divisional Court held that the Secretary of State was entitled to make new regulations banning oral snuff in the UK even though the government had previously encouraged the applicants to set up as the sole manufacturer of oral snuff in the UK. It was held that the applicants' legitimate expectation entitled them to a hearing to challenge the medical evidence against 'snuff dipping' which had prompted the new regulations.

3 *MFK* case (above, n 1).

4 *British Telecom* (above, n 1); *R v Secretary of State for the Home Department, ex p Patel* [1991] Imm AR 14.

5 *R v Jockey Club, ex p RAM Racecourses Ltd* [1990] COD 346. Cf *R v Bradford City Metropolitan Council ex p Wilson* [1989] 3 All ER 140 at 151; *R v Secretary of State for the Home Department, ex p Doody* [1993] 1 All ER 151 at 162.

6 *R v Swale Borough Council, ex p Royal Society for the Protection of Birds* (above, n 2); *A–G of Hong Kong v Ng Yuen Shiu* (above, n 13, p 8).

7 [1987] 1 All ER 1118 at 1170.

8 [1987] 2 All ER 518, [1987] 1 WLR 1482.

9 Above, n 19, p 9.

10 [1992] 1 QB 353, [1992] 1 All ER 212.

Apart from that the normal rule that the government was entitled to change its policy provided that it acts rationally and fairly must be applied.

In *R v Birmingham City Council, ex p Sheptonhurst Ltd*[11] the applicant who previously held a sex shop licence argued that in the absence of a change in circumstances the authority must renew his licence. It was held that the authority could look at all the circumstances afresh provided that it gave due weight to the fact that the applicant was a previous licence holder.

It is a basic principle that a public authority cannot be fettered by estoppel, or by a previous policy, or by agreement from exercising a statutory discretion.[12] The legitimate expectation doctrine makes inroads on this although in principle there is no reason why an authority should not undertake that it will *normally* exercise its discretion in a particular way. The approach taken by Parker LJ in *R v Secretary of State for the Home Department, ex p Khan*[13] may provide an acceptable compromise between the two principles. His Lordship took the view that a policy could be changed to the detriment of a legitimate expectation only if justified on the basis of an 'overriding public interest'.

The court is unlikely to weigh the public interest for itself so that the question is one of how the authority should structure its discretion. The essential principle seems to be that the onus is on the authority (a) to show that it has weighed the legitimate expectation against the public interest and (b) to justify overriding the legitimate expectation upon a specific ground over and above the government's undoubted general right to change policy. Where the authority's act is equivalent to a breach of contract or a breach of a specific representation the presumption that it is binding is especially strong but even here it cannot be absolute. Fairness is the overriding principle.[14]

## THE OLD APPROACH—THE ULTRA VIRES DOCTRINE

Before Lord Diplock's convenient categories, review had developed within the broad framework of the ultra vires doctine—the notion that the court could intervene only if the decision maker acted beyond the limits upon its powers prescribed by statute. In the absence of any concept of citizens' rights or limits upon Parliamentary powers this was the only constitutionally acceptable excuse for judicial interference with the executive.

The merits of government decisions were not the concern of the courts. However within the framework of ultra vires there was considerable scope for judicial creativity. Notions of fair procedure (natural justice) and basic rights of the individual could be developed as implied limits upon statutory powers, reinforced by presumptions of statutory interpretation, for example against taxation.[15] In the absence of drafting that clearly and unambiguously

11 [1990] 1 All ER 1026, CA.

12 Below p 19.

13 [1985] 1 All ER 40 at 48. See also *R v Liverpool Corpn, ex p Liverpool Taxi Fleet Operators' Association* [1972] 2 QB 299, sub nom *Re Liverpool Taxi Owners' Association* [1972] 2 All ER 589; *A-G of Hong Kong v Ng Yuen Shiu* [1983] 2 All ER 346 at 350; *Hughes v Department of Health and Social Security* [1985] AC 776.

14 See cases cited above, n 1.

15 This remains important eg *Congreve v Home Office* [1976] QB 629, [1976] 1 All ER 697, CA; *McCarthy & Stone v London Borough of Richmond-upon-Thames* [1991] 4 All ER 897 at 900. See also *Hall & Co Ltd v Shoreham-by-Sea UDC* [1964] 1 All ER 1, [1964] 1 WLR 240, CA.

authorises the conduct that is challenged, the ultra vires doctrine is an oven into which any judicial recipe could have been placed.

In the context of challenges to the powers of inferior courts and other judicial tribunals the language of 'jurisdiction' rather than that of ultra vires was usually employed. This led to confusion because 'jurisdiction' could be given a narrow meaning confined to limits upon the persons, place and subject matter over which the tribunal has competence. According to this 'pure theory of jurisdiction', once a tribunal has established its competence, defects which it might commit in the course of its proceedings such as behaving unfairly, are not truly 'jurisdictional' and therefore might escape challenge.[16] This difficulty was sometimes avoided by using the concept of 'abuse of jurisdiction'. Indeed the 'pure theory of jurisdiction' is arguably misconceived since the operative moment at which to decide whether power is validly exercised is surely the end and not the beginning of the process, ie the time at which the decision purports to take effect. In any event the speeches of Lord Reid and Lord Pearce in *Anisminic Ltd v Foreign Compensation Commission*[17] have become widely accepted as establishing that all reviewable defects including errors of law go to jurisdiction.[18] This made the terms jurisdiction and ultra vires largely meaningless[19] and paved the way for Lord Diplock's reorganisation in the *GCHQ* case.

Nevertheless the ultra vires principle remains an important underpinning of judicial review. At a fundamental level it places emphasis upon drawing boundaries between the legal and the political domains. On the other hand recent developments in relation to procedural fairness and the exercise of discretion go some way towards a broader 'balancing of interests' approach although as yet this is rudimentary.

It can also be argued that there is a difference between a decision that is ultra vires in the narrow sense and one the validity of which depends upon ulterior evidence of improper purposes, unfairness or irrationality. This may be relevant to the court's willingness to allow defences or other forms of collateral attack to ostensibly valid decisions.[19]

As a general underpinning for judicial review the ultra vires doctrine is widely regarded as inadequate.[20] Not only is it often merely an empty form but it poses serious conceptual problems in relation to the broad, discretionary nature of judicial review. Strictly speaking an ultra vires decision must be a complete nullity with no legal consequences at all—void ab initio. This principle is in practice unworkable. It is necessary to resort to the courts to expose invalid government action. The court may refuse a remedy in its discretion or because of lack of standing. Even if the court does declare, say, a planning permission invalid, what of third parties—developers, contractors etc—who have already relied upon it? The rationale of the Ord 53 procedure is that challenges to government action raise especially sensitive balancing considerations that justify a special procedure. The ultra vires doctrine by contrast presupposes that without the shield of statutory power officials are no different from any other person. The ultra vires doctrine is of course an important mechanism for protecting the rights of individuals in cases where an official acts outside the

16 See *R v Bolton* (1841) 1 QB 66; cf *Anisminic Ltd v Foreign Compensation Commission* [1969] 2 AC 147, [1969] 1 All ER 208, HL.
17 [1969] 2 AC 147, [1969] 1 All ER 208, HL.
18 *O'Reilly v Mackman* [1982] 3 All ER 1124 at 1129.
19 See pp 40, 47, 96, 114.
20 See eg Dawn Oliver *Public Law* [1987] p 543.

substantive area of his power but judicial review raises issues more complex and wide ranging than this.

The ultra vires doctrine is also difficult to relate to the extended reach of judicial review into non-statutory powers under the royal prerogative or powers exercised by voluntary bodies such as the City Takeover Panel who create and apply their own rules. In the latter case it has been suggested that even the Diplock formula is too rigid and that a broader approach should be taken based upon the desirability of the court interfering.[1]

## THE DIPLOCK CATEGORIES—ILLEGALITY

It is convenient to deal with illegality under four broad heads. All depend upon the construction of the governing legislation or, in the case of prerogative powers, the ambit of the power in question.

### 1. Substantive ultra vires

This is where the official performs an act which is not authorised by the governing legislation. There is some leeway. This is due to the 'reasonably incidental' doctrine under which certain acts, even though not expressly authorised by the legislation, are lawful if they are reasonably incidental to acts which are expressly authorised.[2] Section 111(1) of the Local Government Act 1972 relating to acts which facilitate or are conducive or incidental to 'functions' of a local authority has been said to be a statutory version of the same principle.[3] The reasonably incidental doctrine has not been generously interpreted. In *McCarthy & Stone (Developments) Ltd v London Borough of Richmond-upon-Thames*[4] the House of Lords held that a local authority is not entitled to charge for giving advice to the public without express statutory authority. Part of the reasoning was that the giving of advice is itself 'incidental' and the doctrine does not stretch to what is incidental to the incidental. Furthermore, it is not enough to show that the act in question might benefit an activity which is expressly authorised. In *Hazell v Hammersmith and Fulham London Borough Council*[5] local authority interest rates swaps were held to be ultra vires because they were transactions which did not have a sufficiently close relationship to the statutory function of borrowing as opposed to 'debt management' which is not a statutory function.

The statutory context is all important. Where an activity is governed by what purports to be a comprehensive regime there may be no room for the 'reasonably incidental' doctrine.[6] There are also presumptions of statutory interpretation which require clear statutory language in order to impose a tax or charge, or to restrict what the courts regard as basic rights.[7]

1 Below, p 35.

2 *A-G v Great Eastern Rly Co* (1880) 5 App Cas 473 at 478; *A-G v Fulham Corpn* [1921] 1 Ch 440.

3 *Hazell v Hammersmith and Fulham London Borough Council* [1992] 2 AC 1, [1991] 1 All ER 545 at 554, HL.

4 [1992] 2 AC 48, [1991] 4 All ER 897.

5 Above, n 3. See also *A-G v Crayford UDC* [1962] Ch 575, [1962] 2 All ER 147, CA; *A-G v Mersey Rly Co* [1907] AC 415, HL.

6 *Hazell* case (above, n 3).

7 *McCarthy & Stone (Developments) Ltd v London Borough of Richmond-upon-Thames* [1992] 2 AC 48, [1991] 4 All ER 897; *Chertsey UDC v Mixnam's Properties* [1965] AC 735, [1964] 2 All ER 627—freedom of contract; *Hall & Co Ltd v Shoreham-on-Sea UDC* [1964] 1 All ER 1, [1964] 1 WLR 240—property. This kind of argument also applies in the context of irrationality (below).

## 2. Errors of law

Despite considerable academic doubts and some judicial reservations,[8] it is widely accepted that any mistake of law in construing the governing legislation makes a decision ultra vires or, which is the same thing, goes to jurisdiction.[9] This is said to be the result of *Anisminic Ltd v Foreign Compensation Commission*[10] although Lord Wilberforce in that case expressly rejected the proposition and Lords Reid and Pearce impliedly did so.

Nevertheless their Lordships' reasoning in *Anisminic* has been taken to mean that all errors of law made by administrative bodies go to jurisdiction. The rationale appears to be that all errors of law necessarily involve either taking an irrelevant factor into account or failing to take a relevant factor into account, both of which are well established heads of ultra vires.

Before *Anisminic* errors of law were reviewable only in two cases. Both remain in place but have probably become superfluous at least in relation to administrative bodies. The first case was where the error could be classified as a 'jurisdictional error', that is an error in relation to a matter which defines the tribunal's area of power. For example where a rent tribunal could fix rents only in relation to a 'tenancy', the meaning of tenancy was a jurisdictional question. This mystifying doctrine may have disappeared in relation to questions of law but survives in relation to questions of *fact* (below).

The second case where an error of law could be reviewed was that of error of law on the face of the record. This applied where there was a clear error of law which could be discovered from reading the official record of the tribunal without recourse to extrinsic evidence. Error of law on the face of the record is an aspect of the law of certiorari and will be discussed in that context.

Suffice it to say now that both doctrines, that of jurisdictional error and that of the record, were intended to reflect the undesirability of the courts re-examining substantive issues. As Lord Wilberforce pointed out in *Anisminic*,[11] sometimes a specialist tribunal may be in a better position to decide even questions of law than the High Court. The wide '*Anisminic*' approach to errors of law permits the court to substitute its own views on the matter as opposed to confining its intervention to cases of unreasonableness. Arguably the concept of unreasonableness provides an adequate safeguard. Indeed even where errors of law are reviewable there is still a judicial unwillingness to intervene except in clear cases. This is now expressed in other ways, for example by classifying an issue as one of fact not law, or refusing to intervene as a matter of discretion.[12]

In *Re Racal Communications*[13] Lord Diplock advocated a modified version of the *Anisminic* principle, first by explaining that the error of law doctrine is merely a

8 *R v Registrar of Companies, ex p Central Bank of India* [1986] QB 1114 at 1175–6; *South East Asia Fire Bricks Sdn Bhd v Non Metallic Mineral Products Manufacturing Employees Union* [1981] AC 363, [1980] 2 All ER 689, PC; cf *Pearlman v Keepers and Governors of Harrow School* [1979] QB 56, [1979] 1 All ER 365, CA. See Beatson and Matthews *Administrative Law Cases and Materials* pp 91–102.

9 *O'Reilly v Mackman* [1983] 2 AC 237, [1982] 3 All ER 1124 at 1133; *R v Chief Immigration Officer Gatwick Airport, ex p Kharrarzi* [1980] 3 All ER 373, [1980] 1 WLR 1396. See *Gould* [1970] PL 358.

10 [1969] 2 AC 147, [1969] 1 All ER 208, HL.

11 Ibid at 210, 246.

12 See *Puhlhofer v Hillingdon London Borough Council* [1986] AC 484, [1986] 1 All ER 467, HL; *R v Preston Supplementary Benefits Appeal Tribunal, ex p Moore* [1975] 2 All ER 807, [1975] 1 WLR 624, CA.

13 [1981] AC 374, [1980] 2 All ER 634, HL; *Re E's Application* [1983] RPC 231 at 253 (obiter in both cases).

presumption and second by limiting the presumption to administrative bodies as opposed to inferior courts. However, Lord Diplock's subsequent formulation in *O'Reilly v Mackman*[14] did not include these qualifications. The House of Lords has recently endorsed the wide *'Anisminic'* principle in relation to administrative bodies and statutory tribunals but has also recognised Lord Diplock's *'Racal'* qualification about courts.[15] The matter is probably concluded for practical purposes although the conceptual and policy issues have not been confronted. Among its many difficulties, the wide *Anisminic* doctrine appears to make statutory appeals on a point of law superfluous. One obvious disadvantage of Lord Diplock's approach in *Racal* is that the meaning of 'court' is far from clear.[16]

### 3. Mistakes of fact

The *Anisminic* reasoning could, as a matter of logic, also apply to questions of fact. However this has not been attempted. The position as regards errors of fact is uncertain. There are conflicting dicta in the House of Lords. In *Secretary of State for Education and Science v Tameside Metropolitan Borough Council*[17] Lord Wilberforce suggested that a decision made on a false basis of fact was reviewable but in *R v Independent Television Commission, ex p TSW Broadcasting Ltd*[18] Lord Templeman denied that the court could investigate findings of fact. The difference between the two may be that the court will interfere where an error of fact is undisputed but will not resolve disputed questions of fact by looking at primary evidence or fresh material. As we have seen the judicial review procedure is designed to inhibit factual investigation without excluding it altogether.

An error of fact may be reviewable if it falls within another relevant ground of judicial review. These are as follows:

(a) *Collateral questions.* The doctrine of the collateral question is based upon the presumed intention of Parliament to limit a tribunal's powers to cases where a given state of affairs 'exists'. The same concept is sometimes labelled 'jurisdictional fact' or 'precedent fact'. The question whether that state of affairs exists cannot, according to this theory, be decided conclusively by the tribunal, because that would make nonsense of the limitation. The question whether the state of affairs exists is therefore a condition precedent to the tribunal's jurisdiction. As a matter of practical necessity the tribunal may have to decide the question, but a wrong decision in this matter cannot give it jurisdiction, and anything it does thereafter will be a nullity.[19] For example, some tribunals' powers can be exercised only in prescribed geographical areas, some can deal only with defined classes of persons (the Home Secretary can normally deport only non-citizens) or things (rent officers' jurisdiction over premises 'let as a separate dwelling-house') and in other cases there are special exclusions from the tribunal's

14 Above n 9.

15 See *Page v Hull University Visitor* [1993] 1 All ER 97, HL, cf below, p 82.

16 *A-G v BBC* [1981] AC 303, [1980] 3 All ER 161.

17 [1977] AC 1014 at 1047, [1976] 3 All ER 665 at 681–682. See also *Mason v Secretary of State for the Environment* [1984] JPL 332; *Jazendorf and Trott v Secretary of State for the Environment* [1985] JPL 771.

18 (1992) Times, 30 March, HL.

19 *R v Rent Officer for Camden, ex p Ebiri* [1981] 1 All ER 950, [1981] 1 WLR 881; *R v Judge Pugh, ex p Graham* [1951] 2 KB 623, [1951] 2 All ER 307; *R v Fulham, Hammersmith and Kensington Rent Tribunal, ex p Zerek* [1951] 2 KB 1, [1951] 1 All ER 482; *Bunbury v Fuller* (1853) 9 Exch 111 at 140. See *R v Shoreditch Assessment Committee, ex p Morgan* [1910] 2 KB 859 at 880 per Farwell J.

powers (compulsory purchase of land other than 'parkland').[20] A collateral question can be either a question of law or fact, although the court will be less likely to upset a finding of fact.[1] Nevertheless this is one context where the courts can look at facts de novo and accept fresh evidence.

Normally the language of the governing statute will indicate what matters are collateral, since they will be formulated as conditions precedent. There may be language indicating that the tribunal itself is to be the judge of whether a condition precedent is satisfied,[2] although the courts will be reluctant to draw this inference from general language alone.[3] A broad approach must be taken including such matters as the kind and level of expertise possessed by the tribunal, the nature of the issue (subjective judgments are unlikely to be treated as jurisdictional),[4] the remaining matters to be decided by the tribunal (if the matter in question is the most important thing it has to decide, it is unlikely to be jurisdictional) and the existence of other remedies, including statutory rights of appeal.[5] The collateral question doctrine reflects the policy that even in relation to matters of law the courts should sometimes defer to the expertise of an administrative tribunal. The court is less likely to show deference where civil liberties are in issue,[6] but will be deferential in cases where specialist or political judgments are involved.[7]

The collateral question doctrine may be logically vulnerable, in that there is no conceptual distinction between any of the various matters on which any given tribunal is required to form an opinion. If, however, it is remembered that the real question is whether the tribunal or the court is the body best qualified to determine a given matter the doctrine makes sense and is reasonably practicable.

Difficulties with the collateral question doctrine have led to a search for an alternative approach, for example, the general principle of 'unreasonableness'.[8] However, the House of Lords has affirmed that where jurisdictional matters (described as precedent facts) are concerned the court will not confine itself to reasonableness but will probe deeper. The standard to be applied is the civil standard of proof but this must be applied flexibly in the light of the gravity of the case.[9]

20 *Re Ripon (Highfield) Housing Order, 1938, White and Collins v Minister of Health* [1939] 2 KB 838, [1939] 3 All ER 548, CA.

1 *Khawaja v Secretary of State for the Home Department* [1983] 1 All ER 765 at 774, [1983] 2 WLR 321 at 333. The standard of proof is the civil standard, but the degree of probability required depends on the gravity of the matter. See also *R v Fulham, Hammersmith and Kensington Rent Tribunal, ex p Zerek* [1951] 2 KB 1, [1951] 1 All ER 482. See further below, p 191.

2 *R v Income Tax Special Purposes Comrs* (1888) 21 QBD 313 at 319 per Lord Esher.

3 *R v Woodhouse* [1906] 2 KB 501, 75 LJKB 745, CA. See also *R v Ludlow, ex p Barnsley Corpn* [1947] KB 634, [1947] 1 All ER 880; *Brittain v Kinnaird* (1819) 1 Brod & Bing 432 at 442; *Tithe Redemption Commission v Wynne* [1943] KB 756, [1943] 2 All ER 370, CA; *Secretary of State for Education and Science v Tameside Metropolitan Borough Council* [1977] AC 1014, [1976] 3 All ER 665.

4 See *Puhlhofer v Hillingdon London Borough Council* [1986] AC 484; *R v Secretary of State for the Home Department, ex p Muboyayi* [1991] 4 All ER 72 at 89–90; *Bugdaycay v Secretary of State for the Home Department* [1987] AC 514, [1987] 1 All ER 940, HL.

5 *R v Surrey Coroner, ex p Campbell* [1982] QB 661, [1982] 2 All ER 545.

6 *Khawaja v Secretary of State for the Home Department* [1984] AC 74, [1983] 1 All ER 765, HL.

7 See *R v Secretary of State for the Home Department, ex p Bugdaycay* [1986] 1 All ER 458 at 465–6; *Dowty Boulton Paul Ltd v Wolverhampton Corpn (No 2)* [1976] Ch 13 at 26–27.

8 *Ashbridge Investments Ltd v Minister of Housing and Local Government* [1965] 3 All ER 371, [1965] 1 WLR 1320.

9 *Khawaja v Secretary of State for the Home Department*, see above, n 1. See also *R v Hampshire County Council, ex p Ellerton* [1985] 1 All ER 599 at 608.

In other cases, unless there is misconduct, fresh evidence is not available, and the validity of the decision must be judged on the basis of material that was or should have been before the decision-maker at the time.[10] Judicial review is to do with the quality of decision-making and not with whether with the aid of hindsight a better decision could have been made. The underlying general principle could be that the decision-maker has failed to take proper steps to acquaint himself with the facts.[11]

(b) *Where there is no relevant evidence.* The error then becomes one of law.[12] This can arise in two main ways. First, there are cases where no supporting evidence at all is offered for the tribunal's finding. The court will look at all the circumstances, including in particular the extent to which the finding in question is a matter of value judgment or opinion, the extent to which the tribunal is entitled to rely on its own expert professional judgment, and whether more than one conclusion can reasonably be drawn.

Second, there are cases where evidence is adduced but it is not reasonably relevant to the decision.[13] Here the matter will normally be an ordinary error of law because a mistake of this kind often comes out of a misconstruction of the meaning of a legal term.

(c) *Where a failure to disclose a relevant fact can be treated as a breach of natural justice.* In this connection the decision is invalid whether or not the decision-maker was a party to the defect.[14]

(d) *Where the fact in question was one of which the decision-maker should have been aware,* for example, if knowledge can be attributed to the decision-maker because the relevant information was known or should have been known to a servant or agent.[15] This defect is essentially that of taking irrelevant factors into account or failing to take relevant factors into account.

(e) *A factual error disclosed in a statement of reasons.* This could be regarded as making the statement of reasons defective for the purpose of compliance with a statutory duty to give reasons.

(f) *Where a finding of fact is perverse.*[16]

10 *Hollis v Secretary of State for the Environment* (1982) 47 P & CR 351; *Glover v Secretary of State for the Environment* [1981] JPL 110.

11 Eg *Tameside* case (above, n 17) at 696 1065. *R v Secretary of State for the Environment, ex p Powis* [1981] 1 All ER 788, [1981] 1 WLR 584, *Bath Society v Secretary of State for the Environment* [1992] 1 All ER 28 [1991] 1 WLR 1303, CA.

12 See *R v Panel on Take-overs and Mergers, ex p Guinness plc* [1989] 1 All ER 509 at 539 per Woolf LJ. See also *Secretary of State for Employment v Associated Society of Locomotive Engineers and Firemen (No 2)* [1972] 2 QB 455, 493; *R v Hillingdon London Borough, ex p Thomas* (1987) 19 HLR 196, 200; *Smith v Inner London Education Authority* [1978] 1 All ER 411, 415; *Secretary of State for Education v Tameside Metropolitan Borough Council* [1977] AC 1014 at 1030; *Armah v Government of Ghana* [1968] AC 192 at 234, *sub nom Re Kwei Armah* [1966] 2 All ER 1006; *Coleen Properties Ltd v Minister of Housing and Local Government* [1971] 1 All ER 1049, [1971] 1 WLR 433, CA.

13 *R v Deputy Industrial Inquiries Comr, ex p Moore* [1965] 1 QB 456, [1963] 1 All ER 81, CA.

14 *R v Leyland Justices, ex p Hawthorn* [1979] QB 283, [1979] 1 All ER 209; *R v Blundeston Prison Board of Visitors, ex p Fox-Taylor* [1982] 1 All ER 646; *Mahon v Air-New Zealand* [1984] AC 808, [1984] 3 All ER 201, PC. But see *Al Mehdawri v Secretary of State for the Home Department* [1990] 1 AC 876 [1989] 3 All ER 843 (applicant's lawyer at fault).

15 *Hollis v Secretary of State for the Environment* (1982) 48 P & CR 351; *Secretary of State for Education and Science v Tameside Metropolitan Borough Council* [1977] AC 1014, [1976] 3 All ER 665, HL; *East Hampshire District Council v Secretary of State for the Environment* [1979] JPL 533, CA; *GE Simplex (Holdings) Ltd v Secretary of State for the Environment* (1988) 57 P & CR 306, CA.

16 *Shamer v B & R Residential Lettings Ltd* [1992] IRLR 317.

*The distinction between law and fact*

The distinction between law and fact can readily be drawn at its extremes. A question of law involves an inquiry into the meaning of a statutory provision or a question of the interpretation of a document such as a planning permission or a policy circular. A question of fact on the other hand is a question which can be answered by evidence from the senses (primary facts) or by inferences drawn from such evidence without reference to legal concepts or rules (secondary facts). It is therefore possible to decide whether a given matter is one of law or fact only within a particular context and many issues will involve a mixture of legal and factual elements. Questions of law and fact may also be mixed up with subjective policy judgments with which the court is reluctant to interfere.[17] Indeed the whole question of the law and fact distinction is heavily influenced by policy considerations. These centre upon whether judicial intervention is appropriate, for example to secure consistency upon matters of general importance, or where specialist expertise is involved.

*The application of law to facts*

The application of a rule of law to facts is prima facie a question of law since it is a question of construction. However, sometimes such questions are treated as questions of fact. This is where the matter is of a kind which the High Court is not necessarily in a better position to resolve than the tribunal. Against the status and expertise of a tribunal must be balanced the desire for consistency and the importance of the issue in question. The vital initial question as to which category a given issue falls into is of course entirely a question of law for the court.

Questions of construction which are treated as questions of fact fall into three broad categories. First, there are cases where terms used in a statute are not technical legal terms but represent ordinary everyday usage.[18] Here the tribunal of fact may be free to define what the term means. In some cases, however, the court will decide that a term which appears to have an everyday flavour must be given a specific technical meaning, thus becoming a matter of pure law.[19]

Second, there are terms which are inherently indefinable in the sense that they involve broad, nebulous or heavily value-laden concepts in relation to which more than one view can reasonably be taken, eg a 'fair rent', 'building', 'adventure in the nature of a trade', or that they involve questions of degree, eg a 'material change of use', a 'separate' unit of land. Again it is open to the court to impose a rigid defining criterion but in general this kind of issue will be treated as a question of fact.[20]

17 *Puhlhofer v Hillingdon London Borough Council* [1986] AC 484. Cf *R v Secretary of State for Transport, ex p Gwent County Council* [1987] 1 All ER 161 at 166–7; *Bushell v Secretary of State for the Environment* [1981] AC 75, [1980] 2 All ER 608, HL.

18 *Brutus v Cozens* [1973] AC 854 at 866, HL; *Stephens v Cuckfield RDC* [1960] 2 QB 373 at 382; *R v National Insurance Comrs, ex p Secretary of State for Social Services* [1974] 3 All ER 522, [1974] 1 WLR 1290; *W v L* [1974] QB 711 at 719, [1973] 3 All ER 884 at 890.

19 *Rolls-Royce Ltd v Jeffrey (Inspector of Taxes)* [1962] 1 All ER 801, [1962] 1 WLR 425.

20 *Edwards v Bairstow* [1956] AC 14 at 33–36; *Woodhouse v Peter Brotherhood Ltd* [1972] 2 QB 520, [1972] 3 All ER 91 (but cf the judgment of Lord Denning MR apparently blurring this distinction); *Bean v Doncaster Amalgamated Collieries Ltd* [1944] 2 All ER 279 at 283–284; *Cole Bros Ltd v Phillips* [1982] 2 All ER 247 at 253; *East Barnet UDC v British Transport Commission* [1962] 2 QB 484, [1961] 3 All ER 878; *Burdle v Secretary of State for the Environment* [1972] 3 All ER 240, [1972] 1 WLR 1207; *McPhail v Islington London Borough Council* [1970] 2 QB 197, [1970] 1 All ER 1004, CA.

Third, there are cases where a statutory term has a precise technical meaning in the sense that its meaning corresponds to some technical concept which exists independently of the law, for example, a scientific or land valuation term. Here the question will again be one of fact.

## 4. Relevance

There are several overlapping concepts. They include acting in bad faith, acting for an improper purpose, failing to take relevant factors into account or taking irrelevant factors into account. Acting for an improper purpose in its turn shades into 'irrationality'. The question of what factors are relevant to be taken into account depends upon the scope and purpose of the governing legislation. The courts give leeway to the decision-maker in four main ways:

(a) the onus of proving irrelevance is on the objector;[1]

(b) the court will set aside the decision only if, taking a broad view, the factor that has been ignored or the irrelevant factor taken into account is material in the sense that it has substantially affected the outcome.[2] To this extent the line between merits and legality is blurred. There is a danger that the courts will trespass into the forbidden territory of 'weighting' the various factors, this being *par excellence* a matter for the decision-maker;

(c) there may be some factors that are relevant in principle but which the court leaves to the decision-maker to decide whether they are relevant in the particular circumstances, for example the extent to which economic factors or alternative sites should be taken into account in planning decisions.[3] Here the ground of intervention becomes one of reasonableness; and

(d) where a statute imposes very wide discretionary powers the court will be reluctant to impose its own criteria of relevance[4] and will confine review to bad faith.

### *Fettering discretion*

Closely connected with the notion of failing to take relevant factors into account is the principle that a public authority cannot tie its hands by a promise, a policy, or an agreement. This applies to all discretionary powers, whether individual or based upon a series of similar applications.[5] As regards contracts, these can bind public authorities on the basis of ordinary principles

1 *Bristol District Council v Clark* [1975] 3 All ER 976, [1975] 1 WLR 1443, CA; *R v Swale Borough Council, ex p Royal Society for the Protection of Birds* [1991] JPL 39.

2 *R v Secretary of State for Social Services, ex p Wellcome Foundation Ltd* [1987] 2 All ER 1025, [1987] 1 WLR 1166; *Westminster Corpn v London and North Western Rly Co* [1905] AC 426, HL; *R v Broadcasting Complaints Commission, ex p Owen* [1985] QB 1153 at 1176; *R v Lewisham London Borough Council, ex p Shell UK Ltd* [1988] 1 All ER 938.

3 See *Sovmots Investments v Secretary of State for the Environment* [1977] QB 411; *Vale of Glamorgan Borough Council v Secretary of State for Wales and Rhys-Williams* (1985) 52 P & CR 418; *Re Findlay* [1985] AC 318 at 334; *CREEDNZ Inc v Governor-General* [1981] 1 NZLR 172.

4 *British Oxygen Co Ltd v Minister of Technology* [1971] AC 610, [1970] 3 All ER 165, HL; *Tower Hamlets London Borough Council v Chetnik Developments Ltd* [1988] 1 All ER 961 at 967.

5 *R v Secretary of State for the Environment, ex p Brent London Borough Council* [1983] 3 All ER 321 at 353–4.

up to the point at which the contract frustrates the proper performance of a statutory function. This is a question of fact.[6]

Similarly a public authority cannot be absolutely bound by an estoppel.[7] As regards policies, whether emanating from published statements, election mandates or party political arrangements, it is clear that decision-makers can give them very great weight. There is a thin line between the decision-maker closing his mind completely to countervailing considerations and considering but rejecting contrary points of view. Thus the fettering of a discretion is closely related to ideas of natural justice and fairness. For example, local councillors cannot be forced to vote in a particular manner nor should they vote blindly in accordance with party policy. Short of that a majority group can adopt a policy of favouring the party line and where a committee is necessarily political it can even select its membership on the basis of their political preferences.[8]

As we have seen, the emerging notion of legitimate expectation does not fundamentally affect this principle. The existence of a legitimate expectation, particularly where an individual promise is given, may require the decision-maker to give special weight to the interest concerned but cannot override the basic principle that statutory duties including the duty to exercise a proper discretion cannot be overridden.

## THE DIPLOCK CATEGORIES—IRRATIONALITY

Irrationality includes cases where a decision is perverse, lacks logic or violates fundamental values of the community.[9] It is sometimes suggested that the concept of irrationality is superfluous since a decision that is flawed to such an extent is likely to be tainted by some other defect such as irrelevance. Nevertheless, irrationality plays a useful role. It allows the court to condemn extreme governmental malpractice outright without resorting to the language of less serious or technical irregularities. Moreover in some cases the court will review for illegality but not for irrationality.[10]

Decisions have been set aside for irrationality where the court has taken the view that they were without any conceivable justification[11] but irrationality has also included decisions which violated basic judicial values by imposing

6 *Ayr Harbour Trustees v Oswald* (1883) 8 App Cas 623, HL; *Re Staines UDC's Agreement, Triggs v Staines UDC* [1969] 1 Ch 10; *Stourcliffe Estates Co Ltd v Bournemouth Corpn* [1910] 2 Ch 12; *Birkdale District Electricity Supply Co Ltd v Southport Corpn* [1926] AC 355, HL. A power exercised under one statute can restrict can restrict a power arising under another. See *R v Hammersmith and Fulham London Borough Council, ex p Beddoes* [1987] QB 1050, [1987] 1 All ER 369, CA; *Dowty Boulton Paul Ltd v Wolverhampton Corpn* [1971] 1 WLR 204 at 210.

7 *Western Fish Products Ltd v Penwith District Council* [1981] 2 All ER 204, CA.

8 *R v Waltham Forest London Borough Council, ex p Baxter* [1988] QB 419, [1987] 3 All ER 671; *R v Greenwich London Borough Council, ex p Lovelace* [1991] 3 All ER 511, [1991] 1 WLR 506, CA. Contrast *Brunyate v Inner London Education Authority* [1989] 2 All ER 417—(school governors); *Bromley London Borough Council v Greater London Council* [1983] 1 AC 768, [1982] 1 All ER 129, HL—electoral mandate cannot bind but can be given particular weight. Compare *Secretary of State for Education and Science v Tameside Metropolitan Borough Council* [1977] AC 1014, [1976] 3 All ER 665.

9 *Council of Civil Service Unions v Minister for the Civil Service* [1984] 3 All ER 935 at 951. See also *Secretary of State for Education and Science v Tameside Metropolitan Borough Council* [1977] AC 1014, [1976] 3 All ER 665; cf *R v Devon County Council, ex p G* [1988] 3 WLR 49 at 51.

10 Below, p 38. For a good example of the difference, see *R v Lewisham Borough Council, ex p Shell UK Ltd* [1988] 1 All ER 938.

11 Eg *R v Secretary of State for Defence, ex p Sancto* (1992) Times, 19 September; *R v Cornwall County Council, ex p Cornwall and Isles of Scilly Guardians ad Litem and Reporting Officers Panel* [1992] 2 All ER 471, [1992] 1 WLR 427; *R v Secretary of State for the Home Department, ex p Cox* [1992] COD 72; cf *R v Secretary of State for the Home Department, ex p K* [1991] 1 QB 270, [1990] 3 All ER 562, CA.

excessive burdens upon individuals[12] or by using administrative powers for purposes of punishment.[13] The standard *Wednesbury* formula, 'so unreasonable that no reasonable body would have made the decision' is helpful in as much as it emphasises that a decision should not be set aside for irrationality if it has any rational justification at all. Nevertheless it is difficult to escape the conclusion that 'unreasonableness' invites the court to set aside a decision of which it strongly disapproves.

In his speech in *Council of Civil Service Unions v Minister for the Civil Service* the GCHQ case[14] Lord Diplock suggested that an additional ground of review based upon the European notion of 'proportionality' might develop. Proportionality requires a reasonable relationship between the measures taken and the lawful objective to be achieved. However, in *R v Secretary of State for Home Department, ex p Brind*[15] the House of Lords was reluctant to introduce this concept into English law. The question was whether the blanket ban introduced by the Home Secretary upon broadcasts of direct speech by supporters of Northern Ireland terrorist organisations was justifiable. Their Lordships recognised that there may have been an element of overkill in the ban but preferred to apply the concepts of unreasonableness. Against this standard the decision was not so irrational as to be perverse. Their Lordships did not completely close the door to the idea of proportionality, but warned that the concept might encourage judges to second guess government policies. The notion of *Wednesbury* unreasonableness is specifically intended to avoid this by its stress upon the idea that if a government decision can conceivably be justified it should be upheld. Thus extreme cases of disproportionality would probably be unreasonable in *Wednesbury* terms.[16] Where issues of European law are involved the courts would be required to apply the proportionality doctrine as such.[17]

*Brind* is also important in that their Lordships refused to use the European Convention on Human Rights as a benchmark for assessing the legality or rationality of government action. The Convention can be used only where the governing UK legislation is ambiguous. Here the legislation unambiguously gave the Secretary of State a very wide discretion.

Lord Greene's judgment in *Wednesbury* emphasised that the various grounds of judicial review of discretionary powers overlap. In addition to unreasonableness, a discretionary decision can be set aside if it is made for an improper purpose, if irrelevant factors are taken into account or if relevant factors are not taken into account. These grounds, all being dependent upon the scope of the governing legislation, fall within the concept of 'illegality' and not that of irrationality. It is important to make this distinction because review is more stringent when it comes to illegality.[18] Unreasonableness must also be measured against the scope of the governing legislation but the notion of

12 *Hall & Co Ltd v Shoreham-by-Sea UDC* [1964] 1 All ER 1, [1964] 1 WLR 240, CA; *R v Hillingdon London Borough Council, ex p Royco Homes Ltd* [1974] QB 720, [1974] 2 All ER 643; *Bromley London Borough Council v Greater London Council* (above, n 8).

13 *Wheeler v Leicester City Council* [1985] AC 1054.

14 Above, n 9 at 950.

15 [1991] 1 AC 696, sub nom *Brind v Secretary of State for the Home Department* [1991] 1 All ER 720.

16 Eg *R v Barnsley Metropolitan Borough Council, ex p Hook* [1976] 3 All ER 452, [1976] 1 WLR 1052; *Luby v Newcastle-under-Lyme Corpn* [1964] 2 QB 64, [1964] 1 All ER 84. See also C-145/88: *Torfaen Borough Council v B and Q (Retail) plc: C 145/88* [1990] 2 QB 19, [1990] 1 All ER 129, ECJ.

17 European Communities Act 1972 s 3.

18 Below, p 38.

unreasonableness extends into the sphere of political and moral value judgments. In the GCHQ case,[19] Lord Diplock defined 'irrationality' to include a decision which is so outrageous in its denial of '. . . accepted moral standards that no sensible person who had applied his mind to the question to be decided could have arrived at it'. His Lordship went on to say that '(w)hether a decision falls within this category is a question that the judges by their training and experience should be well equipped to answer'. He also rejected attempts to squeeze 'irrationality' within one of the other heads of review by explaining that 'by now it can stand on its own feet as an accepted ground on which a decision can be attacked'.[20]

## European law as a ground of review

Apart from proportionality, the relationship between European Community law and judicial review is undeveloped. It can be argued that breach of European Community rights is in itself enough to justify review. The *Factortame* case forced the English courts to grant interim relief against the Crown in a case where a UK statute conflicted with a directly effective provision of the Treaty of Rome. The reasoning in *Factortame* rests upon the obligation imposed on member states by European Community law to provide effective remedies in respect of Community matters and is not confined to Community laws having direct effect.[1] The Advocate General in *Factortame* did not regard the distinction between judicial review proceedings and ordinary proceedings as necessarily of any importance in this context.[2] The principle is that domestic law must fashion remedies to give effect to Community rights.

Other areas where English law may be unduly restrictive in relation to the protection of Community rights include the availability of compensation and other monetary remedies against the state,[3] the operation of ouster clauses,[4] the exclusion of review by alternative remedies, the giving of reasons and the

19 Above, n 9.

20 See ibid *East Berkshire Health Authority v Matadeen* [1992] ICR 723, [1992] IRLR 336, EAT; *British Telecommunications v Sheridan* [1990] IRLR 27, CA; *Piggot Bros & Co Ltd v Jackson* [1992] ICR 85, [1991] IRLR 309, CA; *Neale v Hereford and Worcester County Council* [1986] ICR 471, [1986] IRLR 168, CA.

1 Art 5 EC Treaty. European Communities Act 1972 ss 2(1), 3(1). *Simmenthal* Case (1978) EC 629 at 644. *R v Secretary of State for Transport, ex p Factortame Ltd (No 2) C-213/89:* [1991] 1 AC 603, sub nom *Factortame Ltd v Secretary of State for Transport (No 2)* [1991] 1 All ER 70, ECJ. See below, p 147. UK legislation implementing European law must be interpreted in the light of European law and there may be an obligation to interpet all UK law, whether statute or subordinate legislation, in such a way. See *Marleasing SA v La Comercial Internacional de Alimentacion SA: C-106/89* [1990] ECR I-4135, ECJ. Compare *Duke v GEC Reliance Ltd (formerly Reliance Systems Ltd)* [1988] AC 618.

2 [1991] 1 All ER 70 at 88.

3 Below, ch 8. However, in *Garden Cottage Foods Ltd v Milk Marketing Board* [1983] 2 All ER 770 at 777, a majority of the House of Lords took the view obiter that the treaty should in principle give rise to a cause of action for breach of statutory duty, but cf Lord Wilberforce at 783. See also Oliver LJ's dissent in *Bourgoin SA v Minister of Agriculture, Fisheries and Food* [1986] QB 716, [1985] 3 All ER 585. See also 127/73: *Belgische Raide en Televisie and Société Belge des Auteurs Compositeurs et Éditeurs (BRT) v SV SABAM and NV Fonior* [1974] ECR 51 at 62. C-6/90: *Francovich v Italian Republic* [1992] IRLR 84—damages for failure to implement a directive but perhaps supporting a more general principle. *Woolwich Equitable Building Society v IRC* [1992] 3 All ER 737 at 763–4; *Kirklees Metropolitan Borough Council v Wickes Building Supplies Ltd* [1992] 3 All ER 717 at 734, HL.

4 222/84: *Johnston v Chief Constable of the Royal Ulster Constabulary* [1987] QB 129, [1986] 3 All ER 135, ECJ.

law of locus standi. The latter is particularly important in relation to the European Community Directive on Environmental Impact Assessment, some aspects of which may have direct effect.[5] The English courts appear to take the view that even where a Community provision is of direct effect and the applicant or plaintiff is a person whose interests are intended to be protected by that provision, the applicant must still show that he has suffered specific damage as a result of failure to comply with the European provision.[6]

## THE DIPLOCK CATEGORIES—PROCEDURAL IMPROPRIETY

Procedural impropriety has two aspects. First, the disregard of express statutory procedural requirements, and second, violation of general principles of fair procedure implied by the common law.

### Express statutory requirements

The violation of express procedural requirements is essentially an aspect of the ultra vires doctrine but raises special considerations because of the relatively trivial nature of some procedural irregularities. Would it be reasonable for example to set aside a school reorganisation scheme because a notice was not placed in the correct place at the school gates, particularly if those affected knew of the scheme anyway?

The courts have traditionally approached this kind of problem by distinguishing between mandatory and directory procedural requirements. A mandatory requirement is essential and breach makes the decision invalid. A directory requirement is relatively unimportant. If a directory requirement is broken the court may overlook the matter, if for example the procedure has been 'substantially' complied with or there is no injustice or hardship. The courts had great difficulty in deciding which particular procedural requirements were mandatory and which directory. The only guide was the particular statutory language helped by presumptions in favour, for example, of informing citizens of their rights.[7]

The courts have recently avoided this formalistic approach by relying upon the discretionary nature of judicial review and the presumption that a decision should be treated as valid unless and until it is formally set aside. The court should look at all the circumstances including the importance of the procedural requirement, the impact on the applicant, the interests of third parties and the consequences to government and ask itself whether it would be fair, just and convenient to set aside the decision.[8] This issue is closely bound up with the difficulties created by the proposition that an ultra vires decision is a nullity[9] and reveals a retreat from the rigidity of the ultra vires doctrine.

An aspect of procedural impropriety which overlaps with the rule against

5 Directive 85/337.

6 See *Twyford Parish Council v Secretary of State for the Environment* [1992] 1 CMLR 276, CO/759/40.

7 *Coney v Choyce* [1975] 1 All ER 979, [1975] 1 WLR 422.

8 Ibid. *R v Secretary of State for Social Services, ex p Association of Metropolitan Authorities* [1986] 1 All ER 164, [1986] 1 WLR 1; *London and Clydesdale Estates Ltd v Aberdeen District Council* [1979] 3 All ER 876, [1980] 1 WLR 182; *Main v Swansea District Council* (1984) 49 P & CR 26; *R v Lambeth London Borough Council, ex p Sharp* (1988) 55 P & CR 232, CA; *R v Doncaster Metropolitan District Council, ex p British Railways Board* [1987] JPL 444; *Lovelock v Minister of Transport* (1980) 40 P & CR 336, CA.

9 Above, p 12.

the fettering of discretion is the presumption against delegation. Power given to a designated person must be exercised personally and cannot be delegated to another person (*delegatus non potest delegare*). If this principle were to be applied strictly it would make government unworkable. Exceptions have therefore been created, so many indeed that there is little left of the general principle.

1. Unless a statute states otherwise a civil servant can exercise any departmental function on behalf and in the name of a minister. This is because of the doctrine of ministerial responsibility. Subject perhaps to the test of reasonableness, the courts will not investigate the allocation of decision-making within government departments.[10] On the other hand a minister cannot transfer decision-making power to other ministers.[11] There is no reason, however, why a minister should not consult with other ministers or indeed with anyone he wishes. Furthermore, any power given to a Secretary of State may be exercised by any other Secretary of State.
2. Local authorities have wide powers of delegation to committees, sub committees, officers or other local authorities.[12]
3. Many statutes confer special powers of delegation.
4. A power to delegate may be implied from the particular legislation where for example it would be impractical for the decision-maker to consider cases personally.[13]
5. In other cases, a distinction (often difficult to apply in practice) is made between judicial, legislative and administrative powers. A 'judicial' power for this purpose means a decision made by a court or a similar body which is, deciding disputes affecting the rights of individuals by reference to rules of law. A judicial power cannot be delegated at all.[14] The same applies to legislative powers, that is, making general rules of law. In the case of 'administrative' powers, for example giving grants and permissions and making discretionary decisions, the matter depends on the context. Decisions that are virtually mechanical and involve little discretion can be delegated at least to subordinates[15] but important discretionary powers must be exercised by the body specified in the statute.[16]

In all cases, however, a decision-maker can entrust the tasks of preliminary fact finding, investigation, giving advice and making recommendations to others (for example its staff) provided that it reserves the power to make the final decision itself. In other words it must not rubber-stamp the recommendations of others.[17]

10 *Re Golden Chemical Products* [1976] Ch 300, [1976] 2 All ER 543. Cf *Bushell v Secretary of State for the Environment* [1981] AC 75. *R v Secretary of State for the Home Department, ex p Doody* [1993] 1 All ER 151.

11 *H Lavender & Son Ltd v Minister of Housing and Local Government* [1970] 3 All ER 871, [1970] 1 WLR 1231.

12 Local Government Act 1972 s 101.

13 *Provident Mutual Life Assurance Assocation v Derby City Council* [1981] 1 WLR 173, HL; *Nelms v Roe* [1969] 3 All ER 1379, [1970] 1 WLR 4.

14 *Vine v National Dock Labour Board* [1957] AC 488, [1956] 3 All ER 939, HL. All members of a tribunal must participate in its decisions unless the governing legislation prescribes a quorum.

15 *Provident Mutual Life Assurance v Derby City Council* [1981] 1 WLR 173, HL.

16 *Allingham v Minister of Agriculture and Fisheries* [1948] 1 All ER 780.

17 *Jeffs v New Zealand Dairy Production and Marketing Board* [1967] 1 AC 551, [1966] 3 All ER 863, PC; *R v Greater London Council, ex p Blackburn* [1976] 3 All ER 184, [1976] 1 WLR 550, CA.

## Natural justice or fairness

*The right to a hearing (audi alteram partem)*

Until the leading case of *Ridge v Baldwin*[18] it was believed that a citizen had a right to be heard only in the case of 'judicial' decisions. This caused many problems not least because the idea of a 'judicial' decision was (and remains) hard to pin down. Major areas of government activity—granting licences, paying subsidies, discretionary immigration decisions, housing, public employment and prison discipline—were excluded from the basic safeguard of a fair hearing.

*Ridge v Baldwin* set the law on a new course. The Chief Constable of Brighton had been dismissed by the local police authority without a hearing. They had statutory power to deprive him of his position for incapacity or misconduct but not otherwise. The House of Lords held that he was entitled to a hearing for two reasons: (i) he had been deprived of a public office (not just an ordinary job) and (ii) the power to dismiss was limited by statute so that the authority did not have a policy discretion to dismiss him. Lord Reid in particular emphasised that the right to be heard should depend upon the consequences of the decision to the individual and not upon whether the decision is administrative or judicial. A government decision which causes serious harm to an individual ought in principle to attract the right to be heard.

The terminology of the law has changed from 'natural justice' to 'fairness'.[19] This has two broad implications. First, it allows the law to develop beyond the traditional concepts of *audi alteram partem* (hear the other side) and *nemo iudex in causa sua* (bias) towards wider notions of fairness including a duty to give reasons for a decision and also possibly substantive notions of fairness.[20] Second, flexibility has been achieved at the price of certainty. There is no right to be heard as such, merely a nebulous obligation to be fair, which need not involve a hearing at all. The courts have consciously refused to prescribe objective standards of fairness or even minimum procedural rights but have consistently held that what is fair depends entirely on the circumstances of each case.[1]

The ingredients of a fair hearing can be broken down into advance notice of charges or accusations, a right to see factual evidence in the possession of the decision-maker, and the right to make representations, but each of these is heavily dependent upon context. The court must balance the purpose of the power in question, the width of the decision-maker's discretion and the impact of the decision upon the applicant's interests. There is a desire to avoid formality. Fairness is therefore a minimal entitlement only. Fairness is what is *necessary* to do justice in the particular context and no more. Although the concept of acting judicially is no longer a conclusive factor, fairness leans heavily upon the notion of depriving individuals of rights or making accusations of misconduct.[2] Fairness does not include an obligation to consult

18 [1964] AC 40, [1963] 2 All ER 66, HL.

19 *O'Reilly v Mackman* [1982] 3 All ER 1124 at 1127, HL; *Lloyd v McMahon* [1987] 1 All ER 1118 at 1161, HL; *Council of Civil Service Unions v Minister for the Civil Service* [1984] 3 All ER 935 at 954. Cf *R v Panel on Take-overs and Mergers, ex p Guinness plc* [1990] 1 QB 146, [1989] 1 All ER 509, CA.

20 Eg *Wheeler v Leicester City Council* [1985] AC 1054.

1 *Lloyd v McMahon* loc cit, above, n 19; *Maxwell v Department of Trade and Industry* [1974] 2 All ER 122 at 132–2, CA.

2 *R v Civil Service Appeals Board, ex p Cunningham* [1991] 4 All ER 310, CA; *Norwest Holst v Secretary of State for Trade* [1978] Ch 201, [1978] 3 All ER 280.

people merely because they are adversely affected by policy decisions.[3] There is no right to be heard in what have been called 'pure application cases', ie where a permission or benefit is being sought which can be withheld for policy reasons.[4] Even here, however, an applicant may be entitled to make representations that the policy should not apply in his case.[5]

Corporate or public bodies such as local authorities are not denied the benefits of a right to be heard but have to fit the analogy of the individual. In *Hammersmith and Fulham London Borough Council v Secretary of State for the Environment* it was held that a local council had no right to be heard in relation to a central government decision setting the council's budget on the ground that the council was not accused of misbehaviour nor was its existing property being confiscated.[6] The council's interests were affected only in the sense that it would be less able to fulfil its public goals.

There may be a right to be heard in relation to government inquiries and investigations, but again the right is limited to personal grievances or allegations of misconduct or bad character.[7] The law is therefore restrictive and narrowly focused, geared towards individual rather than group interests and not concerned with notions of democratic participation.

Fairness prevails over administrative convenience[8] but gives way where it frustrates legitimate governmental objectives. For example, confidentiality and national security may override any right to disclosure of information[9] and it has been emphasised that the citizen can claim only the minimum necessary to be fair. Neither an oral hearing nor legal representation are automatic ingredients of fairness,[10] although where a judicial hearing is held fairness will normally include a right to cross examination.[11]

Strictly speaking, the question of fair procedure is a separate matter from the outcome of the decision and to an extent the courts have recognised this. Judges have issued strong warnings against rejecting a right to be heard because a hearing would not have affected the outcome.[12] However, they have also, as a matter of discretion, refused to set aside a decision where the applicant has suffered no prejudice[13] or where it is shown, not merely with hindsight, that a hearing could have made no difference to the result.[14] Indeed

3 *Re Westminster City Council* [1986] AC 668; *R v Devon County Council, ex p Baker* (1992) Times, 20 October.

4 *McInnes v Onslow Fane* [1978] 3 All ER 211, [1978] 1 WLR 1520—aliter if misconduct is involved. *R v Gaming Board, ex p Benaim and Khaida* [1970] 2 QB 417, [1970] 2 All ER 528, CA.

5 *Sagnata Investments Ltd v Norwich Corpn* [1971] 2 All ER 1441 at 1447–8.

6 [1990] 3 All ER 589 at 637–8.

7 *Maxwell v Department of Trade and Industry* [1974] QB 523, [1974] 2 All ER 122, CA; *R v Commission for Racial Equality, ex p Cottrell and Rothon* [1980] 3 All ER 265, [1980] 1 WLR 1580. See also *Mahon v Air New Zealand* [1984] AC 808, [1984] 3 All ER 201, PC. In the case of planning inquiries statute gives broader rights.

8 *R v Board of Visitors of Hull Prison, ex p St Germain (No 2)* [1979] 3 All ER 545, [1979] 1 WLR 1401. Cf *R v Blundeston Prison Board of Visitors, ex p Fox-Taylor* [1982] 1 All ER 646.

9 *Council of Civil Service Unions v Minister for the Civil Service* [1985] AC 374, [1984] 3 All ER 935, HL; *R v Gaming Board* (above, n 4).

10 *R v Board of Visitors of HM Prison, The Maze, ex p Hone* [1988] AC 379, sub nom *Hone v Maze Prison Board of Visitors* [1988] 1 All ER 321, HL; *Lloyd v McMahon* (above, n 1).

11 Cases cited above, n 8.

12 Cases cited above, page 8, n 9; *R v Thames Magistrates Courts, ex p Polemis* [1974] 2 All ER 1219, [1974] 1 WLR 1371.

13 *Glynn v Keele University* [1971] 2 All ER 89, [1971] 1 WLR 487. See *R v Secretary of State for Transport, ex p Gwent County Council* [1987] 1 All ER 161 at 166; *R v Panel on Take-overs and Mergers, ex p Guinness plc* [1989] 1 All ER 509 at 533 per Lloyd LJ, 543–4 per Woolf LJ.

14 *Cheall v Association of Professional, Executive, Clerical and Computer Staff* [1983] QB 126, [1982] 3 All ER 855, CA. Cf *Cinnamond v British Airports Authority* [1980] 2 All ER 368, [1980] 1 WLR 582, CA.

it has sometimes been argued that the test of fairness is not objective but is related to unreasonableness in the sense that a decision will be set aside only if no reasonable body could have regarded it as fair. It seems clear, however, that the question of fairness must be judged objectively even though broadly. The outcome of the decision is relevant in the sense that the applicant must show that he or she has suffered injustice.[15] Where an appeal is provided, then if it involves a full de novo inquiry, this may cure an unfair first instance decision.[16] The nebulous concept of 'fairness', unlike stricter notions of due process, invites the court to take a broad view of the issues.

Finally, fairness involves no more than an opportunity to be heard. An applicant deprived of a hearing due to the fault of his own legal adviser cannot challenge the decision on that ground.[17]

*The bias rule*

A citizen is entitled to assume that the decision-maker is reasonably free from irrelevant biases. Complete impartiality is of course an impossible ideal, so the law has to compromise. Furthermore, where decisions are entrusted to politicians some kinds of bias are inevitable. For example a local council decision can be biased in favour of party political policy provided that the councillors involved do not close their minds to other arguments. The main principles are as follows.

1. A personal financial interest, however small, will automatically disqualify the decision-maker. The only exception is where no other decision-maker is qualified to act in which case Parliament must be taken to have impliedly authorised the bias.[18]
2. A judicial decision of a court or tribunal must not appear to be biased, whether or not the judge is actually biased. Justice 'must manifestly and undoubtedly appear to be done'.[19] A decision will be quashed if there is a 'real likelihood' or 'reasonable suspicion' of bias. Whether there is any significant difference between these two phrases is questionable. It seems the test is as follows: 'Would a reasonable person knowing *all* the facts available to the court suspect that the decision-maker *might* be biased?'[20] Examples of disqualifying bias include participating in the case in more than one capacity, as advisor or prosecutor or at an earlier stage being involved in previous cases involving the same parties. Personal relationships may also disqualify but not political views as such nor loyalty to an organisation whose rules the applicant is accused of breaking, unless the decision-maker actually behaves unfairly.
3. The bias rule has only a limited application in the sphere of administrative decisions made by political bodies. Bias in favour of the political objects of

15 See *Bushell v Secretary of State for the Environment* [1981] AC 75 at 100, HL; *R v Panel on Take-overs and Mergers, ex p Guinness plc* [1990] 1 QB 146 at 178, 200, CA; *General Medical Council v Spackman* [1943] AC 627 at 644–645, HL.

16 See *Lloyd v McMahon* [1987] 1 All ER 1118 at 1144–5 (Woolf LJ); *Calvin v Carr* [1980] AC 574, [1979] 2 All ER 440, PC; cf *Leary v National Union of Vehicle Builders* [1970] 2 All ER 713 at 719–20; *Ridge v Baldwin* [1964] AC 40, [1963] 2 All ER 66, HL.

17 *Al-Mehdawi v Secretary of State for the Home Department* [1990] 1 AC 876, [1989] 3 All ER 843, HL —Aliter if the defect is the other side's fault, *R v Leyland Justices, ex p Hawthorn* [1979] QB 283, [1979] 1 All ER 209.

18 *Grand Junction Canal v Dimes* (1852) 3 HL Cas 759; *Wilkinson v Barking Corpn* [1948] 1 KB 721, [1948] 1 All ER 564, CA.

19 *Metropolitan Property Co (FGC) Ltd v Lannon* [1969] 1 QB 577, [1968] 3 All ER 304, CA; *R v Sussex Justices, ex p McCarthy* [1924] 1 KB 256 at 259.

20 *R v Liverpool Justices, ex p Topping* [1983] 1 All ER 490, [1983] 1 WLR 119; *Reza v General Medical Council* [1991] 2 AC 182, [1991] 2 All ER 796, PC.

the dominant political party within local or central government is necessarily implied in connection with any statutory function imposed upon local authorities or ministers.[1] Moreover, local authorities may have conflicting priorities so that, for example, a bias in favour of a particular form of development cannot in itself vitiate a planning decision.[2] Quite rightly, the law does not require an internal separation of powers or the construction of chinese walls within a local authority. The same applies to prison visitors who have both administrative and judicial duties.[3]

In these cases of institutional bias a decision will be invalid only where the decision-maker actually fetters its discretion by failing to consider all relevant factors. The reasonable likelihood test is effectively displaced by a test of actual bias, or by the ordinary rules relating to the fettering of discretion.

## REASONS FOR DECISION

There is no general duty upon government to give reasons for its decisions.[4] However, in recent years, due largely to the development of flexible notions of 'fairness', this has been substantially qualified. Before looking at these qualifications two distinctions must be made.

First, there is a distinction between 'reasons' and 'grounds'. An authority may have to disclose the evidence it holds against the applicant as part of the normal duty to give a fair hearing. This is not the same as a duty to give reasons for its decision after it has been made.[5] The distinction between grounds and reasons also arises where a statute requires that action can be taken only on specified grounds, for example the deportation of an alien. In such a case the authority must disclose its grounds in order to bring itself within the statute but need not necessarily give supporting reasons as such.[6]

The second distinction arises from the judgment of Lord Donaldson MR in *R v Lancashire County Council, ex p Huddleston.*[7] His Lordship held that once an applicant has been given leave to apply for judicial review, the respondent authority has a duty to give the court sufficient information to help it to do justice. In some cases this involves a duty to give reasons. This 'cards on the table' approach is very limited; indeed, to take advantage of it the applicant must already have obtained leave and must therefore have some evidence of illegality. There is still no duty to give reasons to the public or to the complainant as such. Second, the duty is limited to the subject matter of the particular

1 See cases cited above, p 20, n 8. *Franklin v Minister of Town and Country Planning* [1948] AC 87, [1947] 2 All ER 289, HL.

2 *R v Sevenoaks District Council, ex p Terry* [1985] 3 All ER 226; *R v St Edmundsbury Borough Council, ex p Investors in Industry Commercial Properties Ltd* [1985] 3 All ER 234, [1985] 1 WLR 1157.

3 *R v Frankland Prison Visitors, ex p Lewis* [1986] 1 All ER 272, [1986] 1 WLR 130.

4 *Lonrho plc v Secretary of State for Trade and Industry* [1989] 2 All ER 609, HL; *Public Service Board of New South Wales v Osmond* (1986) 63 ALR 559; *McInnes v Onslow Fane* [1978] 3 All ER 211, [1978] 1 WLR 1520; *R v Civil Service Appeals Board, ex p Cunningham* [1991] 4 All ER 310, CA—'beyond argument'. *R v Secretary of State for the Home Department, ex p Doody* [1993] 1 All ER 151. But see *R v Secretary of State for the Home Department, ex p Creamer* (1992) Independent, 23 October where Rose J mentioned an 'apparent judicial climate in recent years tending towards openness'.

5 See *Breen v Amalgamated Engineering Union* [1971] 2 QB 175, [1971] 1 All ER 1148, CA.

6 *R v Secretary of State for the Home Department, ex p Cheblak* [1991] 2 All ER 319, [1991] 1 WLR 890, CA.

7 [1986] 2 All ER 941, CA. See also *R v Civil Service Appeals Board, ex p Cunningham* [1991] 4 All ER 310, CA.

allegations made by the applicant and does not require the decision as such to be explained or justified. The reasons need be no more than sufficient to dispel the allegations made. The *Huddleston* duty is therefore of little relevance to the general question of whether public authorities should give reasons for their decisions, either as an independent principle of openness or as an aspect of established principles of fairness.

The absence of a general duty to give reasons has been justified on the basis of administrative convenience, including the 'embarrassment' of having to give reasons[8] upon the 'undesirability' of encouraging challenge to decisions, upon the practical problems of multi-member tribunals and upon the subjective element in decision-making.[9] It is arguable that these matters, if they are credible at all, to the extent of the duty, rather than to the duty itself. It has also been said that the giving of reasons after a decision has been made does not affect the fairness of the decision-making process itself. This can be countered by pointing out that the existence of a duty to give reasons is capable of working through and structuring the decision-making process and also that fairness arguably includes sufficient information to be able to challenge the decision.

The modern principle of 'fairness' is sufficiently flexible and independent of the traditional concept of *audi alteram partem* to form the basis of a duty to give reasons. Moreover, European Community law imposes a duty to give reasons in many cases.[10] The English courts have rejected any general rule that fairness includes a duty to give reasons[11] and also the argument, derived from *Padfield v Minister of Agriculture, Fisheries and Food*,[12] that a refusal to give reasons in itself justifies the court in inferring that there are no adequate reasons for a decision.[13]

It therefore must be affirmatively shown that, in the particular circumstances, 'fairness' requires the giving of reasons. In *R v Parole Board, ex p Wilson*[14] the Court of Appeal departed from established principle in holding that the Parole Board should disclose to the applicant the material before it in relation to a forthcoming review of his case. However, this is a case of 'grounds' rather than reasons as such and the refusal of a discretionary benefit based on broad public interest considerations does usually require reasons.[15]

A legitimate expectation based upon past practice or undertakings might attract a duty to give reasons.[16] Reasons have been required where the decision

8 *R v Secretary of State for Social Services, ex p Connolly* [1986] 1 All ER 998, [1986] 1 WLR 421, CA.

9 *McInnes v Onslow Fane* (above, n 4).

10 See Art 190 Treaty of Rome. *R v Secretary of State for the Home Department, ex p Dannenberg* [1984] QB 766, [1984] 2 All ER 481, CA.

11 *R v Immigration Appeal Tribunal, ex p Khan (Mahmud)* [1983] QB 790, [1983] 2 All ER 420, CA; *R v Civil Service Appeals Board, ex p Bruce* [1988] 3 All ER 686 at 695–6.

12 [1968] AC 997.

13 *Lonrho plc v Secretary of State for Trade and Industry* [1989] 2 All ER 609.

14 [1992] 1 QB 740, [1992] 2 All ER 576. Wilson involved a discretionary life prisoner. In *R v Secretary of State for the Home Department ex p Doody* [1993] 1 All ER 151, the Court of Appeal held that a mandatory lifer might also have a right to reasons if there is an exceptionally large gap between the trial judge's tariff and the review period set. There is a right to be informed of the tariff, but not generally to reasons. See also Criminal Justice Act 1991 s 34 (discretionary lifers only).

15 *McInnes v Onslow Fane* (above, n 4).

16 See *R v London Borough of Enfield, ex p TF Unwin (Roydon) Ltd* (1989) 46 B LR 1; *Breen v Amalgamated Engineering Union* [1971] 2 QB 175, [1971] 1 All ER 1148, CA; *McInnes v Onslow Fane* [1978] 3 All ER 211, [1978] 1 WLR 1520.

involves the deprivation of an existing right or accusations of misconduct or bad character.[17] There may be a duty to give reasons where a decision departs from a usual practice, even where there is no legitimate expectation proper, if it would otherwise be impossible to challenge the decision.[18] A formal judicial procedure may attract a duty to give reasons.[19]

The existence of a right of appeal cuts both ways. If the appeal is a full de novo hearing the first instance tribunal may not be required to give reasons. Where there is only a limited right of appeal or no appeal at all there may be an inference in favour of reasons since otherwise it might be impossible to challenge the decision.[20]

## Statutory duties to give reasons

Duties to give reasons for decisions are imposed by about 450 statutes or statutory instruments. Most notable among these is the duty imposed by the Tribunals and Inquiries Act 1992 s 12 upon the tribunals listed in Schedule 1 of the Act to give reasons, if requested, on or before the notification of its decision. The same duty applies to decisions taken by a minister where a statutory public inquiry is held or could be required to be held. In most cases the duty is expressed as a duty to give 'reasons'. In some cases the duty extends to a 'clear and precise statement of full reasons'. In other cases it is limited to 'such reasons as the decision-maker considers appropriate'. However, the standard of reasons required under this formula is no different from that required by an unqualified duty to give reasons.[1]

It is not clear whether a failure to give adequate reasons required by statute counts as a point of law in its own right, for the purpose, for example, of an appeal on a point of law or whether an inadequate statement of reasons is merely the basis from which to infer some other defect.[2] A complete failure to give reasons is a procedural defect which justifies either setting aside the decision itself or an order of mandamus.

## The standard of reasons

There are numerous dicta which attempt to define the nature of an adequate statement of reasons. The statement of Megaw J in *Re Poyser and Mills Arbitration* has commanded widespread and eminent support.[3] This emphasises a minimalist and relativist approach. There is no universal objective standard of reason giving. The statement of reasons must be sufficient to tell persons affected by the decision whether they have grounds of challenge. Indeed the court will scrutinise the statement of reasons from the perspective of the particular applicant and will assess the reasons on the basis of prejudice to the

17 *R v Gaming Board for Great Britain, ex p Benaim and Khaida* [1970] 2 QB 417, [1970] 2 All ER 528, CA; *R v Secretary of State for Foreign and Commonwealth Affairs, ex p Everett* [1989] QB 811, [1989] 1 All ER 655, CA.

18 *R v Civil Service Appeals Board, ex p Cunningham* (above, n 4); *R v Secretary of State for the Home Department, ex p Doody* (above, note 14).

19 *R v Civil Service Appeals Board, ex p Cunningham* (above, n 4).

20 Ibid at 318, 325. See also *Bone v Mental Health Review Tribunal* [1985] 3 All ER 330 at 333.

1 *Bromsgrove District Council v Secretary of State for the Environment* (1991) 62 P & CR 297.

2 *Crake v Supplementary Benefit Commission* [1982] 1 All ER 498.

3 'The reasons must not only be intelligible but must deal with the substantial points raised.' *Save Britain's Heritage v Secretary of State for the Environment* [1991] 2 All ER 10 at 159–160; *Westminster City Council v Great Portland Estates plc* [1984] 3 WLR 1035 at 1045, HL. See also *Alexander Machinery (Dudley) Ltd v Crabtree* [1974] ICR 120 at 122; *R v Immigration Appeal Tribunal, ex p Khan (Mahmud)* [1983] 2 All ER 420 at 423, CA.

applicant's interests rather than according to fixed standards.[4] The main findings of fact must be set out and the issues between the parties identified. The tribunal's conclusions material to its decision must be expressed but not its findings on every point. The logical chain of reasoning must be complete, subjective value judgments must be identified, but neither these nor findings of fact need be justified in detail. In *R v Secretary of State for the Home Department, ex p Swati*[5] Parker LJ said that there was no right to 'reasons for the reasons'.

The House of Lords has approved a dictum of Phillips J in *Hope v Secretary of State*[6] where he said of a planning appeal that 'the decision must be such that it enables the applicant to understand on what ground the appeal had been decided and be in sufficient detail to enable him to know what conclusions the inspector has reached on the principal important controversial issues'. Finally, a statement of reasons can assume that the reader is fully aware of the background circumstances of the case and has any necessary technical knowledge, including apparently legal knowledge.[7]

4 *Save Britain's Heritage* (above, n 3).

5 [1986] 1 All ER 717 at 728. There the statement of reasons was little more than a recital of statutory grounds but where the applicant exercised a right of appeal (which in the circumstances was very difficult) he would have been entitled to more comprehensive reasons. See also *R v Secretary of State for the Home Department, ex p Cheblak* [1991] 2 All ER 319 at 329.

6 (1975) 31 P & CR 120 at 123. (*Save Britain's Heritage*, above, n 3 at 22.)

7 *Godden v Secretary of State for the Environment* [1988] JPL 99, *London Residuary Body v Secretary of State for the Environment* [1988] JPL 637 at 647.

CHAPTER 3

# Excluding and limiting judicial review

## GENERAL CONSIDERATIONS

The balance between the judiciary and the executive is a delicate one touching at times on some raw constitutional nerves. The courts are reluctant to see their powers of review excluded or eroded. But there are cases where judicial review would either be inappropriate or acceptable only to a limited degree. Until the 1960s the courts attempted to deal with this issue by manipulating conceptual categories of governmental activity. Classification as 'administrative', 'managerial', 'disciplinary' and 'prerogative' for example would be used to justify a policy of restraint. Today the courts prefer not to rely on such pigeonholes but to use the flexible and discretionary nature of the law in order to deal with problems of justiciability.[1] In principle all types of government power are reviewable including prerogative powers,[2] purely advisory statements,[3] other voluntary activities, disciplinary powers and managerial functions.[4] Some decisions have been held to be unreviewable because of their subject matter. In other cases a more restricted level of review is applied than normal. This is achieved mainly through the vague concepts of 'unfairness' and 'unreasonableness' and also through the choice of remedy. In particular a non-enforceable declaration is sometimes preferred to a formal quashing by certiorari or restraint by prohibition.

Thus Lord Donaldson MR has said[5]

> in considering how the courts of law have acted in particular situations as recorded in the reports it is important not to overlook the discretionary element. . . . In many, and perhaps most of the reported cases, the courts will not have been concerned to differentiate between a case in which they have no jurisdiction and one in which, whilst they may well have had jurisdiction, as a matter of discretion that jurisdiction would never be exercised.

In general the court will avoid entering into broad questions of policy formation particularly where competing claims upon resources are involved.[6] Local government, whose activities are increasingly circumscribed by statute,

1 See *Leech v Deputy Governor of Parkhurst Prison* [1988] 1 All ER 485 at 500, 517; *R v General Council of the Bar, ex p Percival* [1990] 3 All ER 137 at 149–152; *R v Panel on Take-overs and Mergers, ex p Datafin plc* [1987] 1 All ER 564 at 568–9.

2 *Council of Civil Service Unions v Minister for the Civil Service* [1985] AC 374, [1984] 3 All ER 935, HL.

3 *Gillick v West Norfolk and Wisbech Area Health Authority* [1986] AC 112, [1985] 3 All ER 402, HL.

4 *R v Criminal Injuries Compensation Board, ex p Lain* [1967] 2 QB 864, [1967] 2 All ER 770; *R v Panel on Take-overs and Mergers, ex p Datafin plc* [1987] QB 815, [1987] 1 All ER 564, CA.

5 *R v Hull University Visitor, ex p Page* [1991] 4 All ER 747 at 751, CA. See also *R v Secretary of State for Social Services, ex p Child Poverty Action Group* [1989] 1 All ER 1047 at 1055. See also n 1 above.

6 See *Nottingham County Council v Secretary of State for the Environment* [1986] AC 240, [1986] 1 All ER 199, HL; *Essex County Council v Minister of Housing and Local Government* (1967) 66 LGR 23; *Council of Civil Service Unions v Minister for the Civil Service* [1985] AC 374; *Bushell v Secretary of State for the Environment* [1981] AC 75, [1980] 2 All ER 608, HL.

is more accessible to review than central government. In the case of policy the application of existing policy to individual cases is more stringently reviewed than is a change of policy.[7] The courts are also prepared to interpret statements of policy, while at the same time recognising that a broader approach is required than is the case with legislation proper.[8]

At the other end of the scale, English law has no tradition of formally protected rights which can be overcome only if the government can show a compelling interest. The European Convention of Human Rights is binding on the UK but, subject to some dissenting voices, the courts do not treat this as significantly different from other treaties. They are prepared to apply the convention in judicial review cases only where the governing legislation is ambiguous. Officials are not required to exercise discretionary powers in accordance with the Convention.[9] However there is some indication that, at least at the evidential level, cases involving personal freedom attract a stringent standard of review.[10] By contrast freedom of speech does not appear to enjoy special protection.[11]

The deprivation of property rights is also given special weight but not necessarily restrictions upon the use of property.[12] More generally, cases involving interference with existing rights or interests are subject to a more stringent level of review, particularly in relation to procedural fairness than so called 'application cases' where an individual is applying for some benefit or permission from the state.[13] Cases involving financial exactions are also stringently reviewed.[14]

Until the 1960s, classification of a governmental activity as 'administrative' as opposed to 'judicial' sometimes excluded judicial review. Formal classification is no longer crucial but the old idea lingers on in the sense that 'judicial' functions may command a more rigorous standard of procedural fairness. Classification as 'judicial' is also relevant to immunity in the law of tort.

It is arguable that more rigorous standards should apply where governmental decisions frustrate a binding requirement or objective of European Community law. The House of Lords was forced to grant interim relief against the Crown in respect of a rule of European law[15] and the same argument might be drawn upon in other contexts. However in *R v Secretary of State for Employment, ex p Equal Opportunities Commission*[16] it was held that the court had no

7 *R v Secretary of State for Foreign and Commonwealth Affairs, ex p Everett* [1989] 1 QB 811, [1989] 1 All ER 655, CA; *Re Findlay* [1985] AC 318, [1984] 3 All ER 801, HL.

8 See eg *Waverley Borough Council v Secretary of State for the Environment and Clarke Homes (Southern) and Clarke Homes (South Eastern)* [1987] JPL 202.

9 Cmd 8969 (1953). *R v Secretary of State for the Home Department, ex p Brind* [1991] 1 AC 696 sub nom *Brind v Secretary of State for the Home Department* [1991] 1 All ER 720; cf *R v Secretary of State for the Home Department, ex p Phansopkar* [1976] QB 606, (Scarman LJ). See also *Waddington v Miah* [1974] 1 WLR 683 at 694 per Lord Reid. *R v Secretary of State for the Home Department, ex p K* [1990] 3 All ER 562 at 569; the European Convention could be of binding effect in relation to European Community law issues but see *Kaur v Lord Advocate* 1981 SLT 322.

10 *Khawaja v Secretary of State for the Home Department* [1984] AC 74, [1983] 1 All ER 765, HL.

11 *Wheeler v Leicester City Council* [1985] 2 All ER 1106 at 1112, HL.

12 *Hall v Shoreham-by-Sea UDC* [1964] 1 All ER 1, [1964] 1 WLR 240, CA; *Westminster Bank v Minister of Housing and Local Government* [1971] AC 508, [1970] 1 All ER 734, HL.

13 *McInnes v Onslow Fane* [1978] 3 All ER 211, [1978] 1 WLR 1520 subject to the 'legitimate expectation' argument (above, p 8 *et seq*).

14 Eg *McCarthy & Stones (Developments) Ltd v London Borough of Richmond upon Thames* [1992] 2 AC 48, [1991] 4 All ER 897, HL.

15 Below, p 147 *et seq*.

16 [1992] 1 All ER 545 at 561.

jurisdiction to compel by mandamus the Secretary of State to introduce legislation for the purpose of amending a UK statute to comply with European law. This was because an order of mandamus would be an unconstitutional restriction upon the independence of Parliament. The court's jurisdiction is limited to declaring rights and obligations under the existing law.

Judicial review is a remedy of last resort. Where there is an adequate alternative remedy, particularly one provided by statute, the court will normally exercise its discretion to refuse leave or to refuse a remedy. The matter of the adequacy of the alternative is likely to be dealt with at the hearing rather than at the leave stage. The court will examine the pros and cons of the alternative remedy in detail including questions of delay and cost effectiveness.[17]

## NON-JUSTICIABLE DECISIONS

Certain kinds of decision are wholly unreviewable. This depends upon subject matter rather than a priori classification or source of power (although they mainly involve the royal prerogative). They have been said to involve matters of high policy. The rationale for their exclusion probably lies in their political sensitivity and in the absence of objective principles. They involve the royal prerogative, but by no means include all prerogative powers. According to Lord Roskill in *Council of Civil Service Unions v Minister for the Civil Service*[18] they exclude the following: 'the making of treaties, defence, the prerogative of mercy (sed quaere), the grant of honours, the dissolution of Parliament, the appointment of ministers as well as others'. It has also been held that the Attorney General's powers to initiate legal proceedings in the public interest is non-justiciable.[19] The court has a residual power to refuse to review on public policy grounds.[20]

## OUSTER CLAUSES

There are statutory provisions that purport to exclude judicial review. The courts lean against ouster of their jurisdiction and construe such provisions restrictively. For example a provision that a decision be 'final' does not prevent judicial review at all but merely removes any statutory appeal that would otherwise exist and perhaps prevents revocation.[1] Less plausibly, it has been consistently held that a provision stating that a decision or a determination, order etc 'shall not be questioned in any court of law' does not prevent challenge on the ground that the decision is ultra vires. Being a complete nullity it is not a 'decision' within the meaning of the Act.[2] Coupled with the proposition that all reviewable defects can result in nullity this imposes an obligation upon the draftsman to be explicit in restricting the jurisdiction of the courts.

17 See *R v Secretary of State for Employment, ex p Equal Opportunities Commission* [1992] 1 All ER 545; *R v Chief Constable of Merseyside Police, ex p Calveley* [1986] QB 424, [1986] 1 All ER 257, CA; *R v Panel on Take-overs and Mergers, ex p Guinness plc* [1990] 1 QB 146, [1989] 1 All ER 509, CA and below p 122 *et seq*.

18 [1985] AC 374 at 418. See also *R v Secretary of State for Foreign and Commonwealth Affairs, ex p Everett* [1989] 1 All ER 655 at 660.

19 *Gouriet v Union of Post Office Workers* [1978] AC 435, [1977] 3 All ER 70, HL.

20 See *R v General Council of the Bar, ex p Percival* (above, n 1) at 152.

1 *R v Medical Appeal Tribunal, ex p Gilmore* [1957] 1 QB 574 *sub nom Re Gilmore's Application* [1957] 1 All ER 796, CA. But see *Page v Hull University Visitor* [1993] 1 All ER 97, HL.

2 *Anisminic Ltd v Foreign Compensation Commission* [1969] 2 AC 147, [1969] 1 All ER 208, HL.

Two types of ouster clause have proved to be effective. One is the 'six weeks time limit clause' that permits review within the time limit by means of a special procedure but bans all other forms of challenge in the courts. This excludes other forms of review completely and is very strictly applied.[3] The second is a 'conclusive evidence' clause. This does not exclude review as such but makes it impossible to establish grounds for review by providing that a physical act, for example entry on a register or a signature, shall be 'conclusive evidence' that the decision is valid and within the statutory powers.[4] It may be, however, that the conclusive evidence clause cannot withstand an allegation of bad faith or possibly of breach of natural justice, ie it can be construed as protecting only the substantive decision.

Ministers are often given statutory power to alter or to insert new provisions in an Act of Parliament. This does not prevent the exercise of the power from being challenged.[5] For this reason an older type of ouster clause that gives regulations the same effect 'as if enacted in the Act' might not be effective.[6]

The Divisional Court has said that, when applying for leave, relevant ouster clauses should be specifically drawn to the court's attention.[7]

## SPECIAL CASES

The level of judicial review and the choice of remedy are highly specific to their context. There are some cases where the courts have expressed a particular reluctance to intervene or where they have applied special principles. These have emerged upon an ad hoc basis and the list is not exhaustive.

### National security

National security issues are not wholly outside judicial review but the court will confine itself to deciding whether the decision-maker, usually a minister, is acting in good faith within the language of the governing legislation if any. The court can also look at evidence that the issue is genuinely one of national security although, probably, this requirement is minimal. Beyond that the court will accept the opinion of the Crown as to what national security requires and a claim of national security will normally suffice to exclude a right to be heard.[8]

### Voluntary regulation

Bodies whose powers do not depend upon any formal legal source but upon voluntary acquiescence are subject to judicial review provided that they are of

3 *R v Secretary of State for the Environment, ex p Ostler* [1977] QB 122, [1976] 3 All ER 90, CA; *R v Cornwall County Council, ex p Huntingdon* [1992] 3 All ER 566 at 574–5. *Griffiths v Secretary of State for the Environment* [1983] 2 AC 51–time runs from date of decision.

4 *R v Registrar of Companies, ex p Central Bank of India* [1986] QB 1114; *Ex p Ringer* (1909) 25 TLR 718.

5 See *Woolwich Equitable Building Society v IRC* [1991] 4 All ER 92, HL.

6 Cf *R v Minister of Health, ex p Yaffe* [1931] AC 494, HL. By virtue of the Tribunals and Inquiries Act 1992 s 14 many ouster clauses passed before 1 August 1958 are repealed as far as certiorari is concerned.

7 *R v Cornwall County Council* (above, n 3) at 576.

8 *Council of Civil Service Unions v Minister for the Civil Service* [1985] AC 374, [1984] 3 All ER 935, HL; *R v Secretary of State for the Home Department, ex p Ruddock* [1987] 1 WLR 1482 at 1490; *R v Secretary of State for the Home Department, ex p Hosenball* [1977] 3 All ER 452, [1977] 1 WLR 766, CA; *The Zamora* [1916] 2 AC 77 at 107; *R v Governor of Brixton Prison, ex p Soblen* [1963] 2 QB 243, [1962] 3 All ER 641, CA; *Chandler v DPP* [1964] AC 763.

a public character.[9] However special problems arise because such bodies make their own rules and because there is a particular need for their decisions to be supported. A broader and less interventionist approach has been applied than in the case of statutory tribunals and the discretionary nature of judicial review has been stressed. First, a distinction has been made between interfering with a contemporary decision-making process and making a ruling after the event which avoids formally quashing the decision. The court should normally allow the proceedings to take their course 'intervening if at all, later and in retrospect by declaratory orders which would enable the panel not to repeat any error and would relieve individuals of the disciplinary consequences of any erroneous findings of breach of the rules'.[10] However, in cases of bias or unfair procedure the court would intervene to quash or restrain a decision. Second, the normal three grounds of review (illegality, irrationality and procedural impropriety) lacking statutory terms of reference are more than usually elusive. In *R v Panel on Take-overs and Mergers, ex p Guinness plc*[11] Lord Donaldson MR suggested that the court should review 'more in the round than might otherwise be the case' and 'whilst basing its decision on familiar concepts should eschew any formal categorisation'.[12] His Lordship suggested 'an innominate ground' formed of an amalgam of the three categories 'with perhaps added elements reflecting the unique nature of the panel . . . the ultimate question would, as always, be whether something had gone wrong of a nature and degree which required the intervention of the court'.[13]

There is some authority, albeit prior to *Datafin*, that purely ex gratia governmental payments of money are not susceptible to judicial review.[14]

Some self-regulatory bodies have a statutory basis. Nevertheless similar arguments in favour of a limited level of judicial review also apply to them.[15]

## Prisons

Until recently it was believed that internal disciplinary and management decisions within prisons were subject only to a limited level of review. The position now appears to be that the normal principles apply not only to decisions by the Home Secretary and external prison visitors, but also to the Parole Board,[16] and internal disciplinary decisions.[17] However, as with all areas of judicial review, context and discretion are important and the court will give special weight to security and efficiency considerations and also to the broader public interest as they see it.[18] In particular, while it has been asserted that prisoners have their civil liberties only to the extent necessarily required

9 *R v Panel on Take-overs and Mergers, ex p Datafin plc* [1987] QB 815, [1984] 1 All ER 564, CA.
10 Ibid at 589.
11 [1990] 1 QB 146, [1989] 1 All ER 509, CA.
12 At 513.
13 At 512–513. See also Woolf LJ at 538–9.
14 *R v Secretary of State for the Home Department, ex p Chubb* [1986] Crim LR 809. Cf a formal system for awarding compensation viz the Criminal Injuries Compensation Board which was held to be subject to judicial review in *R v Criminal Injuries Compensation Board, ex p Lain* [1967] 2 QB 864, [1967] 2 All ER 770, even before the CICB was put on a statutory basis.
15 See *R v Life Assurance and Unit Trust Regulatory Organisation Ltd, ex p Ross* [1992] 1 All ER 422.
16 *R v Parole Board, ex p Wilson* [1992] 1 QB 740, [1991] 2 All ER 576, CA.
17 *Leech v Deputy Governor of Parkhurst Prison* [1988] AC 533, [1988] 1 All ER 485, HL; cf *R v Board of Visitors of HM Prison, The Maze, ex p Hone* [1988] AC 379, sub nom *Hone v Maze Prison Board of Visitors* [1988] 1 All ER 321, HL, *R v Secretary of State for the Home Department, ex p Doody* [1993] 1 All ER 151, CA.
18 Eg *Re Findlay* [1985] AC 318 at 338. See also *Williams v Home Office (No 2)* [1981] 1 All ER 1211.

by statute,[19] the prison rules have been held not to create private law rights.[20] Except in cases involving ordinary torts it would appear that judicial review is effectively a prisoner's only remedy, reinforced by the possibility of an application under the European Convention of Human Rights.

## Child care

The Children Act 1989 has conferred wide discretionary powers on local authorities and social workers thus increasing the possibility of judicial review. In *R v Harrow London Borough Council, ex p D*,[1] a case involving a decision of a local authority to place a child's name on its child abuse register, the Court of Appeal accepted that a decision which was 'utterly unreasonable' should be reviewed but also held that recourse to judicial review ought to be rare and that all concerned in this difficult and delicate area should be allowed to perform their task without looking over their shoulder all the time for the possible intervention of the court. The power of the court to intervene should be kept very much in reserve, perhaps confined to the exceptional case which involves a point of principle which needs to be resolved not only for the individual case but in general.

This cautious approach could equally apply to areas of child care jurisdiction apart from that of child abuse. In particular the court was reluctant to encourage review of the way that case conferences reached their decisions.

## Emergency powers

Emergency powers are not in principle immune from review but the court will interfere only where the applicant can show strong evidence of ultra vires, bad faith or arbitrariness. The rules of natural justice will also apply in an attenuated form.[2]

## Advisory circulars

Government circulars setting out policy guidance have no legal force unless specifically made in pursuance of statutory powers. Where officials apply them in order to determine a particular case their application is reviewable on ordinary grounds. The interpretation of a circular is treated as a matter of law for the court.[3] An authority with discretionary powers to decide individual cases cannot fetter its discretion by relying absolutely upon a policy enshrined in a circular. On the other hand an individual who has reasonably relied on a circular could argue that the circular has created a 'legitimate expectation' in his favour. This means that if the circular is not applied, the individual must be

19 *Raymond v Honey* [1983] 1 AC 1 at 10.

20 *Arbon v Anderson* [1943] KB 252, [1943] 1 All ER 154; cf *Raymond v Honey* [1983] 1 AC 1, [1982] 1 All ER 756, HL; *R v Secretary of State for the Home Department, ex p Herbage (No 2)* [1987] QB 1077, [1987] 1 All ER 324, CA.

1 [1990] 3 All ER 12 at 16–17.

2 *R v Secretary of State for Transport, ex p Pegasus Holdings Ltd* [1989] 2 All ER 481, [1988] 1 WLR 990; *Secretary of State for Employment v Associated Society of Locomotive Engineers and Firemen (No 2)* [1972] 2 QB 455, [1972] 2 All ER 949, CA.

3 *Waverley Borough Council v Secretary of State for the Environment and Clarke Homes (Southern) and Clarke Homes (South Eastern)* [1987] JPL 202.

given a hearing and the authority must justify departing from it.[4] A legitimate expectation cannot however prevent the government from altering or withdrawing a policy provided that this is announced in advance[5] and there is no general obligation to consult or to give a hearing before changing a policy. It might however be arguable that a person with a legitimate expectation created by an undertaking or assurance given to him on an individual basis has a right to be heard to the extent of claiming to be exempted from the change in policy.

A circular or other form of published government advice can also be challenged directly. A declaration is the most appropriate remedy. However a *refusal* to give general advice is probably not reviewable and there is authority that advisory circulars as such should only be reviewed on the ground that they are clearly inconsistent with the general law.[6] Purely informal advice, for example in a letter, is probably not reviewable absent a legitimate expectation.

## Public finance

Central government decisions concerning the allocation of public finance are subject to a lower than normal level of judicial review for unreasonableness. This restriction was imposed by the House of Lords in *Nottinghamshire County Council v Secretary of State for the Environment*.[7] It does not affect review on the grounds of illegality including the taking of irrelevant factors into account or the failure to take relevant factors into account, nor does it affect review on procedural grounds. According to Lord Bridge[8] a statutory power conferred upon a minister which involves 'the formulation and implementation of national economic policy and which can only take effect with the approval of the House of Commons is not open to challenge short of the extremes of bad faith, improper motives or manifest absurdity'. In the words of Lord Scarman it must be shown 'that the Secretary of State had acted in bad faith or for an improper motive or that the consequences of his guidance were so absurd that he must have taken leave of his senses'.[9]

It is not easy to see how there can be a lower standard of irrationality than the 'normal' level formulated by Lord Diplock[10] that a decision must be 'so outrageous in its defiance of logic or of accepted moral standards that no sensible person who had applied his mind to the question to be decided could have arrived at it'. However despite this rhetoric which suggests that instant resignation should be the result of a finding of unreasonableness, the courts in

4 See *HTV Ltd v Price Commission* [1976] ICR 170; *A-G of Hong Kong v Ng Yuen Shiu* [1983] 2 AC 629, [1983] 2 All ER 346, PC; *R v Secretary of State for the Home Department, ex p Asif Khan* [1985] 1 All ER 40, [1984] 1 WLR 1337, CA; *R v Secretary of State for the Home Department, ex p Ruddock* [1987] 2 All ER 518, [1987] 1 WLR 1482. Above p 8 *et seq*.

5 *Re Findlay* [1985] AC 318, [1984] 3 All ER 801, HL; *Hughes v Department of Health and Social Security* [1985] AC 776 at 788, HL; *R v Secretary of State for Health, ex p United States Tobacco International Inc* [1992] 1 QB 353, [1992] 1 All ER 212, but see *R v Secretary of State for the Home Department, ex p Asif Khan* (above, p 11, n 13) per Parker LJ.

6 *Gillick v West Norfolk and Wisbech Area Health Authority* [1986] AC 112 at 193–4. See also *Royal College of Nursing of the United Kingdom v Department of Health and Social Security* [1981] AC 800, [1981] 1 All ER 545. Cf below p 68.

7 [1986] AC 240, [1986] 1 All ER 199, HL.

8 *Hammersmith and Fulham London Borough Council v Secretary of State for the Environment* [1990] 3 All ER 589 at 637.

9 *Nottingham* case (above, n 7 at 202).

10 *Council of Civil Service Unions v Minister for the Civil Service* [1984] 3 All ER 935 at 951.

fact apply a much lower threshold of unreasonableness in non-financial contexts, particularly in the case of local authority decisions and appear to blur the line between unreasonableness as such and unfairness.[11]

More generally cases involving broad or complex discretions concerning the allocation of resources will generally be treated with circumspection. This includes education, housing and social security areas[12] and is particularly the case in relation to the allocation of health resources. Challenges to decisions concerning the allocation of hospital treatment are in practice unreviewable.[13] Such challenges face a combination of broad discretion, the absence of defined legal rights the exercise of professional judgment, and the difficulty of obtaining evidence about the adequacy of medical provision so as to produce any kind of justiciable standard. The fact that an allocation decision is couched in terms of duty makes little difference. Duties which depend upon the allocation of limited resources, for example the provision of sufficient school places,[14] are reviewable only in the event of a total failure to attempt to fulfil the duty or a positive ultra vires act.

## Professional value judgments

The courts are reluctant to interfere with judgments within the special expertise of professional bodies but such decisions are not wholly excluded from review. A distinction can perhaps be made between professional judgments as such and cases where a person is charged with breach of a professional code of conduct involving fraud or other behaviour analogous to an ordinary criminal offence. In the latter case there is no reason for any special deference apart from the court's usual unwillingness to review findings of fact.[15]

## Military tribunals

There are dicta that decisions made by military tribunals will be reviewed only where ordinary civil rights are in issue.[16] However, this may be a matter of discretion. The court will be reluctant to substitute its opinion upon specialist questions of military or spiritual law[17] but there is no reason why the court should refrain from interference in cases of breach of natural justice. A distinction has also been made between tribunals such as courts martial constituted by statute and ad hoc tribunals established by military authorities as part of their command functions. The latter have been said to be entirely

11 See *Wheeler v Leicester City Council* [1985] AC 1054. An example of a strict application is *Secretary of State for Education and Science v Tameside Metropolitan Borough Council* [1977] AC 1014 in favour of a local authority, but the 'reasonableness' standard had to be applied by the Secretary of State not by the court directly.

12 See *Puhlhofer v Hillingdon London Borough Council* [1986] 1 All ER 467 at 474.

13 *R v Secretary of State for Social Services, ex p Hincks* (18 March 1980, unreported) CA; *Re Walker's Application* (1987) Times, 26 November, CA; *R v Central Birmingham Health Authority, ex p Collier* (6 January 1988, unreported).

14 Described as 'target duties' by Woolf LJ in *R v Inner London Education Authority, ex p Ali* [1990] 2 Admin LR 822, 829.

15 *R v General Council of the Bar, ex p Percival* [1990] 3 All ER 137 at 153; *General Medical Council v Spackman* [1943] 2 All ER 337 at 362; *Bhattachanga v General Medical Council* [1967] 2 AC 259 at 265, PC; *Re a Solicitor, ex p Law Society* [1912] 1 KB 302; *Hounslow London Borough Council v Twickenham Garden Developments Ltd* [1971] Ch 233, [1970] 3 All ER 326. But cf *Page v Hull University Visitor* [1993] 1 All ER 97, HL, rejecting this kind of argument.

16 *R v Secretary of State for War, ex p Martyn* [1949] 1 All ER 242; *R v O/C Depot Battalion RASC Colchester, ex p Elliott* [1949] 1 All ER 373.

17 See *R v Hull University Visitor, ex p Page* [1991] 4 All ER 747 at 751–2.

extra legal.[18] However, modern cases extending judicial review beyond the formal legal sources of power throw doubt upon this distinction. A more satisfactory explanation of it may be that it applies only in wartime or in emergency conditions.[19]

## Ecclesiastical courts

These can be reviewed by prohibition and presumably declaration, but not by certiorari.[20]

## Visitors

It has been held that universities have a sufficiently public character to fall within judicial review.[1] However, where under its statute or charter of incorporation the university has appointed a visitor, the visitor's jurisdiction in relation to disputes arising from powers exercised under the university's internal rules is exclusive and disputes must be dealt with initially by the visitor.[2] Decisions made by the visitor can be reviewed on the grounds of unfairness, abuse of power or exceeding jurisdiction in the narrow sense,[3] but not for errors of law even in relation to non-academic matters. The visitors to the Inns of Court are subject to the same principles.[4] The judges act as visitors to the Inns.

By virtue of the Education Reform Act 1988 s 206(1) the visitor's jurisdiction is excluded in relation to employment disputes between a member of a university and its academic staff except where a dispute has been referred to and accepted by the visitor before a date specified in the Act (this being the date on which a Commission will alter the university's governing instrument to impose special appeal arrangements). During this interim period the court therefore has a provisional jurisdiction.[5] Moreover industrial tribunals have a concurrent jurisdiction with the visitor.[6]

## Superior courts

Decisions of superior courts are not subject to judicial review. This is a consequence of the history of the prerogative orders as instruments for controlling the jurisdiction of inferior tribunals by the royal courts. There is little doubt, however, that the same applies to the declaration and injunction.[7] The High Court itself is in a special position as a court of unlimited jurisdiction whose decisions can be challenged only on appeal, or by application to the

18 *Re Clifford and O'Sullivan* [1921] 2 AC 570, HL.
19 *R v Criminal Injuries Compensation Board, ex p Lain* [1967] 2 QB 864 at 886.
20 Below p 54. *R v North, ex p Oakey* [1927] 1 KB 491, CA.
1 *R v Hull University Visitor, ex p Page* [1991] 4 All ER 747 at 751.
2 *Thomas v University of Bradford* [1987] AC 795, [1987] 1 All ER 834, HL.
3 Above, p 12.
4 *Page v Hull Univesity Visitor* [1993] 1 All ER 97; *R v Visitors to Lincoln's Inn, ex p Penaud* (1993) Times, 26 January, CA.
5 See *Pearce v University of Aston in Birmingham* [1991] 2 All ER 461, CA. See also *Oakes v Sidney Sussex College, Cambridge* [1988] 1 All ER 1004, [1988] 1 WLR 431; *R v HM the Queen in Council, ex p Vijayatunga* [1990] 2 QB 444, *sub nom R v University of London Visitor, ex p Vijayatunga* [1989] 2 All ER 843, CA.
6 *Thomas v University of Bradford* (above, n 2) at 849.
7 *Re Racal Communications* [1980] 2 All ER 634 at 638, 641, 646, HL. *R v Cripps, ex p Muldoon* [1984] QB 68, [1983] 3 All ER 72.

court to set aside its own decision.[8] Other superior courts can in principle act outside their jurisdiction and it might be possible to challenge such a decision collaterally. A superior court judge can be liable in damages for *knowingly* exceeding jurisdiction.[9]

One hallmark of a superior court is that its decisions are presumed to be within its jurisdiction unless the contrary can be shown whereas an inferior court (or other public body) must show that it is acting within its jurisdiction.[10]

In some cases the governing statute states expressly whether or not the body in question is a superior court. The Crown Court provides a complex example of a special statutory case and will be discussed below. County courts and magistrates' courts are inferior courts. Where the statute is silent 'it is necessary to look at all the relevant features of the tribunal' in order to determine its status.[11] One important feature is whether, looked at broadly, the tribunal should be subject to judicial review, eg where there is no right of appeal. Other factors are whether the membership of the tribunal includes a High Court judge and the width of the jurisdiction of the tribunal. According to Ormod LJ in *Sirros v Moore*[12] there is a presumption that a body is not a superior court if its jurisdiction is limited by person, place or subject matter.

A special problem arises in the case of the Crown Court. Decisions of the Crown Court are sometimes reviewable even though the Crown Court is a superior court[13] but only by the prerogative orders. Section 29(3) of the Supreme Court Act 1981 provides that: 'in relation to the jurisdiction of the Crown Court, other than its jurisdiction in matters relating to trial on indictment, the High Court shall have all such jurisdiction to make orders of mandamus, prohibition or certiorari as the High Court possesses in relation to the jurisdiction of an inferior court'.[14]

The jurisdiction of the Crown Court in relation to 'trial on indictment' is not therefore reviewable. The meaning of 'in relation to' in this context has caused considerable difficulty in connection with the Crown Court's power to make decisions about peripheral and ancillary matters such as costs, jury empanelling and bail.[15] *Re Smalley*[16] is the leading case. The question there was whether an order estreating a recognisance of a surety where the defendant had jumped bail was reviewable. The House of Lords held that it was reviewable. They applied what Lord Bridge called a 'helpful pointer' (while suggesting that a precise test was impossible).[17] The helpful pointer was in favour of a narrow construction that did not unduly restrict rights of challenge in cases where no other right existed. The test was whether the decision to be challenged affected the actual conduct of the trial.[18] The rationale behind this is to avoid delay

8 *Isaacs v Robertson* [1985] AC 97, [1984] 3 All ER 140, PC; *Hadkinson v Hadkinson* [1952] 2 All ER 567 at 565, CA.
9 Below, p 95.
10 See *Peacock v Bell and Kendall* (1667) 1 Saund 69; *R v Judge Pugh, ex p Grahame* [1951] 2 KB 623, [1951] 2 All ER 307; *London Corpn v Cox* (1867) LR 2 HL 239 at 262. The distinction between courts of record (which include some inferior courts such as magistrates) and courts not of record may also be relevant.
11 *R v Cripps, ex p Muldoon* [1984] QB 68, [1983] 3 All ER 72—election court is an inferior court.
12 [1975] QB 118 at 150, CA.
13 Courts Act 1971 s 4(1).
14 See also Prosecution of Offences Act 1985 s 22(13); cf Criminal Justice Act 1988 s 159.
15 See Ward [1990] PL 50 for a valuable overview to which we are indebted.
16 [1985] AC 622 *sub nom Smalley v Crown Court at Warwick*, [1985] 1 All ER 769, HL.
17 Ibid at 643–4, 780.
18 Ibid at 643, 779.

bearing in mind that the accused has a right of appeal and by tradition the prosecution is without remedy in relation to trials in the Crown Court.

*Smalley* was followed in *R v Central Criminal Court, ex p Randle*[19] where it was held that a decision not to stay proceedings as an abuse of process was not a matter relating to a trial of indictment whereas a decision to quash a trial because of a defective indictment would be, as would a decision that an indictment be not proceeded with without leave. There is therefore a distinction between a decision that a trial does not take place at all and a decision concerning the time and manner of trial.

Lord Bridge's 'helpful pointer' is not exhaustive. In *Sampson v Crown Court at Croydon* an order that the defendant pay £250 towards his legal aid costs was held to relate to a trial on indictment because it was 'an integral part of the trial process'.[20] This was after the trial and could not therefore affect its conduct. Moreover, their Lordships refused to distinguish between costs orders as such and legal aid orders, both being affected by what happens at the trial itself.[1] This seems to override other policy arguments since there was no question of delay in the *Sampson* case which also left the applicant without remedy.

## PARLIAMENT

Approval by Parliament does not in itself prevent judicial review and is strictly irrelevant to the question of legality.[2] The existence of parliamentary control can, however, influence the court indirectly. In a borderline case the fact that a decision is subject to approval by the House of Commons (however illusory) might tip the balance away from a finding of unreasonableness or unfairness.[3]

Decisions made by either House of Parliament concerning its internal proceedings[4] cannot be challenged in the courts. Nor can the court prevent a matter being submitted to Parliament.[5] On the other hand parliamentary approval does not exclude judicial review as such either before the matter goes to Parliament or afterwards. Where review is sought before a matter goes to Parliament a declaration will normally be the only remedy since it would be improper to prevent Parliament from considering the matter.[6]

19 [1992] 1 All ER 370, [1991] 1 WLR 1087 (The *Burgess Masterminders* case). See also *R v Central Criminal Court, ex p Raymond* [1986] 2 All ER 379, [1986] 1 WLR 710.

20 [1987] 1 All ER 609 at 613, HL.

1 See also *R v Smith (Martin)* [1975] QB 531 per Megew LJ at 545—possible distinction where order made against third party. *R v Southwark Crown Court, ex p Cohen* (1989) Independent 7 November. A distinction could also be made in the case of contribution orders under the Legal Aid Act 1982.

2 *Hoffman-La Roche (F) and Co AG v Secretary of State for Trade and Industry* [1975] AC 295, [1974] 2 All ER 1128, HL; cf *R v Secretary of State for the Environment, ex p Hackney London Borough Council* [1984] 1 All ER 956, [1984] 1 WLR 592, CA—discretion not to interfere.

3 See *R v Secretary of State for Employment, ex p Equal Opportunities Commission* [1992] 1 All ER 545. *R v HM Treasury, ex p Smedley* [1985] QB 657, [1985] 1 All ER 589, CA; *R v Boundary Commission, ex p Foot* [1983] QB 600 at 626, CA.

4 *Bradlough v Gossett* (1884) 12 QBD 271.

5 *Bilston Corpn v Wolverhampton Corpn* [1942] Ch 391, [1942] 2 All ER 447.

6 *R v Boundary Commission, ex p Foot* (above, note 3).

CHAPTER 4

# Administrative finality: revocation and res judicata

As an alternative to direct challenge an aggrieved person may request a decision-maker to revoke his decision. This would raise the issue of whether the decision is capable of being revoked. Alternatively the aggrieved person may decide to leave the decision unchallenged but challenge it at a later date—by way of collateral attack in different proceedings. This latter course may raise the issue of res judicata or 'issue estoppel'. We will consider both of these problems which concern the finality or otherwise of administrative decisions.

## REVOCATION

Where a decision is ultra vires then no question of revocation arises. The previous decision can be challenged in the courts and mandamus issued to compel the authority to make a fresh decision. However, where an authority has the power to revoke its own decisions this may provide a convenient method of securing redress in respect of an unsatisfactory decision. An improper refusal to revoke a decision could itself be challenged.

Authorities on the question of revocation are sparse. It may be that the view of one eminent commentator that the matter is essentially pragmatic and policy oriented is correct.[1] In the present state of the law, it is only possible to suggest some general lines of argument. There are many and diverse cases where statute provides an express power of revocation. Some are limited, expressly or impliedly, to cases of fraud or mistake. Some require a special procedure and/or the payment of compensation.

One provision of general import is contained in the Interpretation Act 1978, s 14. This creates a presumption that a power to make a statutory instrument or other subordinate legislation implies the power to revoke, amend or re-enact the same.

Before determining whether a decision can be revoked we must first decide when that decision becomes effective. Only at that point does the decision-maker become *functus officio* and the decision perhaps irrevocable. The matter depends upon the construction of the governing legislation. What is the final operative act which completes the decision-making process? Subject to the provisions of the particular statute, the choice lies between the performance by the decision-maker of the final act in this process (eg a resolution completed or confirmed or a document signed) or the notification of the decision to the persons affected by it, including of course sub-issues as to what counts as notification.[2] In *R v Yeovil Borough Council, ex p Trustees of Elim Pentecostal Church*[3] it was

1 SA de Smith *Judicial Review of Administrative Action* (4th edn, 1980) by JM Evans, pp 107–108.
2 See *Ringwood Investments Ltd and Courtburn v Secretary of State for the Environment* (1979) 40 P & CR 99. See Interpretation Act 1978, s 7; RSC Ord 55, r 4(4).
3 (1971) 23 P & CR 39, 70 LGR 142. See *Slough Estates v Slough Borough Council (No 2)* [1971] AC 958, [1970] 2 All ER 216. See also [1969] 2 Ch 305 at 315.

held that a planning permission becomes effective only when it is notified to the applicant, so that even after a local planning authority had formally resolved to grant permission, it was free to change its mind at any time before notification of the decision. This case may have confused the question of what constitutes a planning permission for purposes of construction with the question of when the permission takes effect, but nevertheless it is consistent with cases decided in other contexts in favour of a presumption that a decision takes effect only when it is notified.[4] Where this presumption is rebutted, the authority's final formal act may make the decision binding.[5]

## Irrevocable decisions

Whether a valid decision can be revoked depends primarily upon the nature and effect of the decision. The governing distinction is between on the one hand a decision which is (a) based on the application of rules of law, and (b) declares the existing rights of the citizen (a judicial decision), and on the other hand a decision involving a discretion to allocate benefits and privileges.

A judicial decision cannot generally be revoked. Thus in *Re 56 Denton Road, Twickenham*,[6] the War Damage Commission classified the plaintiff's property as a non-total-loss. This entitled the plaintiff to a more favourable level of compensation than would be the case with a 'total loss' classification. The Commission later purported to alter the classification. It was held that once the decision had been communicated 'in terms which are not expressly preliminary or provisional it is final and conclusive'. Vaisey J emphasised that the principle here had nothing to do with estoppel.

## Revocable decisions

There appear to be four exceptions to the principle that a judicial decision cannot be revoked. First, a judicial decision can be revoked with the consent of all the affected parties. Second, it appears that a tribunal can preserve a power of revocation by communicating its decision in terms that are expressly stated to be provisional.[7] Third, it is said that a decision procured by fraud can always be revoked.[8] This is hardly an exception, because a decision tainted by fraud is ultra vires even where the decision-maker itself is not a party to the fraud. The final exception is a 'slip rule' which permits ambiguities or minor errors to be amended. It may be, however, that this requires a statutory basis.[9]

4 *Bailey v Williamson* (1873) LR 8 QB 118, 42 LJMC 49; *Norfolk County Council v Secretary of State for the Environment* [1973] 3 All ER 673, [1973] 1 WLR 1400; *Co-operative Retail Services Ltd v Taff-Ely Borough Council* (1979) 39 P & CR 223 CA; affd (1981) 42 P &CR 1, HL; *Miller v Weymouth and Melcombe Regis Corpn* (1974) 118 Sol Jo 421, 27 P & CR 468; *Re 56 Denton Road, Twickenham* [1953] Ch 51, [1952] 2 All ER 799.

5 *R v Criminal Injuries Compensation Board, ex p Tong* [1977] 1 All ER 171, [1976] 1 WLR 1237, CA; *Griffiths v Secretary of State for the Environment* [1983] 2 AC 51.

6 [1953] Ch 51, [1952] 2 All ER 799. See also *R v Epping and Harlow General Comrs, ex p Goldstraw* [1983] 3 All ER 257, [1983] STC 693, CA; *Punton v Ministry of Pensions and National Insurance (No 2)* [1964] 1 All ER 448, [1964] 1 WLR 226, CA; *IRC v Soul* (1976) 51 TC 86; *Livingstone v Westminster Corpn* [1904] 2 KB 109, 73 LJKB 434.

7 *Re 56 Denton Road, Twickenham* [1953] Ch 51, [1952] 2 All ER 799.

8 *Lazarus Estates Ltd v Beasley* [1956] 1 QB 702, [1956] 1 All ER 341, CA.

9 *R v Income Tax General Comrs for Morleston and Litchurch, ex p G. R. Turner Ltd* (1951) 32 TC 335. But cf *R v Cripps, ex p Muldoon* [1984] QB 68, [1984] 2 All ER 705; *Preston Borough Council v Secretary of State for the Environment and ELS Wholesale Wolverhampton* [1978] JPL 548.

**Administrative decisions involving the exercise of discretion may be revocable**

This kind of power does not affect pre-existing rights and duties and may involve the allocation of scarce public resources, so that there are cogent arguments for preserving a degree of governmental flexibility. The leading case is the decision of the Court of Appeal in *Rootkin v Kent County Council*.[10] The defendant authority had a statutory obligation to pay travelling expenses to children whose journey to school was more than three miles, but a discretion in other cases. The authority mistakenly believed that the plaintiff's child lived outside the three-mile limit and made a payment on that basis. Having discovered its mistake, it revoked the decision. It was held that the authority was entitled to do so on the ground that on a correct view of the facts the child had no right to payment. Thus had the child actually lived more than three miles from school, payment would have been as of right and revocation would not have been permissible even in the event, for example, of a mistake as to the amount payable. Similarly a decision to waive liability to tax is revocable,[11] whereas an assessment is not. It is not enough that the decision is discretionary. In *Rootkin* the decision involved the making of a payment by the State. Some discretionary powers may involve interference with existing legal rights. It is arguable that this kind of power is not revocable.[12]

The doctrine of estoppel cannot restrict the exercise of a statutory discretion and cannot prevent revocation of a decision or changes of policy. However, the existence of a prior representation is a relevant factor to be considered when exercising a valid discretion to revoke. Thus where an individual has reasonably relied on a particular practice or policy to his detriment the authority must justify its decision to revoke and give an opportunity to be heard.[13] To this extent the standard of 'reasonableness' may be higher than usual and there may be an obligation to give reasons.

## RES JUDICATA

The doctrine of res judicata prevents the same issue being redetermined between the same parties in new proceedings once a valid decision has been made and in the absence of changed circumstances. The main application of the doctrine is in judicial proceedings. It has two limbs. First, 'cause of action estoppel' prevents the same claim from being repeated. Second, 'issue estoppel' prevents a finding of fact or law from being challenged in later proceedings even where those proceedings are not of the same kind. The governing principle is not really one of estoppel but an application of the simple proposition that valid decisions are binding.

The *res judicata* doctrine does not involve challenging the initial decision

10 [1981] 2 All ER 227, [1981] 1 WLR 1186. See also *R v Metropolitan Police Comr, ex p Parker* [1953] 2 All ER 717 at 719, [1953] 1 WLR 1150 at 1154.

11 *R v IRC, ex p Preston* [1984] 3 All ER 625, [1984] 3 WLR 945, CA. See also *Lund v Thompson* [1959] 1 QB 283, [1958] 3 All ER 356.

12 See *Heron Corpn Ltd v Manchester City Council* (1976) 33 P & CR 268. There are express statutory powers relating to the revocation of planning permission.

13 *HTV Ltd v Price Commission* [1976] ICR 170, CA; *R v Liverpool Corpn, ex p Liverpool Taxi Fleet Operators' Association* [1972] 2 QB 299, *sub nom Re Liverpool Taxi Owners' Association* [1972] 2 All ER 589, CA. Contrast *Re Findlay* [1985] AC 318, [1984] 3 All ER 801, HL. See also *Council of Civil Service Unions v Minister for the Civil Service* [1985] AC 374, [1984] 3 All ER 935, HL.

which remains binding. However, an invalid decision cannot give rise to a *res judicata*. In this sense an argument that a matter is not res judicata may be a form of collateral challenge and can therefore be raised outside Order 53.

Res judicata is not confined to decisions of courts nor to judicial tribunals. However, the doctrine involves the existence of a binding decision and cannot therefore apply to purely advisory or investigative activities.[14] The particular statutory context is also important. For example, a tax assessment may relate only to a particular year and cannot therefore form the basis of res judicata in respect of other years.[15]

Res judicata applies only to findings of fact and law. It does not apply to policy or value judgments, it being a basic democratic principle that policy can be changed.

In *Thrasyvoulou v Secretary of State for the Environment*[16] the House of Lords held that the findings of an inspector in a planning enforcement appeal could not be challenged. The inspector held that a finding that the appellant had an established use right, was binding as was a finding that certain premises constituted a 'hostel' within the meaning of the Act. However, a decision as to whether a particular use is harmful could not create res judicata.

The developing doctrine of legitimate expectation may give some protection against misuse of policy. Where a policy has been announced and the applicant has reasonably relied upon it the policy cannot be departed from without justification and the applicant may be entitled to a hearing. This does not, however, prevent the policy from being changed and the court is unlikely to evaluate the strength of the reason given for departing from the policy.[17]

There is no general obligation to consult before policy is made or changed. However, a duty to consult could arise as a result of a previous practice of consultation provided that this was sufficiently specific.[18]

## DOUBLE JEOPARDY

The principle that no one should be placed at risk twice for the same offence has important consequences in relation to judicial review for the purpose of challenging decisions in criminal cases. The double jeopardy principle means that a person cannot be retried following a valid conviction or acquittal. Thus an argument that a conviction is ultra vires circumvents the double jeopardy principle. There must have been a complete concluded trial.[19] Where the case stated procedure is available, this must normally be resorted to rather than judicial review and the plea of double jeopardy cannot be raised.

However case stated is appropriate only for substantive or procedural errors of law or complete lack of jurisdiction. It cannot be used for defects such as

14 See *Thoday v Thoday* [1964] P 181 at 197, CA.

15 *Caffoor (Trustees of the Abdul Caffoor Trust) v Income Tax Comr, Colombo* [1961] AC 584, [1961] 2 All ER 436, PC; *Society of Medical Officers v Hope* [1960] AC 551, [1960] 1 All ER 317, HL.

16 [1990] 2 AC 273, [1990] 1 All ER 65. See also *R v Wychavon District Council and Secretary of State for the Environment, ex p Saunders* (1991) 64 P & CR 120.

17 *Council of Civil Service Unions v Minister for the Civil Service* [1985] AC 374, [1984] 3 All ER 935, HL; *R v Secretary of State for the Home Department, ex p Khan* [1985] 1 All ER 40, [1984] 1 WLR 1337, CA; *R v Secretary of State for the Home Department, ex p Ruddock* [1987] 2 All ER 518, [1987] 1 WLR 1482. See further above, pp 8 *et seq*.

18 *Re Westminster City Council* [1986] AC 668; *R v Brent London Borough Council, ex p Gunning* (1985) 84 LGR 168; *CCSU* case above, n 17.

19 *Re Harrington* [1984] AC 473, sub nom *Harrington v Roots* [1984] 2 All ER 474, HL.

unreasonableness, unfairness or fraud which have to be proved by affidavit.[20] For judicial review purposes these defects make a decision ultra vires or, which means the same, go to the jurisdiction of the justices. On a purist view an acquittal thus defective is a nullity and the plea of double jeopardy should not be available.

The double jeopardy principle has only a limited application to appellate decisions. In *Weight v MacKay*[1] the House of Lords held that the quashing of an acquittal by the Crown Court on appeal from justices did not attract the double jeopardy principle. This was because the effect of such a quashing was not to place the accused at risk but only to restore the original and only conviction. It would appear to make no difference for this purpose whether the appeal is by way of rehearing or determined on the basis of documents.

Their Lordships in the *Weight* case also drew another distinction which although discussed only in the context of the quashing of an appellate decision could in principle be of wider application. The appeal proceedings in question were quashed because the hearing was aborted by the Crown Court without hearing relevant evidence. Their Lordships distinguished between this kind of case where no decision on the merits was made and cases where an appeal tribunal does reach a decision on the merits, the double jeopardy principle applying only where a decision is made on the merits.

On the other hand the courts have been reluctant to quash acquittals so as to place the accused in double jeopardy. In *Re Harrington*[2] the House of Lords applied a narrow concept of 'jurisdiction'. They held that a complete failure by justices to adjudicate upon an essential issue did go to jurisdiction so that the accused could be retried. However, their Lordships took the view that other defects would not go to jurisdiction. In that case a refusal by magistrates to hear the prosecution case completely was held to go to jurisdiction, but their Lordships took the view that breach of natural justice as such would not do so.

In an earlier case which was not cited, the Divisional Court had held that an abuse of power involving a failure to hear the whole of the evidence did go to jurisdiction but declined to interfere as a matter of discretion, taking into account the rationale of the double jeopardy principle.[3] In *R v Hendon Justices, ex p DPP*[4] a three-judge Divisional Court held that an unreasonable acquittal by justices on the grounds of prosecution delays was ultra vires and could be quashed by certiorari and mandamus could go to order a new trial irrespective of double jeopardy. In deciding whether to quash an acquittal the court would exercise its discretion in the light of all the circumstances including the length of time that had elapsed since the trial. This discretionary approach seems preferable to the application of an artificial distinction between jurisdictional and non-jurisdictional defects.

20 *Crane v DPP* [1921] 2 AC 299 at 332; *DPP v Nasralla* [1967] 1 All ER 161 at 166, PC. Cf *Williams v DPP* [1991] 3 All ER 651, [1991] 1 WLR 1160. Retrial is discretionary, see *Griffiths v Jenkins* [1992] 2 AC 76, [1992] 1 All ER 65, HL.

1 [1984] 2 All ER 673, [1984] 1 WLR 980, HL.

2 [1984] AC 473, sub nom *Harrington v Roots* [1984] 2 All ER 474. See also *R v Sutton Justices, ex p DPP* [1992] 2 All ER 129.

3 *R v Birmingham Justices, ex p Lamb* [1983] 3 All ER 23, [1983] 1 WLR 339.

4 [1992] NLJR 1303.

CHAPTER 5

# Certiorari

## INTRODUCTION

The function of certiorari is to quash an invalid decision. Even where a decision is a nullity, so that certiorari is strictly unnecessary, certiorari can be granted so as to remove any question of the decision being ostensibly valid.[1] Certiorari is not appropriate for giving general guidance beyond the facts of a particular decision.[2] Certiorari is the primary judicial review remedy and the court will issue other remedies only where certiorari does not provide adequate relief.[3] The other prerogative orders of prohibition and mandamus have specialised purposes, but before the Ord 53 reforms the declaration and injunction were often treated as flexible alternatives to certiorari and indeed were sometimes seen as superseding the prerogative orders.[4]

In this chapter we will examine the scope of certiorari. Some aspects of certiorari law, viz, the question of locus standi, the discretionary powers of the court and the exclusion of the remedy raise considerations common to all the remedies and will be treated in separate chapters.

The classic statement of the general scope of certiorari is the much quoted dictum of Lord Atkins in *R v Electricity Comrs, ex p London Electricity Joint Committee Co (1920) Ltd.*[5] This is one of those judicial statements that are sometimes treated as if contained in a statute and therefore subjected to detailed semantic construction. However, Lord Atkins' dictum is now subject to so much gloss and qualification that it could, taken literally, seriously mislead.

## DECISIONS AGAINST WHICH CERTIORARI LIES

The scope of certiorari is governed by the following criteria.

(i) The decision must be of a 'public' as opposed to a private character.

(ii) The decision must affect the interests of the applicant. These are not confined to legal rights in a strict sense.[6]

(iii) Certiorari was at one time thought to be limited to government functions

1 See *R v Hendon Justices, ex p DPP* [1992] NLJR 1303.

2 *R v Harrow Justices, ex p DPP* [1991] 3 All ER 873 at 876.

3 *O'Reilly v Mackman* [1983] 2 AC 237, [1982] 3 All ER 1124, HL; *Cocks v Thanet District Council* [1982] 3 All ER 1135 at 1139, HL.

4 *Pyx Granite Co Ltd v Minister of Housing and Local Government* [1960] AC 260 at 290, HL.

5 [1924] 1 KB 171 at 205, CA: 'Wherever any body of persons having legal authority to determine questions affecting the rights of subjects and having the duty to act judicially.' Cf *R v Manchester Legal Aid Committee, ex p Brand & Co Ltd* [1952] 2 QB 413, [1952] 1 All ER 480; *Ridge v Baldwin* [1964] AC 40 at 76, [1963] 2 All ER 66 at 78–79.

6 *R v Criminal Injuries Compensation Board, ex p Lain* [1967] 2 QB 864, [1967] 2 All ER 770; *R v Panel on Take-overs and Mergers, ex p Datafin plc* [1987] QB 815, [1987] 1 All ER 564, CA.

which could be classified as 'judicial' in the sense that they were analogous to the functions of a court of law. This is no longer the case. It seems that certiorari will lie in respect of all government decisions which have adverse consequences for persons, even apparently general legislation. It has been emphasised that the scope of certiorari is not fixed.[7]

(iv) Certiorari lies only in respect of a written document which qualifies as a binding 'decision'. Thus purely oral decisions and ministerial acts which invoke no substantial element of choice or discretion are excluded. It is arguable that certiorari does not apply to decisions which are not binding in the sense that they are merely preliminary, advisory or not enforceable.

(v) Certiorari does not lie against the Crown as such.

## Public functions

This limitation has been extended to apply to all the Ord 53 remedies and the general nature of a 'public' function will be discussed in Chapter 10. Certiorari does not lie in respect of contractual powers nor powers derived from property rights, these being regarded as private law matters.[8]

### *Prerogative powers*

Powers derived from the royal prerogative are public law powers. In principle certiorari is available in respect of prerogative powers although the substantive law of judicial review may be of limited application to the royal prerogative because of the nature of the subject matter covered by prerogative powers.[9] Moreover, the prerogative orders issuing as they do in the name of the Crown do not lie directly against the Crown. Thus a prerogative power will be reviewable by certiorari only where the power is delegated to a specific official or tribunal. There is no embargo upon certiorari issuing against a servant or agent of the Crown, provided that the power in question is exercised by the servant or agent specifically as persona designata, for example under a prerogative order in council. In the case of statutory powers this is the normal practice. However, in the case of a prerogative power a declaration may usually be preferable because declarations are freely available against the Crown.

### *Voluntary bodies*

Provided that a particular voluntary body is public in character certiorari will lie even though the powers of the body do not derive from any specific legal source but rely upon acquiescence alone. However, in practice a declaration may be a preferable remedy.[10]

7 *O'Reilly v Mackman* [1983] 2 AC 237 at 279; *Leech v Deputy Governor of Parkhurst Prison* [1988] 2 WLR 290 at 317. *R v Panel on Take-overs and Mergers, ex p Datafin plc* [1987] QB 815 at 849.

8 See below, pp 111 *et seq*. See also *R v Post Office, ex p Byrne* [1975] ICR 221.

9 *R v Criminal Injuries Compensation Board, ex p Lain* [1967] 2 QB 864, [1967] 2 All ER 770; *Council of Civil Service Unions v Minister for the Civil Service* [1985] AC 374, [1984] 3 All ER 935, HL. See further above, ch 3.

10 See below, p 76.

## Judicial functions

Certiorari is no longer confined to decisions which can be classified as judicial.[11] Nevertheless judges still speak of judicial functions in connection with certiorari and it remains true that if a public decision-making process can be characterised as judicial certiorari will normally be available whereas in the case of non-judicial functions the availability of certiorari will be more open to argument. In a borderline case characterisation as judicial may therefore assist in argument.[12]

It is not necessary to attempt an exhaustive analysis of a judicial function. Indeed the variety and range of public decision-making processes employed in this country do not easily lend themselves to conceptual classification. Thus the term quasi-judicial is often used to refer to a decision that does not fully qualify as judicial but which is treated for some purposes as if it were judicial.[13] Another difficulty is that the term judicial appears to mean different things in different contexts, a problem which is compounded by the absence of consistent terminology.

As a matter of description rather than definition there are two broad approaches to the task of identifying a judicial decision. One approach concentrates on procedure and looks for a formal 'lis' or dispute between parties which is conclusively settled by an adjudicator who applies an existing rule of law to the facts as established by evidence and argument.[14] The second approach concentrates upon the effect of the decision and requires that the decision be binding as opposed to merely advisory and that it affect the legal rights of the parties.[15] Certiorari law has fluctuated between the two approaches. Lord Atkins' dictum[16] has sometimes been taken to mean that for certiorari to apply the decision must both affect 'rights' and be 'judicial' and sometimes merely that a decision which affects 'rights' is therefore judicial.[17] Today neither approach seems helpful. Certiorari is not confined to cases involving 'rights' in any strict legal sense. Nor is it limited to 'subjects' as in Lord Atkins' formulation. It is probably preferable to abandon the use of the term 'judicial' altogether in this context.

## Binding decisions

A more serious limitation upon the scope of certiorari is that the decision in question must be 'binding'. However, modern cases suggest that this requirement is a liberal one. There are three broad kinds of case to consider. First, there

11 *O'Reilly v Mackman* [1983] 2 AC 237 at 279, [1982] 3 All ER 1124 at 1129–1130; *R v Hillingdon London Borough Council, ex p Royco Homes Ltd* [1974] QB 720, [1974] 2 All ER 643; *R v Liverpool Corpn, ex p Liverpool Taxi Fleet Operators' Association* [1972] 2 QB 299, sub nom *Re Liverpool Taxi Owners' Association* [1972] 2 All ER 589, CA.

12 *R v Criminal Injuries Compensation Board, ex p Lain* (n 9, above); *R v Board of Visitors of Hull Prison, ex p St Germain (No 2)* [1979] 3 All ER 545, [1979] 1 WLR 1401.

13 See Wade *Administrative Law* (6th edn, 1988), pp 504–520; *Johnson & Co (Builders) Ltd v Minister of Health* [1947] 2 All ER 395 at 399 per Lord Greene MR. Two-stage processes involving a formal public inquiry or hearing followed by a discretionary, administrative decision are subject to this analysis—but see *Franklin v Minister of Town and Country Planning* [1948] AC 87, [1947] 2 All ER 289, HL. See *Vine v National Dock Labour Board* [1957] AC 488 at 510, [1956] 3 All ER 939, HL.

14 *Johnson's* case (above, n 13).

15 Eg *R v Manchester Legal Aid Committee, ex p RA Brand & Co Ltd* [1952] 2 QB 413, [1952] 1 All ER 480. Cf *Jeffrey v Evans* [1964] 1 All ER 536, [1964] 1 WLR 505.

16 Above, n 5. See also *Nakkuda Ali v M F De S Jayaratne* [1951] AC 66, PC; *R v Metropolitan Police Comr, ex p Parker* [1953] 2 All ER 717, [1953] 1 WLR 1150.

17 *Ridge v Baldwin* [1964] AC 40 at 71–79, [1963] 2 All ER 66 at 77–78.

are decisions which are entirely extra-legal. Second, there are decisions which, although statutory, are merely advisory, such as reports and recommendations following inquiries. Third, there are decisions, for example, a decision to prosecute, which are preliminary to the taking of further statutory action but which do not purport to affect legal rights in themselves. The law appears to have reached the position that in all these cases certiorari will be available provided that the decision in question in fact has adverse consequences for the applicant.

*Extra-legal decisions*

Certiorari lies in respect of a decision which in fact affects the interests of individuals even though the decision results only in an unenforceable payment. In *R v Criminal Injuries Compensation Board, ex p Lain*,[18] the Criminal Injuries Compensation scheme was held to be reviewable by certiorari. This was a landmark case which extended certiorari to non-statutory governmental activities but in the present context its importance lies in the fact that the rules under which the Criminal Injuries Compensation Board operated did not purport to create legally enforceable rights. At most they created the Board's authority as an agent of the Crown for the purpose of dispensing government money and thus made a payment lawful, which would otherwise have been unlawful. Lord Parker CJ thought it sufficient that the Board's decision in fact affected the individual's interests, although Diplock LJ left open the question whether certiorari would lie in a case where no legal rights were involved at all.

The rules of the Criminal Injuries Compensation scheme were promulgated as mandatory, but certiorari will also lie in respect of advisory rules which are, in fact, misapplied. For example, a misconstruction of a ministerial circular has been held reviewable by certiorari.[19] Certiorari will also lie where non-statutory and non-binding arrangements for providing hearings in deportation cases are applied unfairly.[20]

In many cases, voluntary codes of practice or advisory rules are applied by officials in connection with statutory decision-making processes. Here there is no particular problem about certiorari. The material in question will be reviewable as a factor which the decision-maker must take into account on ordinary principles relating to fairness, reasonableness and relevance.

An example is provided by the extra-statutory system of tax concessions. Once a voluntary tax concession, or indeed any other governmental practice or concession, has been relied upon, the government is bound to apply the concession fairly and correctly. Errors of construction will be treated as errors of law and the concession cannot be unreasonably withdrawn.[1] This is an aspect of the legitimate expectation doctrine which is considered in Chapter 2.

In cases which involve no statutory power at all, the position may be different. Early cases suggest that certiorari is not available in respect of decisions taken entirely outside a legal framework[2] but these can be questioned

18 [1967] 2 QB 864, [1967] 2 All ER 770.

19 *R v Worthing Borough Council, ex p Burch* [1984] JPL 261.

20 *R v Secretary of State for the Home Department, ex p Hosenball* [1977] 3 All ER 452, [1977] 1 WLR 766, CA.

1 *R v IRC, ex p Preston* [1984] 3 All ER 625, CA; *HTV v Price Commission* [1976] ICR 17; *R v Board of Inland Revenue, ex p MFK Underwriting Agencies Ltd* [1990] 1 All ER 91.

2 *R v Barnstable Justices, ex p Card* [1938] 1 KB 385, [1937] 4 All ER 263. See *R v Secretary of State for the Home Department, ex p Chubb* [1986] Crim LR 809—no 'judicial' element of formal rules. See Wade, *Administrative Law* (6th edn, 1988) pp 637 et seq.

in the light of *ex p Lain*. Moreover, in *R v Worthing Borough Council, ex p Burch*[3] Griffiths J extended certiorari to an (at the time) entirely voluntary government practice embodied in DOE Circular 69/63 concerning proposals to develop Crown land. The basis of his Lordship's reasoning was that the circular was in practice though not in law intended to be binding. Review of such non-statutory codes is arguably limited to the question whether the code is being construed correctly and applied fairly although there seems to be no reason in principle why the reasonableness of such a code should not be challenged. However, the absence of a statutory context against which to assess reasonableness could influence the courts' willingness to intervene.[4]

### *Investigatory and advisory functions*

Older cases support the proposition that certiorari does not lie in respect of functions which do not culminate in any kind of final decision. These include the range of governmental inquiries and investigations which may result only in factual reports or recommendations. However, it is now clear that natural justice and other substantive judicial review principles apply to these investigatory matters[5] and there appears to be no reason in principle to exclude certiorari.

Where a fact finding or advisory function can lead to legal consequences, for example, the proceedings of a coroner's court or 'ombudsman', certiorari will certainly lie.[6] Similarly certiorari is available where a fact finding investigation is a required element in a larger statutory process which culminates in a binding decision, at least where the findings of the investigation are conclusive.[7] It appears, therefore, that certiorari will be excluded only where the advisory decision or report has no significant impact upon anyone's interests.

Advisory functions may also provide a context where the notion of a judicial function is still relevant. If an advisory procedure is required to adopt a judicial form this may in itself suffice to attract certiorari.

### *Preliminary decisions*

There are many kinds of preliminary decisions. These include decisions to prosecute or institute proceedings, decisions which require confirmation by another body and preliminary recommendations or reports which are conditions precedent to further action. It is reasonably clear that certiorari lies in respect of all these kinds of decisions if it can be shown that the decision in question is a genuine condition precedent to some further action[8] and if the

3 [1984] JPL 261.

4 Cf *British Oxygen Co v Minister of Technology* [1971] AC 610 at 623–625, [1970] 3 All ER 165 at 169–170, HL.

5 *Selvarajan v Race Relations Board* [1976] 1 All ER 12; *Re Pergamon Press* [1971] Ch 388, [1970] 3 All ER 535, CA; *Hillingdon London Borough Council v Commission for Racial Equality* [1982] AC 779, [1982] 3 WLR 159, HL.

6 *R v Surrey Coroner, ex p Campbell* [1982] 2 QB 661, [1982] 2 All ER 545; Coroners Act 1887, s 6; *R v West Yorkshire Coroner, ex p Smith* [1983] QB 335, [1982] 3 All ER 1098, CA; *R v Local Comr for Administration for the North and East Area of England, ex p Bradford Metropolitan City Council* [1979] 1 QB 287, [1979] 2 All ER 881, CA.

7 *R v Boycott, ex p Keasley* [1939] 2 KB 651, [1939] 2 All ER 626; *R v Postmaster General, ex p Carmichael* [1928] 1 KB 291, 96 LJKB 347; *R v St Lawrence's Hospital Caterham Statutory Visitors, ex p Pritchard* [1953] 2 All ER 766, [1953] 1 WLR 1158; *R v Kent Police Authority, ex p Godden* [1971] 2 QB 662 sub nom *Re Godden* [1971] 3 All ER 20, CA.

8 *R v Electricity Comrs, ex p London Electricity Joint Committee Co (1920) Ltd* [1924] 1 KB 171, 93 LJKB 390.

preliminary decision has in itself an impact on the applicant's interests so that certiorari would serve a useful purpose. This applies even if the decision in question is only an initial investigation leading to another fuller investigation which itself is preliminary to the taking of further proceedings.[9] The circumstances in which the court will interfere with investigations into crime, however, are severely limited.[10]

## Ministerial acts

Certiorari is not appropriate to challenge ministerial acts in the sense of acts of a mechanical nature where the official has little or no discretion or power to decide between alternatives, for example, issuing a warrant.[11] Indeed, the contrast between these functions and judicial functions was probably influential in producing the belief that certiorari lies only in respect of the latter. In other words, the notion of 'judicial' was to be contrasted with ministerial not with administrative or legislative and was thus a liberalising rather than a restricting concept. Mandamus is the appropriate remedy for ministerial orders.

## Legislative functions

It has been suggested that certiorari will not lie in respect of legislation such as statutory instruments. Before 1977 other remedies, injunction and declaration in particular, were freely available in respect of subordinate legislation so that the question has been of little importance. Under the modern Ord 53 procedure there is much to be said in favour of making certiorari available in respect of subordinate legislation. Certiorari has been held applicable to compulsory purchase schemes classified as legislative (which contain a judicial element as part of their procedure[12]) and even the leading case in support of the contrary view is strictly irrelevant. In *R v Church Assembly Legislative Committees, ex p Haynes-Smith*,[13] it was held that prohibition did not lie in respect of the activities of the Assembly. These were, however, purely deliberative, the function of the Assembly being merely to initiate proposals for legislation to be placed before Parliament. Moreover, the reasoning of the Divisional Court leaned heavily upon the discredited belief that certiorari lies only in respect of judicial functions. Indeed in *R v Secretary of State for Health, ex p United States Tobacco International Inc*[14] the Oral Snuff (Safety) Regulations 1989 were quashed by certiorari on the ground of procedural unfairness without this point being discussed.

9 *Hillingdon London Borough Council v Commission for Racial Equality* [1982] AC 779, [1982] 3 WLR 159, HL.

10 *IRC v Rossminster Ltd* [1980] AC 952, [1980] 1 All ER 80, HL; *R v Serious Fraud Office, ex p Nadir* [1990] TLR 701, (1990) Times, 5 November.

11 *Hetherington v Security Export Co Ltd* [1924] AC 988, 94 LJPC 1.

12 *R v Minister of Health, ex p Yaffé* [1930] 2 KB 98.

13 [1928] 1 KB 411, 97 LJKB 222.

14 [1992] 1 QB 353, [1992] 1 All ER 212; see also *R v Secretary of State for Social Services, ex p Association of Metropolitan Authorities* [1986] 1 All ER 164, [1986] 1 WLR 1.

## PERSONS AND BODIES NOT AMENABLE TO CERTIORARI

### The Crown

Certiorari was originally a Royal demand for information. It later became used to remove proceedings of inferior courts to the royal courts for a variety of purposes including quashing or even for a decision in the matter. This latter appellate function no longer exists[15] but it remains the case that the Crown is technically the instigator of certiorari proceedings so that neither certiorari nor the other prerogative orders will lie against the Crown. However, modern statutes normally confer powers on ministers, departments or agencies rather than the Crown as such and certiorari will undoubtedly lie against them. This is a convenient albeit highly artificial way of dealing with a historical anomaly.[16]

*Interim relief against the Crown*

Under Ord 53, r 3(10) the court, when granting leave to apply for certiorari and prohibition, can give interim relief by directing a stay of the proceedings being challenged until the determination of the application or until the court otherwise orders. As we discuss below, this kind of interim relief might be available against ministers despite the apparent general rule that interim orders cannot be made either against the Crown itself or Crown servants.[17]

### The ecclesiastical courts

This appears to be a special case arising out of the long history and special characteristics of an ecclesiastical court as administering an exotic system of law outside the ordinary common law. Certiorari will not lie against an ecclesiastical court in respect of errors of law but prohibition will lie to restrain an excess of jurisdiction.[18] The position of the ecclesiastical court cannot therefore be used as the basis of any general principle.

### Visitors

The ancient office of visitor is held by a person who under the terms of the governing instrument represents the founder of certain types of charitable or benevolent corporation, most notably universities. Among other functions a visitor determines disputes between the corporation and its members relating to the internal affairs of the corporation and to the corporation's own rules, but not disputes involving non-members or arising out of the general law. The Visitors' decision can itself be reviewed but only on limited grounds which do not include errors of law.[19]

15 But see County Courts Act 1984, ss 83 and 84.

16 Cf *Town Investments Ltd v Department of Environment* [1978] AC 359, [1977] 1 All ER 813, HL—dealing with artificiality of distinguishing between ministers and the Crown as such. See also *Department of the Environment v Fox* [1980] 1 All ER 58, EAT.

17 Below, p 145.

18 *R v St Edmundsbury and Ipswich Diocese Chancellor, ex p White* [1948] 1 KB 195, [1947] 2 All ER 170, CA. See also *R v Cripps, ex p Muldoon* [1984] QB 68, [1983] 3 All ER 72.

19 *Page v Hull Univesity Visitor* [1993] 1 All ER 97, HL. See above, p 40. The suggestion that mandamus or prohibition but not certiorari will lie is probably obsolete.

## Oral decisions

There is authority that a purely oral decision or order is not subject to review by certiorari.[20] The basis of this appears to be the historical relationship between certiorari and the notion of the record. However, it is now clear that oral reasons can be regarded as part of the record. Indeed, the court may possess an inherent power to require an oral decision to be reduced to writing.

It has been said that certiorari is the only remedy appropriate to convictions before justices.[1] This may be because justices are a court of record and that there is a need formally to set aside the record. For other purposes, however, prohibitions and mandamus have been issued against justices as well as declarations.[2]

## THE GROUND ON WHICH CERTIORARI LIES—ERROR OF LAW ON THE FACE OF THE RECORD

Certiorari is unique among the judicial review remedies in that it lies not only where a decision is ultra vires but also where an error of law exists upon the face of the record. Whether this exceptional ground of review remains of practical importance depends upon whether we are prepared to accept that *Anisminic Ltd v Foreign Compensation Commission*[3] effectively turned all errors of law into jurisdictional defects. It may be that the face of the second doctrine is still applicable to decisions made by inferior courts proper. It remains useful, therefore, to examine this topic. Error on the record has sometimes been ridiculed as a meaningless technicality out of place in the modern law. However, it reflects a policy that has been widely accepted, that of avoiding opening up decisions made by experts to a reconsideration of the merits, and limiting the courts to a broad supervisory role.

To be reviewable by certiorari an error must either be jurisdictional, in which case it is immaterial whether or not it appears on the record, or it must be an error of law which can be discovered from a perusal of the material which makes up the tribunal's 'record'. However, affidavit or other extrinsic evidence may be admissible even in a face of the record case if the record is unclear or incomplete but only in order to establish the basis of the tribunal's decision and not for the purpose of contradicting or supplementing the record.[4]

Statutory rights of appeal to the High Court on a point of law are frequently available.[5] In such cases the error need not appear on the record so that this remedy may be preferable to certiorari. A statutory right of appeal usually lies

20 *R v Newington Licensing Justices, ex p Conrad* [1948] 1 KB 681, [1948] 1 All ER 346. Cf Ord 53, r 9(2).

1 *Pyx Granite Co Ltd v Minister of Housing and Local Government* [1960] AC 260 at 290 per Lord Goddard.

2 *R v Kent Justices* (1889) 24 QBD 181; *R v Felixstowe Justices, ex p Leigh* [1987] QB 582, [1987] 1 All ER 551; *R v Hendon Justices, ex p DPP* [1992] NLJR 1303.

3 [1969] 2 AC 147, [1969] 1 All ER 208, HL; *Page v Hull University Visitor* [1993] 1 All ER 97, HL; *Re Racal Communication Ltd* [1981] AC 374, [1980] 2 All ER 634, HL. See above, p 14.

4 *R v Crown Court at Knightsbridge, ex p International Sporting Club (London) Ltd* [1982] QB 304, [1981] 3 All ER 417; *R v Crown Court at Knightsbridge, ex p Aspinall Curzon Ltd* (1982) Times, 16 December; *R v Liverpool City Council, ex p Liverpool Taxi Fleet Operators' Association* [1975] 1 All ER 379, [1975] 1 WLR 701; *R v Patents Appeal Tribunal, ex p Swift & Co* [1962] 2 QB 647 at 686–687, 688–691.

5 Below, Ch 11.

to a single judge and unlike certiorari proceedings leave is not always required. Moreover, a reviewing court in a certiorari case is likely to be less willing to intervene than would be the case where the matter reaches the court in its appellate capacity. Under Ord 53 the court will normally quash a decision only in cases of clear error, or where the matter is of general import requiring consistency, or where the tribunal below is divided.[6] In any event where a convenient statutory appeal is available the court may refuse to intervene in its discretion under Ord 53.[7]

Certiorari has one clear practical advantage over an appeal in that ancillary relief can be given by quashing other decisions which although not themselves defective were made in reliance on a previous invalid decision.[8]

## The record

The notion of the record has recently become increasingly liberal. When this head of judicial review was 'rediscovered' in the case of *R v Northumberland Compensation Appeal Tribunal, ex p Shaw*[9] it was generally believed that the record comprised only the written documents containing the tribunal's formal decision, and the documents which initiated the case. Thus if the record did not disclose full reasons for the decision the court would be unable to interfere. The evidence itself was not part of the record.

However, a combination of statute, technological advances and the court's willingness under the new Ord 53 procedure to eschew formalism means that an application will now rarely fail solely on the ground that an error does not appear on the record.[10]

On the other hand an appellant may be under a heavy onus to establish that an error has been committed, for example that a material factor was not taken into account, since the presumption of validity will favour the tribunal.[11]

In *R v Preston Supplementary Benefits Appeal Tribunal, ex p Moore*[12] Lord Denning MR said that all the material before the tribunal constitutes part of its record, and it is likely that this is now the position. First, the Tribunals and Inquiries Act 1992, s 10 imposes a duty upon many tribunals and also upon ministers following a statutory inquiry to give reasons, in writing if requested, these reasons forming part of the record. The reasons must be reasonably comprehensive and disclose the facts upon which the tribunal relied as well as its conclusions. The standard required is that the reasons must be sufficient to enable the court to discover whether the tribunal fell into error in a way that

6 *R v Preston Supplementary Benefits Appeal Tribunal, ex p Moore* [1975] 2 All ER 807, [1975] 1 WLR 624, CA; *R v National Insurance Comr, ex p Michael* [1977] 2 All ER 420, [1977] 1 WLR 109, CA; *R v National Insurance Comr, ex p Stratton* [1979] QB 361, [1979] 2 All ER 278, CA; *R v Peterborough Supplementary Benefits Appeal Tribunal, ex p Department of Health and Social Security* [1978] 3 All ER 887.

7 Below, p 123.

8 *R v West Kent Quarter Sessions Appeal Committee, ex p Files* [1951] 2 All ER 728 at 732; *R v Kings Lynn Justices, ex p Fysh* [1964] Crim LR 143.

9 [1952] 1 KB 338, [1952] 1 All ER 122, CA.

10 *R v Knightsbridge Crown Court, ex p International Sporting Club (London) Ltd* [1982] QB 304, [1981] 3 All ER 417.

11 *Baldwin and Francis v Patents Appeal Tribunal* [1959] AC 663, [1959] 2 All ER 433, HL.

12 [1975] 2 All ER 807 at 811, [1975] 1 WLR 624 at 628.

affects the applicant's interests.[13] Second, oral reasons can now be treated as part of the record.[14] Technological advances in transcribing, together with the court's power in Ord 53 proceedings to order discovery of documents and the attendance of witnesses, have made contrary dicta questionable. Indeed the form in which reasons are given does not seem to matter. An informal letter to a third party for example has been treated as part of the record.[15]

In the absence of a statutory duty reasons do not generally have to be given for a decision.[16] However, if reasons are in fact given the court may permit incomplete or unintelligible reasons to be supplemented by affidavit evidence, and to order the tribunal to complete its record.[17] It is settled that any document actually referred to in the tribunal's formal record is thereby included in the record and the prevailing liberal approach would support Lord Denning's view that, even if not expressly incorporated, any document which is necessary to explain the decision also forms part of the record.[18]

Finally the parties can consent to treat any matter as part of the record.[19]

13 *R v Immigration Appeal Tribunal, ex p Mahmud Khan* [1983] QB 790, [1983] 2 All ER 420; *Bone v Mental Health Review Tribunal* [1985] 3 All ER 330; *Re Poyser and Mills Arbitration* [1964] 2 QB 467, [1963] 1 All ER 612; *Mountview Court Properties Ltd v Devlin* (1970) 21 P & CR 689; *Alexander Machinery (Dudley) Ltd v Crabtree* [1974] ICR 120; *R v Lancashire County Council, ex p Huddlestone* [1986] 2 All ER 941; *Save Britain's Heritage v Secretary of State for the Environment* [1991] 2 All ER 10, HL. Failure to give adequate reasons may be evidence of error of law but is probably not in itself error of law. See *Crake v Supplementary Benefits Commission* [1982] 1 All ER 498.

14 *R v Crown Court at Knightsbridge, ex p International Sporting Club (London) Ltd* [1982] QB 304, [1981] 3 All ER 417.

15 *R v Supplementary Benefits Commission, ex p Singer* [1973] 2 All ER 931, [1973] 1 WLR 713.

16 Above, pp 28 et seq.

17 *R v Crown Court at Knightsbridge, ex p Aspinall Curzon Ltd* (1982) Times, 16 December.

18 *R v Medical Appeal Tribunal, ex p Gilmore* [1957] 1 QB 574 at 582 sub nom *Re Gilmore's Application* [1957] 1 All ER 796 at 800, CA.

19 *R v Southampton Justices, ex p Green* [1976] QB 11, [1975] 2 All ER 1073, CA.

CHAPTER 6

# Prohibition and mandamus

## INTRODUCTION

Prohibition, mandamus and certiorari form the triumvirate of prerogative orders that together dominate the scope of Ord 53. Of these certiorari is pre-eminent and prohibition and mandamus are, therefore, likely to be issued only to serve purposes that cannot be achieved by certiorari. In theory there is considerable overlap between the three prerogative orders and now that the scope of certiorari has broadened to include non-judicial functions the other remedies can be regarded as specialised or supplementary.

This chapter will therefore consider the remedies of prohibition and mandamus by comparing the scope of these remedies with that of certiorari. Prohibition and mandamus are in a sense complementary to each other as well as supplementary to certiorari. Prohibition issues to prevent a public body from exceeding its jurisdiction while mandamus requires an authority to perform a public duty, and so can require a tribunal to make a decision within its jurisdiction. Like certiorari, prohibition and mandamus apply only to decisions of a public nature and despite some early inconsistent dicta[1] there is no reason to believe that the concept of 'public' will be applied differently in the case of prohibition or mandamus than in certiorari cases.[2] Similarly none of the prerogative orders issues directly against the Crown.

## PROHIBITION

Prohibition issues at an earlier stage than certiorari and lies to prohibit a body with limited jurisdiction from exceeding its jurisdiction. Prohibition is not available in respect of concluded decisions but the courts treat this limitation generously and the order will issue as long as there remains something *other than merely ministerial* to be done to give effect to it.[3] In this respect certiorari and prohibition overlap since certiorari will lie once a binding decision has been made. Prohibition probably lies in advance of a defect being committed as long as there is evidence to show that the tribunal is very likely to exceed its jurisdiction.[4] Prohibition can also issue conditionally and in interim form.[5]

1 *Ex p Napier* (1852) 18 QB 692 at 695; *R v Bank of England Governor & Co* (1819) 2 B & Ald 620.

2 *R v Criminal Injuries Compensation Board, ex p Clowes* [1977] 3 All ER 854, [1977] 1 WLR 1353; *R v Industrial Court, ex p ASSET* [1964] 1 QB 377, [1964] 3 All ER 130.

3 *Estate and Trust Agencies (1927) Ltd v Singapore Improvement Trust* [1937] AC 898 at 917–919.

4 *London Corpn v Cox* (1867) LR 2 HL 239, 36 LJ Ex 225; *R v Electricity Comrs, ex p London Electricity Joint Committee Co (1920) Ltd* [1924] 1 KB 171, 93 LJKB 390, CA; *R v Local Comr for Administration for the North and East Area of England, ex p Bradford City Council* [1979] QB 287, [1979] 2 All ER 881, CA; *R v Tottenham and District Rent Tribunal, ex p Northfield (Highgate) Ltd* [1957] 1 QB 103 at 107–108.

5 *R v Liverpool Corpn, ex p Liverpool Taxi Fleet Operators' Association* [1972] 2 QB 299, *sub nom Re Liverpool Taxi Owners' Association* [1972] 2 All ER 589, CA.

## Limitations upon prohibition

It has been said that prohibition and certiorari differ only in as much as prohibition is available at an earlier stage.[6] This is still generally true but there are some detailed differences between the two orders which derive from their different origins. Thus prohibition lies only in respect of jurisdictional defects and not on the ground of error of law on the face of the record.[7] This is because certiorari originated in the power vested in the King's Bench to scrutinise the records of inferior tribunals, whereas prohibition owes its origin to the power of the Royal Courts to prevent limited jurisdictions from trespassing outside their preserves. In a certiorari case, although review for jurisdictional defects goes beyond the record, the notion of a record is still the basis of the jurisdiction. Thus even where a jurisdictional defect is alleged certiorari will not lie in respect of a purely oral act or decision but prohibition is not subject to this limitation.[8] Prohibition is not limited to judicial functions and will lie, for example, to prevent an invalid report being made.

## Advantages of prohibition

1. Certiorari is limited to bodies which are technically inferior courts. Prima facie all persons exercising limited powers are inferior courts for this purpose so that this has few practical consequences. However, there are certain bodies which, although exercising a limited jurisdiction, are superior courts by virtue either of statute or the common law. These include ecclesiastical courts[9] and, for some purposes, the Crown Court.[10] In theory a superior court could act ultra vires although the High Court is in a special position with power to determine the limits of its own jurisdiction.[11] Prohibition will lie against an ecclesiastical court but it is unlikely that any of the prerogative orders will lie against superior courts.[12] Prohibition and mandamus will however lie in respect of the specialised jurisdiction exercised by the visitor in relation to charitable corporations but only on limited grounds.[13]

2. The locus standi requirement for prohibition may be slightly wider than that for certiorari. This will be discussed later.[14]

3. The courts may have less discretion to refuse mandamus than is the case with certiorari or prohibition.[15]

6 *R v Electricity Comrs, ex p London Electricity Joint Committee Co (1920) Ltd* [1924] 1 KB 171 at 206.

7 Except in relation to ecclesiastical courts; *ex p Smyth* (1835) 3 Ad & El 719 at 724. See also *R v Comptroller-General of Patents, ex p Parke Davis & Co* [1953] 1 All ER 862 at 866, [1953] 2 WLR 760 at 765 (sed quaere).

8 Above, p 55.

9 *R v Edmundsbury and Ipswich Diocese Chancellor, ex p White* [1948] 1 KB 195, [1947] 2 All ER 170.

10 See above, p 41.

11 *R v Cripps, ex p Muldoon* [1984] QB 68, [1984] 2 All ER 705. *Isaacs v Robertson* [1985] AC 97, [1984] 3 All ER 140, PC.

12 See above, p 40.

13 *Page v Hull Prison Visitors* [1993] 1 All ER 97; *A-G v Dedham School* (1857) 23 Beav 350, 26 LJ Ch 497; *R v Bishop of Lincoln* (1785) 2 Term Rep 338 (above, p 40).

14 See below, p 100.

15 See below, p 120.

## MANDAMUS

Mandamus has been described as the most elusive of the prerogative writs and orders.[16] Mandamus issued originally out of the King's Bench and commanded a person or body to perform a public duty. Unlike certiorari and prohibition mandamus has no necessary connection with courts and jurisdictions superior or inferior, but depends upon the notion of a public duty. However, because all public authorities can be said to have a duty to act lawfully the scope of mandamus and certiorari overlap. Mandamus can lie in respect of an ultra vires decision and can take the form of an order to a tribunal or authority to make a new decision, this time in accordance with the law.[17] Mandamus has never been confined to judicial functions so that, for example, in cases involving discretionary licensing powers mandamus is traditionally used as a mechanism for exposing invalidity.[18] Mandamus should also apply to legislative functions.[19] It used to be common practice to apply for certiorari and mandamus in tandem, certiorari to quash and mandamus to order the tribunal to make another decision,[20] although where a decision is ultra vires certiorari is strictly unnecessary because the decision in question is a nullity. On the other hand where error of law within jurisdiction is (assuming such a concept still exists following *Anisminic Ltd v Foreign Compensation Commission*[1]) alleged certiorari is necessary and in any event will often avoid the problems of distinguishing between jurisdictional and non-jurisdictional error.[2] Moreover, under the Supreme Court Act 1981, s 31(5) the Court has power where it quashes a decision by certiorari 'to remit the matter to the court, tribunal, or authority concerned with a direction to reconsider it and reach a decision in accordance with the findings of the High Court'. In many cases this will obviate the need to consider mandamus although in cases where the authority is held to have a duty to make a specific decision in the applicant's favour,[3] mandamus would still be appropriate. Usually, however, the quashing of a decision does not commit the authority to make any particular decision in the future but only to reconsider the matter, in accordance with guidelines laid down by the court.

### Duties

The scope of mandamus depends upon the tribunal or authority having a legal duty to perform some act. Before mandamus will issue performance must be demanded and refused.[4] This can sometimes be implied by the conduct of the

16 *IRC v National Federation of Self Employed and Small Businesses Ltd* [1981] 2 All ER 93 at 111.
17 An ultra vires decision is for this purpose equated with a refusal to make a decision. See *R v Port of London Authority, ex p Kynoch Ltd* [1919] 1 KB 176 at 183.
18 *R v Adamson* (1875) 1 QBD 201, 45 LJMC 46; *R v Cotham* [1898] 1 QB 802, 67 LJQB 632.
19 Provided that there is a duty to make the legislation in question: see *R v Secretary of State for the Environment, ex p Greater London Council* (1983) Times, 2 December.
20 Eg *R v Epsom Justices, ex p Gibbons* [1984] QB 574, [1983] 3 All ER 523; *R v Poole Justices, ex p Fleet* [1983] 2 All ER 897, [1983] 1 WLR 974.
1 [1969] 2 AC 147, [1969] 1 All ER 208, HL, above p 14.
2 Unless the error does not appear on the record: *Gleaves v Deakin* [1979] 2 WLR 665 at 676. See above, p 56.
3 See below.
4 *R v Bristol and Exeter Rly Co* (1843) 4 QB 162, 12 LJKB 106; *R v Board of Comrs of Public Utilities, ex p Halifax Transit Corpn* (1971) 15 DLR (3d) 720.

parties[5] and a demand will be dispensed with if it would serve no useful purpose.[6] There is authority that for the purpose of mandamus the duty in question must be to perform some positive act required by law rather than any general duty to undo an unlawful act.[7]

*Powers and duties*

Mandamus depends upon the imposition of a positive duty upon a public authority. However, governmental functions cannot neatly be divided into powers and duties. The range of governmental duties can best be seen as a spectrum. In each case an interpretation of the particular legislation determines the extent to which a duty exists. Words like 'shall' or 'may', although they raise presumptions, are not conclusive and the purpose of the particular statutory provisions must be examined.[8] The court will take into account such factors as the money or other resources available to the authority, the amount of choice available as to the means of fulfilling the duty, the existence of competing priorities and physical practicality.[9] At one end of the spectrum there are duties that are effectively absolute, for example a statutory duty to give reasons or other information. At the other extreme are duties that are so vague as to be non-justiciable since it would be impossible (or at least too politically controversial) for a court of law to impose specific requirements. These include general duties imposed upon nationalised industries and local authorities to provide adequate or efficient services.[10] However, even in these cases the court can interfere where a clear abuse of power has occurred.[11]

Between these extremes lies a range of specific duties. These fall into three groups. First, there are duties to provide services and benefits, for example education and housing duties. This kind of duty depends upon the availability of resources and often includes the need to balance competing duties or duties against resources. Mandamus will not issue in vain and the court will not normally compel an authority to perform a duty which it has no resources to fulfil.[12] Similarly where an authority is required to choose between competing duties it will have a discretion as to how to fulfil its obligations and a decision to

5 *R v Tower Hamlets London Borough Council, ex p Kayne-Levenson* [1975] QB 431, [1975] 1 All ER 641, CA; *R v Lancaster Inhabitants* (1900) 64 JP 280.

6 *R v Hanley Revising Barrister* [1912] 3 KB 518, 81 LJKB 1152.

7 *Ex p Nash* (1850) 15 QB 92, 19 LJQB 296. But cf *R v Hanley Revising Barrister* [1912] 3 KB 518, 81 LJKB 1152; *R v Greater London Council, ex p Burgess* [1978] ICR 991.

8 *Julius v Lord Bishop of Oxford* (1880) 5 App Cas 214, 49 LJKB 577; *Miller v Weymouth and Melcombe Regis Corpn* (1974) 118 Sol Jo 421, 27 P & CR 468; *R v Secretary of State for the Environment, ex p Greater London Council* (1983) Times, 2 December; *Padfield v Minister of Agriculture, Fisheries and Food* [1968] AC 997, [1968] 1 All ER 694, HL.

9 *R v Bristol Corpn, ex p Hendy* [1974] 1 All ER 1047, [1974] 1 WLR 498, CA; *R v Metropolitan Police Comr, ex p Blackburn* [1968] 2 QB 118, [1968] 1 All ER 763, CA; *R v Metropolitan Police Comr, ex p Blackburn (No 3)* [1973] QB 241, [1973] 1 All ER 324, CA; *Buckoke v Greater London Council* [1971] 1 Ch 655, [1971] 2 All ER 254, CA.

10 Eg Coal Industry Nationalisation Act 1946, s 1(1)(b), Independent Broadcasting Authority Act 1973, ss 2 and 4. See above, p 38.

11 Eg *R v Independent Broadcasting Authority, ex p Whitehouse* (1984) Times, 14 April.

12 *R v Kensington and Chelsea (Royal) London Borough Council, ex p Birdwood* (1976) 74 LGR 424; *R v Bristol Corpn, ex p Hendy* [1974] 1 All ER 1047, [1974] 1 WLR 498, CA; *R v Secretary of State for Social Services, ex p Child Poverty Action Group* [1990] 2 QB 540, [1989] 1 All ER 1047, CA; *West Glamorgan County Council v Rafferty* [1987] 1 All ER 1005, [1987] 1 WLR 457, CA; *R v Inner London Education Authority, ex p Ali* [1990] 2 Admin LR 822 per Woolf LJ at 828—target duties. See also *Glossop v Heston and Isleworth Local Board* (1879) 12 Ch D 102, 49 LJ Ch 89, CA (distinction between mandamus and enforcement in private law).

sacrifice one duty in favour of another will not be unlawful provided that the discretion is exercised properly according to the normal principles governing the review of discretionary powers, and that the authority has done its best to perform its statutory responsibilities.[13]

The second kind of non-absolute duty concerns regulatory or enforcement duties such as police duties, or the duty imposed on the Internal Revenue Commissioners to collect taxes. Here the question of limited resources and competing priorities may also be relevant particularly in the case of the police and the same general principle therefore applies. Thus mandamus will issue only if the authority has failed to do its best to fulfil its duty given the resources available to it and a proper exercise of its discretion to balance competing priorities. In this kind of case the authority may also be excused from strict compliance with a duty if it can establish that the costs of implementing the duty outweigh the benefits to be obtained, for example, in connection with tax collection.[14]

The third kind of non-absolute duty arises where the authority has a discretion to decide whether the applicant has satisfied requirements which are prescribed by statute in order for the duty in question to arise. For example, under the Housing Act 1988, a duty to provide housing exists only if the authority is satisfied that the applicant fulfils specified requirements, including a requirement that he is not intentionally homeless.[15]

In such cases the normal principles of judicial review apply. Thus mandamus will issue only if the authority's decision as to the existence of the requirements is invalid and the court will then require the authority to redetermine the matter.

There may, on the other hand, be cases where there is only one decision that can lawfully be made on the facts and in such a case the court may issue mandamus to require a decision to be made in favour of the applicant.[16] A declaration of the applicant's rights may also be appropriate in such circumstances, and there may, exceptionally, be a right to damages.[17]

## Mandamus and certiorari as alternatives

We have seen that mandamus and certiorari may sometimes overlap. Indeed in many cases mandamus will be unnecessary, since an offending decision can be quashed by certiorari and remitted to the authority for reconsideration in accordance with the decision of the court.

On the other hand, where there has been an actual refusal to make a decision, provide a service, or confer a benefit, mandamus would be appropriate because certiorari requires the exercise in writing of a decision-making power. However, in *R v Hillingdon Borough Council, ex p Streeting*[18] certiorari was

13 Cf *R v Kerrier District Council, ex p Guppys (Bridport) Ltd* (1976) 32 P & CR 411.

14 *IRC v National Federation of Self Employed and Small Businesses Ltd* [1982] AC 617, [1981] 2 All ER 93; *R v Board of Inland Revenue, ex p MFK Underwriting Agencies Ltd* [1991] 1 All ER 91.

15 *Cocks v Thanet District Council* [1983] 2 AC 286, [1982] 3 All ER 1135, HL. See also *R v Metropolitan Police Comr, ex p Holloway* [1911] 2 KB 1131, CA.

16 *Eastleigh Borough Council v Betts* [1983] 2 AC 613, [1983] 2 All ER 1111, HL; *R v Kingston Justices, ex p Davey* (1902) 86 LT 589; *R v City of London Licensing Justices, ex p Stewart* [1954] 3 All ER 270, [1954] 1 WLR 1325; *Padfield v Minister of Agriculture, Fisheries and Food* [1968] AC 997, [1968] 1 All ER 694.

17 *Thornton v Kirklees Metropolitan Borough Council* [1979] QB 626, [1979] 2 All ER 349, CA. See below, pp 89–91.

18 [1980] 3 All ER 413, [1980] 1 WLR 1430.

issued in respect of a refusal to consider an application made under the Housing (Homeless Persons) Act 1977 so that a liberal view of the notion of a 'decision' is possible.

Where both mandamus and certiorari are available certiorari may be preferable for the following reasons:

(i) to avoid the possibility that the defect is not jurisdictional;
(ii) the locus standi requirement for certiorari is arguably broader (see ch 9, below);
(iii) the difficulty in borderline cases of drawing the line between discretion and duty.

## Mandamus coupled with certiorari

The applicant for judicial review may seek all or any of the available remedies either in the alternative or cumulatively. It might be useful to apply for certiorari and mandamus together. There will usually be a time lag between quashing the old decision and making the new one which could cause inconvenience. However, the court can in its discretion bridge the gap by postponing certiorari until a new decision has been made.[19] It is difficult to see how there can be a duty or indeed any power to make another decision while the previous one still exists but this is one of many examples of the conceptual problems posed by the courts' equivocal attitude to the concept of nullity.[20]

## Mandamus and the Crown

Mandamus, like the other prerogative orders, will not lie against the Crown or a Crown servant acting as such. Where a duty is owed by the Crown a declaration and sometimes damages is the appropriate remedy. However, a statutory function imposed specifically upon a named Crown servant including a minister is enforceable by mandamus against the designated person upon the dubious theory that the person in question is presumed to be designated independently of his position as a Crown servant.[1] Apart from this the general principle applies that an act performed by a servant or agent of the Crown is to be treated as an act of the Crown itself[2] and will thus presumably be beyond the reach of mandamus. However, mandamus has issued against the Criminal Injuries Compensation Board[3] even though at the time this body had existence only as an agent of the Crown and had no statutory status. The rationale of this appears to be the formal constitution of the Board as a distinct entity. The rule that mandamus does not lie against the Crown is explicable historically but serves no convincing policy purpose. The 'persona designata' theory is therefore a useful device, but could be readily circumvented by the draftsman.

Mandamus will not normally issue against a minister, this being regarded

19 *R v Paddington Valuation Officer, ex p Peachey Property Corpn Ltd* [1966] 1 QB 380, [1965] 2 All ER 836, CA. Cf *Punton v Ministry of Pensions and National Insurance (No 2)* [1964] 1 All ER 448, [1964] 1 WLR 226 (declaration).

20 See above, pp 11–13.

1 *R v Secretary of State for War* [1891] 2 QB 326 at 334, CA; *R v Treasury Lords Comrs* (1872) LR 7 QB 387, 41 LJQB 178; *R v IRC, Re Nathan* (1884) 12 QBD 461, sub nom *R v Income Tax Special Comrs, ex p Cape Copper Mining Co Ltd* 53 LJQB 229, CA; *R v Income Tax Special Purposes Comrs* (1888) 21 QBD 313, 57 LJQB 513, CA. See also *R v Secretary of State for the Home Department, ex p McWhirter* (1969) Times, 21 October.

2 Cf *Town Investments Ltd v Department of the Environment* [1978] AC 359, [1977] 1 All ER 813, HL, but concerning a contractual function and not a statutory power.

3 Eg *R v Criminal Injuries Compensation Board, ex p Clowes* [1977] 3 All ER 854, [1977] 1 WLR 1353.

as 'unnecessary and discourteous'.[4] The normal practice is to make a declaration which is unenforceable but puts moral pressure on the minister. This is a matter of discretion rather than law. There is no reason in principle to withhold mandamus from ministers and the courts' stance reveals the deferential attitude to government which underlies English public law.

4 *R v Secretary of State for Employment, ex p Equal Opportunities Commission* [1992] 1 All ER 545 at 560.

CHAPTER 7

# The declaration and injunction

## GENERAL BACKGROUND

Before 1977 the Ord 53 procedure concerned only the prerogative orders. An important aspect of the 1977 reforms was to empower the Queen's Bench Division to make declarations or grant injunctions in addition to or instead of the prerogative orders, and to provide a uniform procedure for all the remedies under Ord 53. The law relating to these remedies has not otherwise been altered and the declaration and injunction remain available in other proceedings. The prerogative orders are still available only in Ord 53 proceedings.

In this chapter we will examine the substantive law relating to the declaration and injunction and also the relationship between these remedies and the prerogative orders. A later chapter will consider the circumstances in which a declaration or injunction may be sought against a public authority in another forum.

The declaration and injunction originated as private law remedies. The injunction is an equitable remedy and this gives it a special character. The declaration is also said to be an equitable remedy since it originated as part of the inherent jurisdiction of the Court of Chancery. However, the modern jurisdiction to make declarations derives from the Judicature Act 1873 and from what is now RSC Ord 15, r 16. This can be regarded as a sufficiently important reform to justify treating the declaration as being in effect a new statutory remedy.[1] The point is of practical importance in connection with the courts' discretionary powers, since, if the declaration does retain its equitable character then the equitable requirements embodied in the maxims of equity must be applied and the courts' discretion may be less flexible than is the case with the prerogative orders.[2]

The private law origins of the declaration and injunction raises a different set of problems than those associated with the prerogative orders. The emphasis of private law is more upon the rights of the applicant than the nature of the decision challenged. This has caused difficulty in a public law context and it may be that these remedies have only a subsidiary function within the Ord 53 process. From about 1911 when the well-known *Dyson*[3] case was decided, until the mid 1970s, the declaration enjoyed considerable favour as a public law remedy. The scope of certiorari was still linked to the notion of a judicial function and the prerogative orders were subject to serious procedural limitations which sometimes made them ineffective. The declaration appeared to be

1 For the present statutory basis see the Supreme Court Act 1981. *Hordern Richmond Ltd v Duncan* [1947] KB 545 at 552; *Guaranty Trust Co of New York v Hannay & Co* [1915] 2 KB 536, 84 LJKB 1465, CA; *Chapman v Michaelson* [1909] 1 Ch 238 at 243.

2 See *Tito v Waddell (No 2)* [1977] Ch 106 at 259, [1977] 3 All ER 129 at 256, suggesting that this is not the case.

3 *Dyson v A-G* [1911] 1 KB 410, 80 LJKB 531, CA.

a broader and less technical remedy[4] and the courts were willing to grant declarations both where certiorari was not available[5] and as an alternative to certiorari.[6] Indeed, it was predicted that the declaration and injunction would supersede the prerogative orders, since on the face of it a declaration and injunction seemed to be able to fulfil most if not all of the functions of certiorari, prohibition and mandamus. This has not happened. On the one hand the prerogative orders have become broader in scope while on the other serious difficulties have been experienced with the declaration and injunction. Moreover, the language of the Supreme Court Act 1981 has been narrowly construed as demoting the declaration and injunction in judicial review proceedings to the subordinate task of supplementing the prerogative orders. However in recent years this attitude has been less prevalent.[7]

## THE DECLARATION—GENERAL SCOPE

A declaration is a statement of the legal relationship between the parties. It is unique among the remedies in two fundamental ways. First, a declaration as such cannot be enforced and disobedience is not a contempt of court. Second, a declaration is not constitutive. That is, it records only existing legal rights and cannot change the legal position in any way. Such force as it has appears to depend on the doctrine of res judicata. Thus unlike certiorari a declaration cannot quash a decision.[8] The chameleon notion of nullity must therefore be called upon. Originally the declaration was not a suitable public law remedy because it has to be linked to another cause of action such as a claim for damages. However, Ord 15, r 16, provided that a declaration could be made even though no other consequential relief was or *could* be claimed. In *Dyson v A-G*[9] a declaration was successfully sought that a demand for information made by the Inland Revenue was ultra vires. The plaintiff could have raised a defence when prosecuted for refusing to provide the information but the court held that the declaration was an appropriate way of challenging the decision, thus saving the plaintiff the inconvenience of criminal proceedings. The court emphasised the discretionary and flexible character of the declaration, a theme taken up in later cases to escape the restrictive time limits and the exclusion of discovery and cross-examination which then applied to certiorari. The high water mark of the declaration came with *Pyx Granite Co Ltd v Ministry of Housing and Local Government*[10] where the House of Lords appeared to allow a declaration to lie in a case where certiorari might have served the same purpose and where a statutory remedy was also provided.

Until the complications introduced by the 1977 reforms, the declaration applied equally to public and private law matters without the need to draw a formal distinction between them, but this advantage has been removed because of the need to decide whether to seek a declaration under Ord 53 as a matter of public law, or by an ordinary private law action. Other advantages of

4 *Barnard v National Dock Labour Board* [1953] 2 QB 18 at 41–42, [1953] 1 All ER 1113 at 1119.
5 Ibid.
6 *Pyx Granite Co Ltd v Ministry of Housing and Local Government* [1960] AC 260, [1959] 3 All ER 1, HL. See also *Payne v Lord Harris of Greenwich* [1981] 2 All ER 842, [1981] 1 WLR 754, CA.
7 *Cocks v Thanet District Council* [1982] 3 All ER 1135 at 1139, HL; *R v Edmonton Licensing Justices, ex p Baker* [1983] 2 All ER 545 at 550–551. Cf *O'Reilly v Mackman* [1982] 3 All ER 1124 at 1132–3.
8 *Punton v Ministry of Pensions and National Insurance (No 2)* [1964] 1 All ER 448, [1964] 1 WLR 226, CA.
9 [1911] 1 KB 410, 81 LJKB 217, CA.
10 [1960] AC 260, [1959] 3 All ER 1.

the declaration have also disappeared. For example, many procedural restrictions affecting the prerogative orders have been removed in favour of a uniform procedure applicable to all the remedies. Indeed the declaration is now more restrictive than certiorari since no interim declaration can be made.[11] Certiorari is no longer confined to judicial decisions and unlike the declaration certiorari lies in respect of errors within jurisdiction as well as ultra vires decisions. The cumulative effect of these considerations seems to be that the declaration will rarely be preferable to the prerogative orders as a general judicial remedy but is likely to find its main role as an ancillary remedy for the purpose of clarifying the applicant's private rights, or where an enforceable remedy is inappropriate.

## AGAINST WHOM CAN A DECLARATION BE MADE?

In some respects the declaration is the most liberal of all the remedies. This is especially so in respect of the range of persons and decisions against which a declaration can be made. The emphasis in declaration cases is upon the right of the plaintiff rather than the nature of the defendant. The declaration is in principle available against any person or body public or private, including tribunals and enforcement officers.

### The Crown

In particular the declaration is the only Ord 53 remedy which is available against the Crown.[12] However, until the 1977 reforms of Ord 53 the 'appropriate authorised government department', rather than the Crown itself was the correct defendant. If none of the authorised government departments is appropriate or the person instituting the proceedings has any reasonable doubt whether there are any and if so which of these departments is appropriate, the declaration lies against the Attorney General.[13] Thus unlike the prerogative orders declarations should not strictly have been made against ministers as such. However, this requirement of the Crown Proceedings Act 1947 may have been affected by the 1977 reforms which seem to have the effect of allowing the court in its discretion to make a declaration against a person to whom the prerogative orders apply. This can include ministers.[14]

## DECISIONS SUBJECT TO THE DECLARATION

A declaration can be made in respect of any kind of decision, legislative, administrative, judicial and ministerial. Therefore, to avoid any doubts as to whether certiorari and prohibition lie to challenge subordinate legislation the declaration has been treated as the usual remedy in respect of statutory instruments and local byelaws. There are early dicta that a declaration is not appropriate to challenge decisions of a purely advisory character.[15] This is

11 Below, p 75, 147.
12 Crown Proceedings Act 1947, s 21(1).
13 Ibid, s 17.
14 See *Minister of Foreign Affairs, Trade and Industry v Vehicles and Supplies Ltd* [1991] 4 All ER 65 at 70, PC.
15 *Maxwell v Department of Trade and Industry* [1974] QB 523 at 542, [1974] 2 All ER 122 at 134. See also *Malone v Metropolitan Police Comr* [1974] Ch 344.

because the applicant's rights are not sufficiently affected to form the subject matter of a declaration. This is, however, too narrow a view and declarations have been made in relation to government advice albeit where the advice impinged upon legal rights.[16] Indeed this is one of the most valuable functions of the declaration. For example, in *R v Secretary of State for Employment, ex p Equal Opportunities Commission*[17] the Secretary of State's opinion expressed in a letter to the effect that certain statutory thresholds were not in breach of European Community law was held to be reviewable by means of a declaration. The Divisional Court took the view that even if the letter was just an informal expression of the Secretary of State's views it could nevertheless be treated as an alleged refusal to carry out a statutory duty. However the context was that of a statutory body entitled by statute to make representations to the Secretary of State about matters affecting its powers. Informal correspondence as such may not normally be reviewable.

## Hypothetical matters

Because the declaration is not tied to any other form of relief, special rules have been developed to discourage people from seeking declarations which have no practical consequence. English law does not encourage the giving of advisory opinions by the courts[18] and so the principle has developed that a declaration will not issue in respect of academic or hypothetical issues or where it would serve no useful purpose. It is not clear whether this group of rules is a matter of jurisdiction or discretion. In this respect a distinction could perhaps be drawn between cases where the matter is theoretical or premature in the sense that the facts upon which the dispute is premised do not exist at the time proceedings are instituted,[19] and cases where there turns out to be no practical benefit from making a declaration.[20] The former case is appropriate to be treated as a matter of jurisdiction but the latter principle, which also applies to prerogative orders, appears more suitable to be governed by the court's discretion. The court is best able to weigh the issues involved once it has heard the merits of the case. For example, even though the making of a declaration may be too late to protect the applicant's existing position, the declaration may serve a persuasive or educational purpose or give guidance for the future or settle the question of costs.[1]

Essentially there must be a genuine dispute between the parties based upon existing facts, where a declaration will have a practical effect.

16 See *Gillick v West Norfolk and Wisbech Area Health Authority* [1986] AC 112, [1985] 3 All ER 402, HL; *Royal College of Nursing of the United Kingdom v Department of Health and Social Security* [1981] AC 800, [1981] 1 All ER 545, HL.

17 [1992] 1 All ER 545. The Secretary of State's view on the substantive issue was upheld.

18 *Ainsbury v Millington* [1987] 1 All ER 929 at 930–931, HL.

19 Eg *Draper v British Optical Association* [1938] 1 All ER 115; *Argosam Finance Co Ltd v Oxby* [1965] Ch 390, [1964] 3 All ER 561, CA—no declaration merely to guide a future course of action.

20 See below, n 6.

1 Eg *Eastham v Newcastle United Football Club* [1964] Ch 413, [1963] 3 All ER 139. See also *Hampshire County Council v Shonleigh Nominees Ltd* [1970] 2 All ER 144, [1970] 1 WLR 865. Cf *Williams v Home Office (No 2)* [1981] 1 All ER 1211 at 1248. *R v Secretary of State for the Home Department, ex p Ruddock* [1987] 2 All ER 518, [1987] 1 WLR 1482; *R v Greenwich London Borough Council, ex p Lovelace* [1991] 3 All ER 511 at 521, CA.

A matter will be treated as theoretical or hypothetical in at least the following circumstances:

1. where the defendant does not dispute the plaintiff's claim;[2]
2. where the defendant has already rectified the wrong complained of, or for some other reason the applicant has suffered no injury;[3]
3. where the facts upon which the dispute is based are either not fully known or contingent;[4]
4. where it is not reasonably probable that the authority is intending to take the action complained of;[5] or
5. where it is impossible or inconvenient to give the applicant any practical relief.[6]

## Declarations in advance

A declaration may in a suitable case be made in advance of apprehended action. Indeed this is one of the advantages of the declaratory judgment.[7] However, as well as raising the possibility that the matter is too remote or hypothetical the court must also be satisfied that the balance of convenience is in favour of intervening in advance. This was clearly the case in *Dyson v A-G*[8] but in *Square Meals Frozen Foods Ltd v Dunstable Borough Council*[9] the court refused to make a declaration in a case where the plaintiff was threatened with an enforcement notice by a local planning authority. This was partly because the matter involved a mixture of legal and factual issues which were better determined by the executive before reaching judicial review.

## THE GROUNDS ON WHICH A DECLARATION WILL ISSUE

A declaration will lie on all the normal grounds of judicial review. In this respect the declaration is capable of achieving the same result as any of the prerogative orders. Like certiorari or prohibition it can expose the nullity of an existing or prospective decision and like mandamus can declare that the authority has a duty to decide according to principles laid down by the court. The applicant's private rights can also be declared.

2 *Re Carnarvon Harbour Acts 1793 to 1903, Thomas v A-G* [1937] Ch 72, sub nom *Thomas v A-G* [1936] 2 All ER 1325; *Ruislip-Northwood UDC v Lee* (1931) 145 LT 208, CA.
3 *Whyte, Ridsdale & Co v A-G* [1929] 1 Ch 548, 96 LJ Ch 351; *Earl of Dysart v Hammerton & Co* [1914] 1 Ch 822, 83 LJ Ch 530, CA; revsd sub nom *Hammerton v Earl of Dysart* [1916] 1 AC 57, 85 LJ Ch 33, HL; *Williams v Home Office (No 2)* [1981] 1 All ER 1211 at 1248.
4 *Draper v British Optical Association* [1938] 1 All ER 115; *Faber v Gosforth UDC* (1903) 88 LT 549. See also n 19, above.
5 *Lever Bros & Unilever Ltd v Manchester Ship Canal Co* (1945) 78 Ll L Rep 507. Cf *Pharmaceutical Society of Great Britain v Dickson* [1970] AC 403, [1968] 2 All ER 686, HL.
6 *A-G v Colchester Corpn* [1955] 2 QB 207, [1955] 2 All ER 124. Cf *Chief Constable of North Wales Police v Evans* [1982] 3 All ER 141, [1982] 1 WLR 1155, HL; *Merricks v Nott-Bower* [1965] 1 QB 57 at 67, [1964] 1 All ER 717 at 721, CA.
7 *Dyson v A-G* [1911] 1 KB 410, 80 LJKB 531, CA; *Gouriet v Union of Post Office Workers* [1978] AC 435 at 497, 499–500, [1977] 3 All ER 70 at 97, 98–99, HL.
8 Above, n 7.
9 [1974] 1 All ER 441, [1974] 1 WLR 59, CA.

## Errors of law

During the 1960s it was held by the Court of Appeal that a declaration did not lie in respect of errors of law.[10] This is because the decision was not treated as a nullity and a declaration is not capable of quashing a decision. It is almost certainly the case, following *Anisminic Ltd v Foreign Compensation Commission*,[11] that all errors of law committed by government officials and administrative tribunals are now regarded as making the decision a nullity so that this rule is no longer reliable except perhaps in relation to inferior courts proper.

It is not clear from the cases whether the embargo on extending the declaration to errors within jurisdiction is a matter of jurisdiction or discretion. It can plausibly be argued that this rule is an aspect of the general notion that a declaration will not issue where it will serve no useful purpose, this being a matter of discretion.[12] Thus, if a declaration is made that a decision is erroneous this will normally be useless since the decision will remain fully valid and effective. However, if the tribunal in question has a power to revoke its own decisions a declaration could serve a useful purpose so as to persuade the court to exercise its discretion in favour of making the declaration.[13] In any event, given the liberal approach now taken to certiorari for error of law, the matter may be of little practical importance.

### *The effect of the Supreme Court Act 1981*

Whatever view is taken upon the question of whether a declaration can be made in respect of a non-jurisdictional error the Supreme Court Act 1981, s 31(2) does not appear to have affected the question. This provides that the court may grant a declaration where having regard to the availability of the prerogative orders and to all the circumstances of the case it would be 'just and convenient to do so'. It can be argued that this equates the scope of the declaration to that of certiorari but this seems unlikely given that the Act and Ord 53 are concerned only with procedural matters. The general language of the subsection does not seem capable of affecting the substantive law governing the remedies at all.[14] The purpose of s 31(2) is to govern the question of choice of remedy, not to alter the law relating to individual remedies. However, if a declaration is now available in respect of an error of law, it would follow that the error need not appear on the record.

## WHO CAN OBTAIN A DECLARATION?

Not long before the reformed Ord 53 was introduced the House of Lords in *Gouriet v Union of Post Office Workers*[15] affirmed the long established principle that, apart from specific statutory provisions, a declaration and injunction can

10 *Punton v Ministry of Pensions and National Insurance (No 2)* [1964] 1 All ER 448, [1964] 1 WLR 226, CA; cf *R v Medical Appeal Tribunal, ex p Gilmore* [1957] 1 QB 574 at 584, sub nom *Re Gilmore's Application* [1957] 1 All ER 796 at 804; *Healey v Minister of Health* [1955] 1 QB 221, [1954] 3 All ER 449, CA.

11 Above, p 4.

12 *Bousefield v North Yorkshire County Council* (1982) 44 P & CR 203 at 209; *Stevenson v United Road Transport Union* [1977] 2 All ER 941 at 951–952, [1977] ICR 893 at 905–906, CA (a contract case in respect of which arguments based on nullity are less compelling).

13 See *Taylor v National Assistance Board* [1956] P 470, [1956] 2 All ER 455.

14 *IRC v National Federation of Self Employed and Small Businesses Ltd* [1982] AC 617 at 647–648, [1981] 2 All ER 93 at 109, but see ibid at 639, 103.

15 [1978] AC 435, [1977] 3 All ER 70. See also Local Government Act 1972, s 222.

be obtained only by the Attorney General or by a person whose private rights are affected by the act complained of. This 'private rights' rule could be considered a matter of locus standi, but is arguably more fundamental and concerns the substance of the declaration itself. A 'bare' declaration is on this view unknown to the law because a declaration can by definition declare only legal or equitable rights.[16] It has however been argued that the declaration has a separate 'supervisory' role which is geared to the invalidity of a decision rather than to a specific right vested in the plaintiff. There is little direct authority for this[17] and it seems clear that at least in cases commenced by writ under RSC Ord 15, r 16, a declaration can be granted only in relation to private rights. It could therefore be argued that because the Ord 53 procedure is not intended to alter the substantive law about the remedies, then the declaration is still limited to private rights cases.[18]

It is, however, arguable, and indeed this now seems to be the better view, that the Supreme Court Act 1981, s 31, has altered the law by permitting the court to make a declaration in purely public law cases. The *Gouriet* case is readily distinguishable not only because it was decided before the 1977 reforms but also because public law was not involved. Section 31 does not restrict declarations to declarations of 'right' and the distinctive concept of a 'supervisory' declaration has long been recognised.[19]

If this view is correct then the nature of the declaration has changed in relation to a public law matter and any restrictions upon the persons who may obtain a declaration must be discovered by reference to the law of locus standi.

Nevertheless, the relationship between the declaration and private rights remains important. First, if an applicant has a private right he will not only satisfy the standing requirement for Ord 53 but will also qualify for the purpose of an ordinary action. It might therefore be advantageous to establish standing under this head. Second, there are dicta which suggest that, independently of the question of standing, the particular role of the declaration in Ord 53 proceedings is to protect private rights. Where no private rights are involved certiorari is therefore the more appropriate remedy and, as a matter of discretion, a declaration will usually be granted only for the purpose of protecting private rights.[20]

## The meaning of private right

This topic is fraught with confusion partly because the approach of English law is through providing a remedy for a particular set of facts rather than through general concepts of rights. There are conflicting dicta but according

16 *Nixon v A-G* [1931] AC 184, 100 LJ Ch 70, HL; *London Passenger Transport Board v Moscrop* [1942] AC 332 at 342; *Guaranty Trust Co of New York v Hannay & Co* [1915] 2 KB 536 at 705, [1914–15] All ER Rep 38 at 39, CA.

17 See *Healey v Minister of Health* [1955] 1 QB 221 at 227–228, [1954] 3 All ER 449 at 451, CA. Perhaps *Anisminic Ltd v Foreign Compensation Commission* [1969] 2 AC 147, [1969] 1 All ER 208, HL is an example. The appellant had a right under the statute but not enforceable.

18 See *R v Secretary of State for the Environment, ex p Ward* [1984] 1 WLR 834 at 844. RSC Ord 53, r 9(5) reflects the private law nature of the declaration and the injunction.

19 See *Healey v Minister of Health* [1955] 1 QB 221, [1954] 3 All ER 449, CA.

20 *R v Secretary of State for the Environment, ex p Ward* [1984] 2 All ER 556 at 565; *O'Reilly v Mackman* [1982] 3 All ER 1124 at 1133. See below p 113 et seq.

to the majority in *Garden Cottage Foods Ltd v Milk Marketing Board*[1] the notion of a right without the possibility of damages is unknown at common law.

In the context of the declaration the following have been recognised as private rights:

1. Rights which are actionable in damages will always be amenable to a declaration either instead of or in addition to damages.
2. Cases where the applicant's legal position is affected by governmental action, for example regulations[2] or tax demands.[3] This kind of right is sometimes confused with a purely 'public right' because numerous other people may be similarly affected. However, apart from the possibility of initiating representative proceedings[4] it is irrelevant that numerous other people are in the same position, as long as the plaintiff's legal position is in fact affected.
3. Where the applicant is entitled to a benefit under a statute. It appears that a private right is established once the applicant fulfils any of the required criteria even if the final decision depends on the discretion of a public authority.[5] By contrast where the applicant has not yet established any entitlement he may in certain circumstances have a 'legitimate expectation' sufficient to attract procedural protection such as the right to be heard, but has no 'private right'.[6] Where on the other hand there is a *duty* to confer the benefit in question, then there will be a private right.[7]
4. *Special damage.* Even where the applicant's legal position in the strict sense is not affected, he may still be able to obtain a declaration where he can establish that he has suffered 'special damage' as a result of a breach of statutory duty or other unlawful conduct by a public authority.[8] Special damage for this purpose means a substantial harm or injury of a kind or extent[9] greater than that suffered by the public generally as a result of the unlawful conduct. The same appears to apply to the injunction.[10] Thus the notion of special damage, although it falls short of conferring a public right of action, can extend the concept of a private right in a flexible way.

   Although special damage need not be quantifiable in pecuniary terms[11] it seems that purely moral or social interests do not qualify. For example in

1 [1984] AC 130, [1983] 2 All ER 770, HL. Cf *Booth & Co (International) Ltd v National Enterprise Board* [1978] 3 All ER 624 at 636; *Meade v London Borough of Haringey* [1979] 2 All ER 1016, [1979] 1 WLR 637, CA; *Gouriet v Union of Post Office Workers* [1978] AC 435 at 494, 497, 499–500, 506, 517, 518; *Abbott v Sullivan* [1952] 1 KB 189, [1952] 1 All ER 226, CA; *Bradbury v London Borough of Enfield* [1967] 3 All ER 434, [1967] 1 WLR 1311, CA; *ex p Island Record* [1978] Ch 122, [1978] 3 All ER 824, CA.

2 *Brownsea Haven Properties v Poole Corpn* [1958] Ch 574, [1958] 1 All ER 205, CA; *Nichols v Tavistock UDC* [1923] 2 Ch 18.

3 *Dyson v A-G* [1911] 1 KB 410, 80 LJKB 531, CA.

4 *Duke of Bedford v Ellis* [1901] AC 1, HL.

5 *Roy v Kensington, Chelsea and Westminster Family Practitioner Committee* [1992] 1 AC 624, [1992] 1 All ER 705, HL.

6 *O'Reilly v Mackman* [1982] 3 All ER 1124 at 1126, HL.

7 *Cocks v Thanet District Council* [1983] 2 AC 286, [1982] 3 All ER 1135, HL.

8 *Gravesham Borough Council v British Railways Board* [1978] Ch 379 at 397–399; *Steeples v Derbyshire County Council* [1984] 3 All ER 468; *Charles Roberts & Co Ltd v British Railways Board* [1964] 3 All ER 651; *Birmingham and Midland Motor Omnibus Co v Worcestershire County Council* [1967] 1 All ER 544, [1967] 1 WLR 409.

9 *Boyce v Paddington Borough Council* [1903] 1 Ch 109.

10 Ibid. See also *Bradbury v London Borough of Enfield* [1967] 3 All ER 434, [1967] 1 WLR 1311, CA; *Coney v Choyce* [1975] 1 All ER 979, [1975] 1 WLR 422.

11 Eg parents in school closure cases, n 10, above.

*Malone v Metropolitan Police Comr*[12] telephone tapping by the police was held not to be susceptible to a declaration on the ground that privacy is not a right known to the law. However, if the officers had violated the relevant Home Office instructions it is arguable that a declaration might have been appropriate.[13]

Special damage in the present sense is not generally sufficient to create liability in tort. However the two contexts are sometimes confused. For example in *Gregory v Camden London Borough Council*[14] Paull J held that a neighbour who objected to an ultra vires grant of planning permission had no cause of action in damages and 'therefore' no right to a declaration. In *Lonrho v Shell Petroleum Co Ltd (No 2)*[15] the House of Lords also interpreted the notion of 'special damage' restrictively. However, *Lonrho* was an action for damages in tort brought in respect of financial loss arising out of violations of a sanctions order made in respect of oil supplies to Rhodesia. The wider question of the declaration was not discussed. Confusion is further compounded because 'special damage' is a substantive ingredient of the tort of public nuisance. There is no necessary reason to assimilate tort liability with special damage for the purpose of declaratory relief.

The notion of special damage depends essentially upon the scope and purpose of the particular statutory power in issue. Thus in the *Lonrho* case the sanctions order was not concerned with the position of customers of sanctions violators who should therefore be left to the ordinary law of contract or tort. On the other hand, one purpose of planning controls is to protect the amenities of local residents. Thus in *Steeples v Derbyshire County Council* Webster J, refusing to follow the *Gregory* case, held that a local resident who can show particular injury should be able to obtain a declaration, whether or not his property rights in the strict sense are affected.[16] *Thorne RDC v Bunting*[17] also supports this view. There Megarry J held that the scope of the declaration depends not upon the existence of a cause of action as such, but whether the declaration can provide the plaintiff with real and effective relief.

5. *Quasi-proprietary rights*. Finally, there appears to be a separate category of 'right' consisting of interests or expectations which the courts are prepared on policy grounds to protect even though they fall within none of the recognised categories of legal interest. There are only two cases which unequivocally support the existence of this kind of right. Both involved economic interests related to the plaintiff's livelihood and these rights have been regarded as 'proprietary', a classification reminiscent of the notion of the 'new property' which has developed in American jurisprudence and which signifies a social interest regarded by the law as especially important, even though outside the recognised categories of proprietary interest.

12 [1979] Ch 344, sub nom *Malone v Metropolitan Police Comr (No 2)* [1979] 2 All ER 620. Cf *Francome v Mirror Group Newspapers* [1984] 2 All ER 408, [1984] 1 WLR 892, CA.
13 See above, p 67 et seq.
14 [1966] 2 All ER 196, [1966] 1 WLR 899. But see now *Steeples v Derbyshire County Council* [1984] 3 All ER 468 at 496–500.
15 [1982] AC 173, [1981] 2 All ER 456, HL. Contrast the *Gouriet* case (above, n 1).
16 Above, n 14.
17 [1972] Ch 470, [1972] 1 All ER 439. See also *Tito v Waddell (No 2)* [1977] Ch 106 at 260, [1977] 3 All ER 129, 256–257.

In *Nagle v Fielden*[18] (an application for an interlocutory injunction) the Court of Appeal held that the plaintiff's 'right to work' could entitle her to have her application for a trainer's licence considered by the Jockey Club despite a club ruling excluding women from entitlement to a trainer's licence. There was no express or implied contract between the plaintiff and the club upon which the normal principles of unreasonable restraint of trade could operate. This was, therefore, a bold decision which depended upon the court's willingness to recognise an independent right vested in the plaintiff. Similarly, in *ex p Island Records*[19] the Court of Appeal made a declaration that the plaintiffs, a group of musicians,had a right to benefit from a recording of a concert given by them which had been 'bootlegged' by the defendants. The practice of bootlegging—that is, recording live performances without permission—infringed no copyright laws nor did it violate any contract. Nevertheless Lord Denning MR and Lawton LJ regarded the right to benefit from a profession or calling as in itself a proprietary right capable of forming the subject of a declaration.

## Statutory rights

It is important to distinguish between decisions taking away existing rights and those which purport to create new rights. There is a presumption against excluding the jurisdiction of the courts. Thus where a governmental decision purports to take away existing rights a declaration will lie in support of these rights unless excluded by clear statutory language.[20] On the other hand where a statute creates a new right and also provides machinery for determining the circumstances in which that right is to come into existence a declaration will not lie, since only the statutory machinery can create the right.[1] *Pyx Granite Co Ltd v Ministry of Housing and Local Government*[2] (declaration that plaintiff's land was not subject to planning control) and *Ealing London Borough Council v Race Relations Board*[3] (declaration that plaintiff's conduct was not capable of falling within the Race Relations Act 1968) provide examples of the first kind of case. *Shah v Barnet London Borough Council*[4] is an example of the second kind of case. However if there is only one possible decision that can be made on the facts of the case a declaration may be made to the effect that the statutory body is bound to confer the benefit in question.[5]

18 [1966] 2 QB 633, [1966] 1 All ER 689.

19 [1978] Ch 122, [1978] 3 All ER 824. But this decision was criticised in *Lonrho v Shell Petroleum* (above, n 12), although *Lonrho* concerned a common law claim in tort; see also *RCA Corpn v Pollard* [1982] 2 All ER 468, [1982] 1 WLR 979.

20 *Pyx Granite Co Ltd v Ministry of Housing and Local Government* [1960] AC 260, [1959] 3 All ER 1, HL.

1 *Barraclough v Brown* [1897] AC 615, [1895–99] All ER Rep 239; *Argosam Finance Co Ltd v Oxby* [1965] Ch 390, [1964] 1 All ER 791; *Harrison v Croydon London BC* [1968] Ch 479, [1967] 2 All ER 589.

2 Above, n 20. See also *Roy v Kennington and Chelsea and Westminster Family Practioner Committee* [1992] 1 AC 624, [1992] 1 All ER 705, HL (below p 117).

3 [1972] AC 342, [1972] 1 All ER 105, HL.

4 [1983] 2 AC 309, [1983] 1 All ER 226, HL (grant entitlement); see also *Healey v Minister of Health* [1955] 1 QB 221, [1954] 3 All ER 449, CA.

5 *Anisminic Ltd v Foreign Compensation Commission* [1969] 2 AC 147, [1969] 1 All ER 208, HL; *Barty-King v Ministry of Defence* [1979] 2 All ER 80.

## INTERIM RELIEF

There is no power to make an interim declaration either against the Crown or any other body or person.[6] This embargo is not based on any specific statutory provision but is said to be inherent in the nature of the declaration. The notion of a 'provisional' declaration of rights is seen as contradictory[7] and in the case of a declaration and injunction, interim relief in Ord 53 proceedings is available only where such relief would be available in an ordinary action.[8]

However, the declaration need not necessarily be postponed until the final determination of all the issues in the case. A final declaration can be granted on an interlocutory application[9] though the power to do so will only be used sparingly.[10] There is no reason in principle why such a declaration may not be made against the Crown.

## FLEXIBLE NATURE OF THE DECLARATION—RELATIONSHIP WITH THE PREROGATIVE ORDERS

In deciding whether to make a declaration or grant an injunction the court must 'have regard to':

(a) the nature of the matters in respect of which 'relief may be granted by order of mandamus, prohibition and certiorari';

(b) the 'nature of the persons and bodies against whom relief may be granted by such orders'; and

(c) all the circumstances of the case. It must consider that it would be 'just and convenient' to make a declaration or grant an injunction.[11]

As we have seen certiorari lies only in respect of a written 'decision' and although a 'decision' for this purpose can include preliminary decisions, certiorari is not available in respect of all unlawful governmental action. A declaration can state the rights of the parties and expose any unlawful behaviour and the court has a discretion as to how to formulate its declaration. For example, in *Chief Constable of North Wales Police v Evans*[12] the Chief Constable unlawfully threatened to dismiss the applicant policeman who thereupon resigned. The House of Lords, believing that a blatant illegality should be formally recognised, made a declaration that the applicant was entitled to the same rights except reinstatement as if he had been wrongfully dismissed. In cases such as this to which the prerogative orders do not neatly apply the declaration comes into its own.

A declaration is also suitable for advisory statements or non-statutory rules contained, for example, in circulars or letters.[13]

6 *IRC v Rossminster Ltd* [1980] 1 All ER 80 at 89, 95–96, 105–106.

7 *International General Electric Co of New York Ltd v Customs and Excise Comrs* [1962] Ch 784, [1962] 2 All ER 398, CA.

8 RSC Ord 53, r 10(6); see *R v Secretary of State for the Home Department, ex p Herbage* [1987] QB 872, [1986] 3 All ER 209 (overruled in its main point but construing r 10(6) broadly).

9 RSC Ord 15, r 16; *Re St Nazaire Co* (1879) 12 Ch D 88, CA; *Clarke v Chadburn* [1985] 1 All ER 211, [1985] 1 WLR 78. *Malone v Metropolitan Police Comr (No 2)* [1979] 2 All ER 620 at 650; *IRC v Rossminster Ltd* (above, n 6).

10 *Meade v London Borough of Haringey* [1979] 2 All ER 1016 at 1026, [1979] 1 WLR 637, 648–649.

11 Supreme Court Act 1981 s 31(2).

12 [1982] 3 All ER 141, [1982] 1 WLR 1155.

13 *R v Secretary of State, ex p Equal Opportunities Commission* [1992] 1 All ER 545 at 555.

Similarly if coercion is undesirable, for example to avoid inconvenience or where an enforceable order would inhibit parliamentary proceedings or the activities of informal bodies, a declaration is appropriate.[14]

A declaration is also suitable in politically sensitive areas where the court wishes to give guidance as to proposed action but not necessarily to give a coercive remedy, particularly against a minister.[15] Indeed in cases where only the broadest guidelines can be given, the courts' judgment may be enough without any remedy.[16]

There are dicta that a declaration or injunction cannot be granted unless the matter is within the scope of the prerogative orders.[17] This has arisen in the context of the 'public law' issue and there are contrary dicta.[18] If applied generally, this restriction is probably too rigid. It would frustrate the purpose of the reforms to Ord 53 of combining the advantages of all the remedies. It would follow, for example, that a declaration could no longer be made against the Crown in judicial review proceedings whereas it could in ordinary civil proceedings.[19] The scope of the prerogative orders is required to be taken into account as a discretionary factor but there seems to be no justification for a more rigid approach.

## THE INJUNCTION

The injunction is the least used among the judicial review remedies. Like the declaration it is geared to the protection of private rights and is, of course, widely used in private law contexts. Despite the wide language of the Supreme Court Act 1981, s 37(1), the injunction lacks the flexibility of the declaration. Its main advantage over the declaration, that it carries enforceable sanctions, is counterbalanced by the fact that it is not available against either the Crown or Crown servants. In this latter respect the injunction is the most restrictive of all the remedies.

### Forms of injunction

#### *Interlocutory injunction*

An interlocutory injunction (an interim injunction is the same thing) can be used to stay the governmental action complained of pending a full trial.

14 *R v Boundary Commission for England, ex p Foot* [1983] 1 All ER 1099 at 1116, CA; *R v HM Treasury, ex p Smedley* [1985] QB 657, [1985] 1 All R 589, CA; *R v Panel on Take-overs and Mergers, ex p Datafin plc* [1987] QB 815, [1987] 1 All ER 564, CA.

15 Above, pp 36, 64.

16 *R v Secretary of State for Social Services, ex p Child Poverty Action Group* [1989] 1 All ER 1047 at 1055, CA. This might also apply where there is no locus standi (ibid). See also *Re F* [1990] 2 AC 1, sub nom *F v West Berkshire Health Authority* [1989] 2 All ER 545.

17 *Davy v Spelthorne Borough Council* [1984] AC 262, [1983] 3 All ER 278 at 288, HL; *IRC v National Federation of Self-Employed and Small Businesses Ltd* [1982] AC 617 at 629, 639, 647–648. *R v Secretary of State for the Home Office, ex p Dew* [1987] 2 All ER 1049, [1987] 1 WLR 881.

18 *R v Panel on Take-overs and Mergers, ex p Datafin plc* [1987] QB 815 per Lloyd LJ; *R v BBC, ex p Lavelle* [1983] 1 WLR 23 at 31. See also *Law v National Greyhound Racing Club Ltd* [1983] 3 All ER 300, [1983] 1 WLR 1302, CA; *R v Bromley London Borough Council, ex p Lambeth London Borough Council* (1984) Times, 16 June. (Early dicta were before this provision had statutory force, cf s 31(4).)

19 See *R v Secretary of State for the Home Department, ex p Herbage* [1987] QB 872.

Ord 53 expressly provides for interim relief in certiorari or prohibition cases but as far as other remedies are concerned the matter depends upon the general law.[20] Thus, where it is alleged that a local byelaw is unlawful it may be that an injunction is the most suitable remedy. The declaration cannot give interim relief, and there are still doubts as to whether prohibition or certiorari applies to subordinate legislation. Injuctions are not available against the Crown.

The court will exercise its discretion in favour of granting an interim injunction only where it is established that:

(a) the applicant has an arguable case (not necessarily a prima facie case);
(b) the balance of convenience is in favour of altering the status quo. (Thus it is more difficult to obtain an interim mandatory than a prohibitory injunction.);[1] and
(c) damages are not in the circumstances an adequate remedy.[2]

The court will take into account the public interest when applying the balance of convenience test where a public authority is involved.[3]

### *Mandatory injunction*

A mandatory injunction requires a person to perform a positive act and thus overlaps with mandamus. In relation to the performance of a positive statutory duty mandamus will normally be the more appropriate remedy and has the advantage of lying against a Crown servant in cases where the duty has been specifically conferred upon the servant in question. On the other hand mandamus will not lie solely to compel the consequences of an unlawful act to be undone and here a mandatory injunction would be appropriate. Moreover, as in the case of all equitable remedies an injunction operates in personam against any individual involved in the illegality in question, whereas mandamus is available only against the body on which the duty is specifically conferred.

As a matter of discretion however the court is unlikely to grant a mandatory injunction in relation to a duty which involves a substantial exercise of discretion and which the court is not in a position to supervise.[4] This can represent a major weakness in the judicial review procedure when attempting to enforce the more complex duties of public bodies. So far the court has failed to find a solution.

A mandatory injunction is available only to a person whose specific legal rights are in issue.

20 RSC Ord 53, r 3(10)6 and Ord 29, r 1.

1 See *De Falco v Crawley Borough Council* [1980] 1 All ER 913 at 924, CA; *R v Kensington and Chelsea Royal London Borough Council, ex p Hammell* [1989] QB 518, [1989] 1 All ER 1202, CA.

2 *American Cyanamid Co v Ethicon Ltd* [1975] AC 396, [1975] 1 All ER 504, HL; *Hubbard v Pitt* [1976] QB 142, [1975] 3 All ER 1, CA; *XAG v A Bank* [1983] 2 All ER 464, [1983] 2 Lloyd's Rep 535. However, where no conflict of evidence is involved as will often be the case in judicial review proceedings the court may be prepared in interlocutory proceedings to go further towards weighing the parties' respective cases.

3 *Smith v Inner London Education Authority* [1978] 1 All ER 411, CA. Cf *Bradbury v London Borough of Enfield* [1967] 3 All ER 434, [1967] 1 WLR 1311, CA.

4 *Meade v London Borough of Haringey* [1979] 2 All ER 1016 at 1028–1029, 1034–1035, [1979] 1 WLR 637 at 651, 658, CA. See also *R v Secretary of State for the Environment, ex p Lee and Bond* (1985) 54 P & CR 311.

*Prohibitory injunction*

A prohibitory injunction restrains a person from committing an unlawful act. The most useful role of the prohibitory injunction as an Ord 53 remedy is therefore to prevent the enforcement or implementation against the applicant of an ultra vires order or regulation. Because an injunction issues in personam it can be granted directly against the implementing official.

In the case of an ultra vires decision prohibition would fulfil the same purpose as an injunction more efficiently because it lies against the tribunal as such, whereas unless the tribunal is incorporated the injunction lies only against its individual members.[5]

On the other hand an injunction can reach beyond prohibition. An order of prohibition lies only against the tribunal itself whereas an injunction can in principle attach to any unlawful conduct, for example, to restrain a person from initiating proceedings, to prevent a witness from giving false or inadmissible evidence, or to prevent multiplicity of proceedings.

*Quia timet injunction*

This form of injunction restrains the commission of an unlawful act which has not yet occurred but which is threatened. A very high likelihood is required that the feared act will occur and the anticipated injury to the applicant must be substantial.[6] This illustrates the private law orientation of the injunction.

*Quo warranto injunction*

This is a special form of injunction provided for by s 30 of the Supreme Court Act 1981 and unlike other kinds of injunction is available only in Ord 53 proceedings.[7] It is the successor of the former prerogative writ and later information of quo warranto and thus has common law rather than equitable origins. The purpose of a quo warranto injunction is to restrain a person who is not entitled to do so from acting in a public office. The office in question must be of a substantive character in the sense that powers and duties are attached to it and must be permanent in character. It must either be held under the Crown or created by statute or Royal Charter. Thus, apart from some local authority office holders, and members of statutory tribunals, it is arguable that the police and judges fall within this category since whether or not they are strictly Crown servants the functions of both derive from the Crown.[8] An office holder must be distinguished from a servant, the test apparently being that the person concerned must enjoy a status protected by law and must not be

5 Eg *Davis v Carew Pole* [1956] 2 All ER 524, [1956] 1 WLR 833. Cf *Barnard v National Dock Labour Board* [1953] 2 QB 18 at 41–42, [1953] 1 All ER 1113 at 1119, CA; *Land Comr v Pillai* [1960] AC 854, [1960] 3 WLR 626.

6 *Hooper v Rogers* [1975] Ch 43, [1974] 3 All ER 417, CA; *Redland Bricks Ltd v Morris* [1970] AC 652, [1969] 2 All ER 576, HL; *A-G v Wellingborough UDC* (1974) 72 LGR 507, CA; *A-G v Nottingham Corpn* [1904] 1 Ch 673, 73 LJ Ch 512.

7 Supreme Court Act 1981, s 31(1)(c); *A-G for New South Wales v Perpetual Trustee Co Ltd* [1955] AC 457 at 480, PC. In the context of membership of local authorities this form of injunction has been replaced by statutory provisions: Local Government Act 1972, s 92. See RSC Ord 53, r 11.

8 *Lewis v Cattle* [1938] 2 KB 454, [1938] 2 All ER 368; *Fisher v Oldham Corpn* [1930] 2 KB 364, 99 LJKB 569.

dismissible at will. Thus employees of some nationalised industries may be office holders but ministers and civil servants are not since as a matter of law both are dismissible at pleasure.[9] The various distinctions that are required are therefore sometimes arbitrary in the context of the objectives of judicial review.

Unlike other forms of injunction a quo warranto injunction is a public remedy and not limited to protecting individual rights. It appears that any member of the public can apply for a quo warranto injunction subject to the court's discretion to refuse the remedy to a person with no genuine interest in the matter.[10]

## Authorities amenable to the injunction—the position of the Crown

At common law an injunction did not lie against the Crown, but could possibly be granted against a Crown servant.[11] Under the Crown Proceedings Act 1947, s 21(1)(a) an injunction is not available against the Crown. Nor is an injunction available against a servant or officer of the Crown if to grant the remedy would give relief which would otherwise not be available against the Crown.[12] Thus unlike prerogative order cases even if a minister or other Crown servant is exercising a statutory function conferred on him specifically, an injunction still cannot be granted. One qualification is that a statute could be construed as conferring upon a Crown servant a power or duty to be exercised independently of his position as such. There is however a strong presumption against this.[13]

Despite the foregoing it is arguable that the Crown Proceedings Act 1947, s 21(2) does not apply to Ord 53 proceedings at all. The argument is that s 21(2), which forbids injunctions issuing against Crown servants, applies only to 'civil proceedings' and 'civil proceedings' are defined in s 38(2) (subject to context) not to include 'proceedings on the Crown side of the King's Bench Division'. Order 53 proceedings are proceedings on the Crown side, and it seems that Parliament intended to leave judicial review proceedings outside the Crown Proceedings Act. The context of s 38(2) does not help since in 1947, injunctions were not available in judicial review proceedings. Contextual arguments pull both ways. However, the House of Lords has taken the view that since no injunction could issue against the Crown at common law before the Crown Proceedings Act, injunctions are not available against either the Crown or individual officers irrespective of the scope of s 21 except where European Community law makes this remedy necessary.[14]

9 See *Vine v National Dock Labour Board* [1957] AC 488, [1956] 3 All ER 939, HL; *R v East Berkshire Health Authority, ex p Walsh* [1985] QB 152 [1984] 3 All ER 425, CA, per May LJ. But see Crown Proceedings Act 1947 s 38(2).

10 *R v Speyer* [1916] 1 KB 595, 613.

11 See de Smith, *Judicial Review of Administrative Action* (4th edn) p 445. See also below pp 148–9.

12 Crown Proceedings Act 1947, s 21(2).

13 *Harper v Secretary of State for the Home Department* [1955] Ch 238 at 254; [1955] 1 All ER 331 *Merricks v Heathcoat-Amory and the Minister of Agriculture, Fisheries and Food* [1955] Ch 567, [1955] 2 All ER 453. Cf *R v Secretary of State for the Home Department, ex p Herbage* [1987] QB 872 at 884; *Padfield v Minister of Agriculture, Food and Fisheries* [1968] AC 997, [1968] 1 All ER 694, HL sometimes cited *contra* was a *mandamus* case.

14 *Factortame Ltd v Secretary of State for Transport* [1990] 2 AC 85, [1989] 2 All ER 692, HL; *Factortame Ltd v Secretary of State for Transport (No 2)*. See also s 23(2) further limiting 'civil proceedings'.

## Who can obtain an injunction?

An injunction, unlike the other Ord 53 remedies, is a personal inter partes remedy. The dicta conflict but the better view is that an injunction lies in favour of a plaintiff who has suffered either injury to a legal or equitable right or special damage.[15] It is sometimes said, however, that a *mandatory* injunction lies only in favour of an applicant or a plaintiff who has a cause of action for damages.[16] However this does not seem to apply where a public authority has committed a positive act of misfeasance or acted ultra vires.[17]

## Role of the injunction

The main use of the injunction in Ord 53 cases is probably to obtain a speedy remedy against enforcement officers where physical interference has taken place or is anticipated. It is no defence that the authority has not sufficient resources to prevent physical injury but an injunction can be temporarily suspended.[18]

It is also important to remember that the court can award damages instead of or in addition to an injunction independently of any cause of action in tort.[19] This form of equitable damages is sometimes overlooked, attention being focussed upon the problems of tortious liability in public law.

15 *Ashby v Ebdon* [1985] Ch 394, [1984] 3 All ER 869; *Chief Constable of Kent v V* [1983] QB 34, [1982] 3 All ER 36, CA.

16 *Stockport District Waterworks Co v Manchester Corpn* (1862) 7 LT 545, 9 Jur NS 266; *Glossop v Heston and Isleworth Local Board* (1879) 12 Ch D 102, 49 LJ Ch 89, CA.

17 *Meade v London Borough of Haringey* [1979] 2 All ER 1016, [1974] 1 WLR 637, CA.

18 *Pride of Derby and Derbyshire Angling Association Ltd v British Celanese Ltd* [1953] Ch 149, [1953] 1 All ER 179, CA.

19 Supreme Court Act 1981, s 50; *Garden Cottage Foods Ltd v Milk Marketing Board* [1984] AC 130 at 144. Supreme Court Act 1981, s 31(4) does not seem to prevent this.

CHAPTER 8

# Damages

## GENERAL CONSIDERATIONS

Damages can be awarded in Ord 53 proceedings only if two general conditions are fulfilled. First, the claim for damages must be joined with an application for at least one of the other Ord 53 remedies and must 'arise out of any matter to which the application relates'.[1] Thus ordinary actions in tort, for example arising out of public works, are not within the scope of Ord 53, even though public law issues in the sense of questions involving the ambit of statutory powers or duties may be involved.

The meaning of the expression 'arising out of any matter' is not clear. The court may possibly award damages even though the offending governmental action is not found to be invalid, for example in cases involving negligent misstatement of the effect of a governmental policy. However, where a claim for damages rests primarily on a private law cause of action such as negligence and the question of validity is only incidental, the court is likely to permit proceedings to be instituted by writ.[2] Indeed if there is no substantial issue concerning the validity of a governmental decision but only an ordinary claim in tort the court will strike out a judicial review action. New proceedings must be commenced. The court's power to treat an application for judicial review as if it were an ordinary action under RSC Ord 53, r 9(5) is limited to cases where there is a public law issue to be decided, for example where complex factual issues have arisen for which a full trial is more appropriate.[3] Indeed given that the assessment of damages may involve complex factual issues, the award of damages in Ord 53 proceedings is likely to be unusual.

The second requirement is that the court must be satisfied that 'if the claim had been made in an action begun by the applicant at the time of making his application he would have been awarded damages'.[4] Thus no new head of liability is created and the applicant must rely on the general law. An award of damages is a matter of private law, and a form of collateral challenge. Damages can therefore be sought in ordinary proceedings. If the main purpose of the litigation is to seek damages it is doubtful whether there would be any advantage in taking Ord 53 proceedings particularly where there are factual issues to be resolved.

1 Supreme Court Act 1981, s 31(4)(a).
2 *Davy v Spelthorne Borough Council* [1984] AC 262, [1983] 3 All ER 278, HL.
3 *R v Secretary of State for the Home Office, ex p Dew* [1987] 2 All ER 1049, [1987] 1 WLR 881; *R v Liverpool County Council, ex p Coade* (1986) Times, 10 October; *R v East Berkshire Health Authority, ex p Walsh* [1985] QB 152, [1984] 3 All ER 425, CA.
4 Supreme Court Act 1981, s 31(4)(b).

## Other monetary remedies—restitution

Order 53 does not permit claims for money due as such.[5] There is no reason why an application for damages in lieu of an injunction should not be made in Ord 53 proceedings. This has the advantage that no cause of action in tort need be established. On the other hand this remedy is discretionary.

Restitution is available against a public authority where money has been paid as a result of an unlawful demand. In *Woolwich Equitable Building Society v IRC*[6] the House of Lords, by a three to two majority, allowed the appellants to recover excessive tax assessments, despite the traditional private law rule that money paid under a mistake of law is not recoverable (except where there is compulsion or an implied or express agreement to repay). The rationale behind this important change in the law was essentially constitutional—the fundamental principle of no taxation without the authority of Parliament. Lord Goff also pointed out that the citizen's right to recover overpaid charges would otherwise be more restricted under domestic law than under EC law.[7] In many cases there is also a statutory right to reimbursement.

However, their Lordships distinguished between a payment that was ultra vires and therefore a nullity and a payment made as a result of error of fact or law. Payments made as a result of error of fact are generally recoverable. As regards error of law, this is yet another case which throws doubt upon the *Anisminic* principle that all errors of law make a decision ultra vires.[8]

Now that restitution is in principle available it may be possible to mitigate the injustice of the rule that there can be no damages in respect of payments made to a local authority under an ultra vires contract.

## Actions in tort generally

There is no general law of governmental liability.[9] The Ord 53 applicant must therefore being his arguments within a recognised category of the law of torts. This branch of the law has developed mainly in private law contexts, and English law has not traditionally recognised the existence of public law as such. This has been judicially recognised to be 'notoriously unsatisfactory from a plaintiff's point of view'.[10] A straightforward example is where an official commits an invasion of the applicant's person or property which would constitute a trespass or nuisance. Here the matter is one of collateral attack. The authority must justify its invasion by reference to statutory powers, and it cannot do this if its decision is ultra vires. In collateral attack cases it is the physical invasion and not the invalid decision as such that constitutes the cause of action. This may be important from the point of view of the running of time[11] and because the enforcement official may be liable as well as the decision-maker.

Throughout this area of law the cases illustrate a common theme, that of

5 *Roy v Kensington, Chelsea and Westminster Family Practitioner Committee* [1992] 1 AC 624, [1992] 1 All ER 705, HL.

6 [1992] 3 All ER 737, [1992] 3 WLR 366, HL.

7 Above at 763–4; see 199/82: *Amministrazione delle Finanze dello Stato v San Giorgio SpA* [1983] ECR 3595, [1985] 2 CMLR 658, ECJ.

8 Above, p 14.

9 *R v Knowsley Metropolitan Borough Council, ex p Maguire* [1992] NLJR 1375, (1992) Times, 26 June, where damages for 'maladministration' were refused in the absence of a course of action at common law.

10 *R v Knowsley Metropolitan Borough Council, ex p Maguire* [1992] NLJR 1375.

11 *O'Connor v Isaacs* [1956] 2 QB 288, [1956] 2 All ER 417, CA.

judicial reluctance to impose wide-ranging liability upon public authorities. However, arbitrary or oppressive governmental conduct is one of the few cases where exemplary damages can be awarded. A deliberate interference with the plaintiff's rights is required so that exemplary damages cannot be recovered in a negligence action.[12]

## Invalidity and illegality—private rights

An ultra vires decision does not in itself create liability in tort. One reason offered for this is that a tort is an unlawful act and an ultra vires decision is merely void but not unlawful.[13] An unlawful act takes place only where the plaintiff's rights are infringed in purported reliance on a void decision. This analysis fits the enforcement cases which have been mentioned above, but is difficult to apply to cases where no recognised kind of common law right is infringed, for example, the refusal of a benefit or licence. In such cases liability, if it occurs at all, depends upon negligence.[14] In *Malone v Metropolitan Police Comr*[15] a plaintiff had no remedy in connection with telephone tapping by the police, since no right vested in him had been infringed. No trespass or criminal offence was involved, and English law recognises no right to privacy.

However, in some cases a private right for the purpose of damages may be created solely by the statute which confers the power or duty in question. The separate tort of breach of statutory duty is based upon the assumption that Parliament intended to create a cause of action in damages because of a failure to perform a statutory obligation. Also a duty of care in negligence can arise out of a statutory function and be defined by reference to that function.[16]

## Causation

Another reason why an invalid decision does not sound in damages concerns causation. An ultra vires decision is void and can therefore be ignored. The plaintiff who obeys it can be regarded as the author of his own injury. The courts have sometimes applied this somewhat artificial reasoning,[17] but it can be circumvented. First, losses arising independently of the purported legal effect of the decision, eg injury to reputation, should in principle be recoverable.[18] Second, this argument cannot apply to the refusal, as opposed to the revocation, of a benefit to which the plaintiff is entitled.[19] Third, and most importantly, it is arguable that the nullity argument applies only in cases where it would be unreasonable for the plaintiff to obey the decision. Where

12 *Rookes v Barnard* [1964] AC 1129, [1964] 1 All ER 367, HL; *Cassell & Co Ltd v Broome* [1972] AC 1027, [1972] 1 All ER 801, HL; *AB v South West Water Services Ltd* [1992] 4 All ER 574.

13 *Polley v Fordham* [1904] 2 KB 345, 73 LJKB 687; *Dunlop v Woollahra Municipal Council* [1982] AC 158, [1981] 1 All ER 1202, PC; *Bourgoin SA v Ministry of Agriculture, Fisheries and Food* [1986] QB 716, [1985] 3 All ER 585, CA.

14 See *Tate and Lyle Industries Ltd v Greater London Council* [1983] 2 AC 509, [1983] 1 All ER 1159, HL.

15 [1980] QB 49, [1979] 1 All ER 256, CA; cf *Francome v Mirror Group Newspapers Ltd* [1984] 2 All ER 408, [1984] 1 WLR 892, CA—breach of confidence.

16 *Ministry of Housing and Local Government v Sharp* [1970] 2 QB 223, [1970] 1 All ER 1009, CA.

17 *O'Connor v Isaacs* [1956] 2 QB 288, [1956] 2 All ER 417, CA; *Wood v Woad* (1874) LR 9 Exch 190, 43 LJ Ex 153; *Dunlop v Woollahra Municipal Council* [1982] AC 158, [1981] 1 All ER 1202, PC; *Stott v Gamble* [1916] 2 KB 504, 85 LJKB 1750; *Polley v Fordham* [1904] 2 KB 345 at 348.

18 *Beaurain v Scott* (1812) 3 Camp 388.

19 *Thornton v Kirklees Metropolitan Borough Council* [1979] QB 626, [1979] 2 All ER 349, CA. The position is different where the plaintiff has no entitlement to the benefit in question, the matter being discretionary.

the plaintiff reasonably relies on the decision or cannot conveniently ignore it, the decision can be regarded as the cause of the plaintiff's injury.[20] However the chain of causation is broken if the applicant neglects to exercise a right of appeal or some other convenient remedy, or if the decision is confirmed by a higher body, or if enforcement requires a court order.

## THE MAIN HEADS OF TORT LIABILITY

In *Lonrho plc v Tebbit*,[1] Browne-Wilkinson V-C summarised the conditions under which liability exists in private law for the improper exercise of statutory power as follows:

(a) if the defendant acted knowingly in excess of such powers or maliciously;
(b) if the statute was passed for the protection of a specific class of the public to which the plaintiff belongs; or
(c) the power has been exercised negligently in breach of a private law duty of care to the plaintiff.

Browne-Wilkinson V-C did not discuss the question of liability for nuisance or under the rule in *Rylands v Fletcher*. Because of the factual issues involved these kinds of liability are unlikely to arise in the context of Ord 53. Indeed *Rylands v Fletcher* may not apply at all where public bodies are exercising statutory functions.[2] Furthermore the governing legislation may deal openly with the question of liability. There is no liability for damage which is necessarily authorised by the governing legislation and to this extent public law issues may arise.

Browne-Wilkinson V-C's summary equally applies to statutory duties where there might be liability for negligence or under the separate tort of breach of statutory duty. However statutory provisions which exclude or limit liability are construed more liberally in the case of duties than in the case of powers.[3]

## NEGLIGENCE

In *Fellows v Rother District Council*,[4] Robert Goff J summarised as follows the principles governing an action in negligence at common law against a public body or official purporting to exercise statutory powers.

The plaintiff must show:

(a) that the act complained of was not within the limits of a discretion bona fide exercised under the relevant power;
(b) that, having regard to all the circumstances (including the legislation creating the relevant power), there was sufficient proximity between the plaintiff and the defendant to create a duty of care on the part of the defendant to avoid damage to the plaintiff of the type complained of;

20 *Roncarelli v Duplessis* (1959) 16 DLR (2d) 689; *McGillivray v Kimber* (1915) 52 SCR 146, 26 DLR 164; *O'Connor v Isaacs* [1956] 2 QB 288 at 303, 367. Perhaps there will be liability if the decision is good on its face. See *DPP v Head* [1959] AC 83, [1958] 1 All ER 679, HL per Lord Denning.
1 [1991] 4 All ER 973 at 980; affd [1992] 4 All ER 280, CA.
2 See *Dunne v North Western Gas Board* [1964] 2 QB 806, [1963] 3 All ER 916, CA. Wade *Administrative Law* (6th edn) p 770.
3 *Department of Transport v North West Water Authority* [1984] AC 336.
4 [1983] 1 All ER 513.

(c) that there was no ground for negating, reducing or limiting the duty of care;
(d) that it was reasonably foreseeable that the act of the defendant or those for whom he was vicariously responsible was likely to cause damage of the type in fact suffered by the plaintiff by reason of such act.

These requirements will be examined in turn.

## Ultra vires

Ordinary negligence in the sense of failure to take reasonable care is not, as such, the standard of liability to be applied to a public authority. Early cases such as *Geddis v Bann Reservoir (Proprietors)*,[5] which suggest that an authority can be liable for exercising its powers negligently in the sense of failing to prevent foreseeable and avoidable injury, must now be treated with caution. According to more recent cases, where an authority exercises a statutory discretion a different standard applies, namely that of public law. It must be shown that the authority has exceeded or abused its powers in the normal judicial review sense, because this determines the appropriate level of judicial interference. To apply a more stringent test in an action for damages is said to be anomalous.[6] However, this ultra vires requirement may itself be anomalous.

An ultra vires act or a breach of statutory duty is therefore an essential prerequisite of liability. Beyond that the following three general considerations are relevant.

### *(a) Powers and duties*

In the case of statutory powers, ie where an authority has no obligation to do anything at all, the House of Lords has emphasised that the public law ultra vires standard of liability applies.[7]

In the case of *duties* where the authority is bound to act, it appears that accidental injuries are actionable on proof of negligence. It has been said in this context that negligence has a special meaning, the test being that the operation be conducted 'with all reasonable regard and care for the interests of other persons'.[8] However, where statutory duties are coupled with a power in the sense that they involve the exercise of discretion as to the level and manner of compliance, ultra vires will be the test for liability. Indeed it may be difficult to draw a clear line between powers and duties since many duties involve a considerable measure of discretion as to how they are performed, particularly when it comes to weighing competing priorities.[9]

For many years it was believed that a distinction must be drawn between a power and a duty, to the effect that a public authority, because it is not obliged to exercise a power, should, if it does in fact exercise it, be liable only for

5 (1878) 3 App Cas 430, HL.
6 *Home Office v Dorset Yacht Co Ltd* [1970] AC 1004 at 1031, 1037, 1067, [1970] 2 All ER 294 at 301, 306, 332, HL; *Lonrho plc v Tebbit* [1991] 4 All ER 973 at 892 (with reluctance).
7 *Anns v Merton London Borough Council* [1978] AC 728, [1977] 2 All ER 492, HL. *Anns* was overruled in *Murphy v Brentwood District Council* [1991] 1 AC 398, [1990] 2 All ER 908, HL, as regards liability for economic loss, but what was said in *Anns* about the ultra vires principle does not seem to have been affected. See *Lonrho plc v Tebbit* (above, n 6) at 984.
8 *Allen v Gulf Oil Refining Ltd* [1981] AC 1001 at 1011, HL; *Tate and Lyle Industries Ltd v Greater London Council* [1983] 2 AC 509 at 538, HL.
9 See *R v Metropolitan Police Comr, ex p Blackburn* [1968] 2 QB 118 at 136, CA; *R v Secretary of State for Social Services, ex p Child Poverty Action Group* [1989] 1 All ER 1047 at 1054–1055, CA.

additional injury to the plaintiff over and above the injury which would have occurred had the power not been exercised at all.[10] It was also believed that there could be no liability in tort for a refusal to exercise a power as opposed to a negligent exercise of a power.

However, in *Anns v Merton London Borough Council*[11] both these propositions were rejected. It was held first that there can be liability for failing to prevent damage, and that the 'additional damage' rule applies, if at all, only where the exercise of the power is intrinsically harmful. Second, a majority agreed with Lord Wilberforce that there can in principle be liability for failing to exercise a power. However, Lord Salmon took the view that in cases involving a total failure to exercise a power (as opposed to a duty), damages should not be available and the matter should be left to the prerogative orders.[12] The issue was not material in *Anns* itself, and there is much to be said for Lord Salmon's view. For example, it does not follow because there has been an ultra vires refusal to exercise a power, that the power must in fact be exercised. Precisely what damage has been caused? There are difficulties in establishing liability for economic loss. Mandamus or a declaration appear to be more appropriate remedies.

### *(b) The standard of care*

The exercise of a power must be ultra vires before the question of liability can arise. Where the decision is ultra vires solely because it is unreasonable in the public law sense of 'arbitrary or capricious',[13] the speeches in *Anns v Merton London Borough Council*[14] and *Home Office v Dorset Yacht Co Ltd*[15] indicate that this in itself constitutes negligence. As regards other kinds of defect, breach of natural justice, irrelevant consideration, etc, the position is different. These defects could be committed bona fide without carelessness.[16] It is submitted therefore that the plaintiff is also required to establish (a) that there has in fact been negligence and (b) that the negligence relates to the specific ultra vires defect complained of.

### *(c) Policy and operational matters*

A further distinction must be drawn. In *Anns v Merton London Borough Council*[17] Lord Wilberforce distinguished between policy decisions and operational acts. This distinction draws upon American jurisprudence, where it has been employed with little success.[18] A policy decision is one where the governing statute confers a discretion upon the authority 'involving the weighing of competing public interests, particularly financial or economic interests'.[19] An operational act concerns matters of implementation which do not involve the exercise of a statutory discretion, and which usually correspond to private

10 *East Suffolk Rivers Catchment Board v Kent* [1941] AC 74, [1940] 4 All ER 527, HL.
11 [1978] AC 728, [1977] 2 All ER 492, HL. See above, n 7.
12 At 762, 507.
13 *Associated Provincial Picture Houses Ltd v Wednesbury Corpn* [1948] 1 KB 223, [1947] 2 All ER 680, CA.
14 Above, n 7.
15 Above, n 6.
16 Eg *Hall & Co Ltd v Shoreham-by-Sea UDC* [1964] 1 All ER 1, [1964] 1 WLR 240, CA; *Webb v Minister of Housing and Local Government* [1965] 2 All ER 193, [1965] 1 WLR 755, CA.
17 [1978] AC 278, [1977] 2 All ER 492, HL. See above, n 7.
18 Eg *Johnson v State of California* 447 P (2d) 352 (1968).
19 *Rowling v Takaro Properties* [1988] AC 473, [1988] 1 All ER 163, PC.

activities, eg maintaining or inspecting a road or building. The activities of the building inspector in *Anns v Merton London Borough Council* (above) could be regarded as operational, whereas the decision whether or not to adopt the system of inspections would be a policy matter.

The distinction between policy and operational matters is imprecise and Lord Wilberforce conceded that it is probably one of degree only. Thus, as the implementation of policy extends down the administrative hierarchy, progressively less discretion is involved. Relatively simple examples come easily to hand—for example, the distinction between deciding whether to provide a closed or open prison and the day to day task of administering the prison. The former is 'policy', the latter *may* be operational in a case where, for example, a guard falls asleep on duty. If for example the prison was staffed by inexperienced officers because of a decision to save public money the matter could be regarded as one of policy. In *Lonrho v Tebbit*[20] it was held that the decision when to release Lonrho from an undertaking, as opposed to the decision to release itself, could become an operational matter where the public interest was not involved.

The scope of the distinction between policy and operational decisions is not clear. Recent cases suggest that the distinction is far from conclusive. While a policy decision may not be actionable, it does not follow that all operational decisions are actionable.[1] On one possible analysis even in the case of operational acts the act must be the result of an ultra vires decision as a precondition of liability. However if operational acts do not involve the specifically public law element of an exercise of a public interest discretion, it is difficult to see why the standard should not be the ordinary private law standard. Lawful authority to do an act is not authority to do it negligently.

Another possible analysis of *Anns* is that liability in the policy sphere applies, if at all, only where there has been an ultra vires decision in the public law sense but operational liability depends on ordinary principles. Contrary to what Browne-Wilkinson V-C said in *Lonrho v Tebbit*,[2] policy decisions are sometimes justiciable but the court cannot substitute its views of the merits for those of the authority. In *Meade v Haringey London Borough Council*[3] it was said that private law liability could arise in relation to a statutory discretion where the defendants had acted ultra vires. The point of the policy/operational distinction is to preserve the legitimate area of official discretion. Once outside this area there seems no reason in principle to give immunity from negligence liability. It is important to remember that there is no automatic duty of care. Irrespective of the policy/operational distinction the existence of a duty of care depends on the particular circumstances (below). For example no duty of care arises in relation to the grant or refusal of planning permissions, since this kind of function is imposed for the public benefit at large and not for the protection of specific individuals.[4] the other hand where the exercise of a governmental power creates a physical danger a duty of care will normally arise.[5]

20 *Lonrho plc v Tebbitt* [1991] 4 All ER 973 at 981.
1 *Rowling v Takaro Properties* (above, n 19). See also below p 88.
2 Above, n 20.
3 [1979] 2 All ER 1016, [1979] 1 WLR 637, CA.
4 *Buxton v Minister of Housing and Local Government* [1961] 1 QB 278, [1960] 3 All ER 408. See also *Evans v LCC* (1960) 12 P & CR 172; *Strable v Dartford Borough Council* [1984] JPL 329, CA. See below, n 15.
5 *Haydon v Kent County Council* [1978] QB 343, [1978] 2 All ER 97, CA even though resource allocation was in issue.

## Proximity

Robert Goff J's second requirement is that there must be sufficient proximity between the plaintiff and the defendant. It appears that the question of proximity is to be determined by reference to the scope and purpose of the governing legislation and is an aspect of the question of whether a duty of care exists.[6] It concerns the relationship of the parties to the particular kind of injury that has occurred. The courts are reluctant to impose liability for purely economic loss but this is not an absolute rule. The matter seems to be pragmatic. For example, there can be a duty of care in respect of economic loss caused by a failure to carry out an official search of the land register properly.[7] The relationship here is clearly one of reliance and is essentially economic. Liability for economic loss is not necessarily limited to liability for statements.

In *Hills v Chief Constable for West Yorkshire*[8] it was held that the police owed no duty of care to the victims and their relatives for failing to catch the Yorkshire Ripper because the relationship between the police and the suspect was not sufficiently proximate. By contrast there can be a duty of care to persons in the immediate vicinity in respect of damage caused by a prisoner in custody or who has escaped. The criterion seems to be that of some special degree of risk over and above the general public duties owed by the police.[9] The police may also be liable in respect of exceptionally high risk activities but the standard of care will reflect the operational pressures involved.[10]

Robert Goff J's dictum presupposes that there is a general principle capable of establishing the existence of a duty of care which might be outweighed by other factors. This is no longer the case and the question whether a duty of care exists is a matter of incremental development based upon established categories. The criteria to be applied are pragmatic. 'The situation must be one in which the court considers it to be fair just and reasonable to impose a duty of a given scope on the one party for the benefit of the other.'[11]

In the context of a statutory power exercised by a public authority the following factors militate against liability:[12]

(a) an adequate judicial review remedy or an adequate internal remedy;
(b) 'overkill', the need to discourage officials from excessive caution;
(c) the likelihood of an error being committed by the official concerned; and
(d) the difficulty of requiring a minister to seek legal advice.

In *Rowling v Takaro Properties*[13] the New Zealand Finance Minister had refused consent to a share issue to an overseas company. The Minister was held not to have been negligent on the facts but the Privy Council doubted whether there was a duty of care mainly because of the consequences for the

6 See *Caparo Industries plc v Dickman* [1990] 1 All ER 568 at 573–40, HL; *Lonrho plc v Tebbit* [1991] 4 All ER 973 at 985–6; *Murphy v Brentwood District Council* [1990] 2 All ER 908 at 433–4, HL.
7 *Ministry of Housing and Local Government v Sharp* [1970] 2 QB 223, [1970] 1 All ER 1009, CA.
8 [1988] QB 60, [1987] 1 All ER 1173, CA.
9 See *Home Office v Dorset Yacht Co Ltd* [1976] AC 1004, [1970] 2 All ER 294, HL.
10 *Rigby v Chief Constable of Northamptonshire* [1985] 2 All ER 985, [1985] 1 WLR 1242. See also *Clough v Bussan* [1990] 1 All ER 431, [1990] RTR 178; *Alexandrou v Oxford* (1990) Times, 19 February, CA.
11 *Caparo Industries* (loc cit, above, n 6); *Murphy v Brentwood District Council* [1991] 1 AC 398, [1990] 2 All ER 908, HL; *Rowling v Takaro Properties* [1988] 1 All ER 163 at 172, PC.
12 *Rowling v Takaro Properties* (above, n 11); *Lonrho plc v Tebbit* (above, n 6) at 983; *Calveley v Chief Constable of the Merseyside Police* [1989] 1 All ER 1025 at 1030, HL.
13 Above, n 11.

public interest of delay. A similar view was taken in *Dunlop v Woollahra Municipal Council.*[14]

Another important factor is the scope of the statutory power in issue and whether it is intended to benefit or protect persons in the position of the plaintiff against particular enquiries.[15]

In *Lonrho plc v Tebbit*[16] Browne-Wilkinson V-C refused to strike out the action but thought that the question depended upon a detailed factual analysis appropriate for a full trial. It may therefore follow that Ord 53 is not often appropriate to deal with allegations of negligence.

### Causation

Robert Goff J's final criterion was that of causation, and seems to be an application of ordinary private law principles of negligence. However, causation raises special problems in connection with governmental decisions, because of the theory that an ultra vires decision is a nullity. We have already discussed these.

## BREACH OF STATUTORY DUTY

A breach of statutory duty may result in acts which give rise to an action for negligence or nuisance, and in some cases be actionable as a separate tort in its own right.

It is important to distinguish between cases where the applicant claims damages and those where he is concerned only with establishing locus standi for the purpose of Ord 53 remedies or an ordinary action. As we shall see, the locus standi requirements, for the purpose of Ord 53, are becoming increasingly liberal, but even where proceedings are instituted outside Ord 53, a plaintiff can arguably obtain a declaration and injunction where he can establish special damage arising out of a failure to perform a public duty. However it is not clear how far the 'special damage' cases create a remedy in tort as opposed to standing for a declaration or injunction.[17]

### Establishing a right to damages for breach of statutory duty

Whether damages can be obtained in respect of a breach of statutory duty depends upon 'a consideration of the whole Act and the circumstances, including the pre-existing law, in which it was enacted'.[18] Thus the matter depends upon the court's inferences as to the intention of the legislature and

14 [1982] AC 158 at 171, PC.

15 *Governors of the Peabody Donation Fund v Sir Lindsay Parkinson & Co Ltd* [1985] AC 210—the purpose of statute to safeguard occupiers not developers; *Curren v Northern Ireland Co-ownership Housing Association Ltd* [1987] AC 718, [1987] 2 All ER 13, HL—purpose of statute to safeguard public funds not to protect builders. *Calveley v Chief Constable of Merseyside Police* [1989] AC 1228 [1989] 1 All ER 1025, HL—procedural protection only.

16 [1991] 4 All ER 973–5, 987, affd [1992] 4 All ER 280, CA.

17 *Lonrho Ltd v Shell Petroleum Co Ltd (No 2)* [1982] AC 173, [1981] 2 All ER 456, HL; *Garden Cottage Foods Ltd v Milk Marketing Board* [1984] AC 130, [1983] 2 All ER 770, HL.

18 *Cutler v Wandsworth Stadium Ltd* [1949] AC 398 at 407, [1949] 1 All ER 544 at 548, HL; *Lonrho Ltd v Shell Petroleum Co Ltd (No 2)* [1982] AC 173, [1981] 2 All ER 456, HL.

policy considerations relating to the interests of governmental efficiency play a part.[19] There are certain pointers but none is conclusive.

First, where a statutory method of enforcing the duty is provided it will normally be presumed that a right to damages is not intended, and the absence of a statutory method of enforcement will support the case for damages.[20] The presumption against damages can be rebutted where the statutory remedy will not give the plaintiff adequate relief due to some special circumstances or special damage, for example physical injury.[1] In *Meade v London Borough of Haringey*[2] the Court of Appeal said that a statutory remedy would not be exclusive where there was a positive act of misfeasance or where the authority used its powers for an improper purpose. The rationale for these exceptions is not clear. A common law action for negligence may also lie.

Second, although a right of action is not excluded merely because performance of the duty involves an element of discretion,[3] a duty which is defined in nebulous terms will be presumed not to be actionable in damages.[4]

Third, the applicant must show that the injury he has suffered is the sort of injury which the statute was intended to guard against.[5] In this connection a member of a specific class upon which a benefit or protection was intended to be conferred is in a stronger position than a person who is attempting to enforce a duty owed to the public at large or who is claiming only procedural protection.[6] Older cases which suggest that a breach of an important public duty is always actionable are unreliable, since they predate the modern notion of breach of statutory duty, and in some instances involved the special ingredient of malice.[7] Particularly where personal injuries are involved, an individual may sometimes sue in respect of a duty owed to the public as such, although this is more likely where the breach takes the form of a positive unlawful act, as opposed to a failure to act. However, even in the case of a failure to act, a cause of action in damages might be implied where there has been a denial of a substantive benefit to which the applicant is entitled under the statute, such as free education or

19 Eg *Williams v Home Office (No 2)* [1981] 1 All ER 1211 at 1242; *Becker v Home Office* [1972] 2 QB 407 at 408, [1972] 2 All ER 676 at 682, CA; *Arbon v Anderson* [1943] KB 252, [1943] 1 All ER 154; *R v Deputy Governor of Parkhurst Prison, ex p Hague* [1992] 1 AC 58, sub nom *Hague v Deputy Governor Parkhurst Prison* [1991] 3 All ER 733, HL.

20 *Thornton v Kirklees Metropolitan Borough Council* [1979] QB 626, [1979] 2 All ER 349, CA; *Wyatt v Hillingdon London Borough Council* (1978) 76 LGR 727, CA; *Ministry of Housing and Local Government v Sharp* [1969] 3 All ER 225; *Booth & Co (International) Ltd v National Enterprise Board* [1978] 3 All ER 624; *Pasmore v Oswaldtwistle UDC* [1898] AC 387, HL; *Robinson v Workington Corpn* [1897] 1 QB 619, 66 LJQB 388, CA.

1 See *Reffell v Surrey County Council* [1964] 1 All ER 743, [1964] 1 WLR 358; *Ching v Surrey County Council* [1910] 1 KB 736, 79 LJKB 481, CA; *Phillips v Britannia Hygienic Laundry Co Ltd* [1923] 2 KB 832 at 841 per Atkin LJ. See also *Lonrho Ltd v Shell Petroleum Co Ltd (No 2)* [1982] AC 173 at 185, HL.

2 [1979] 2 All ER 1016, [1979] 1 WLR 637, CA. There can of course be a duty coupled with an element of discretion. See also *R v Secretary of State for the Environment, ex p Ward* [1984] 1 WLR 834 at 844.

3 *Thornton v Kirklees*, above, n 20.

4 See *Garden Cottage Foods Ltd v Milk Marketing Board* [1984] AC 130, 141, 144, HL.

5 *Gorris v Scott* (1874) LR 9 Exch 125, 43 LJ Ex 92; *Knapp v Railway Executive* [1949] 2 All ER 508, CA.

6 *Groves v Lord Wimborne* [1898] 2 QB 402, 67 LJQB 862, CA. Cf *McCall v Abelesz* [1976] QB 585 at 597, [1976] 1 All ER 727 at 733, CA. Cf *Calveley v Chief Constable of Merseyside Police* (below, n 11).

7 *Ashby v White* (1703) 2 Ld Raym 938, Holt KB 524; *Ferguson v Earl of Kinnoull* (1842) 9 Cl & F in 251, HL.

housing assistance,[8] but is unlikely to implied merely because of a failure to provide a general public service in which the plaintiff shares.[9]

It is arguable also that the requirement of compliance with European Community obligations may confer a right to damages for failure to perform an obligation imposed by European Community law which has direct effect in UK law. It is questionable whether the English courts are still content to apply the ordinary English law rules.[10]

The court will also take into account when deciding whether a statute was intended to create tort liability, the adequacy of the ordinary judicial review remedies.[11] In particular procedural impropriety is unlikely to attract damages.

## MALICIOUS ABUSE OF PUBLIC OFFICE

This is a distinctive kind of liability, which was developed specifically in connection with abuse of power by public officials. Although somewhat uncertain in scope, malicious abuse of public office is our closest equivalent to a public law tort. The decision-maker must perform some act on the strength of a purported exercise of public office and either must be aware that it is acting ultra vires and that injury to the plaintiff is likely or its decision must be affected by spite or ill will.[12] The gist of the action appears to be the malice itself, so that damages are available even if the decision itself is not set aside, because for example, the applicant is out of time,[13] or because the court exercises its discretion against the applicant. Proof of malice seems to entitle a plaintiff to damages in a wide range of cases, including revocation or refusal of a licence[14] without reference to the limitation that an independent 'private right' must be established.

Attempts are sometimes made to distinguish between two kinds of malicious exercise of power, that is, between cases where the authority actually knows that it is acting ultra vires and those where the authority is motivated by spite or ill will. However, in either case it seems that the authority will be liable.[15]

There is some authority in favour of extending the tort of abuse of public office beyond cases of malice and even negligence, so as to allow recovery whenever a public authority abuses its power.[16] Both the Privy Council and

8 *Guardians of the Poor of Gateshead Union v Durham County Council* [1918] 1 Ch 146, 87 LJ Ch 113, CA. Cf *Watt v Kesteven County Council* [1955] 1 QB 408, [1955] 1 All ER 473, CA; *Thornton v Kirklees Metropolitan Borough Council* [1979] QB 626, [1979] 2 All ER 349, CA; *Bremer v Haringey London Borough Council* (1983) Times, 12 May; *Reade v Croydon Corpn* [1938] 4 All ER 631.

9 *Glossop v Heston and Isleworth Local Board* (1879) 12 Ch D 102, 49 LJ Ch 89, CA; *Clegg Parkinson & Co v Earby Gas Co* [1896] 1 QB 592, 65 LJQB 339; *Atkinson v Newcastle and Gateshead Waterworks Co* (1877) 2 Ex D 441; *Hey & Croft Ltd v Lexden and Winstree RDC* (1972) 70 LGR 531; *R v Inner London Education Authority, ex p Ali* [1990] 2 Admin LR 822.

10 *Bourgoin SA v Ministry of Agriculture, Food and Fisheries* [1986] QB 716, [1985] 3 All ER 585, CA. Cf *Garden Cottage Foods Ltd v Milk Marketing Board* [1984] AC 130, HL. *An Bord Bainne Co-operative Ltd v Milk Marketing Board* [1988] 1 CMLR 605, CA, cf *Francovitch v Italian Republic*: C–6/90 [1992] IRLR 84, ECJ. See also *Kirklees Metropolitan Borough Council v Wickes Building Supplies Ltd* [1992] 3 All ER 717 at 734.

11 *Calveley v Chief Constable of Merseyside Police* [1989] 1 All ER 1025 at 1029, HL.

12 *Calveley v Chief Constable of Merseyside Police* [1989] AC 1228, [1989] 1 All ER 1025, HL; *Jones v Swansea City Council* [1990] 3 All ER 737, [1990] 1 WLR 1453; *Dunlop v Woollahra Municipal Council* [1982] AC 158, [1981] 1 All ER 1202, PC.

13 *Smith v East Elloe RDC* [1956] AC 736, [1956] 1 All ER 855, HL.

14 *Roncarelli v Duplessis* (1959) 16 DLR (2d) 689.

15 See cases cited above, n 12.

16 *Beaudesert Shire Council v Smith* (1966) 120 CLR 145.

the House of Lords have disapproved these authorities and upheld the traditional view that malice is an essential requirement.[17]

## VICARIOUS LIABILITY

A public authority may be liable in damages either directly or vicariously. In the case of the tort of breach of statutory duty liability is normally direct. The duty is imposed upon the authority itself, and the fact that the actual performance of the duty is entrusted to subordinates does not affect the position. The authority is bound to see that the duty is performed albeit, depending on the context, this might only be a duty to exercise proper supervision.[18] Different considerations perhaps apply if the decision-maker is empowered to delegate. A delegate as such is neither a servant nor an agent, and while a valid delegation subsists the delegate rather than the principal is liable for any breach of duty, unless statute provides otherwise.

As between a minister and civil servants within his department a special rule applies. Although a minister is not in a master and servant relationship with his subordinates, all being fellow servants of the Crown,[19] he is nevertheless personally and directly liable for their official decisions taken in his name, and the knowledge of a civil servant is directly attributed to the responsible minister.[20] The Crown itself is vicariously liable for the torts committed by its servants, and the civil servant who actually committed the tort remains personally liable.

### Tribunals

The officials who enforce or implement the decisions of courts and tribunals are not the servants or agents of the court or tribunal in question. Therefore a tribunal is not vicariously liable for the actions of its enforcement official, but its members may be directly liable for authorising any tortious act.[1] Unless the tribunal is incorporated its members are individually liable, so that although the tribunal as such is the appropriate respondent to an application for certiorari, prohibition or mandamus, the individual members must be joined as parties in a claim for damages.

### The independent discretion doctrine

A statute often confers a power or imposes a duty upon a designated person. Even if that person is a servant of a public body, the body will not be liable either directly or vicariously for a tort committed by the designated person.[2]

17 *Dunlop v Woollahra Municipal Council* [1982] AC 158, [1981] 1 All ER 1202, PC; *Lonrho Ltd v Shell Petroleum Co Ltd (No 2)* [1982] AC 173, [1981] 2 All ER 456, HL. See also *R v Secretary of State for the Environment, ex p Hackney London Borough Council* [1983] 3 All ER 358, [1983] 1 WLR 524. However in *Calveley v Chief Constable of Merseyside Police* (above, n 11 at 1031) their Lordships stated as a possibility that there might be liability for an act done 'without reasonable cause'.

18 *Ministry of Housing and Local Government v Sharp* [1969] 3 All ER 225; revsd [1970] 2 QB 223, CA.

19 *Bainbridge v Postmaster-General* [1906] 1 KB 178, 75 LJKB 366, CA; *Pfizer Corpn v Ministry of Health* [1965] AC 512, [1965] 1 All ER 450, HL; *Wood v Leeds Area Health Authority (Training)* [1974] ICR 535. It does not follow that every day-to-day act of a civil servant is attributed to the minister.

20 *Bushell v Secretary of State for the Environment* [1981] AC 75, [1980] 2 All ER 608, HL.

1 *O'Connor v Isaacs* [1956] 2 QB 288, [1956] 1 All ER 513.

2 *Stanbury v Exeter Corpn* [1905] 2 KB 838, 75 LJKB 28; *Ministry of Housing and Local Government v Sharp* [1969] 3 All ER 225; revsd [1970] 2 QB 223, CA.

This is because of the 'independent discretion' doctrine. The designated person exercises his functions by virtue of the statute and not the instructions of his employer, who cannot control the exercise of the function. Thus when determining the question of vicarious liability for the exercise of statutory powers or duties the particular power or duty must be looked at in addition to establishing the general relationship between the parties.

There is an important exception to the independent discretion principle. This applies to the Crown. We have already seen that for the purpose of the prerogative order a distinction is made between a function imposed upon the Crown as such, exercised necessarily through Crown servants or agents, and a function imposed upon a minister or other Crown officer or agent as persona designata. This does not apply in the case of actions in tort. The Crown remains vicariously liable for torts committed by officials exercising functions directly conferred on them by statute 'as if those functions had been conferred or imposed solely by virtue of instructions lawfully given by the Crown'.[3]

## Crown service

However, this applies only to a function imposed upon an officer of the Crown 'as such'. It is theoretically possible that a statute could confer a power or impose a duty upon, say, a minister but not in his capacity as a Crown servant. There would, however, be a strong presumption against this.[4] Indeed in *Town Investments Ltd v Department of the Environment*[5] a majority of their Lordships analysed the relationship between the Crown and its ministers in terms of identity. On this analysis the Crown is to be treated as a corporation aggregate synonymous with the 'government' of which ministers are not only servants but members and directing arms. Thus their acts could be attributed directly to the Crown.

This analysis is difficult to reconcile with the Crown Proceedings Act 1947, which presupposes a service or agency relationship between the Crown and those who act on its behalf. The Act distinguishes between the monarch in her personal capacity and the Crown, but appears to treat the Crown in the traditional way as a corporation sole. Indeed, the Act makes little sense in relation to tort liability on any other view. The popular notion that the Act has 'removed' the Crown's common law immunity is misleading. The effect of the Act is to impose liability in tort upon the Crown 'as if it were a private person', but only in certain cases: one such is vicarious liability for the torts of servants and agents,[6] but there is no general provision imposing direct liability. This kind of liability is confined to certain common law and statutory duties,[7] and arguably to actions to recover property.[8]

3 Crown Proceedings Act 1947, s 2(3).
4 *Merricks v Heathcoat-Amory and the Minister of Agriculture, Fisheries and Food* [1955] 2 All ER 453 at 456.
5 [1977] 1 All ER 813 at 818, 830–834, [1977] 2 WLR 450 at 456–457, 471–475, HL. Cf Lord Morris at 828, 467–469, and *International Rly Co v Niagara Parks Commission* [1941] 2 All ER 456 at 462, PC. See also *Pearce v Secretary of State for Defence* [1987] 2 WLR 782.
6 Crown Proceedings Act 1947, s 2(1)(a).
7 Ibid, s 2(1)(b), (c), (2).
8 Ibid, s 1. In cases where before the Act a petition of right would lie.

*The definition of a Crown servant*

The question of who is a Crown servant depends in the first instance on the particular statute which may specifically deal with the matter.[9] A distinction must be made between vicarious liability cases, where a strict master and servant relationship must be established, and cases where the benefit of some Crown immunity is claimed. In the latter context it may be sufficient that the person or body in question, even if not a Crown servant in the technical sense, is in '*consimili casu*' with the Crown for the purpose of the particular immunity claimed, in the sense of exercising governmental functions of a kind which are traditionally associated with the Crown.[10] Apart from such cases, which have been regarded as anomalous, the tests used to define the relationship between a given body and the Crown are essentially those appropriate to the relationship of master and servant. They focus upon the degree of control which the Crown under the relevant legislation is entitled to exercise over the activities of the body in question. Actual control through political or economic pressures is apparently irrelevant. The test is whether the Crown has the legal power to control on a day-to-day basis the manner in which the body carries out its functions.[11]

*The Crown as defendant*

Once it has been established that a tortfeasor is a Crown servant, then the Crown itself and not an intermediate body becomes vicariously liable. There can be no master and servant relationship between one Crown servant and another[12] although liability may be created by statute. Under the Crown Proceedings Act 1947 the designated defendant is a government department certified by the Treasury as appropriate. In the absence of an appropriate department, or in the event of reasonable doubt as to the appropriate department, the Attorney-General may be joined as a defendant.[13]

*Personal liability of Crown servants*

As we have seen, an individual Crown servant is liable in his individual capacity for torts committed both within and without the scope of his duties. He cannot claim the benefit of Crown immunities, so that although execution and attachment are not possible against the Crown or Crown assets, his personal assets are vulnerable.

## IMMUNITY FROM LIABILITY IN TORT

There are special cases where a public authority enjoys immunity from liability in tort.

9 Eg Post Office Act 1969, s 6(5).

10 See *Bank voor Handel en Scheepvaart NV v Administrator of Hungarian Property* [1954] AC 584, [1954] 1 All ER 969, HL.

11 *Pfizer Corpn v Ministry of Health* [1965] AC 512, [1965] 1 All ER 450, HL; *BBC v Johns* [1965] Ch 32, [1964] 1 All ER 923, CA; *Tamlin v Hannaford* [1950] 1 KB 18, CA. Cf *Fisher v Oldham Corpn* [1930] 2 KB 364, 99 LJKB 569. See Police Act 1964, s 48.

12 *Bainbridge v Postmaster-General* [1906] 1 KB 178, 75 LJKB 366, CA.

13 Crown Proceedings Act 1947, s 17.

## Crown immunities

These are well discussed elsewhere,[14] and we will content ourselves here with summarising such immunities as are particularly relevant to Ord 53 proceedings.

1. The absence of interim relief against the Crown. This will be described later.[15]
2. The Crown is bound by statutes only by express language or necessary implication.[16]
3. The Crown is immune from liability in tort unless the tort falls within either s 1 or s 2 of the Crown Proceedings Act 1947.[17]
4. The Crown is immune from liability relating to judicial responsibilities. It is not clear what 'judicial' means in this context, but the term may be confined to judicial responsibilities in the narrow sense of decisions taken in the manner of a court of law.[18]
5. The Crown is immune from liability in tort for the acts, neglects, or defaults of its officers unless they have been appointed and paid wholly out of funds provided by Parliament.[19]
6. The Crown is vicariously liable only where the individual Crown servant or agent is also liable.[20]
7. The Crown is liable for breach of statutory duty only where the duty binds persons other than the Crown (and subject to 2, above).[1]
8. No injunction or other coercive remedy is available against the Crown.[2]
9. No execution, attachment or analogous process is available for enforcing the payment of damages or other debts against the Crown.[3]

## Judicial immunity

It has long been settled that officials exercising judicial functions are immune from liability in tort. This is to encourage them to perform their duties without fear or favour. Despite some dicta that this immunity extends to any public duty which affects individual rights,[4] in this context, a judicial function is one

14 See Garner *Administrative Law* (5th edn, 1974) pp 308–310; Hogg *Liability of the Crown* (1971).
15 Below p 147 et seq.
16 *Bombay Province v Bombay Municipal Corpn* [1947] AC 58, [1947] LJR 380, PC. Cf Crown Proceedings Act 1947, s 40(2)(f). The relationship between this immunity and from liability generally may cause problems in relation to statutes which reform the common law area of tort, see Treitel [1957] PL 321 at 322–326. The Crown can, it appears, take the *benefit* of any statute. Cf *Crooke's Case* (1691) 1 Show 208.
17 Crown Proceedings Act 1947, s 2(5). See also Crown Proceedings (Armed Forces) Act 1987.
18 However, the cases normally cited in favour of this proposition do not relate to the present context. Eg *Royal Aquarium and Summer and Winter Garden Society v Parkinson* [1892] 1 QB 431 at 452, CA; *Addis v Crocker* [1960] 1 QB 87, [1959] 2 All ER 773. The term 'judicial' is not used consistently and given the existence of judicial immunity it may be that s 2(5) requires a wide meaning. See de Smith, op cit, p 77. *A-G v BBC* [1981] AC 303, [1980] 3 All ER 161, HL.
19 Crown Proceedings Act 1947, s 2(6). 'Officer' includes ministers and servants. Ibid, s 38(2). This immunity applies only to liability under s 2.
20 Crown Proceedings Act 1947, s 2(2).
1 Ibid, s 2(5).
2 Ibid, s 21.
3 Ibid, s 25(4).
4 *Everett v Griffiths* [1921] 1 AC 631 at 695, HL.

exercised by a court of law or an analogous body determining a pre-existing dispute.[5]

In the case of justices, tribunals, arbitrators and other inferior courts the immunity applies only as long as they are acting within their jurisdiction. In this context exceeding jurisdiction has its narrow traditional meaning, limited to violating statutory limits upon the exercise of the power, as opposed to its wide meaning for ordinary judicial review purposes.[6]

Magistrates are entitled to be indemnified from public funds where they acted honestly and in good faith.[7] Moreover, where, despite the excess of jurisdiction, the accused is rightly convicted or penalised their liability is limited to 1p.[8] Their record must also be formally quashed before liability can arise. However, this is merely a condition of actionability and nothing to do with the cause of action itself, so that time runs from the date of the actual ultra vires decision.[9]

In the case of superior courts the immunity applies even to acts outside jurisdiction although a superior court judge loses immunity if he or she acts entirely outside her judicial capacity or acts in bad faith knowing that the act is unlawful.[10] The High Court is in a special position in as much as it has unlimited jurisdiction as to subject matter (as opposed to remedy and procedure). The Crown Court is an example of a superior court with limited jurisdiction. We have seen that the decisions of a superior court are not subject to judicial review in Ord 53 proceedings.[11]

There are also specific statutory immunities.[12]

5 *Arenson v Casson, Beckman, Rutley & Co* [1975] AC 405, [1975] 3 All ER 901, HL.
6 *Re M^cC (A minor)* [1985] AC 528 at 542, 543, 544, 546–7; cf *R v Manchester City Magistrates' Court, ex p Davies* [1988] 1 All ER 930, [1988] 1 WLR 667. Possibly gross breaches of natural justice could also be jurisdictional.
7 Justices of the Peace Act 1979, s 53. See also sections 50, 51.
8 Ibid, s 52. See *R v Waltham Forest Justices, ex p Solante* [1986] QB 983, [1986] 2 All ER 981.
9 *Re M^cC (A minor)*, above, n 6 at 540, 541; *Sirros v Moore* [1975] QB 118, [1974] 3 All ER 776, CA (overruled on the *inferior* court question). *Anderson v Gorrie* [1895] 1 QB 668, CA.
10 See *Isaacs v Robertson* [1985] AC 97, [1984] 3 All ER 140, PC.
11 Above, p 40.
12 Eg Mental Health Act 1983, s 139.

CHAPTER 9

# Locus standi

## GENERAL BACKGROUND

In order to obtain leave to apply for judicial review, an applicant must have 'sufficient interest' in the matter to which the application relates.[1] This reflects the adversarial character of the English law of judicial review in the sense that the courts' primary function is to resolve disputes between citizen and government and not to control the administration. A member of the public has no automatic access to the courts, it being a basic principle of English law that public rights are a matter for the Crown.

There are however certain 'mechanisms' by which litigation can be instituted directly or indirectly on behalf of the public. Chief among these is the power of the Attorney General, in his role as guardian of the public interest, to apply to the court either upon his own motion or on the relation of any member of the public. This power can be exercised in respect of any unlawful or ultra vires act that causes public harm, but although relator proceedings are available against the Crown, in practice the Attorney General does not intervene against other branches of the central government, presumably for reasons of constitutional propriety. The Attorney General's discretion whether or not to take action is unreviewable[2] and the fact that the Attorney General has failed to intervene or cannot be contacted in time does not confer any residual standing upon a citizen who unsuccessfully seeks the Attorney General's support.[3] If the Attorney General does intervene at the request of a relator, the relator has *de facto* responsibility for the actual conduct of the proceedings and also for costs, but the Attorney General retains full powers of control at all times.[4] The Attorney General's power to initiate proceedings is not affected by whether the relator has standing in his or her own right.

A local authority has power under s 222 of the Local Government Act 1972 to institute any legal proceedings on behalf of the inhabitants of its area, and while this is most commonly employed against private persons in respect of criminal offences, it can also be used against other public bodies. The Attorney

1 Supreme Court Act 1981, s 31(3).

2 *Gouriet v Union of Post Office Workers* [1978] AC 435, [1977] 3 All ER 70, HL; *LCC v A-G* [1902] AC 165 at 168–169, although the court may still withhold a discretionary remedy upon other grounds; *A-G v Harris* [1961] 1 QB 74, [1960] 3 All ER 207, CA; *A-G (on the relation of Hornchurch UDC) v Bastow* [1957] 1 QB 514, [1957] 1 All ER 497.

3 *A-G (ex rel McWhirter) v Independent Broadcasting Authority* [1973] QB 629, [1973] 1 All ER 689.

4 *Gouriet*, above, n 2, [1978] AC 435 at 477–481, [1977] 3 All ER 70 at 80–82, per Lord Wilberforce.

General's consent is not required.[5] The Audit Commission also has power, under s 161 of the same Act, to seek a declaration in respect of unlawful expenditure by a local authority.

Finally, any person can bring a private prosecution in respect of a criminal offence other than an offence where the power to prosecute is limited by statute. However, this does not confer standing on a citizen for the purpose of any other remedy,[6] so that its importance in administrative law is confined to cases involving the criminal offence of failing to perform a statutory duty.[7]

Before the 1977 reforms of Ord 53 the individual remedies generated their own standing requirements. This has been one of the most confusing areas of the law. Within each remedy, there are conflicting lines of authority although there had been attempts, notably by Lord Denning,[8] to develop a uniform concept of locus standi applicable to all the remedies. Given that the different remedies fulfil different functions, these are not entirely convincing.

The leading case on locus standi for the purpose of Ord 53 is the decision of the House of Lords in *IRC v National Federation of Self-Employed and Small Businesses Ltd*[9] (the '*Fleet Street Casuals* case').

Their Lordships undertook a general review of locus standi in relation to Ord 53. Unfortunately, although the decision itself was unanimous, there were important differences of emphasis between the five speeches. It seems reasonably clear, however, that the locus standi requirements are now considerably more liberal than earlier cases would suggest.

The *Fleet Street Casuals* case has significance beyond the sphere of locus standi. Their Lordships recognised first that the Ord 53 procedure was intended to facilitate the elimination of unnecessary technical differences between the individual remedies, and second that, independently of Ord 53, the law of judicial review has changed so much over the last 30 years that older cases must be treated with caution and should be reassessed in the light of changing circumstances.[10]

Locus standi is a matter of the jurisdiction of the court and cannot be conferred by consent. However locus standi appears to relate to the question of remedy and the High Court, having unlimited jurisdiction over subject matter, can give its opinion on the merits even if it cannot issue a remedy.[11]

5 Unlike the case with the Attorney General this power is reviewable. See *Waverley Borough Council v Hilden* [1988] 1 All ER 807, [1988] 1 WLR 246. It has been suggested that this power can only be used as a last resort. See *Stoke-on-Trent County Council v B and Q (Retail) Ltd* [1984] AC 754, [1984] 2 All ER 332, HL; *Runnymede Borough Council v Smith* [1986] JPL 592. As with the Crown the court may in its discretion grant an interlocutory injunction to a local authority under s 22 without a cross undertaking in damages; *Kirklees Metropolitan Borough Council v Wickes Building Supplies Ltd* [1992] 3 All ER 717, [1992] 3 WLR 170, HL.

6 *Gouriet*, above, n 2.

7 A failure by a public authority to perform a statutory duty is an indictable offence, unless excluded by statute (eg Highways Act 1959, s 59(1)) at least where public harm is occasioned. See de Smith *Judicial Review of Administrative Action* (4th edn, 1980) by J. M. Evans, pp 557–558.

8 Eg *R v Greater London Council, ex p Blackburn* [1976] 3 All ER 184, [1976] 1 WLR 550, CA.

9 [1982] AC 617, [1981] 2 All ER 93.

10 [1982] AC 617 at 637–638, 645–646, 657, 662, [1981] 2 All ER 93 at 102, 108, 116, 119 ('older' seems to mean pre-1950s). This advice has not been followed in the interim relief cases (below p 147)

11 See *R v Secretary of State for Social Services, ex p Child Poverty Action Group* [1989] 1 All ER 1047 at 1055–6, CA.

## THE STATUTORY PROVISIONS

The Supreme Court Act 1981, s 31(3) provides that 'No application for judicial review shall be made unless the leave of the High Court has been obtained in accordance with rules of court; and the court shall not grant leave to make such an application unless it considers that the applicant has a sufficient interest in the matter to which the application relates'.

Their Lordships agreed in the *Fleet Street Casuals* case that this 'sufficient interest' requirement at the preliminary leave stage was merely a threshold requirement to exclude clearly unmeritorious cases and that locus standi could be investigated in detail at the subsequent full hearing.[12] This is because the locus standi question cannot be considered in the abstract, but is inseparable from the substantive grounds and seriousness of the application. It does not follow that locus standi has vanished by being absorbed into other concepts. Subsequent cases have dealt with standing as a separate issue. Sometimes however standing has been conceded without argument, and in some cases the court having denied the applicant standing has nevertheless dealt with the substantive issues, without of course granting a remedy.[13] Public interest pressure groups may be prepared for this reason to resort to litigation for tactical or publicity purposes.

We must briefly consider the law as it stood prior to their Lordships' speeches. Given that a majority of their Lordships were in general agreement that older cases should be treated with caution, we can dispense with an attempt to reconcile the confusing maze of cases, but shall treat the old law as providing only general guidelines.[14]

## THE INDIVIDUAL REMEDIES

The traditional distinction is between the prerogative orders on the one hand and the declaration and injunction on the other. The prerogative orders originated as administrative writs issued by the Crown and therefore embody a strong public element. A restricted locus standi requirement is not appropriate and in theory the orders can issue upon the application of any person. The declaration and injunction on the other hand originated as private law remedies and it is therefore more difficult to extend standing beyond persons whose private rights have been affected by the decision in question.[15]

### Certiorari

Certiorari has traditionally been regarded as embodying a liberal standing requirement. Any member of the public is eligible in the court's discretion, and as a matter of right a person whose interests are particularly affected by the decision in question is entitled to apply for the remedy.[16] 'Interests' are not confined to legal rights in the strict sense but may include other adverse

12 [1982] AC 617 at 630, 643–664, 649, 659, [1981] 2 All ER 93 at 96–97, 105–106, 107, 110, 115.
13 See also *R v Monopolies and Mergers Commission, ex p Argyle Group plc* [1986] 1 WLR 763 at 773–4. *R v Secretary of State for the Environment ex p Rose Theatre Trust Ltd* [1990] 1 QB 504, [1990] 1 All ER 754.
14 See [1982] AC 617 at 645–646, [1981] 2 All ER 93 at 108.
15 See above, pp 70 et seq.
16 *R v Surrey Justices* (1870) LR 5 QB 466, 39 LJMC 145; *R v Richmond Confirming Authority, ex p Howitt* [1921] 1 KB 248.

consequences—inconvenience,[17] economic loss,[18] loss of amenity,[19] even though the grievance may be shared with large numbers of other people. It appears that in certiorari law only the busybody is excluded. It is now arguable that this broad test which previously applied to certiorari governs all the remedies.

## Prohibition

The locus standi requirement can generally be regarded as the same as that for certiorari. However there is older authority that if the defect appears on the face of the record, prohibition can be obtained as of right by any member of the public, subject to the court's discretion to refuse the remedy on other grounds, such as delay.[20]

## Mandamus

The cases involving locus standi for mandamus conflicted. Mandamus was generally regarded as a more limited remedy than certiorari and prohibition. One line of cases embodied a narrow test which required the applicant to show that his strict legal rights were directly affected by the breach of duty complained of.[1] However, this may have been the result of confusion between the prerogative order of mandamus, the mandatory injunction and the analogous but now obsolete common law order of mandamus.[2] The latter two remedies are concerned with private rights, but there seems to be no reason in principle why the prerogative order should be similarly limited.

The other line of cases required the applicant to establish only that his 'interests' had been affected by the breach of duty, even though this did not involve legal rights in the strict sense. For example an unsuccessful objection to the grant of a liquor licence was held to have standing,[3] as was an insurance company whose business was likely to be affected by a failure to make local traffic regulations.[4] The *Fleet Street Casuals* case primarily concerned mandamus and their Lordships unanimously held that mandamus was not limited to claims based upon strict legal rights.[5]

## The declaration and injunction

Apart from special considerations relative to Ord 53 it is clear from *Gouriet v Union of Post Office Workers*[6] that these remedies are available only to a person whose legal rights are in issue or who has suffered special damage.

In the *Fleet Street Casuals* case, a majority of their Lordships took the view

17 *R v Bradford-on-Avon UDC, ex p Boulton* [1964] 2 All ER 492, [1964] 1 WLR 1136, but dubitante.
18 *R v Thames Magistrates' Court, ex p Greenbaum* (1957) 55 LGR 129, CCA.
19 *R v Hendon RDC, ex p Chorley* [1933] 2 KB 696, 102 LJKB 658.
20 *Farquharson v Morgan* [1894] 1 QB 552 at 558–559, CA; *Ricketts v Bodenham* (1836) 4 Ad & El 433 at 441. See *R v Greater London Council, ex p Blackburn* [1976] 3 All ER 184, [1976] 1 WLR 550, CA.
1 *R v Lewisham Union* [1897] 1 QB 498 at 500–501; *R v London City Assessment Committee* [1907] 2 KB 764, 76 LJKB 1087, CA; *R v Hereford Corpn, ex p Harrower* [1970] 3 All ER 460, [1979] 1 WLR 1424; *R v Russell, ex p Beaverbrook Newspapers* [1969] 1 QB 342, [1968] 3 All ER 695.
2 Cf *Glossop v Heston and Isleworth Local Board* (1879) 12 Ch D 102, 49 LJCh 89, CA.
3 *R v Cotham* [1898] 1 QB 802 at 808.
4 *R v Manchester Corpn* [1911] 1 KB 560, 80 LJKB 263. See also *R v Customs and Excise Comrs, ex p Cooke and Stevenson* [1970] 1 All ER 1068, [1970] 1 WLR 450.
5 [1982] AC 617 at 631, 646, 650, 662, [1981] 2 All ER 93 at 97, 108, 111, 119–120.
6 [1978] AC 435, [1977] 3 All ER 70, HL.

that in Ord 53 proceedings the declaration is not limited to cases involving private rights and that the reasoning in *Gouriet* is not applicable. There appear to be two related explanations for this. First their Lordships agreed, albeit with considerable differences of emphasis, that the question of locus standi is at least partly one of discretion,[7] and depends upon a weighing of all the circumstances of the case. Second it was said that as a result of Ord 53 the standing requirement for the declaration is now linked to that of the prerogative orders.[8] Lord Scarman in particular took the view that the court was now able to make a declaration in circumstances where before the changes in Ord 53 a prerogative order could have been made. His Lordship emphasised that the court has a 'complete discretion' to select and grant the appropriate remedy.[9]

There now appear to be two separate tests of standing for the declaration and injunction. For the purposes of Ord 53, the matter is governed by the criteria discussed in the *Fleet Street Casuals* case. These will be discussed below. For the purposes of an ordinary action, however, the *Gouriet* case applies in full. This can be justified because there is no preliminary 'filter' mechanism for an ordinary action.[10]

## THE PRESENT STATE OF THE LAW: THE *FLEET STREET CASUALS* CASE

In *IRC v National Federation of Self-Employed and Small Businesses Ltd*[11] the applicants were a pressure group representing taxpayers concerned about the alleged unfairness of certain concessions made by the Revenue to a group of Fleet Street print workers. Their Lordships held that the applicants had not demonstrated 'sufficient interest' in the subject matter to qualify for relief. All five members of the court agreed that the applicants could show no grounds for their allegations that the Revenue had acted ultra vires. Extra-statutory tax concessions are not ultra vires unless it can be shown that they have been made for some extraneous purpose unrelated to the efficient administration of the Revenue service and the applicants produced no evidence that this was the case. In addition, three of their Lordships[12] thought that except possibly in rare cases of grave and widespread illegality, a taxpayer as such has insufficient interest in the affairs of other taxpayers to qualify for relief, on the ground that the governing legislation was not concerned with the rights of taxpayers inter se, and contained specific provisions protecting the confidentiality of individual taxpayers.

Their Lordships were unanimous in emphasising that locus standi cannot be determined in the abstract, but is inextricably bound up with the subject matter of the particular allegations. In other contexts therefore a taxpayer may have standing.[13]

There was less agreement on other matters. First, different views were expressed upon the question whether locus standi was a matter of law or

7 [1982] AC 617 at 631, 642, 648, 653, [1981] 2 All ER 93 at 97, 105, 109, 113.

8 [1982] AC 617 at 629, 639, 647–648, [1981] 2 All ER 93 at 96, 103, 109.

9 [1982] AC 617 at 647–648, [1981] 2 All ER 93 at 109.

10 *Barrs v Bethell* [1982] Ch 294, [1982] 1 All ER 106. But cf *Steeples v Derbyshire County Council* [1984] 3 All ER 468, [1985] 1 WLR 256.

11 [1982] AC 617, [1981] 2 All ER 93.

12 Lord Wilberforce, Lord Fraser and Lord Roskill.

13 *R v HM Treasury, ex p Smedley* [1985] QB 657, [1985] 1 All ER 589, CA—validity of payment to EC, very serious issue. *R v A-G, ex p ICI plc* [1987] 1 CMLR 72, CA—valuation of products for tax purposes, locus as competitor.

discretion. At one extreme, Lord Diplock regarded the matter as entirely one of discretion,[14] while Lord Fraser apparently took the opposite view.[15] The other members of the court treated locus standi as a mixed question of law and fact. This is probably the best approach, and we will explain it more fully below.

Second, different views were expressed as to whether the same principles should apply to all the remedies. We shall also examine this below.

Third, there was a difference of approach between Lord Wilberforce, Lord Fraser and Lord Roskill on the one hand and Lord Diplock and Lord Scarman on the other. The former adopted a less liberal stance, regarding standing as dependent upon the scope of the particular legislation under which the action complained of was taken. The essential question is what range of interests the governing legislation is intended to protect. The latter, particularly Lord Diplock, went further towards developing a general public right of action. Lord Diplock thought that, at least in serious cases, there would be a gap in our public law if there was no public right of standing to enforce duties owed to the public at large. A majority seems to have supported this approach at least in the case of widespread and serious illegality.

We shall now consider the general principles arising out of their Lordships' speeches.

## Locus standi and substance

It is sometimes suggested that the *Fleet Street Casuals* case has effectively abolished locus standi as a separate requirement by merging it with the merits of the applicants' allegations. Thus, according to Lord Diplock and Lord Scarman,[16] had the applicants been able to show some grounds for their allegations, they would have been granted leave to apply. It is submitted, however, that their Lordships' speeches taken as a whole are not consistent with this proposition. While much emphasis was placed upon the lack of substance in the applicants' allegations, none of their Lordships treated this as the only relevant criterion. Lord Fraser and Lord Diplock in particular emphasised the distinction between this lack of substance and locus standi as such.[17] The other members of the Court examined the general scope of the legislation and Lord Wilberforce, Lord Fraser and Lord Roskill would not have awarded standing to a taxpayer at all, except in cases involving exceptionally grave or widespread illegality. Thus locus standi remains an analytically distinct matter, depending upon the balancing of several factors, including the nature and gravity of the allegations and the applicant's connection with the purpose of the decision-making power in question. For example, an applicant might more easily be able to establish standing where the allegation is of bad faith than where he is alleging that another person should have been given a hearing. In *R v Legal Aid Board, ex p Bateman*[18] Nolan J said that 'in some cases it will be necessary to decide whether the application for judicial review is well founded in substance before determining the question of the applicant's interest.' His Lordship went on to say that in the *Fleet Street Casuals* case 'the Federation had no locus standi because it had no sufficient interest in the

14 [1982] AC 617 at 642, [1981] 2 All ER 93 at 105, HL.
15 [1982] AC 617 at 646, [1981] 2 All ER 93 at 108, HL.
16 See particularly [1982] AC 617 at 654–655, [1981] 2 All ER 93 at 114 per Lord Scarman. Cf ibid at 645, 107 per Lord Diplock.
17 Ibid at 644–645, 107.
18 [1992] 3 All ER 490 at 493.

manner in which the Commissioners exercised their *lawful* discretion in relation to other taxpayers'.[19]

### Differences between the individual remedies

The same general approach to locus standi now applies to all the remedies. The *Fleet Street Casuals* case concerned mandamus and the declaration, but their Lordships discussed the question of standing in general terms. Once again Lord Diplock took the broadest view, emphasising the width of the court's discretion. On the other hand Lord Wilberforce, with whom Lord Fraser and Lord Roskill agreed, stated that an applicant who seeks to enforce the performance of a duty by mandamus is not necessarily in the same position as regards standing as one who seeks merely to expose the invalidity of a decision.[20] All their Lordships emphasised that technical differences between remedies should no longer rigidly be adhered to. However, the nature of the relief sought is clearly a relevant factor. Thus standing may be liberal for certiorari, prohibition and the declaration but less liberal for mandamus which requires the performance of a positive act.[1] In the case of the injunction, because of the drastic nature of this remedy and the well-established body of law surrounding it, standing may be limited to a person whose legal or equitable rights are affected.

### The criteria to be applied

Apart from cases involving obvious busybodies, the locus standi issue must be decided at the full *inter partes* hearing. The matter involves a mixture of law, fact and discretion. On this basis the criteria to be applied are matters of law, but the weight to be given to the various criteria is a matter for the discretion of the court. The more serious and substantial are the allegations, the more liberal will be the standing requirement. The following appear to be the governing criteria:

1. The scope and purpose of the particular statutory power or duty is probably the single most important consideration. On this basis an applicant must show that he possesses an interest which as a matter of construction the governing legislation recognises. However the courts seem to have resisted the conclusion that legislation intended to protect the general public as such, for example environmental legislation, should without more generate a public right of standing (below).

2. The gravity of the allegations. Thus an applicant who fails the first test may have standing to challenge exceptionally serious governmental misdeeds.

3. The strength of the applicant's case and the relevance of the grounds of challenge to the applicant's interests.

4. The public interest in the governmental act challenged. The law on the question of public rights remains in confusion.[2]

5. The nature of the remedy sought.

6. The nature and gravity of the applicant's injury. Where the applicant's

19 Ibid (my italics). See Beatson and Matthews *Administrative Law Cases and Materials* (2nd edn, 1989) p 511. However this distinction does not reflect what was said in *Fleet Street Casuals*.

20 [1982] AC 617 at 631, [1981] 2 All ER 93 at 97, HL.

1 See *R v Felixstowe Justices, ex p Leigh* [1987] QB 582, [1987] 1 All ER 551—public spirited citizen eligible for declaration but not mandamus in relation to the disclosure of Justices' names.

2 See below, n 4.

interests have not been adversely affected then, irrespective of standing considerations, the court is likely to refuse a remedy in its discretion.[3]

7. Financial or other substantial prior involvement with the matter in hand. Pressure groups may sometimes qualify under this head, but it seems that a pressure group which is formed in the public interest in order to contest the particular decision does not have standing.[4]

## RECENT DEVELOPMENTS

The law of locus standi depends so much on particular facts that the cases can provide little more than signposts. Writing extrajudicially, Sir Konrad Schiemann has pointed out that the uncertainty of the standing rules reflects uncertainty about the purpose of standing and how far judicial review should restrain the activities of government as an end in itself.[5] His Lordship summarised the advantages of an open system such as that supported by Lord Diplock in the *Fleet Street Casuals* case. An open system would strengthen accountability by enlisting the energies of pressure groups. A closed system which limits standing to people clearly affected by a decision has efficiency and financial advantages. A closed system may also do justice in the sense that courts are not in a position to weigh the public interest in governmental decisions that affect many people in widely different ways.

Among the recent cases the problem of persons who seek standing purely upon the ground that they are asserting the public interest is probably the most acute. There is some authority in favour of standing upon the basis of the public interest alone[6] but the cases involving both pressure groups and individuals, if not actually in conflict, remain highly dependent on the court's discretion.

### Pressure groups

In *R v Secretary of State for the Environment, ex p Rose Theatre Trust*[7] Schiemann J held that a pressure group which was created purely to represent the public interest in preserving an Elizabethan site against developers did not have standing. By contrast, organisations with established pedigrees and representing specific sectional or local interests, both environmental[8] and social,[9] have been successful. A track record of financial or other direct involvement seems to be an important factor. Direct relationships with individuals affected

3 See below, p 127 et seq.

4 *R v Secretary of State for the Environment, ex p Rose Theatre Trust* [1990] 1 QB 504, [1990] 1 All ER 754 (see below); cf the *Fleet Street Casuals* case [1982] AC 617 at 644 per Lord Diplock; *R v Hammersmith and Fulham London Borough Council, ex p People Before Profit Ltd* (1980) 80 LGR 322; *R v Horsham Justices, ex p Farquharson* [1982] QB 762 at 787.

5 [1991] PL 342. See also Hough [1992] JPL 319.

6 *R v Felixstowe Justices, ex p Leigh* [1987] QB 582, [1987] 1 All ER 551; *R v Legal Aid Board, ex p Bateman* [1992] 3 All ER 490 at 496; *R v HM Treasury, ex p Smedley* (above, n 13, p 101). See also above, n 4.

7 Above, n 4.

8 *R v Poole Borough Council, ex p Beebee* [1991] JPL 643; *R v Westminster City Council, ex p Monahan* [1990] 1 QB 87, [1989] 2 All ER 74, CA.

9 *R v Secretary of State for Social Services, ex p Child Poverty Action Group* [1989] 1 All ER 1047 at 1056, CA—but not argued. Cf *Scottish Old People's Welfare Council (Age Concern), Petitioners* (1987) SLT 179; *R v Secretary of State for Employment, ex p Equal Opportunities Commission* [1972] 1 All ER 545.

by the government action in question may also be important[10] but it is clear that persons without standing as individuals cannot improve their position by forming an organisation. The more generalised the group's objectives are, the less likely is the group to be successful. English law is essentially concrete and practical.

## Individual standing

It is not necessary to show a financial or legal interest but at the other extreme a moral or social concern is not enough.[11] Nor is it relevant that the applicant is an acknowledged expert in the area.[12] The applicant must be affected by the decision in question in some concrete sense.[13] The degree of involvement might affect the choice of remedy rather than exclude standing altogether. In the case of serious allegations taxpayers and ordinary citizens might have standing provided that their interests are affected, even if no differently from the rest of the public.[14] Standing might also be conferred by relying upon the doctrine of 'legitimate expectation' or that of unfairness where particular assurances or undertakings have been given or where the applicant is within the terms of a previously announced policy. Here the question of standing may be especially bound up with the substantive issues in the case such as the right to be heard.[15] A complainant as such does not have standing unless there is some other moral, legal or social interest involved.[16]

## Statutory remedies

The standing requirement for statutory rights of appeal and other forms of statutory challenge depends of course upon the particular statutory provisions. The six weeks' time limit provisions[17] for challenging planning and other land use decisions incorporate the phrase 'persons aggrieved' as a test of standing. During the 1960s this was confined to persons whose legal rights were affected by the decision in question.[18] More recent cases have taken a more liberal approach. Indeed it is arguable that the 'persons aggrieved' formula is, if anything, more generous than the 'sufficient interest' required under Ord 53.[19] Pressure groups representing general public concerns have usually been successful even in the case of 'single issue' groups comparable to the group denied standing in the *Rose Theatre Trust* case.[20] Persons who made

10 See *R v Chief Adjudication Officer, ex p Bland* (1985) Times, 6 February; *Royal College of Nursing of the United Kingdom v Department of Health and Social Security* [1981] AC 800, [1981] 1 All ER 545.
11 *R v Legal Aid Board, ex p Bateman* (above, n 6)—client could not challenge taxation of solicitor's costs.
12 *R v Secretary of State for the Environment, ex p Rose Theatre Trust* (above, n 4).
13 Albeit minimally; *R v Independent Broadcasting Authority, ex p Whitehouse* (1984) Times, 14 April—TV viewer. Cf *Holmes v Checkland* (1987) Times, 15 April, CA.
14 *R v HM Treasury* (above, n 6); cf *Felixstowe* case (above, n 1).
15 Above, p 8 et seq.
16 See *R v General Council of the Bar, ex p Percival* [1991] 1 QB 212, [1990] 3 All ER 137. See also *R v International Stock Exchange of the United Kingdom and the Republic of Ireland ex p Else (1982) Ltd* [1993] 1 All ER 420 at 432.
17 Below, p 186.
18 *Buxton v Minister of Housing and Local Government* [1961] 1 QB 278, [1960] 3 All ER 408.
19 See Hough [1992] JPL 319.
20 Above, n 4. Compare *Lewin and Rowley v Secretary of State for the Environment* [1992] JPL 342. See also *Hildenborough Village Preservation Association v Secretary of State for the Environment and Hall Aggregates* [1978] JPL 708.

formal representations or who participated in the public inquiry that usually precedes controversial land use decisions have also been regarded as 'persons aggrieved'[1] but this might also suffice to confer standing under Ord 53. A person must be 'aggrieved' by the outcome of the decision that is being challenged and not merely by some aspect of its reasoning.[2] However under both procedures an applicant whose interests have not been adversely affected will be denied relief as a matter of discretion, irrespective of standing.

## Conclusion

*Fleet Street Casuals* has broadened and diversified the law of standing but has produced considerable uncertainty. This is compounded because the standing question is sometimes not fully argued. Given the discretionary power of the court to refuse a remedy where the applicant has suffered no damage, it is questionable whether there is a need for a separate standing requirement apart from the relatively uncontroversial filtering of hopeless cases at the leave stage. In any case there seems to be no need for the standing requirement to differ in the case of statutory challenges (as opposed to appeals) from the position under Ord 53.

1 *Turner v Secretary of State* (1973) 72 LGR 380, 28 P & CR 123; cf *Bizony v Secretary of State for the Environment* [1976] JPL 306; *Wilson v Secretary of State for the Environment* [1988] JPL 540. In *Save Britain's Heritage v Secretary of State for the Environment* [1991] 2 All ER 10 an established pressure group was given standing by the House of Lords under s 288 of the Town and Country Planning Act 1990 but without discussion. It would probably also have qualified under Ord 53 (above, n 8, p 104).

2 *Greater London Council v Secretary of State for the Environment and Harrow London Borough Council* [1985] JPL 868.

CHAPTER 10

# Choice of forum: 'public' v 'private' law

## GENERAL BACKGROUND

The prerogative orders of prohibition, certiorari and mandamus are within the sole jurisdiction of the High Court. They can only be sought in that Court and are not obtainable in the county court or any other court. The grant of those prerogative orders is governed by the exclusive procedures set out in the Rules of the Supreme Court with which this book is concerned. The prerogative orders are not available in an action by writ nor by an ordinary originating summons.

Public body decisions may be challenged collaterally without resort to the prerogative powers of the High Court, for example in an action in tort. In this way, void decisions may be treated as being of no effect. However, unless and until a court has confirmed that a decision of an inferior body is void, the individuals who may be affected by it remain at risk and at the very least are subject to uncertainty. Further, if a person affected by a void decision fails to act to establish its invalidity then he may lose his right to seek relief from the courts by his delay. In order to protect his position an affected person may seek a declaration as to the validity of the decision and as to his own rights. The application may be made in the High Court under Ord 15, r 16 of the Rules of the Supreme Court or in the county court as ancillary relief to a claim for damages. Such a course does not involve any exercise of the prerogative powers. The court may even give effect to their declaratory judgments by granting appropriate injunctions, except as against the Crown. In so doing a court may, in effect, be achieving the result available by use of the prerogative orders without actually invoking them.

We have already seen that declaratory judgments, injunctions and indeed damages are available under the Ord 53 procedure whether with or without relief by prerogative order. Although these remedies are available under Ord 53 it has always been, and in principle remains, possible to seek declaratory and injunctive relief by ordinary action by writ or by ordinary originating summons where no prerogative order is required. Following the decision of the House of Lords in *O'Reilly v Mackman*,[1] however, it is an abuse of the process of the Court to attempt to obtain any remedy which is available as a matter of 'public' law by any procedure other than an application for judicial review under Ord 53. Although other proceedings are technically possible, therefore, they are liable to be struck out under Ord 18, r 19(c) of the Rules of the Supreme Court, save in exceptional cases. Their Lordships' decision in *O'Reilly v Mackman* reversed what had been in effect the practice hitherto of

1 [1983] 2 AC 237, [1982] 3 All ER 1124.

treating the choice of procedure as a matter for the option of the applicant. It was the procedural improvements which had been made to Ord 53 in 1977[2] which, according to the judgment of Lord Diplock, rendered attempts to use other procedures an abuse. It is, therefore, necessary to consider in brief the relevant effects of these changes.

## THE POSITION BEFORE 1977

Before the major reconstruction of Ord 53 in 1977 it was not possible to seek an injunction, declaration or damages under Ord 53. In these circumstances there had been no doubt that it was possible to bring an action by writ or originating summons claiming relief similar in effect to a prerogative order available under Ord 53. There are many examples of such actions. Much of the case law in which English administrative law was developed arose out of claims brought by ordinary action rather than under Ord 53. For example the claim in *Anisminic Ltd v Foreign Compensation Commission*[3] was for a declaration. In practice the ordinary action was accepted as a normal method of reviewing administrative decisions and the procedural accuracy of this method was never fully argued or judicially dealt with.

Prior to 1977 the procedure under Ord 53 posed a number of insuperable hurdles rendering it an inadequate remedy in many cases:

1. a claim for damages could not be added;
2. no injunction or declaration could be sought;
3. there was no provision for discovery or interrogatories; and
4. there was no express provision for cross-examination of deponents upon evidence contained in affidavits, nor was such cross-examination in practice ordered.

Even before 1977, however, no option existed where an applicant sought to quash a decision which was merely voidable and, therefore, valid until set aside by a court, rather than void and thus null and of no effect. Whereas a court could declare a decision to be void and thereby provide a remedy without further action, a declaration that a decision was voidable would have left it standing as a valid decision and still requiring an order of certiorari to set it aside. In those circumstances the Court would not grant declarations which would be of no effect when certiorari existed as a more appropriate and effective remedy. Thus when an applicant sought to set aside a decision on the basis of an error on the face of the record this could only be on the basis that the error entitled him to certiorari.[4] It is probable, however that the face of the record rule is obsolete except in relation to courts.[5] When an applicant seeks to quash a conviction before justices the only appropriate remedy is that of certiorari.[6] This is because the formal record must be removed.

2 See ch 1, above.
3 [1969] 2 AC 147, [1969] 1 All ER 208, HL.
4 *R v Northumberland Compensation Appeal Tribunal, ex p Shaw* [1952] 1 KB 338, [1952] 1 All ER 122.
5 *Bousfield v North Yorkshire County Council* (1982) 44 P & CR 203; as to an alleged error on the face of an entry in a register of common land. But see above pp 14–15, 55–57.
6 *Pyx Granite Co Ltd v Ministry of Housing and Local Government* [1960] AC 260 at 290, [1959] 3 All ER 1 at 89 per Lord Goddard.

## THE EFFECT OF THE 1977 CHANGES TO ORD 53

The changes to Ord 53 in 1977 allowed an applicant to combine a claim for injunctions, declarations or damages with a claim for a prerogative order under Ord 53 and made express provision for discovery, interrogatories and cross-examination. Despite this change to the rules the practice of allowing an applicant an option of whether to proceed by Ord 53 or by ordinary action remained. For example, in *Thornton v Kirklees Metropolitan Borough Council*[7] the Court of Appeal held that decisions of local housing authorities under the Housing (Homeless Persons) Act 1977 were reviewable by the courts in an ordinary action. They did so in proceedings for damages and an injunction commenced in a county court and then transferred to the High Court when the defendant attempted to strike out the plaintiff's pleadings as disclosing no cause of action under Ord 18, r 19(a) of the Rules of the Supreme Court. The existence of this option was judicially recognised in a series of cases between 1977 and 1982, though amid growing dispute. The division of opinion is well demonstrated by the case of *Uppal v Home Office*.[8] There an immigration case was commenced in the Chancery Division by an originating summons seeking a declaration. At first instance Sir Robert Megarry V-C accepted the existence of an option:

> Where two or more different types of proceedings are possible in the same court (and of course the Chancery Division and Queen's Bench Division are both parts of the High Court) then I do not see why the plaintiffs should not be free to bring whatever type of proceedings they choose. . . . I do not think the Chancery Division can be regarded as being avid for this jurisdiction: but it would be wrong to turn away or discourage a plaintiff who elects to bring one form of proceedings instead of the other.

But this view was disavowed in the Court of Appeal where Roskill LJ gave a judgment of the Court intended only as guidance to litigants generally since the actual appeal in the case was abandoned by consent. After expressly disagreeing with the Vice-Chancellor, Roskill LJ said:

> It is the Divisional Court which is equipped by reason of its experience, expertise and long practice to deal with these matters and to deal with them expeditiously; and I express the hope that in future it is the Divisional Court to which this type of problem will be submitted and that the temptation to deal with immigration problems by way of Originating Summons in proceedings for a declaration in the Chancery Division will be avoided . . . it would be wrong that this procedure should be adopted in order to by-pass the need for getting leave from the Divisional Court to move for the relevant Order where what in truth is sought is Judicial Review.

Within a month a differently constituted Court of Appeal came to consider the same question in the context of the Housing (Homeless Persons) Act 1977 in *De Falco v Crawley Borough Council*.[9] The Court was not referred to the decision in *Uppal v Home Office*.[10] Far from confirming the guidance of Roskill LJ the

7 [1979] QB 626, [1979] 2 All ER 349, CA.

8 (1978) Times, 21 October; affd (1978) 123 Sol Jo 17, CA, and set out extensively in the judgment of Goulding J in *Heywood v Hull Prison Board of Visitors* [1980] 3 All ER 594, [1980] 1 WLR 1386.

9 [1980] QB 460, [1980] 1 All ER 913.

10 See *O'Reilly v Mackman* [1983] 2 AC 237 at 247f, [1982] 3 All ER 680 at 686, 687, per Peter Pain J.

Court followed *Thornton v Kirklees Metropolitan Borough Council*. The main judgment was given by Lord Denning MR:[11]

> It had been held by this Court that if the Council fails to provide accommodation as required by section 3(4) [of the Housing (Homeless Persons) Act 1977], the applicant can claim damages in the county court. . . . No doubt such a person could, at his option, bring proceedings for Judicial Review under the new RSC Ord 53. In those proceedings he could get a declaration and an injunction equally well. He could get interim relief also. So the applicant has an option. He can either go by action in the High Court or county court: or by an application for Judicial Review.

After reservations about whether the choice of procedure was purely a matter of option for an applicant had been expressed in the House of Lords,[12] however, Lord Denning expressed an altered view in the later case of *Lambert v Ealing London Borough Council*[13] in respect of judicial review of decisions under the Housing (Homeless Persons) Act:

> . . . These cases should be reviewed, if at all, by the process of Judicial Review in the High Court here: not by actions for damages, or injunctions, in the county court. The only way in which a local authority's decision in these cases can properly be interfered with is by way of Judicial Review: applying the well-known principles of Judicial Review to ascertain whether the decision is so unreasonable that it cannot stand. That is the right and proper way of considering these matters.

None of this 'guidance' brought to an end the practice of applicants seeking review of public authority decisions by writ or ordinary originating summons rather than by way of Ord 53 proceedings. It did, however, lead to an increase in the number of defendants who sought to strike out under Ord 18, r 19 of the Rules of the Supreme Court proceedings commenced by ordinary action. Finally the House of Lords, which does not normally concern itself with issues of practice and procedure, came to consider the matter in *O'Reilly v Mackman*.[14]

## THE HOUSE OF LORDS' DECISION IN *O'REILLY v MACKMAN*

In *O'Reilly v Mackman* a number of prisoners sought declarations that a board of prison visitors' decision was ultra vires as having been taken in breach of the rules of natural justice. They did not seek relief by prerogative order and had brought their action either by writ and statement of claim or by ordinary originating summons. They had chosen not to proceed by way of Ord 53. The House of Lords struck the proceedings out on the ground that the proceedings were an abuse of the process of the Court because a person claiming the protection of rights to which he was entitled under public law should use the Ord 53 procedure which was best suited to such actions. The rationale for this decision was that since discovery, interrogatories and cross-examination were now available under Ord 53 (although not automatically) the disadvantages of the previous system had been removed and the remaining safeguards under

11 [1980] QB 460 at 476, [1980] 1 All ER 913 at 920.

12 *Din v Wandsworth London Borough Council* [1983] 1 AC 657 at 666c, [1981] 3 All ER 881 at 885h, per Lord Wilberforce and at 685d and 899–900 per Lord Bridge.

13 [1982] 2 All ER 394 at 399, [1982] 1 WLR 550 at 557.

14 [1983] 2 AC 237, [1982] 3 All ER 1124.

Ord 53, especially the requirements for leave, were necessary to protect 'the public interest in good administration'.

The judgment of the House of Lords was delivered by Lord Diplock. In an earlier decision of the House of Lords in *IRC v Rossminster Ltd*[15] Lord Diplock had already begun to separate the two roles of the Court; one when dealing with Ord 53 applicants and one when trying ordinary actions, which he regarded as dealing with two separate categories of relief. In *O'Reilly v Mackman*, Lord Diplock developed the distinction between the two roles of the Court and based it on a distinction between private law and public law, a distinction on which Lord Denning had also concentrated when *O'Reilly v Mackman* was heard in the Court of Appeal. Lord Diplock held that as a matter of 'private law' none of the prisoners had a remedy against the board of prison visitors since the remission which they were in danger of losing was, under the Prison Rules, an indulgence and not a private right. All the prisoners had was a legitimate expectation which as a public law right gave them a sufficient interest to challenge the legality of the adverse disciplinary award made against them by the board on the grounds that the board had not acted fairly.

The protection given to public bodies by Ord 53 which it is thought to be an abuse to circumvent is:

1. the requirement of obtaining leave ex parte before commencing proceedings;
2. a time limit in the absence of 'good reason' of three months within which to bring proceedings;
3. the absence of provisions for automatic discovery, placing its availability firmly within the discretion of the court;
4. that cross-examination of deponents will only be allowed at the discretion of the Court and not as a matter of course; and
5. that terms may be imposed as to costs and/or security as a condition of granting leave.

## 'PUBLIC LAW'

Not all activities of government fall within public law. This is because of the deep-rooted assumption in English law that governmental officials and private persons are subject to the same general private law framework. Government officials are treated, prima facie, as ordinary persons. At common law the Crown has the same legal capacity as a natural person subject to a miscellaneous collection of special rights, powers and immunities existing under the royal prerogative. Any additional powers exercised by the Crown or its ministers depend on statute. The powers of local authorities and other public bodies depend upon statute. This is true even in the case of local authorities incorporated by royal charter.[16]

There is no single test for distinguishing between private and public law. The matter depends on the nature and effect of the particular decision-making power that is being challenged. In the case of a body which is outside the normal governmental framework, the function of the particular body and especially its connection with government is important. The source of the power in question, whether it performs important public functions, the extent

15 [1980] AC 952, [1980] 1 All ER 80.
16 See *Hazell v Hammersmith & Fulham London Borough Council* [1991] 1 All ER 545 at 563–566.

of its powers and, somewhat illogically, the availability of alternative remedies have been said to be the main factors.[17] The courts are also influenced towards a restrictive approach to the scope of Ord 53 by fears of excessive demands on the procedure.[18] The position can be summarised briefly as follows:

1. Statutory or royal prerogative powers are prima facie public law powers unless perhaps they correspond wholly to activities carried out in the private sector.[19]
2. Powers derived purely from contract or agreement, whether exercised by government or by indepenent bodies such as sports regulatory bodies, are not public law powers[20] unless, perhaps, there is a substantial connection with government activity of a wider kind.
3. Powers which fall into neither category being derived only from custom or political pressure may be public law powers provided that the body in question performs its duties in the public interest and for public purposes and, crucially, that there is evidence that the activities of the body are backed by government proper. This backing need not take the form of specific powers but can be an intention on the part of government to intervene itself, if the body in question did not exist—in other words an implied delegation of public power.[1] The fact that a body is created by Royal Charter does not make it a public law body as such, but may be relevant to the question of a link with government.[2]

This approach has been criticised at Divisional Court level[3] but the doctrine of precedent has prevailed in the form of the Court of Appeal decisions in *Law, Aga Khan* and *Datafin*.[4] In particular it seems artificial and unnecessary to require evidence of government support in respect of bodies such as the Jockey Club which exercise regulatory powers for public purposes and affect many people who have no contractual link with them. Moreover the distinction between contractual and non-contractual powers is artificial. Many governmental powers for example in the public employment field comprise of a mixture of contract, statute, prerogative and policy. Even where a power is essentially contractual, the presence in a given case of an additional statutory element or even the exercise of a general governmental policy might possibly convert a contractual private law issue into one of public law.[5]

17 *R v Panel on Take-overs & Mergers, ex p Datafin plc* [1987] QB 815, [1987] 1 All ER 564, CA; *R v Disciplinary Committee of the Jockey Club, ex p Massingberd-Mundy* [1990] 2 Admin LR 260. The mere absence of a private law remedy is not enough. *R v Lord Chancellor's Department, ex p Nangle* [1992] 1 All ER 897 at 908.

18 *R v Football Association Ltd, ex p Football League Ltd* (1991) Times, 22 August; judicial review of the decision by the Football Association to set up the Premier league refused.

19 *R v Panel on Take-overs and Mergers* (above, n 17); *R v National Coal Board, ex p National Union of Mineworkers* [1986] ICR 791.

20 *Law v National Greyhound Racing Club Ltd* [1983] 3 All ER 300, [1983] 1 WLR 1302, CA; *R v Football Association* (above, n 18); *R v East Berkshire Health Authority, ex p Walsh* [1985] QB 152, [1984] 3 All ER 425, CA; *R v Lord Chancellor's Department, ex p Nangle* [1992] 1 All ER 897.

1 *R v Panel on Take-overs and Mergers* (above, n 17); *R v Football Association* (above, n 18); *R v Advertising Standards Authority Ltd, ex p Insurance Service plc* (1989) 133 Sol Jo 1545; *R v Chief Rabbi of the United Hebrew Congregations of Great Britain and Commonwealth, ex p Wachmann* [1992] 1 WLR 1036.

2 *R v Jockey Club, ex p Massingberd Mundy* (above, n 17); *R v Disciplinary Committee of the Jockey Club, ex p His Highness the Aga Khan*, (1992) Times, 9 December, CA.

3 In *RAM Racecourses* (see n 4) and *ex p Aga Khan* (see n 2).

4 Above n 20, 2 and 17. See *Massingberd-Mundy* (above, n 17); *R v Jockey Club, ex p RAM Racecourses Ltd* [1991] 5 Admin LR 265 (non-contractual); but compare *R v Football Association* (above, n 18).

5 *McClaren v Home Office* [1990] ICR 824 at 837; *R v Lord Chancellor's Department* (above, n 20); *R v Derbyshire County Council, ex p Noble* [1990] ICR 808 at 813, CA.

DEVELOPMENTS SINCE *O'REILLY v MACKMAN*

## Collateral challenge

In *O'Reilly v Mackman* Lord Diplock described a general rule but accepted that there would be exceptions.[6] He expressly mentioned cases where the invalidity of a decision arises as a collateral issue in a claim for infringement of a right of the plaintiff arising under private law. Following *O'Reilly v Mackman* the Divisional Court held that although a stop notice served under s 90 of the Town and Country Planning Act 1971 could only be set aside by proceedings under Ord 53, its validity could be challenged by way of defence in criminal proceedings.[7] Similarly the House of Lords has allowed a defence arising out of public law to be raised in civil proceedings. In *Wandsworth London Borough Council v Winder*[8] a housing authority sought an order for possession against their tenant based on non-payment of rent. The tenant had refused to pay an increased rent because he alleged that the increase was excessive and ultra vires. Since the rent increase was in his view invalid, the tenant denied that he was in arrears with his rent. Although the main issue to be decided was one of public law the Court allowed it to be raised by way of defence.

An example of a collateral challenge had also reached the House of Lords in *Davey v Spelthorne Borough Council.*[9] There a plaintiff in an action by writ sought damages against a local planning authority for negligent advice. He had been served with an enforcement notice under the Town and Country Planning Act 1971 by the defendant council. It was alleged that following negotiations with the plaintiff the council's officers had purported to agree not to enforce the notice. Such an agreement was invalid since it was ultra vires but by relying on it the plaintiff had lost his right to object to the enforcement notice. In the plaintiff's subsequent action by writ the validity of the enforcement notice was one issue in question but only an incidental one. The plaintiff's claim, being one for damages for negligent advice, was an action under the 'private' law of tort. It was, therefore, appropriate to commence proceedings by way of an ordinary action and the writ was not struck out as an abuse of the process.

In *An Bord Bainne Co-operative Ltd (Irish Dairy Board) v Milk Marketing Board*[10] complaint was made as to the price-fixing policy of a public body. The decision to implement a particular price system was a matter of public law but the plaintiff's claim was for damages for breach of statutory duty on the basis that the system contravened regulations of the European Community. Such a claim was actionable in private law[11] and so since the validity of the system was only a collateral issue the plaintiff was permitted to proceed by way of a writ action.

Logically, collateral challenge presupposes that a decision which is incidental to a cause of action is void ab initio, ie a complete nullity with no legal consequences. It does not therefore need to be formally quashed by the court. For example an action for assault against an official purporting to enter property under a warrant must fail if the warrant were treated as valid until

6 [1983] 2 AC 237 at 285f, [1982] 3 All ER 1124 at 1134f, HL.
7 *R v Jenner* [1983] 2 All ER 46, [1983] 1 WLR 873, CA.
8 [1985] AC 461, [1984] 3 All ER 976. Their Lordships regarded a defence as *sui generis* rather than as a collateral challenge; see also *Lonhro plc v Tebbit* [1991] 4 All ER 973 at 987. For examples of 'public law' allegations not amounting to a defence see *Avon County Council v Buscott* [1988] QB 656, [1988] 1 All ER 841 and *Tower Hamlets London Borough Council v Abdi* [1993] 06 EG 102.
9 [1984] AC 262, [1983] 3 All ER 278, HL.
10 [1984] 1 CMLR 519; affd [1984] 2 CMLR 584, CA.
11 *Garden Cottage Foods Ltd v Milk Marketing Board* [1982] QB 1114, [1982] 3 All ER 292, CA, revsd [1984] 1 AC 130, [1983] 2 All ER 770, HL.

quashed. However nullity is a two-edged sword and somewhat unrealistic. In *O'Connor v Isaacs*[12] the plaintiff refused to pay arrears of maintenance on the basis that the magistrate's decision was void. His action for false imprisonment succeeded but his action for the return of money already paid failed on the ground that he should not have obeyed the Order which had no legal effect.

In order to protect public authorities against the capriciousness of the nullity principle the court's toyed with the notion that less serious defects made a decision only voidable, ie only void once formally quashed.[13] This would have prevented collateral challenge. However in *Anisminic Ltd v Foreign Compensation Commission*[14] the House of Lords effectively held that all reviewable defects made a decision completely void. This was in the context of an 'ouster' clause which attempted to exclude judicial review. The problem with the nullity concept is that in some contexts it is attractive[15] while in others, where third parties are involved, it can be seriously unjust and inconvenient. The court's approach therefore lacks consistency. It is generally accepted, however, that even an ultra vires decision might have legal consequences, but that collateral challenge is still possible.[16]

The current orthodoxy is to rely upon a presumption that unless and until government action is challenged in appropriate proceedings it can be treated as valid, but the court in its discretion can treat a decision as wholly void.[17] For example in *R v Panel on Take-overs and Mergers, ex p Datafin plc*[18] Sir John Donaldson MR said

> I think that it is important that all . . . should have well in mind a very special feature of public law decisions such as those of the panel, namely that however lacking in jurisdiction they may be, they remain fully effective unless and until they are set aside by a court of competent jurisdiction. Furthermore the court has an ultimate discretion whether to set them aside and may refuse to do so in the public interest notwithstanding that it holds and declares the decision to have been made ultra vires.

This can be regarded as a principle of 'relative nullity' or 'ostensible validity'. In *R v Hendon Justices, ex p DPP*[19] the Queen's Bench Division held that an acquittal which was defective for unreasonableness, was a complete nullity and the defendant could not therefore plead autrefois acquit. However Mann LJ stressed that whether the decision was to be described as void or voidable was unhelpful but that the issue depended upon the court's willingness to issue the discretionary remedy of mandamus.

## Non-objection

Lord Diplock also accepted in *O'Reilly v Mackman* that cases could proceed,

12 [1956] 2 QB 288, [1956] 1 All ER 513. In the case of magistrates' courts, unless the defect is patent, separate quashing is required before an action can proceed. This does not affect the general principle, eg time runs from the date of the decision. See also *Dunlop v Woollahra Municipal Council* [1982] AC 158, [1981] 1 All ER 1202, PC.

13 Eg *Grand Junction Canal v Dimes* (1852) 3 HL Cas 759; *DPP v Head* [1959] AC 83; *Durayappah v Fernando* [1967] 2 AC 337, [1967] 2 All ER 152, PC; *R v Secretary of State for the Environment, ex p Ostler* [1977] QB 122, [1976] 3 All ER 90, CA; *R v Paddington Valuation Officer, ex p Peachey Property Corpn Ltd* [1966] 1 QB 380, [1965] 2 All ER 836, CA.

14 [1969] 2 AC 147, [1967] 1 All ER 208, HL. Cf p 208.

15 See eg *Ridge v Baldwin* [1964] AC 40, [1963] 2 All ER 66, HL, cf p 125.

16 See *London and Clydendale Estates Ltd v Aberdeen District Council* [1979] 3 All ER 876 at 883; *Chief Constable North Wales Police v Evans* [1982] 3 All ER 141 at 145; *Co-operative Retail Services v Taff-Ely District Council* (1979) 39 P & CR 223 at 239–9.

17 *Hoffman-La-Roche & Co AG v Secretary of State for Trade and Industry* [1975] AC 295 at 341, 350, 358, 365.

18 [1987] QB 815, [1987] 1 All ER 564, CA.

19 [1992] NLJR 1303.

although commenced by writ or ordinary originating summons, where no party objected to the adoption of such procedure. Indeed Lord Diplock appears[20] to have distinguished *Anisminic Ltd v Foreign Compensation Commission*[1] not only on the grounds that it was before the 1977 changes to Ord 53 but also on the grounds that the procedural issue was not fully argued, having been mentioned but not developed in the reply of counsel for the Foreign Compensation Commission,[2] and so was not taken by the Court. Lord Diplock further accepted that there would be other exceptions but left them to be decided on a case to case basis. Lord Denning MR in the Court of Appeal in *O'Reilly v Mackman*[3] gave, as an example of a claim for a declaration by writ which should be allowed to continue as an exception, the case of *Air Canada v Secretary of State for Trade (No 2)*.[4] He did not, however, give his reason for the example, though it may have been that the case was singularly concerned with the discoverability of documents, that issue having already reached the House of Lords.[5] He may simply have wished to avoid confusion in a particular case.

## Express provision

*O'Reilly v Mackman* establishes principles of general application which are overridden by express provision. Thus where a particular statute provides for a particular method by which applications to the High Court may be made, an applicant will not be abusing the process of the Court by making use of that method.[6]

## 'Private' rights

The principles of *O'Reilly v Mackman* were applied directly to problems arising under the Housing (Homeless Persons) Act 1977, in a judgment delivered by the House of Lords on the very same day as *O'Reilly v Mackman*, in *Cocks v Thanet District Council*.[7] In the speech of Lord Bridge, comprising the judgment of the House, *Thornton v Kirklees Metropolitan Borough Council*[8] was distinguished on the grounds that in the earlier case the defendant's application to strike out the plaintiff's pleading was under Ord 18, r 19(a) of the Rules of the Supreme Court only, ie that the pleadings disclosed no reasonable cause of action. Since the question of the proceedings being an abuse of the process of the Court under Ord 18, r 19(c) of the Rules of the Supreme Court was not raised, the Court of Appeal had been deciding a different issue. On the application by Thanet District Council under Ord 18, r 19(c) the House of Lords had to consider the question of abuse in the light of *O'Reilly v Mackman*. It was held that where the validity of a decision of a housing authority was questioned that was a right given to the applicant by 'public' law and was, therefore, a matter for judicial review and not an ordinary action. Where, however, a housing authority had reached a decision, the consequence of which was that it was under a duty to house an applicant, then the performance of that duty was a 'private' law right which, though enforceable by mandamus under Ord 53, could also be enforced by ordinary action.

20 [1982] 2 AC 237 at 278g–279a, [1982] 3 All ER 1124 at 1129e–g.
1 [1969] 2 AC 147, [1969] 1 All ER 208, HL.
2 Reported at [1969] 2 AC 147 at 167.
3 [1983] 2 AC 237 at 259, [1982] 3 All ER 680 at 695g, CA.
4 [1983] 2 AC 394, [1983] 1 All ER 910.
5 Reported together with the Court of Appeal decision, ibid.
6 *Buckley v The Law Society* [1983] 2 All ER 1039, [1983] 1 WLR 985.
7 [1983] 2 AC 286, [1982] 3 All ER 1135. The statutory provisions are now in the Housing Act 1985.
8 [1979] QB 626, [1979] 2 All ER 349.

In many cases this distinction will not be an easy one to make. In *Parr v Wyre Borough Council*,[9] for example, a local housing authority claimed to have fulfilled its duty under the Housing (Homeless Persons) Act 1977 by providing accommodation in the area of another authority 200 miles away. An application was successfully brought under Ord 53. As a matter of definition following *Cocks v Thanet District Council*, though, it is debatable whether that was a case of an authority failing to perform its duty, and thus enforceable by ordinary action, or one of review of the authority's decision that the accommodation offered was appropriate to the needs of the applicant, and thus reviewable only under Ord 53. In practice this dilemma will oblige applicants to proceed under Ord 53 rather than run the risk of having their proceedings struck out.

Thus the result of the House of Lords' decisions is that, whilst the courts have jurisdiction to consider ordinary actions for declarations as to the validity of administrative decisions, such applications are liable to be struck out at the instigation of other parties unless brought under Ord 53.

The restriction applies only to cases where a public law remedy is clearly the appropriate relief and where private rights are not in issue. In *Law v National Greyhound Racing Club Ltd*[10] the Court of Appeal refused to strike out originating summonses issued in the Chancery Division to restore greyhound training licences which were needed by the applicants for their livelihood, on the ground that the basis of the licences and such rights to them as the applicants may have had was contractual and, therefore, enforceable as a matter of 'private' rather than 'public' law. In those circumstances no prerogative order would lie and Ord 53 proceedings would not be appropriate.[11]

The same reasoning was applied where a nurse attempted to quash his dismissal by a health authority by an application for judicial review.[12] The Court of Appeal set aside leave to apply under Ord 53. Since the complaint arose out of the relationship of employer/employee in private law the proper course was to bring a claim for breach of contract or for unfair dismissal before the Industrial Tribunal. The mere fact that an employer is a public body does not necessarily inject public law rights where the duties in question are contractual. It does, however, make it more likely that there may be special statutory restrictions upon dismissal which would bring the matter within the scope of Ord 53.

These decisions conform with Lord Diplock's express comments in *O'Reilly v Mackman* about two earlier decisions of the House of Lords in *Vine v National Dock Labour Board*[13] and *Ridge v Baldwin*.[14] In those cases declarations were granted as to the invalidity of purported dismissals from employment, under a statutory scheme for dock labour in the first case, and of a Chief Constable under the statutory powers of a Watch Committee in the second. In *O'Reilly v Mackman*[15] Lord Diplock distinguished both cases as involving rights under

9 (1982) 2 HLR 71, CA; see also *Tower Hamlets London Borough Council v Abdi* [1993] 06 EG 102, CA.
10 [1983] 3 All ER 300, [1983] 1 WLR 1302.
11 See also *R v BBC, ex p Lavelle* [1983] 1 All ER 241, [1983] 1 WLR 23.
12 *R v East Berkshire Health Authority, ex p Walsh* [1985] QB 554, [1984] 3 All ER 425, CA. But see *R v Secretary of State for the Home Department, ex p Benwell* [1985] QB 152, [1984] 3 All ER 854, HL.
13 [1957] AC 488, [1956] 3 All ER 939.
14 [1964] AC 40, [1963] 2 All ER 66.
15 [1983] 2 AC 237 at 281f, [1982] 3 All ER 1124 at 1131f, HL.

private law. In both cases it would remain appropriate, therefore, to proceed by ordinary action.

In *Roy v Kensington and Chelsea and Westminster Family Practitioner Committee*[16] the House of Lords substantially ameliorated the strict view of *O'Reilly v Mackman*. The House took the view that a litigant whose 'private rights' are in issue is not obliged to use Ord 53. The meaning of 'private rights' is not obvious but their Lordships took a broad view which included any established claim against a public authority even one created only by the particular statutory power that is being challenged. *Roy* concerned a claim to a NHS practice allowance, the amount of which depended upon a discretionary decision by the FPC. The 'private right' arose because Dr Roy had satisfied the first stage of a two-stage discretionary test for eligibility for payment. Thus 'private rights' go well beyond rights that can be asserted against private persons such as claims in contract or tort. The decision in *Roy* effectively allows Ord 53 to be by-passed except by those with no established rights at all, eg claimants for state benefits, those affected by governmental action of an advisory character such as placing names on a register with no specific legal consequences,[17] or third parties such as pressure groups.

In many cases the short time limit and the need for leave makes Ord 53 unattractive although in the field of employment the wider range of remedies provided by Ord 53 may make Ord 53 the preferable option. The 'exclusive' nature of Ord 53 is, after *Roy*, somewhat questionable and their Lordships emphasised their reluctance to force litigants to use Ord 53.[18]

If in doubt as to which procedure is appropriate it is possible to commence both types of proceedings simultaneously. If Ord 53 proceedings are commenced and a declaration or injunction is sought then, by virtue of RSC Ord 53 r 9, if Ord 53 turns out not to be appropriate the court can continue to hear the case as an ordinary action. This applies only where the case involves genuine judicial review issues.[19] There is no specific mechanism to transfer a case wrongly brought elsewhere to Ord 53.[20]

## Caveat

In conclusion it is worth quoting a passage from Lord Wilberforce's speech in *Davey v Spelthorne Borough Council*[1] as a warning against excessive formalism in the application of the distinction between public law and private law:

> The principle remains intact that public authorities and public servants are . . . answerable in the ordinary courts for wrongs done to individuals. We have not yet reached the point at which mere characterisation of a claim as a claim in public law is sufficient to exclude it from consideration by the ordinary courts; to permit this would be to create a dual system of law with the rigidity and procedural hardship for the Plaintiffs which it was the purpose of the recent reforms to remove.

16 [1992] 1 AC 624, [1992] 1 All ER 705.

17 There was a narrower rationale in *Roy* based upon the case being an exception to the general *O'Reilly* rule because inter alia Ord 53 did not provide the monetary remedy sought. But the wider view of *Roy* was endorsed by the Court of Appeal in *Lonhro plc v Tebbit* [1992] 4 All ER 280 at 288.

18 [1992] 1 All ER 705 at 729, 730 per Lord Lowry.

19 See *R v Secretary of State for the Home Department, ex p Dew* [1987] 2 All ER 1049, [1987] 1 WLR 881; *R v BBC, ex p Lavelle* [1983] 1 All ER 241, [1983] 1 WLR 23.

20 But see below, p 158.

1 [1984] AC 262, [1983] 3 All ER 278, HL.

## THE EUROPEAN CONVENTION ON HUMAN RIGHTS

The relationship between the European Convention on Human Rights and the English courts has never been a comfortable one. The convention is not directly enforceable under English law despite the best efforts of the 'Bill of Rights' campaigners. English courts have been reluctant to allow the convention to be enforced indirectly. In *R v Secretary of State for the Home Department, ex p Brind*[2] the House of Lords refused to use the convention as a benchmark for assessing the legality or rationality of government action. The convention can only be used where the governing UK legislation is ambiguous. In *Brind* the governing UK legislation gave the Secretary of State a very wide discretion.

Thus if the provisions of the convention are to be relied upon then it may be necessary to invoke the machinery of the convention. An application to the European Commission on Human Rights and subsequently, if referred by the Commission, the European Court of Human Rights, can be made only after exhausting domestic remedies. This would include judicial review. However, because English judicial review law does not formally recognise the concept of fundamental rights and its discretionary elements arguably fall short of providing an effective protection for the individual there may be cases where an unsuccessful judicial review application can be followed by an application under the convention or judicial review by-passed completely. For example in *X v UK*[3] it was held that the United Kingdom was in breach of art 5(4) of the European Convention because the power to recall a person released from a mental hospital under s 66(3) of the Mental Health Act 1959 was not accompanied by a provision for speedy challenge. This was 'rectified' in s 75(1) of the Mental Health Act 1983 by a provision for reference to a mental health review tribunal.

2 *R v Secretary of State for the Home Department, ex p Brind* [1991] 1 AC 696, sub nom *Brind v Secretary of State for the Home Department* [1991] 1 All ER 720. See also *R v General Medical Council, ex p Colman* [1990] 1 All ER 489, CA.

3 3/1985/89/136: *Weeks v United Kingdom* (1987) 10 EHRR 293, E Ct HR Series A No 114.

CHAPTER 11

# The court's discretion to refuse relief on judicial review

## INTRODUCTION

Except in the case of damages, the Ord 53 remedies are discretionary. This means that even where a decision is ultra vires and in theory void the court can refuse to award a remedy because of a factor such as delay which is independent of the validity of the decision complained of. In such cases therefore, subject to the possibility of collateral challenge,[1] even an ultra vires decision must be treated as effective.

In recent years the court's use of its discretionary powers has become a significant, perhaps a dominant, aspect of judicial review. It is not always easy to determine whether a particular ground for not setting aside a governmental act is a matter of substance or based upon the discretion to refuse a remedy. The question is not merely academic since if the former is the case, collateral challenge is ruled out. This issue has become important in recent years because of the tendency which we have already noted to develop doctrines of substantive validity in broad discretionary terms. For example, it has been held that a decision will be invalid for breach of natural justice only if there is a substantial risk that the applicant would be prejudiced as a result of the defect,[2] and yet the fact that an applicant has not been prejudiced is traditionally a discretionary ground for refusing a remedy. A similar principle has been applied in other contexts[3] and comes near to the court deciding what the governmental decision should have been, since the court is often asking itself whether the decision would have been different in the absence of the defect. The courts have stressed that they do not wish to intervene upon 'theoretical or legalistic grounds' and that they are sensitive to 'good policy making, administration and decision-making' recognising the need to look at the issues broadly.[4]

1 Above, p 113; *R v Secretary of State for Social Services, ex p Association of Metropolitan Authorities* [1986] 1 All ER 164, [1986] 1 WLR 1.

2 *R v Secretary of State for Transport, ex p Gwent County Council* [1987] 1 All ER 161 at 166; *R v Blundeston Prison Board of Visitors, ex p Fox-Taylor* [1982] 1 All ER 646. See also *Cinnamond v British Airports Authority* [1980] 2 All ER 368, [1980] 1 WLR 582, CA.

3 Eg irrelevant considerations only if the decision is actually affected. *R v Secretary of State for Social Services, ex p Wellcome Foundation Ltd* [1987] 2 All ER 1025, [1987] 1 WLR 1166; *R v Broadcasting Complaints Commission, ex p Owen* [1985] QB 1153, [1985] 2 All ER 522; *R v Tottenham District Rent Tribunal, ex p Fryer Bros (Properties) Ltd* [1971] 2 QB 681, [1971] 3 All ER 563, CA. In the case of errors of law the matter has been treated as one of discretion: *R v Crown Court at Knightsbridge, ex p Marcrest Ltd* [1983] 1 All ER 1148, [1983] 1 WLR 300, CA.

4 *Wellcome* case (above, n 3) at 1132; *R v Panel on Take-overs and Mergers, ex p Guinness plc* [1989] 1 All ER 509 at 526; *R v Lancashire County Council, ex p Huddleston* [1986] 2 All ER 941, CA; *R v Monopolies and Mergers Commission, ex p Argyle Group plc* [1986] 2 All ER 257, [1986] 1 WLR 763, CA; *R v Hull Prison Visitors, ex p St Germain* [1979] QB 425 at 455–6, [1979] 1 All ER 701 at 716.

## THE NATURE OF THE COURT'S DISCRETION

The court's discretionary power to refuse relief arises at two different stages in the Ord 53 process. First, at the initial leave to apply stage, the court must decide whether or not to grant leave to apply. This involves a limited exercise of discretion. It is enough that the applicant *might* have an arguable[5] case and is not clearly without locus standi. Some discretionary issues such as the adequacy of alternative remedies can appropriately be considered at this stage. Section 31 of the Supreme Court Act 1981 prescribes special provisions relating to delay in seeking relief and expressly makes these applicable at both stages. At the second inter partes stage, the court will be particularly concerned with choosing the most appropriate remedy. For example, there are several kinds of case where coercive relief would be inappropriate but where a declaration can usefully be made.

The same general grounds for withholding relief are broadly applicable to all the remedies. However, particular characteristics of individual remedies sometimes require differences in the application of the various grounds. In all cases the court's discretion must be exercised judicially in the sense that precedent must be followed. Nevertheless the essence of a discretionary power is a flexible response to the circumstances of the individual case. Thus the guidelines to be discussed in this chapter are concerned with the factors which it is open to the court to take into account, and not generally with the balancing of the relevant factors in the circumstances of a particular case.

In terms of flexibility there may be differences between the individual remedies. For example it has been said that mandamus, being concerned with a duty, is the least discretionary of the remedies,[6] whereas the declaration is often considered to be the most discretionary.[7] It is also arguable that the personal conduct of the applicant is a weightier consideration when it comes to the granting of an injunction than in connection with the prerogative orders because of the equitable character of the injunction, contrasted with the public nature of the prerogative orders.

The grounds of challenge are also important. The court is less likely to exercise its discretion against giving relief where the challenge is based upon the decision being entirely ultra vires as opposed to a challenge based upon procedural impropriety or failure to take relevant factors into account.[8]

In general the court's discretion is very wide. All relevant factors including cost, administrative efficiency and the position of third parties can be taken into account.[9] Financial interests are given more weight than rights to be consulted.

5 *IRC v National Federation of Self-Employed and Small Businesses* [1982] AC 617, [1981] 2 All ER 93, HL; *R v Secretary of State for the Home Department, ex p Swati* [1986] 1 All ER 717, [1986] 1 WLR 477, CA, but cf *R v Civil Service Appeals Board, ex p Cunningham* [1991] 4 All ER 310 at 315 'prima facie case'. *R v Legal Aid Board, ex p Hughes* (1992) Times, 29 October, CA 'prima facie arguable case'.

6 *R v Hounslow London Borough Council, ex p Pizzey* [1977] 1 All ER 305 at 309, [1977] 1 WLR 58 at 62 per Lord Widgery LCJ.

7 *Barnard v National Dock Labour Board* [1953] 2 QB 18 at 41, [1953] 1 All ER 1113 at 1119 per Denning LJ. Cf de Smith *Judicial Review of Administrative Action* (4th edn, 1980) by J M Evans, pp 483–484.

8 *R v Swale Borough Council, ex p Royal Society for the Protection of Birds* [1991] JPL 39 of Env Law 135; *R v Exeter City Council, ex p JL Thomas & Co Ltd* [1991] 1 QB 471, [1990] 1 All ER 413.

9 *R v Monopolies and Mergers Commission, ex p Argyle Group plc* [1986] 2 All ER 257, [1988] 1 WLR 763; *R v Secretary of State for the Environment, ex p Equal Opportunities Commission* [1992] 1 All ER 545 at 558.

## THE GROUNDS ON WHICH A REMEDY CAN BE REFUSED

The various discretionary grounds for refusing a remedy can be classified under three broad heads. These are first, matters related to the conduct of the applicant, second, the availability of alternative remedies, and third, matters relating to the effect of the remedy asked for. We shall examine each of these in turn.

### The conduct of the applicant

Several forms of misconduct may deprive the applicant of a remedy.

#### (i) *Delay*

An applicant's delay in seeking redress has always been an important consideration. The court will not allow delay in applying for relief by way of judicial review. Although the court retains an inherent discretion to refuse relief for delay the position is now principally governed by s 31(6) of the Supreme Court Act 1981.[10] Delay may also affect the grant of leave under the provisions of Ord 53, r 4 and s 31(6) of the Supreme Court Act 1981.[11] The combined effect of these provisions is so significant that they are treated separately in chapter 12.[12]

#### (ii) *Waiver and acquiescence*

An applicant who submits to a decision knowing it to be defective, for example by acting upon a decision vitiated by a procedural defect, or accepting the jurisdiction of a biased or unqualified tribunal has sometimes been denied a remedy.[13] Conceptual difficulties have been perceived in the notion of waiver, it being denied that jurisdiction can be conferred upon a tribunal by any form of consent or acquiescence.[14] In this connection a distinction has sometimes been drawn between 'total want of jurisdiction' in the sense of an absence of any power at all over the subject matter and a 'contingent defect' such as bias or a procedural error, it being argued that the former cannot be waived whereas the latter can be.[15] It is submitted that these difficulties are irrelevant, waiver being a matter of discretion. The courts no longer apply the logic of nullity in a strict sense.

10 In the case of certiorari time runs from the date of the decision: RSC Ord 53, r 4(2). For mandamus it is presumably the refusal to perform the duty following a demand where necessary. In other cases notice of the defect is arguably the correct date.
11 The latter also applies at the trial stage.
12 Below p 135 et seq.
13 *London Corpn v Cox* (1867) LR 2 HL 239, 36 LJEx 225; *R v Williams, ex p Phillips* [1914] 1 KB 608, 83 LJKB 528.
14 *Farquharson v Morgan* [1894] 1 QB 552 at 560, CA.
15 *Essex County Council v Essex Congregational Church Union* [1963] AC 808, [1963] 1 All ER 326, HL. See also *R v Campbell, ex p Nomikos* [1956] 2 All ER 280, [1956] 1 WLR 622 (plea of guilty, no certiorari).

### (iii) *Bad faith*

An applicant for judicial review has a duty *uberrimae fidei* to disclose all relevant information available to him.[16] Should the applicant fail to disclose documents or other evidence of which he is actually aware, the court is entitled in its discretion to refuse a remedy. Here it will be particularly important to balance the public interest against the applicant's own conduct and interests. Similarly an applicant may not obtain a remedy in respect of a decision which is invalid because of his own culpable error.[17] The authority must also make disclosure of its reasoning where relevant.[18]

### (iv) *Misconduct*

The court has a general discretion to take into account the applicant's bad behaviour in relation to the subject matter of the application. Where this takes the form only of delay, then, as we have seen, a special statutory regime applies, but in other cases the court's discretion appears to be at large. For example in *Ward v Bradford Corpn*[19] a student who had been expelled from a college of education as a result of a decision which was held to have contravened the governing regulations was refused an injunction as a matter of discretion. The court appeared to have been influenced by the fact that her alleged misconduct was said to have involved cohabitation with a man, for which reason Lord Denning MR opined that she would never make a teacher.[20] However, the present Master of the Rolls, Sir Thomas Bingham, has stated extrajudicially that misconduct *per se*, unless it is related to the conduct of the proceedings, is an unsatisfactory ground for refusing relief.[1] Indeed such a ground of refusal would come very close to the court trespassing upon the merits of the decision.

## Alternative remedies

There are many methods of challenging governmental decisions apart from Ord 53 proceedings. These range from, at the one extreme, general political remedies, exercisable through Parliament, to statutory provisions for challenge in the High Court before the same judges and upon the same grounds as in the case of Ord 53 applications.[2] In between these extremes, there is a wide range of specific rights of appeal or default powers entrusted to ministers or tribunals.

The governing principle is that the court will refuse to grant a judicial review remedy where another suitable remedy is available. The general principle applies to all the remedies, but its application may differ in particular contexts. Unless the other remedy is clearly made exclusive the court will treat

16 *R v Kensington Income Tax Comrs, ex p Princess de Polignac* [1917] 1 KB 486, 86 LJKB 257, CA; *White v Kuzych* [1951] AC 585, [1951] 2 All ER 435, PC. See also *R v Board of Inland Revenue, ex p MFK Underwriting Agencies Ltd* [1990] 1 All ER 91.

17 *R v Secretary of State for Education and Science, ex p Birmingham District Council* (1984) Times, 18 July.

18 See *R v Lancashire County Council* (above, n 4).

19 (1972) 115 Sol Jo 606, CA.

20 See also *Glynn v Keele University* [1971] 2 All ER 89, [1971] 1 WLR 487 (plaintiff guilty of charge); *Cinnamond v British Airports Authority* [1980] 2 All ER 368, [1980] 1 WLR 582, CA (persistent offences).

1 [1991] PL 64 at 71.

2 Below ch 17.

the matter as one of discretion.[3] It seems that the applicant must show at the leave stage some special reason for not using the statutory machinery[4] but the matter can also be argued in depth at the hearing. As in other discretionary areas the court may at this stage refuse a remedy but deal with the merits.[5]

The various kinds of remedy will be considered in turn.

*Parliamentary remedies*

Parliamentary remedies have no direct effect on judicial review, except in as much as the court cannot interfere with proceedings in Parliament. Legality and political merits are, in theory at any rate, distinct matters, and the availability of an opportunity to complain to a member of Parliament or to the Parliamentary Commissioner will not justify the court withholding a remedy.[6] However, the existence of Parliamentary safeguards may have indirect effect, for example in determining whether a decision is reasonable or a hearing fair,[7] and may affect the choice of remedy.[8]

*Public interest remedies*

There is no reason to believe that the existence of powers vested in the Attorney General or other functionaries to institute legal proceedings has any effect on the right of an individual with locus standi to institute proceedings in his own name, except where an express power is given to enforce a statutory duty.

*Appeals*

Statutory rights of appeal might be given to the High Court itself, or to a tribunal or to a minister. The same basic principle applies in all cases. The court will look at all the circumstances and will require the applicant to exhaust the statutory remedy

> save in exceptional circumstances. By definition exceptional circumstances defy definition but where Parliament has provided an appeal procedure judicial review will have no place unless the applicant can distinguish his case from the run of cases for which the appeal procedure was provided.[9]

The modern approach is more restrictive than the old law which was content to allow judicial review unless the statutory remedy was equally convenient.[10] In *Ex p Swati*[11] judicial review was reformed even though the statutory appeal was less convenient because the applicant would have to leave the country in

3 *Roy v Kensington, Chelsea and Westminster Family Practitioner Committee* [1992] 1 All ER 705 at 714–5; *Leech v Deputy Governor of Parkhurst Prison* [1988] 2 WLR 290 at 306.

4 *R v Secretary of State for the Home Department, ex p Swati* [1986] 1 All ER 717 at 723–4.

5 But see *R v Brentford General Comrs, ex p Chan* [1986] STC 65 per Taylor J.

6 *IRC v National Federation of Self-Employed and Small Businesses Ltd* [1982] AC 617 at 644, [1981] 2 All ER 93 at 107.

7 Above, p 38.

8 *R v HM Treasury, ex p Smedley* [1985] QB 657, [1985] 1 All ER 589, CA. Above, p 42.

9 *R v Secretary of State for the Home Department, ex p Swati* [1986] 1 All ER 717 at 724 per Sir John Donaldson MR. See also *R v Chief Constable of Merseyside Police, ex p Calveley* [1986] QB 424 at 433, 435; *Re Preston* [1985] AC 835 at 952; *R v Epping and Harlow General Comrs, ex p Goldstraw* [1983] 3 All ER 257 at 262.

10 See Wade *Administrative Law* (6th edn 1988) pp 712–6.

11 Above, n 9. Contrast *R v Chief Immigration Officer Gatwick Airport, ex p Kharrazi* [1980] 3 All ER 373, [1980] 1 WLR 1396, CA—applicant unable to return to country.

order to exercise it, but this was not 'exceptional'. However it may be that, in their result the cases are more liberal.[12]

Before looking at the way in which the court exercises its discretion a preliminary difficulty must be mentioned. It has sometimes been held that appeals and reviews are mutually exclusive. If this is correct, then of course no question of discretion arises. The grounds of judicial review could not be raised in appeal proceedings.[13] This is sometimes rationalised by the proposition that there can be no appeal against a nullity,[14] providing another example of the strict jurisdictional concept which is no longer reliable.

This view is not generally supported. First, because judicial review extends to errors of law there is a large overlap between review and appeal, a right of appeal sometimes being restricted to errors of law.[15] Second, the idea that an invalid decision is a nullity for all purposes has been rejected, specifically in relation to appeals.[16] Third, the overwhelming weight of authority treats the relationship between appeal and review as one of discretion.[17] In *Chief Adjudication Officer v Foster*[18] the House of Lords held that an appeal tribunal can determine whether the rules which it is required to apply are ultra vires.

Recent cases assert that where there is a statutory right of appeal, judicial review will be permitted only in exceptional cases, where the appeal machinery is clearly inadequate or the issues are important enough to transcend the particular dispute between the parties.[19] However it has been suggested that this rhetoric may mask a more flexible approach favouring judicial review where there is a strong case on the merits.[20]

The following factors have been held to favour judicial review but none are conclusive:

(i) expense, including the applicant's resources and legal aid matters.[1] Cost effectiveness is openly articulated as an important factor in judicial review cases[2] and one justification for the allegedly strict approach in appeal cases is to ration limited judicial resources. Many statutory appeals are entrusted to deputy judges;

(ii) the significance for third parties of the issues;[3]

12 Eg *Swati* seems to have been an attempt to challenge on the facts. See Bingham (1991) PL 64 at 71. See *R v Birmingham City Council ex p Ferrero* [1993] 1 All ER 530, CA.

13 See *Chapman v Earl* [1968] 2 All ER 1214, [1968] 1 WLR 1315; *Henry Moss of London Ltd v Customs & Excise Comr* [1981] 2 All ER 86 at 90, CA, where the court dealt with the case as one of review.

14 *Ridge v Baldwin* [1964] AC 40, [1963] 2 All ER 66, HL.

15 Above, p 14 et seq.

16 *Calvin v Carr* [1980] AC 574, [1979] 2 All ER 440, PC.

17 *Re Preston* [1985] AC 835 at 862 and below passim.

18 [1993] 2 WLR 292. But see *R v Secretary of State for the Home Department, ex p Malhi* [1991] 1 QB 194, [1990] 2 All ER 357, CA—right of appeal on grounds that no 'power in law' to make decision did not include unfairness. Cf *R v Secretary of State for the Home Department, ex p Oladehinde* [1991] 1 AC 254.

19 *Re Preston* [1985] AC 835 at 852, 862; *R v Epping and Harlow General Comrs, ex p Goldstraw* [1983] 3 All ER 257 at 262; *R v Secretary of State for the Home Department, ex p Swati* [1986] 1 All ER 717 at 723–4; *R v Chief Constable of Merseyside Police, ex p Calverley* [1986] QB 424 at 433, CA.

20 See Wade *Administrative Law* (6th edn) p 714–6; Bingham (1991), PL 64 at 71, 72.

1 *R v IT Special Purposes Comr, ex p Stipplechoice Ltd* [1985] 2 All ER 465 at 470, CA; *R v Inspector of Taxes, ex p Kissane* [1986] 2 All ER 37 at 40; *R v Panel on Take-overs and Mergers, ex p Guinness plc* [1989] 1 All ER 509 at 526f.

2 *R v Secretary of State for Employment, ex p Equal Opportunities Commission* [1992] 1 All ER 545 at 558; *R v Panel on Take-overs and Mergers, ex p Guinness plc* [1989] 1 All ER 509 at 526.

3 *R v Paddington Valuation Officer, ex p Peachey Properties Ltd* [1965] 2 All ER 836 at 840; *R v Huntingdon District Council, ex p Cowen* [1984] 1 All ER 58 at 63; *R v Secretary of State for Social Services, ex p Equal Opportunities Commission* [1992] 1 All ER 545 at 557.

(iii) the novelty or gravity of the issues;[4]
(iv) the more comprehensive remedies available under Ord 53;[5] and
(v) the ability to investigate facts more thoroughly in Ord 53 proceedings.[6]

Other relevant factors include speed,[7] technical expertise[8] and an analogy with private law issues.[9] The court will not permit judicial review merely because the time limit for the appeal has passed.[10] Where the appellate body has a wide jurisdiction to examine all the issues at one sitting this may be preferable to judicial review, particularly where policy issues are involved.[11] The intended scope of the appeal mechanism is a basic consideration.[12]

It may be that where the complaint centres upon the core judicial review issues of fairness and reasonableness, the presence of an appeal procedure will not prevent access to judicial review.[13] In the overwhelming majority of reported cases the courts have allowed judicial review.

The appeal decision is itself susceptible to judicial review on ordinary principles. Some defect must therefore be found in the appeal decision. However this may entail examining the validity of the decision appealed against where, for example, it is sought to show that an initial defect has not been put right on appeal.[14]

*Default powers*

Many statutes confer powers on ministers to intervene in the event of a failure by a local authority to perform a duty. Default powers range from a discretion to take over the activity in question to a statutory power to apply to the court for mandamus. Powers to give directions to the authority are very common. In some cases a default power can be exercised only in the event of 'unreasonableness'. It has been held, perhaps surprisingly, that unreasonableness in this context is the very low standard of *Wednesbury* unreasonableness,[15] thus making the minister's power analogous to that of a reviewing court. In other cases the scope of the power to intervene does not depend upon any finding of wrongdoing.[16]

4 *R v Panel on Take-overs and Mergers, ex p Guinness plc* [1989] 1 All ER 509 at 530; *R v Huntingdon District Council, ex p Cowen* (above, n 3); *R v Chief Constable of Merseyside Police, ex p Calverley* [1986] QB 424, [1986] 1 All ER 257, CA.
5 *Bone v Mental Health Review Tribunal* [1985] 3 All ER 330 at 334; *Leech v Deputy Governor of Parkhurst Prison* [1988] AC 533, [1988] 1 All ER 485, HL.
6 *R v Inspector of Taxes, ex p Kissane* (above, n 1); *R v Secretary of State for Employment, ex p Equal Opportunities Commission* [1992] 1 All ER 545 at 558.
7 This may point in either direction. *R v Secretary of State for Employment, ex p Equal Opportunities Commission* [1992] 1 All ER 545 at 558 but cf *R v Chief Constable of Merseyside Police, ex p Calverley* [1986] QB 424 at 436; *R v Birmingham City Council, ex p Ferrero Ltd* (1991) 155 JP 721, CA.
8 *R v Hallstrom, ex p W* [1985] 3 All ER 775 at 789–90.
9 *R v Civil Service Appeals Board, ex p Bruce* [1988] 3 All ER 686 at 694, 696–7, 701; *R v Lord Chancellor's Department, ex p Nangle* [1992] 1 All ER 897 at 908.
10 *R v Epping and Harlow General Comrs, ex p Goldstraw* above, n 19.
11 *R v Hillingdon London Borough Council, ex p Royco Homes Ltd* [1974] 2 All ER 643 at 648–9. (The statement at 649 that the matter of law must appear on the face of the order is questionable). See Town and Country Planning Act 1990, s 79(1). See also *Square Meals Frozen Foods Ltd v Dunstable Borough Council* [1974] 1 All ER 441, [1974] 1 WLR 59, CA.
12 See *ex p Swati* (above, n 19).
13 Eg *Re Preston* (above, n 19).
14 See *Calvin v Carr* (above, n 16).
15 *Secretary of State for Education and Science v Tameside Metropolitan Borough Council* [1977] AC 1014.
16 Eg *R v Secretary of State for the Environment, ex p Norwich City Council* [1982] QB 808.

The relationship between default powers and judicial review is a politically sensitive one, in that where it is alleged that an authority has failed to perform a statutory duty, the court is sometimes being required in effect to instruct a political body how to spend public money. Indeed it is sometimes suggested on the basis of the decision of the House of Lords in *Pasmore v Oswaldtwistle UDC*[17] that the existence of a statutory method of enforcing a duty is enough in itself to exclude the courts. This is, however, too broad as a distinction exists between two kinds of case. These are first, cases where an applicant is pursuing only a prerogative order, and second, where the applicant is claiming that the duty in question creates a private right vested in the applicant and enforceable by damages.

Where an applicant is seeking a prerogative order, the matter is for the discretion of the court. The general presumption against ousting the jurisdiction of the courts applies, so that express words or necessary implication are necessary to exclude the prerogative jurisdiction altogether.[18]

However, if the statutory remedy is at least as convenient, effective and expeditious, the court is unlikely to intervene. Nor will the court intervene in a case where the duty in question is unsuitable for judicial enforcement. This may be because continuous supervision is required or because the matter involves technical expertise or the exercise of a political discretion such as a choice between financial priorities.[19]

Different considerations arise where a plaintiff or applicant attempts to assert a private law cause of action in respect of a failure to comply with a statutory duty. This was the position in *Pasmore v Oswaldtwistle UDC.*[20] The case did not concern the prerogative order of mandamus but involved the now obsolete common law action for mandamus which was analogous to a mandatory injunction.[1] In this kind of case as we have seen the existence of a statutory default power in the same statute will normally be taken as an indication that Parliament did not intend the duty to confer a cause of action upon an individual.

There are two main exceptions. The first exception is where 'the act complained of constitutes malfeasance and not mere nonfeasance',[2] ie the authority has performed a positive act as opposed to a failure to comply with the duty. This distinction sometimes seems to be merely semantic. For example, a school closure can be classified under either head. In *R v Secretary of State for the Environment, ex p Ward*[3] Woolf J confined this distinction to cases

17 [1898] AC 387, 67 LJQB 635, HL; *Doe d Bishop of Rochester v Bridges* (1831) 1 B & Ad 847 at 859.

18 *R v Hounslow London Borough Council, ex p Pizzey* [1977] 1 All ER 305, [1977] 1 WLR 58; *R v Paddington Valuation Officer, ex p Peachey Property Corpn* [1966] 1 QB 380, [1965] 2 All ER 836, CA.

19 *R v Secretary of State for the Environment, ex p Ward* [1984] 2 All ER 556, [1984] 1 WLR 834; *R v Bristol Corpn, ex p Hendy* [1974] 1 All ER 1047, [1974] 1 WLR 498, CA. See also *R v Poplar Borough Council, ex p LCC* [1922] 1 KB 72 at 94. Beatson and Matthews, op cit at 557–8.

20 Above, n 17.

1 Common Law Procedure Act 1854, ss 68–73. See de Smith *Judicial Review of Administrative Action* (1st edn, 1959) pp 425–428; *Glossop v Heston and Isleworth Local Board* (1879) 12 Ch D 102 at 122, CA and *Kensington and Chelsea London Borough Council, ex p Wells* (1973) 72 LGR 289 appear also to support the distinction between prerogative order cases and private right cases. But see [1898] 387 at 398 per Lord MacNaghten.

2 *Meade v London Borough of Haringey* [1979] 2 All ER 1016, [1974] 1 WLR 637, CA; *Bradbury v London Borough of Enfield* [1967] 3 All ER 434, [1967] 1 WLR 1311, CA; *Cumings v Birkenhead Corpn* [1972] Ch 12, 36.

3 Above, n 19. See also *R v Secretary of State for the Environment, ex p Lee and Bond* (1985) 54 P & CR 311 at 322. *Beatson and Matthews*, op cit 557–8.

involving private law remedies as opposed to prerogative order cases. The rationale of this exception seems to be that there is more than a mere breach of duty, for which the default procedure applies, but an unlawful exercise of discretion, which is a matter for the courts. On this basis the exception also seems relevant to the court's discretion in prerogative order cases.

The second exception is where the applicant has suffered special damage such as personal injuries or been refused some entitlement to which he is specifically entitled.[4] Here again the statutory remedy is unlikely to be adequate. Conversely, where the applicant is representing a general class of people affected by the failure to provide a public service the statutory remedy is likely to be exclusive.

Finally, it is worth remembering that in some cases a failure to comply with a statutory duty may also be tortious at common law, for example if the failure is negligent, or if the authority commits a nuisance.[5] Here the existence of a statutory default power does not in itself affect the question of liability, although it may still be construed either as authorising the tort in question or as conferring a degree of immunity.

## The effect of the remedy

The court will refuse to issue a remedy which serves no useful purpose. The court will also consider the effect of the remedy applied for in terms of the public interest in efficient administration and in practicability. We will examine each of these considerations in turn.

### *No useful purpose*

This has two aspects. First, the particular remedy may not make any difference to the applicant. In *R v Walton General Comrs, ex p Wilson*[6] the applicant sought certiorari to quash an allegedly erroneous PAYE tax coding. It was held that even if an error of law had been committed the court would not award certiorari because the quashing of the decision would not entitle him to a repayment of tax. Under the governing legislation repayments of tax improperly exacted could be made only under prescribed procedures. Similarly mandamus has been refused where the duty in question could not practicably be performed.[7] However, the fact that performance will cause difficulties or may not be effective is not sufficient ground to refuse a remedy.[8]

Another similar discretionary ground concerns cases where the applicant has in the court's eyes suffered no injustice as a result of the decision, so that there is no point in judicial intervention.[9] This is a controversial area of the law since it raises a conflict between the court's duty to ensure that governmental

4 *Ching v Surrey County Council* [1910] 1 KB 736, CA; *Guardians of the Poor of Gateshead Union v Durham County Council* [1918] 1 Ch 146, CA.

5 *Ministry of Housing and Local Government v Sharp* [1970] 2 QB 223, [1970] 1 All ER 1009, CA; *Pride of Derby and Derbyshire Angling Association Ltd v British Celanese Ltd* [1953] Ch 149, [1953] 1 All ER 179, CA.

6 [1981] STC 610 Slade J, affd [1983] STC 464, CA.

7 *R v Bristol Corpn, ex p Hendy* [1974] 1 All ER 1047, [1974] 1 WLR 498, CA.

8 *A-G v (at the relation of Allen) Colchester Corpn (or BC)* [1955] 2 QB 207, [1955] 2 All ER 124; *R v LCC, ex p Corrie* [1918] 1 KB 68, 87 LJKB 303. But see *R v Secretary of State for Social Services, ex p Association of Metropolitan Authorities* [1986] 1 All ER 164, [1986] 1 WLR 1.

9 *R v Secretary of State for Foreign and Commonwealth Affairs, ex p Everett* [1989] 1 All ER 655 at 659.

agencies act lawfully, and the public interest in discouraging unnecessary litigation. It is a fundamental principle that the court will not act in vain, so that a decision will not be quashed where the court takes the view that the defect did not affect the actual decision.[10]

This principle has been applied in cases where it has been held that an applicant denied a hearing has no remedy if the failure has not affected the outcome.[11] Strong reservations have been expressed about this on the ground that due process is of special importance to the rule of law, and also that outcomes are rarely so certain.[12] It probably has to be established with absolute certainty that a hearing would have been futile.

*Administrative convenience*

The courts do not take the maxim *fiat justitia* to extreme lengths. Administrative and public inconvenience is a factor to be weighed in the balance in deciding whether to grant a remedy. Thus in *Coney v Choyce*,[13] Templeman J would have refused an injunction to prevent the reorganisation of a group of schools, stating that he would be 'very slow to introduce the swingeing weapon of an injunction interfering in educational matters of great moment by the sledgehammer of an injunction which would bring to a halt all the co-operation from these two places which had been obtained in the course of the last few years'. However, where private rights are involved, the court is unlikely to refuse a remedy altogether. An injunction or mandamus can be postponed or a declaration can be granted rather than a coercive remedy.[14] Alternatively an undertaking to comply with the law may be obtained.[15]

There appears to be a wide variation in judicial attitudes as regards the weight to be given to considerations of administrative convenience. There are dicta that governmental illegality must be curbed come what may,[16] but the weight of recent authority is in favour of exercising discretion.[17] In this connection, however, there has been little attempt to develop the law of

10 *R v Crown Court at Knightsbridge, ex p Marcrest Ltd* [1983] 1 All ER 1148, [1983] 1 WLR 300, CA.

11 *Glynn v Keele University* [1971] 2 All ER 89, [1971] 1 WLR 487; *Malloch v Aberdeen Corpn* [1971] 2 All ER 1278, [1971] 1 WLR 1578; *Cinnamond v British Airports Authority* [1980] 2 All ER 368, [1980] 1 WLR 582, CA. Cf *Cheal v Association of Professional, Executive, Clerical and Computer Staff* [1983] 2 AC 180, [1983] 1 All ER 1130, HL; *Beatson and Matthews* p 343.

12 *R v Chief Constable of Thames Valley Police, ex p Cotton* [1990] IRLR 344, CA per Bingham LJ; *John v Rees* [1970] Ch 345, 402. *Lloyd v McMahon* [1987] AC 625 at 653, 669; *Ridge v Baldwin* [1964] AC 40, HL; *R v Thames Magistrates Court, ex p Polemis* [1974] 1 WLR 1371 at 1375–6. See Clark (1975) PL 27.

13 [1975] 1 All ER 979 at 991. See also *Meade v London Borough of Haringey* [1979] 2 All ER 1016, [1979] 1 WLR 637, CA; *R v Monopolies and Mergers Commission, ex p Argyle Group plc* [1986] 2 All ER 257 at 266.

14 *Pride of Derby and Derbyshire Angling Association Ltd v British Celanese Ltd* [1953] Ch 149, [1953] 1 All ER 179; *R v Paddington Valuation Officer, ex p Peachey Property Corpn Ltd* [1966] 1 QB 380, [1965] 2 All ER 836, CA; *R v Secretary of State for Social Services, ex p Association of Metropolitan Authorities* [1986] 1 All ER 164, [1986] 1 WLR 1.

15 *St Mary, Islington Vestry v Hornsey Urban Council* [1900] 1 Ch 695, 69 LJ Ch 324, CA; *Hanson v Radcliffe UDC* [1922] 2 Ch 490 at 503; *Guardians of the Poor of Gateshead Union v Durham County Council* [1918] 1 Ch 146 at 164; *Llandudno UDC v Woods* [1899] 2 Ch 705, 68 LJ Ch 623 (triviality).

16 See *R v Paddington Valuation Officer, ex p Peachey Property Corpn Ltd* [1966] 1 QB 380 at 419, [1965] 2 All ER 836 at 852 per Salmon LJ. See also *Bradbury v London Borough of Enfield* [1967] 3 All ER 434 at 442 per Dankwerts LJ.

17 *R v Monopolies and Mergers Commission, ex p Argyle Group plc* [1986] 2 All ER 257, [1986] 1 WLR 763, CA.

damages as a possible alternative to the invalidation of governmental action.[18] The question of public convenience may also manifest itself as a factor relating to substantive questions, for example whether a procedural requirement is to be regarded as mandatory or directory.[19] Administrative convenience cannot in itself justify a failure to comply with natural justice except to the extent that the decision-making process may be frustrated.[20]

*Supervision*

The court will not normally issue a remedy in circumstances where it would be impracticable to supervise its implementation.[1] This discretionary ground has only a limited application in public law cases, but could apply where a mandatory injunction or mandamus is sought in relation to a continuing series of acts. However, in such cases, and in analogous contexts, such as the provision of schools, difficulties of supervision may be a reason for regarding statutory default as a more appropriate remedy. Alternatively judicial intervention could be confined to the prohibition of a formal act such as the closure of a railway or school.

*Employment*

Except in special cases the courts are unwilling to make orders requiring specific performance of contracts of employment. However, this does not prevent mandamus lying to require the restoration of the applicant to a statutory public office, although even here a declaration is often the more appropriate remedy.[2]

## SEVERANCE

Can a decision which is tainted by illegality be upheld in part and the invalid part struck out without affecting what remains? In general, when the court quashes a decision, the authority is free to determine the matter again. For example, where a court quashes a refusal by a minister to grant planning permission, it does not follow that permission must be granted. The position depends upon the nature of the defect and the circumstances. At one extreme, if the only defect consists of a failure to state reasons with sufficient clarity, the minister is entitled to put matters right by issuing another decision later.[3] If on the other hand relevant matters have not been taken into account, or there has been a breach of natural justice, the entire decision-making process may have to be repeated. The minister is entitled, and indeed bound, to redetermine the matter and to take into account new circumstances which have arisen since the

18 See *F Hoffmann-La-Roche & Co A G v Secretary of State for Trade and Industry* [1975] AC 295 at 359, [1974] 2 All ER 1128 at 1148 per Lord Wilberforce.

19 See *Simpson v A-G* [1955] NZLR 271. Above pp 23–24.

20 *R v Board of Visitors Hull Prison, ex p St Germain (No 2)* [1979] 3 All ER 545, [1979] 1 WLR 1401. *General Medical Council v Spackman* [1943] AC 627 at 638, HL.

1 *A-G (at the relation of Allen) v Colchester Corpn (or BC)* [1955] 2 QB 207, [1955] 2 All ER 124; *Meade v London Borough of Haringey* [1979] 2 All ER 1016, [1979] 1 WLR 637, CA.

2 *Chief Constable of North Wales Police v Evans* [1982] 3 All ER 141, [1982] 1 WLR 1155, HL (appellant had resigned).

3 *Price Bros (Rode Heath) Ltd v Department of the Environment* (1979) 38 P & CR 579, 252 Estates Gazette 595; *Ridge v Baldwin* [1964] AC 40 at 92, HL.

decision was made, so that in the case of discretionary decisions the citizen's victory may be shortlived. The court may, however, issue mandamus to require the tribunal to make a new decision. Indeed, if the circumstances are such that there is only one decision that could lawfully be made, a declaration may also be appropriate.[4]

The question of severance arises in two main kinds of case. First, there are cases where a decision goes too far, for example where an ultra vires requirement or penalty is imposed on the citizen, or an order includes a geographical area outside its limits. Second, there are cases where a valid licence or permission is subject to an invalid condition. Although the principles to be applied in each kind of case are broadly similar, the problems raised by conditions are sufficiently specialised to require separate treatment.

## Excessive orders

Dealing first with the question of excessive decisions, these can be severed or even modified provided that what remains is within the substantial purpose and effect of the instrument. The court must be sure that the altered provision would have been made by the decision-maker had he been aware of the limits on his powers.[5] The court is not limited to the old mechanical 'blue pencil' test under which severance is permissible if what remains makes grammatical sense. Indeed the court is not limited to any particular form of drafting. The court can make a declaration stating the effect of the instrument shorn of the invalid part. The court cannot of course do the government's job for it. A crucial limitation on severance is therefore that what is left after severance must be in substance unchanged. It is not clear from the cases whether the requirement that the decision-maker would still have made the altered decision is a reinforcement of or an alternative to this requirement. The better view is that both requirements are necessary in order to prevent the court from usurping the role of the government.[6]

*Thames Water Authority v Elmbridge Borough Council*[7] concerned a compulsory purchase order which included a piece of land to which the appropriate power did not apply. However, the document on its face did not specifically refer to the land in question, and the illegality would be discerned only by knowing the actual user of the land. The court looked at the circumstances, including geography, and upheld a modified order. Similarly in *DPP v Hutchinson*[8] regulations prohibited access to Ministry of Defence land but the statute in question did not authorise control over common land. The regulation was enforced in relation to land other than common land. In *Woolwich Equitable Building Society v IRC*[9] the whole of a regulation was declared void because one of its sub-rules was invalid. This was because, without the offending rule, the tax rate to be charged became unclear and the rewriting of it would be speculative.

4 Eg *Anisminic Ltd v Foreign Compensation Commission* [1967] 2 AC 147, [1969] 1 All ER 208, HL.
5 *Woolwich Equitable Building Society v IRC* [1991] 4 All ER 92, HL; *DPP v Hutchinson* [1990] 2 AC 783, [1990] 2 All ER 836, HL.
6 *Woolwich Equitable Building Society v IRC* (above, n 5) at 104, 108.
7 See also *Dunkley v Evans* [1981] 3 All ER 285, [1981] 1 WLR 1522; *United City Merchants (Investments) Ltd and Glass Fibres and Equipments Ltd v Royal Bank of Canada, Vitrorefuerzos SA and Banco Continental SA (incorporated in Canada)* [1982] 2 All ER 720 at 736, [1982] 2 WLR 1039 at 1051, HL.
8 [1990] 2 AC 783, [1990] 2 All ER 836, HL.
9 [1991] 4 All ER 92 at 104–107.

However the court will lean in favour of upholding the decision and will take into account the needs of good administration.[10]

## The limits of severance

Thus with the aid of the presumption of validity, the court can give effect to a partially defective decision by enforcing it to the extent that it can lawfully be enforced. In cases of physical excesses such as in *Elmbridge* itself, this will usually be straightforward. It will also be possible to enforce decisions which contain several distinct orders of which one or more is unlawful, as in the case of demands for payment or for information.[11] Decisions which impose a single penalty which the court holds to be unreasonable are more difficult. If the court were to reduce the penalty to a more reasonable one, or to the maximum permitted, this would come very near to exercising the tribunal's discretion for it, and goes beyond the sphere of judicial review. In this kind of case, the court will normally quash the entire decision.[12] For the same reason, severance may be inappropriate in cases where the decision is tainted by an abuse of discretion.

Conversely, the statutory duty to give adequate reason for a decision can be regarded as a duty which is separate from the decision itself and although mandatory in the sense that compliance can be compelled, a breach need not necessarily invalidate the decision.[13] Similarly, there is the case of a failure to comply with a statutory duty to consult interested parties before making a decision on a statutory order. In one case, involving this defect, it was held that the order remained valid but was not binding on those who were not consulted.[14] It is arguable that a similar principle applies to a breach of the *audi alteram partem* rule of natural justice.

### *Invalid conditions*

Perhaps the most difficult case of severance is where a licence, or permission, is granted subject to an invalid condition. Here, as a matter of language, it may be relatively easy to sever the condition, but this may have the result that the permission is no longer the sort of permission which the authority would wish to grant. For example, there are cases where a condition is held to be unreasonable but where the policy reason for imposing the condition would itself be lawful so as to justify refusing the permission entirely.[15] In this kind of case, it may be in the public interest to quash the whole permission. The majority of cases concern planning permissions which are arguably a special case because an individual planning condition is part of a larger entity in the sense that it is part of an overall land use strategy and has an impact both on other planning

10 See *Thames Water Authority v Elmbridge Borough Council* [1983] 1 All ER 836 at 844, 847–8, CA.

11 *Potato Marketing Board v Merricks* [1958] 2 QB 316 at 333, [1958] 2 All ER 538 at 547; *Daymond v South West Water Authority* [1976] AC 609, [1976] 1 All ER 39, HL.

12 Eg *R v Barnsley Metropolitan Borough Council, ex p Hook* [1976] 3 All ER 452, [1976] 1 WLR 1052, CA. But see *Jackson Stansfield & Sons v Butterworth* [1948] 2 All ER 558, CA; *Dennis & Co Ltd v Munn* [1949] 2 KB 327, [1949] 1 All ER 616, CA. See the Supreme Court Act 1981, s 43.

13 *Brayhead (Ascot) Ltd v Berkshire County Council* [1964] 2 QB 303, [1964] 1 All ER 149. Cf Crake v Supplementary Benefits Commission [1982] 1 All ER 498.

14 *Agricultural, Horticultural and Forestry Industry Training Board v Aylesbury Mushrooms Ltd* [1972] 1 All ER 280, [1972] 1 WLR 190.

15 Eg *Hall & Co Ltd v Shoreham-by-Sea UDC* [1964] 1 All ER 1, [1964] 1 WLR 240, CA.

permissions and upon any development plan in force in the area.[16] It is arguable, therefore, that a planning condition, at least where it relates to the physical use of the land, should rarely be severed, but the whole permission should fall. This does not necessarily apply, for example, to cinema or trading licences. In all cases, however, the object of the particular legislation is the controlling factor. Thus if the licence minus the offending condition still fulfils the objectives of the Act, the condition should be severable. Indeed, except in the case of planning permissions, the courts appear usually to have regarded conditions as severable, albeit there has been little discussion of the reasons for doing so.[17] In the case of planning permissions, the entire permission has usually been quashed.[18]

The language used in the planning cases is far from precise but there seems to be a presumption against severance and a condition will be struck out only where it is 'trivial' or 'unimportant', or 'not part of the structure of the permission'.[19] Perhaps the most useful guidance is to be found in the speech of Lord Reid in *Kent County Council v Kingway Investments (Kent) Ltd.*[20] His Lordship distinguished between two classes of conditions. First, there are conditions which are imposed for reasons totally unrelated to the proper purposes of the governing legislation. These should always be severable, since ex hypothesi the same reasons could not justify refusing permission.[1] Second, there are conditions which are imposed for proper reasons, but invalid only because they are unreasonably onerous. Here the position depends upon whether the condition physically restricts the use of land. If it does, then the whole permission should fall, since to allow an unconditional permission might frustrate legitimate planning objectives.[2] If on the other hand the condition is unreasonable, but does not physically restrict the use of the land, then the matter depends on the importance of the condition.[3]

16 See *Kent County Council v Kingsway Investments (Kent) Ltd* [1971] AC 72 at 106–107, [1970] 1 All ER 70 at 88 per Lord Guest.

17 Eg *Ellis v Dubowski* [1921] 3 KB 621, 91 LJKB 89; *Associated Provincial Picture Houses Ltd v Wednesbury Corpn* [1948] 1 KB 223, [1947] 2 All ER 680, CA; *Chertsey UDC v Mixnam's Properties Ltd* [1965] AC 735, [1964] 2 All ER 627, HL.

18 If a minister decides the question of severance on appeal, the court will usually not interfere with the exercise of his discretion: *Newbury District Council v Secretary of State for the Environment* [1981] AC 578, [1980] 1 All ER 731, HL.

19 See *Hall & Co Ltd v Shoreham-by-Sea UDC* [1964] 1 WLR 240 at 251, 252, CA; *Kent County Council v Kingsway Investments (Kent) Ltd* [1971] AC 72 at 91, 102, 114, [1970] 1 All ER 70 at 86, 89, 96, HL; *R v Hillingdon London Borough Council, ex p Royco Homes Ltd* [1974] QB 720, [1974] 2 All ER 643.

20 [1971] AC 72, [1970] 1 All ER 70, HL.

1 Eg *Chertsey UDC v Mixnams Properties* [1965] AC 735, [1964] 2 All ER 627.

2 Eg *R v Hillingdon London Borough Council, ex p Royco Homes Ltd* [1974] QB 720, [1974] 2 All ER 643; *Hall & Co Ltd v Shoreham-by-Sea UDC* [1964] 1 All ER 1, [1964] 1 WLR 240, CA.

3 Eg *Kent County Council v Kingsway Investments (Kent) Ltd* [1971] AC 72, [1970] 1 All ER 70.

CHAPTER 12

# Time limits and the effect of delay on applications for judicial review

Applications for judicial review are subject to tight time limits. The court can refuse leave to apply or substantive relief as a result of quite short periods of delay. Indeed one of the purposes of having a leave requirement is to protect public authorities from having to deal with unjustifiably late applications. The provisions for delay can be summarised as follows:

(a) applications for leave must be made promptly and in any event within three months, but the court may extend time if there is a good reason to do so;

(b) if there has been undue delay then the court may refuse leave or substantive relief if the granting of relief would be likely to cause substantial hardship to, or substantially prejudice the rights of, any person or would be detrimental to good administration;

(c) a failure to apply promptly or in any event within three months will be treated as undue delay;

(d) the courts still treat the issue of delay as a matter of discretion within the context of the express provisions summarised above.

The consequences of a refusal to grant relief due to delay may be dramatic. The applicant will lose the right to challenge a decision otherwise than collaterally.[1] This is so even if the challenged decision would otherwise be held to be ultra vires. An invalid decision which the courts refuse to do anything about is given the effect in law of a valid decision.[2] This notion is sometimes glorified by the maxim *omnia praesumuntur rite esse acta*.[3] The continued right to mount a collateral attack (eg by way of defence to possession proceedings) may appear anomalous in this context but it may provide a practical safeguard against unlawful government which would otherwise be unhindered due to procedural irregularities.

## EXPRESS TIME LIMITS

The problem of delay in applying for judicial review is dealt with in two different express provisions. They are RSC Ord 53 r 4(1) and s 31(6) of the Supreme Court Act 1981. Both seek to ensure timely application. It is possible to take too technical a view of these provisions, particularly given the appalling way in which the provisions are drafted and the fact that they were not designed with each other in mind. In the leading case of *Caswell v Dairy Produce Quota*

1 See *Wandsworth London Borough Council v Winder* [1985] AC 461 and p 113 of this work.

2 See *O'Reilly v Mackman* [1983] 2 AC 237, 283F.

3 All acts are presumed to have been done right. 'It is a maxim of the law of England to give effect to everything which appears to have been established for a considerable course of time, and to presume that what has been done was done of right, and not in wrong' per Pollock CB, *Gibson v Doeg* (1857) 2 H & N 615, 623.

*Tribunal for England and Wales*[4] Lord Goff emphasised that questions of delay are best dealt with in depth at the substantive hearing. Leave should, therefore, only be refused in clear cases of unjustifiable delay. In *Caswell* itself leave was granted even though nearly two years had passed. In *R v Comr for Local Administration, ex p Croydon London Borough Council*,[5] Woolf LJ stated that the delay provisions should not be construed technically and should not be invoked strictly against an applicant who has behaved sensibly and reasonably. Nevertheless, an applicant delays at his peril.

## Order 53

Order 53, r 4(1) of the Rules of the Supreme Court provides that:

> An application for leave to apply[6] for judicial review shall be made promptly and in any event within three months from the date when grounds for the application first arose unless the Court considers that there is good reason for extending the period within which the application shall be made.

## The Supreme Court Act

Section 31(6) of the Supreme Court Act 1981 provides:

> Where the High Court considers that there has been undue delay in making an application for Judicial Review, the Court may refuse to grant:
> (a) leave for the making of the application; or
> (b) any relief sought on the application,
> if it considers that the granting of the relief sought would be likely to cause substantial hardship to, or substantially prejudice the rights of, any person or would be detrimental to good administration.

## Two tests

In the fifth edition of his work *Administrative Law*, Professor Wade suggested that the two different tests existed as a result of a Parliamentary oversight. Given the history, this explanation is entirely credible although, in the event, the tests do more than merely repeat each other. The oversight arose following the drastic revision of Ord 53 in January of 1978. The procedure known as 'Application for Judicial Review' was created, bringing together the prerogative remedies of certiorari, mandamus and prohibition and enabling them to be joined with applications for declarations, injunctions and damages. As part of the revision, the former six months' time limit which applied to certiorari only was removed and a test in similar form to the present s 31(6) was introduced. In January of 1981 that test was removed from Ord 53 and replaced by the present test in r 4. The 1978 rule changes were so drastic, however, that there was academic comment that they had been ultra vires the Rules Committee. In order to make the statutory basis for the new Ord 53 clear, express reference was made to the new procedure in the Supreme Court Act 1981 which came into effect on 1 January 1982. In providing an express

4 [1990] 2 AC 738, [1990] 2 All ER 434.
5 [1989] 1 All ER 1033, 1045.
6 The words 'for leave to apply' were inserted by the RSC (Amendment) Rules 1987 (SI 1987 No 1423) following criticism by the Court of Appeal in *R v Stratford-on-Avon District Council, ex p Jackson* [1985] 3 All ER 769, [1985] 1 WLR 1319. Even in the absence of these words the Court of Appeal had concluded that the rule had to be read as intending to refer to applications for leave as being 'the only sensible construction that could be given to the rule'.

statutory authority for Ord 53, however, Parliament enacted in s 31(6) the test regarding delay that had already been removed from Ord 53 in January 1981. Since January 1982, therefore, there have been two separate tests and the courts have had the task of reconciling them.[7]

## CONSTRUCTION OF ORD 53, R 4

The provisions of Ord 53 r 4 apply only at the stage of granting, refusing or setting aside leave to apply for judicial review. The wording 'promptly and in any event within three months' imposes a cumulative time limit. Thus, an application for leave to apply for judicial review made within three months may still be dismissed for delay if it has not been made promptly.[8] The test of whether an applicant has acted promptly requires an objective consideration of the applicant's conduct. If an application has not been made promptly within three months, the court may grant leave if there is good reason to extend the period. This is not necessarily synonymous with there being 'good reason' for the delay. Leave may be refused where the delay is perfectly explicable but, for example, has prejudiced the interests of other parties. In *R v Stratford-on-Avon District Council, ex p Jackson*[9] the Court of Appeal granted an extension notwithstanding nine months' delay. Five weeks elapsed due to the applicant's attempts to secure the assistance of the Secretary of State in a planning dispute. The Court of Appeal refused to criticise the applicant for this delay since the applicant had been following the advice of experienced counsel although the prospect of the Secretary of State intervening had been remote. Thereafter, there was a further delay, through no fault of the applicant, due to an application for legal aid. The court distinguished the judicial guidance relating to similar discretions, eg the renewal of writs after the limitation period has accrued, since judicial review does not concern a *lis inter partes*. The court expressed the hope that legal aid authorities would give special consideration to judicial review applications and act with special expedition.

In permitting the extension of time in *ex p Jackson*, the Court of Appeal emphasised that the delay would still be a matter to be raised at the substantive hearing under s 31(6) of the Supreme Court Act 1981. The granting of an extension of time under Ord 53, r 4 does not, therefore, determine once and for all the effect of prior delay. Indeed if an extension of time is granted ex parte, the respondent need not necessarily await the substantive hearing for a reconsideration of the effect of the delay. A respondent aggrieved by a discretion exercised ex parte may apply on notice for a review of the

7 Clause 43 of the Administration of Justice Bill as originally introduced into the House of Lords in 1982 provided for the repeal of s 31(6) of the Supreme Court Act 1981, thus Ord 53, r 4 would have been left as the only express test relating to delay. Clause 43, however, also contained the more controversial proposal that the right of renewal to the Court of Appeal after a refusal of leave to apply for judicial review be abolished. The proposal met with unprecedented public and judicial outcry (see *R v IT Acts Special Purposes Comr, ex p Stipplechoice Ltd* [1985] 2 All ER 465 and *R v Beverley County Court, ex p Brown* (1985) Times, 25 January). Although the Lord Chancellor reported to Parliament that the Judges who had openly criticised the change had apologised to him, he nevertheless withdrew the whole of Clause 43 and with it went the proposed repeal of s 31(6).

8 *R v Greenwich London Borough Council, ex p Cedar Transport Group Ltd* [1983] RA 173.

9 [1985] 3 All ER 769, [1985] 1 WLR 1319.

discretion.[10] In *R v British Railways Board, ex p Great Yarmouth Borough Council*,[11] for example, an extension of time was overturned on an application by the respondent due to a material non-disclosure in the ex parte application.

In any case where delay has occurred, the reasons for it should be explained in the Notice of Application for Leave and the verifying affidavit. If the proposed respondent consents to an extension of time then such consent should be exhibited to the affidavit, although the fact that the respondent consents is no bar to the court considering the delay of its own motion and refusing to extend time.[12]

Before the recent increase in applications for judicial review it was the practice to give notice to intended respondents of applications for leave where it was proposed to seek an extension of time.[13] Since the introduction of the modern Ord 53, this procedure is not normally adopted and the procedure outlined above and approved by the Lord Chief Justice's *Practice Note* in 1983 is followed. If the court considers that the intended respondent (or any other person) should have an opportunity of resisting an extension of time then it may adjourn the application for leave so that notice can be given and the other parties given an opportunity of attending and being heard.

Order 53, r 4(2) makes express provision that in applications for certiorari, the grounds for the application first arise on the date of any judgment, order, conviction or proceeding being challenged. Since no such express provision exists for mandamus, arguments may arise as to whether an extension of time is necessary in applications for mandamus to oblige a public authority to do its duty. An allegation may be made that a body has failed to act for a considerable time. On one view the grounds for the application first arose within Ord 53, r 4 when the applicant could first have complained to the High Court. It may be necessary to distinguish, for these purposes, between enforcement of continuing duties and challenges to erroneous determinations of an applicant's status as a result of which no duty arises.[14] In the latter case the time for a challenge runs from the date of the determination. Such problems can adequately be dealt with as a matter of discretion. There is no need for the judicial creation of any rule as to when grounds for applications first arise akin to the rule relating to a cause of action arising under the Limitation Act 1980.[15]

## CONSTRUCTION OF S 31(6) OF THE SUPREME COURT ACT 1981

Unlike Ord 53 r 4, which applies only at the leave stage, the provisions of s 31(6) relate to both applications for leave and to substantive applications. The phrase 'an application for judicial review' in the preamble has to be read as 'an application for leave to apply for Judicial Review' where appropriate.[16] The phrase 'undue delay' is similar to, but not synonymous with, the notion of

10 Per Lord Lane CJ, *Practice Note* [1983] 2 All ER 1020.

11 (1983) Times, 15 March.

12 *R v Dairy Produce Quota Tribunal, ex p Wynn Jones* [1987] 2 EGLR 9.

13 See *R v Ashford (Kent) Justices, ex p Richley* (1955) 2 All ER 327n.

14 Eg under the homeless persons provisions of the Housing Act 1985; see *Cocks v Thanet District Council* [1983] 2 AC 286 per Lord Bridge at 292–293.

15 See, for example, *Pirelli General Cable Works Ltd v Oscar Faber & Partners* [1983] 2 AC 1, [1983] 1 All ER 65, HL.

16 Per Lord Goff in *Caswell v Dairy Produce Quota Tribunal for England and Wales* [1990] 2 All ER 434 at 439b.

want of promptness in Ord 53 r 4. In attempting to reconcile the two tests, the House of Lords in *Caswell v Dairy Produce Quota Tribunal for England and Wales*[17] approved the view expressed by the Court of Appeal in *ex p Jackson*[18] that whenever there is a failure to act promptly or within three months, there is necessarily undue delay and, in the words of Lord Goff:

> It follows that when an application for leave to apply is not made promptly and in any event within three months, the Court may refuse leave on the grounds of delay unless it considers that there is good reason for extending the period; but, even if it considers that there is such good reason, it may still refuse leave (or, where leave has been granted, substantive relief) if in its opinion the granting of the relief sought would be likely to cause hardship or prejudice (as specified in s 31(6)) or would be detrimental to good administration.

The fact that the court is satisfied at the leave stage that an applicant has acted promptly, however, does not prevent the court at the substantive hearing from finding that there has been undue delay. In *R v Swale Borough Council, ex p RSPB*[19] Simon Brown J held that 'undue delay' required an objective consideration of all the circumstances surrounding the delay, some of which may not have been known at the leave stage. The case involved an application to quash a planning permission that was made just within the three month time limit. Leave had been granted but at the substantive hearing Simon Brown J held that there was nevertheless undue delay and no clear reason why the applicants could not have applied earlier. At the substantive stage no question of requiring a good reason for extending time arises under the only formal test that applies at this stage, namely s 31(6). To refuse relief under s 31(6) the court must be satisfied that one or other of the two statutory grounds of either substantial hardship or detriment to good administration has been made out. Nevertheless, if a good reason for the delay and/or extending time can be shown, it would be wise to make it known to the court in so far as it does not already appear in the evidence on which leave was granted. In *ex parte RSPB* Simon Brown J refused relief because the adverse economic effects of quashing the permission outweighed the ornathological interests of the applicants.

'Good administration' is not defined by the Supreme Court Act 1981 and the judiciary have not attempted to provide a definition of their own. This reluctance to provide a judicial re-phrasing of the Act is to be encouraged and leaves the court with a wide discretion. It is suggested, however, that 'good administration' means more than mere uninterrupted or smooth running administration but is intended to reflect what Lord Diplock in *O'Reilly v Mackman*[20] expressed as:

> The public interest in good administration requires that public authorities and third parties should not be kept in suspense as to the legal validity of a decision the authority has reached in purported exercise of decision-making powers for any longer period than is absolutely necessary in fairness to the person affected by the decision.

Thus, undue delay may be a ground for refusing leave or substantive relief even if the applicant makes out his case on other grounds. Although s 31(6)

17 [1990] 2 AC 738, [1990] 2 All ER 434.
18 *R v Stratford-on-Avon District Council, ex p Jackson* [1985] 3 All ER 769, [1985] 1 WLR 1319.
19 [1991] JPL 39.
20 [1983] 2 AC 237 at 280–281.

requires its criteria such as substantial hardship to be made out, these in practice are wide enough to cover most, if not all, matters that could influence the court in the exercise of its inherent discretion in any event.

In 1976, when the only express time limit applied to certiorari and specified a six month period without reference to applications being made promptly, Lord Widgery CJ opined that since the remedy was discretionary, the court could impose tighter limits than six months but that anyone seeking to resist certiorari on the basis of lapse of time when less than six months had elapsed would have to make out a strong case.[1] In the light of the recent changes in Ord 53 and s 31, the requirement of a strong case is no longer appropriate. Although the court must have reason for refusing relief due to delay, it will not require one party or another to satisfy any particular burden of proof but will act independently in the public interest.

## EXPRESS TIME LIMITS IN PARTICULAR STATUTES

Any special statutory time limits on applications to the High Court applicable to any particular case will not be affected by the provisions of either Ord 53 r 4 or s 31(6) of the Supreme Court Act 1981.[2] Where a time limit is specified by a particular statute, the court will not be able to extend it by virtue of a general power, but will be able to do so if the interpretation of the particular statute permits. It will, therefore, be a matter of construction of the statute in each case.

1 *R v Herrod, ex p Leeds City District Council* [1976] QB 540.
2 See Ord 53, r 4(3) and s 31(7) of the Supreme Court Act 1981 respectively.

CHAPTER 13

# Applications for leave to apply for judicial review and interim relief

## THE PURPOSE OF LEAVE

Perhaps the feature of applications for judicial review which most distinguishes them from other proceedings is that the permission of the High Court has to be obtained before they can be commenced. Applications for leave to apply for judicial review are made ex parte and so the proposed respondents to any applications are not necessarily put to any trouble or expense at this early stage. The Court may, however, adjourn the application for leave in order that the proposed respondents may be represented to object if need be and to give any reasons why the action should not be allowed to commence.[1] Applications for leave may even be considered by a High Court judge on documents alone without the attendance of any party (even the applicant) though, as will be seen below, no application can be finally dismissed in such a manner. The prime object of the requirement of leave is to filter out the applications of cranks and busybodies who might otherwise impose an excessive burden on the process of legitimate administration. The granting of leave does not prevent a respondent from applying to strike out an application, just as applications to strike out are possible in actions begun by writ or originating summons. The fact that leave is required, however, gives the Court an opportunity to control applications of its own motion, eg refusing leave or permitting them to proceed only in such manner as it may direct. The Court does not require extensive argument on an application for leave but simply needs to be satisfied that the applicant has a prima facie arguable point.[2]

## SUFFICIENT INTEREST

In order to obtain leave to apply for judicial review, an applicant must satisfy the Court that he has a sufficient interest in the matter to which the application relates.[3] This in effect is the filter provided to bar busybodies from pursuing doomed applications through the courts. The effect of this requirement of sufficient interest on the historical development of locus standi in judicial review is considered in full in ch 8, above. Following the House of Lords'

1 *O'Reilly v Mackman* [1983] 2 AC 237 at 280g, [1982] 3 All ER 1124 at 1130j.

2 Eg per Lord Donaldson in *R v Secretary of State for the Home Department, ex p Cheblak* [1991] 1 WLR 890 at 901 D and also in *R v Legal Aid Board, ex p Hughes* (1992) Independent, 27 August, (1992) Times, 29 October, CA in which Lord Donaldson stated that 'Things have moved on since *IRC v National Federation of Self Employed and Small Businesses Ltd* [1982] AC 617, 644, [1981] 2 All ER 93 (the *Fleet Street Casuals* case) where Lord Diplock had stated that leave to move for judicial review ought to be granted if on a quick perusal of the material available the court thought that on further consideration the applicant might have an arguable case.'

3 Ord 53, r 3(7).

decision in *IRC v National Federation of Self Employed and Small Businesses Ltd*,[4] the issue of whether a particular person or body is entitled to ask the Court for relief is closely linked to the merits of the complaint which is being made. In such circumstances the issue of locus standi is not one which can necessarily be determined at the stage of leave or even as a preliminary point on the substantive hearing. Such a course was expressly deprecated by the House of Lords in *ex p Federation of Self Employed*. Leave ought, therefore, to be granted where an applicant can show that he may have locus standi to ask the Court for relief. The effect of the decision in *ex p Federation of Self Employed* is that far from the granting of leave being a final answer in questions of locus standi, they will remain open for the Court to consider at all times and may properly be argued notwithstanding that leave has been granted.

## NOTICE OF APPLICATION FOR LEAVE TO APPLY FOR JUDICIAL REVIEW

The application is made ex parte to a judge of the High Court by filing a notice of application in the Crown Office.

A standard format for the notice of application is prescribed by Form 86A of Appendix A to the Rules of the Supreme Court.[5] Litigants in person will be provided with a standard copy of Form 86A upon request at the Crown Office in the Royal Courts of Justice in the Strand, London. Although the standard forms are prescribed, the required information may be set out separately. This will often be the more convenient course when numerous forms of relief are sought or when numerous grounds are to be relied upon. Order 53, r 3 requires that the following information be set out:

(i) the name and description of the applicant;
(ii) the relief sought and the grounds upon which it is sought;[6]
(iii) the name and address of the applicant's solicitors (if any); and
(iv) the applicant's address for service.

It is important to give proper consideration to the nature of the relief sought at this initial stage since later when the issues may have become blurred by a welter of affidavit evidence and the applicant or the respondent has taken further steps which may alter and confuse the factual matrix of any decision making process, the Court may go back to the original application for leave in order to ask the two questions: what was the thing complained of? and why was it said to be bad?

When specifying the relief sought the limitations of the powers of the Divisional Court should be observed. Where, for example, the exercise of a discretion is complained of, the applicant will rarely be able to seek any relief that the discretion be exercised in his favour. The relief will normally be limited to quashing a purported exercise of discretion and an order that the discretion be exercised properly.[7]

It is not necessary to overburden a notice of application with unrealistic or hypothetical forms of relief so long as the issues for the Court to determine are

4 [1982] AC 617, [1981] 2 All ER 93.
5 See Appendix 2, below. Separate forms previously used by the Crown Office for immigration cases are no longer in use.
6 Where the grounds are settled by Counsel they should be signed by Counsel.
7 As to this distinction see ch 2, above.

clearly set out. Where appropriate the judge hearing an application for leave may allow amendment of the notice in any respect so that an omission will not necessarily be fatal. Although Ord 53, r 6 provides that no grounds can be relied upon or any relief sought at the hearing of the full application for judicial review except as set out in the notice, it also provides express power for the Court to allow an applicant to amend his notice, whether by specifying different or additional grounds or relief or otherwise. If an applicant intends in advance to apply to amend his statement he should give notice of his intention to every other party.[8]

The express power to allow amendment, and indeed the general power of the High Court under RSC Ord 20, r 8 to allow amendment at any time, apply equally to claims for damages in applications for judicial review although Ord 53, r 7 provides that a Court may only award damages in an application for judicial review where they have been included in the statement contained in the applicant's notice of application. Since a liberal granting of permission to amend to include a damages claim in a statement would undermine this protection and because the normal rules of pleading apply to claims for damages under Ord 53 (especially those as to particularity of special damages under Ord 18, r 12) the courts will rarely be prevailed upon to allow such amendments unless made in good time and with adequate notice. Care should therefore be taken to include any claim for damages in the statement when first filed.

## THE SUPPORTING AFFIDAVIT

The notice of application must be accompanied by an affidavit verifying the facts relied upon.[9] The requirement of an affidavit commits an applicant to stating the basis for his case on oath, thus making him liable in perjury. The affidavit must contain all the basic factual material on which reliance will eventually be placed for, if leave is granted, this affidavit will form the basis of the applicant's application for judicial review together with the notice of application. The reasons for any delay in making an application should be explained in the affidavit in order to satisfy the Court that there are 'good reasons' for extending time under Ord 53, r 4 and that the delay is not undue or prejudicial under s 31(6) of the Supreme Court Act 1981.[10]

Since the application is made ex parte, there is a positive duty to disclose all material facts in the supporting affidavit in order to ensure that the Court is not misled. The duty rests primarily upon an applicant but also applies to solicitors and counsel advising applicants since they owe a duty to the Court to be frank in making ex parte applications. Advisers should, therefore, satisfy themselves that they are fully aware of all the material facts which ought to be disclosed.[11] A lack of candour at the ex parte stage may be taken into account by the Court in any later application by the respondent to set aside leave. Where an applicant has misled the Court by suppressing material facts, his application may be dismissed without the merits having been considered.[12]

8 Rule 6(3).
9 Ord 53, r 3(2)(b).
10 See ch 12, above as to the effect of delay.
11 *R v Secretary of State for the Home Department, ex p Mannan* (1984) Times, 29 March.
12 *R v Kensington Income Tax Comrs, ex p Princes De Polignac* [1917] 1 KB 486, 86 LJKB 257, CA.

If an application leads to a substantive hearing then the conduct of the applicant at the ex parte stage may be taken into account where the Court decides whether discretionary remedies under Ord 53 should be granted.[13]

Once the above criteria have been met then, even though the affidavit will later form the basis of the applicant's case, it is neither necessary nor desirable to overburden the supporting affidavit at the stage of leave. The Court may allow further affidavit evidence lodged in support of an application after leave is granted to be referred to by an applicant and such permission is normally granted.[14] Were this not the case there would be little point in making provision for discovery in applications for judicial review. It is not, therefore, necessary to anticipate every possible challenge to the applicant's evidence at the early stage of an application for leave. Once the respondent has challenged some of the applicant's supporting evidence on oath then an affidavit may be lodged in reply. Adopting this approach will lead to a saving in costs and will not overburden the Court with unnecessary unchallenged factual material. Where relevant legislation contains an ouster clause that may arguably bar a right to judicial review[15] this should be brought to the attention of the court even if the applicant is of the view that the ouster clause can be avoided.[16]

## PROCEDURE FOR OBTAINING LEAVE

There are two routes by which an application for leave may be considered. It may be considered at a hearing before a judge or it may first be considered in private by a judge on the documents alone and then only if leave is not granted need there be a hearing. The choice of procedure is made by the applicant at the time of filing the application and depends upon whether or not a hearing is requested in the notice of application. Various factors may affect the exercise of the choice and they are considered on p 143, below.

In either case the application commences by the applicant filing the notice of application and the affidavit in support in the Crown Office. In practice the Crown Office is assisted if the applicant also delivers an index of his documents, although it is not a document required by the rules of Ord 53.

If no hearing is requested then the application will be considered by a High Court judge in private by reading the notice and the supporting affidavit evidence. If the judge considers that the documents reveal an appropriate case for an application for judicial review then leave may be granted without a hearing. A copy of the judge's order will be served on the applicant by the Crown Office. If upon considering the documents the judge refuses leave or grants it on terms, the applicant will be so informed by service of the judge's order and the application may then be renewed by an application in open Court. In a criminal cause or matter the application is renewed by application

13 Per Lord Diplock, *O'Reilly v Mackman* [1983] 2 AC 237 at 280g–281a, [1982] 3 All ER 1124 at 1130j–1131a.

14 It has long been the practice to allow in such additional evidence even though Ord 53 r 6(2) required additional evidence to deal with new matters arising out of an affidavit of a respondent. The Rules of the Supreme Court (Amendment No 2) 1992 SI 1907 (L 9/92) removed this requirement to bring the rule in line with the practice of the court.

15 See p 34.

16 *R v Cornwall County Council, ex p Huntingdon* [1992] 3 All ER 566, 576.

to a Divisional Court of the Queen's Bench Division. In a non-criminal matter the application is renewed by applying to a single judge sitting in open court.[17] In rare cases of extreme public importance, and where the application is to be dealt with inter partes and treated as the substantive hearing, a single judge may direct that the application for leave in a non-criminal matter be renewed before a Divisional Court of the Queen's Bench Division.

After a refusal following consideration of documents alone, the application may be renewed by lodging notice of intention to renew in Form 86B of Appendix A to the Rules of the Supreme Court[18] in the Crown Office within ten days of service of notice of the judge's refusal.[19]

Where the applicant wishes to by-pass consideration of the application for leave on documents alone, he may request a hearing in the notice of application. The application will then go straight to a hearing before a single judge who will normally hear the matter in open court, but may, unlike a renewal of an application after a refusal without a hearing, hear the matter in chambers. If after such a hearing before a single judge either in open court or in chambers the judge refuses leave then there is no provision for renewal of an application in a civil matter, though an application in a criminal cause or matter may be renewed before the Divisional Court. If an application is heard by a single judge it will be before a judge of the Queen's Bench Division assigned to the Crown Office List.

It would be appropriate to request a hearing rather than a consideration of the application on the documents alone where any of the following factors apply:

(i) the application involves a point of law likely to require some argument;
(ii) it is intended that the application be heard inter partes or as if it were a substantive hearing;
(iii) it is thought that the supporting facts or the reasons for the delay need explanation and support by oral submissions;
(iv) the applicant is anxious that should a hearing prove necessary then it should be in chambers;
(v) interim relief is sought[20] or a special direction as to the hearing of the substantive hearing is to be requested.[21]

Oral hearings of applications for leave to apply for judicial review are listed on the footing that the application will take no more than 20 minutes, and that any reply by a respondent who attends will take no more than 10 minutes. Where counsel considers that the hearing of the application will require more than the time allowed he should provide a written estimate and a special fixture must be arranged.[1]

By Ord 53, r 3(6) the judge or court hearing an application for leave has a specific power to allow amendments to the applicant's statement. This power extends to adding completely new heads of relief or grounds. This specific power is expressed to be without prejudice to the general power of the High Court under RSC Ord 20, r 8 to allow amendment of any document in proceedings. The general power may be exercised at any time, though with

17 The distinction between criminal causes or matters and other causes and matters is discussed at p 151, below.
18 See Appendix 1, below.
19 Ord 53, r 3(5).
20 See p 147, below.
21 See p 145, below.
1 *Practice Note* 18 March 1991 [1991] 1 All ER 1055.

both the general and the specific power of amendment the Court may impose such terms as it thinks fit.

Special provision is made by Ord 53, r 3(8) for cases where an application for judicial review by way of an order of certiorari is made to quash any judgment, order, conviction or other proceedings although an appeal procedure is open to the applicant within any specified time limit. The application for leave may in such cases be adjourned until any appeal is determined or the time for appealing has expired. It by no means follows, however, that this procedure will be followed. It may be that any appeal will be adjourned pending the determination of a point of law by the High Court under Ord 53 by way of judicial review.[2]

Appeal to the Court of Appeal from a refusal of leave after all available procedures for renewal have been exhausted is dealt with below at p 176. Where an application for leave to apply for judicial review has been made to and refused by the Court of Appeal, any further application for such leave should be made to the Court of Appeal.[3]

## TIME LIMITS

One of the additional protections given to public bodies in applications for judicial review is that the Court can refuse to entertain or to grant applications which have been delayed. One of the purposes of the requirement for leave is to filter out applications which through inexcusable delay have been left so late as to threaten the consistency and certainty which is thought necessary to good public administration. In any case where delay has occurred, the reasons for it should be explained in the notice of application for leave and the verifying affidavit.

The problem of delay in applying for judicial review is dealt with now in two different provisions, s 31(6) of the Supreme Court Act 1981 and Ord 53 r 4, both of which seek to ensure prompt application. The combined effect of these provisions is so significant that they are considered separately in ch 12.

## GRANTING OF LEAVE ON TERMS

The applicant may be granted leave on such terms as to costs and as to giving security as the Court thinks fit: Ord 53, r 3(9). This is wider than the general powers of the High Court as to security for costs in other actions and proceedings contained in Ord 23, which applies only to very limited cases, and wider also than the power of the Court of Appeal to order security for costs under Ord 59, r 10(5) which requires special circumstances. In practice the power under Ord 53, r 3(9) is more akin to the power under Ord 59, r 10(5).

The fact that an applicant is an assisted person under the Legal Aid Scheme does not prevent the Court from ordering security to be provided for the respondent's costs. It may, however, be taken into account since it may indicate that a full order for costs is unlikely to be made against the applicant

2 As to the interaction of judicial review and appeal procedures generally see ch 17, above.
3 Per Lord Donaldson MR in *M v Home Office* [1992] 2 WLR 73 at 83 but see pp 176–177 below.

and, therefore, the sum for which security may be required will be reduced.[4]

Where an applicant's impecuniosity is due to the act of the body of whom complaint is being made, or, as may often be the case in judicial review, where a new point of law is in issue, the Court may decline to order security when it otherwise would, although the question remains one of discretion in each case.[5] In practice security for costs is rarely required as a condition of granting leave.

SPECIAL DIRECTIONS OR RELIEF

## Hearing by a full Divisional Court

For administrative purposes, pending applications for judicial review are placed in the Crown Office List under the direction of the Master of the Crown Office.[6] Civil cases are normally heard by a single judge but in criminal causes or matters an application will be set down for hearing by a Divisional Court of the Queen's Bench Division. In practice Divisional Courts consist of two judges, one of whom will often be a Lord Justice of Appeal though it may comprise any combination of judges of the High Court. The constitution of Divisional Courts is now provided for by s 66 of the Supreme Court Act 1981 which in sub-s (3) states simply that 'A Divisional Court shall be constituted of not less than two Judges'. Prior to 1979 applications to a Divisional Court would often be made to a court made up of three judges even though the statutory provisions then in force in s 63(6) of the Supreme Court of Judicature (Consolidation) Act 1925 predicated a two-judge court as the normal constitution of Divisional Courts. These courts were frequently presided over by the Lord Chief Justice in person. Such courts are now a rarity in practice although they may be so constituted for cases of particular importance.

Although the Court may arrange for a matter to be listed before a three-judge court, it is for the parties concerned to take the initiative in appropriate cases and to request such a court. The request may be made at the application for leave or at some subsequent time. The request should be made at as early a stage as possible and in any event in sufficient time in advance of a hearing to allow a third judge to be added. The procedure is comparable with that governing the constitution of the Court of Appeal where, on interlocutory appeals or appeals from the county court, appeals may be listed before a two-judge court.[7] The Court of Appeal has indicated that a three-judge court should be requested where a case raises matters of general importance of some complexity and is one upon which there could well be a difference of judicial opinion. While discretion has to be shown in the making of such applications, an obligation rests on counsel and solicitors for the parties to consider making such a request since it may not be apparent from a reading of the papers before the Court that a complex and/or important issue is involved.[8]

4 *Jackson v John Dickinson & Co (Bolton) Ltd* [1952] 1 All ER 104 at 106.
5 *Farrer v Lacy, Hartland & Co* (1885) 28 Ch D 482.
6 *Practice Direction (Trials in London)* (Lord Lane CJ) [1981] 3 All ER 61, [1981] 1 WLR 1296. See ch 19, below.
7 *Practice Note (New Procedure)* [1982] 3 All ER 376 at 383j–384c, [1982] 1 WLR 1312 at 1318.
8 *Wandsworth London Borough Council v Winder* [1985] AC 461, [1984] 3 All ER 83, CA.

## Chambers hearings

In 1980 the organisation of courts for hearing applications for judicial review underwent a streamlining process. As a result civil matters are now heard in the normal course of events by a single judge sitting in open court.[9] The Court may, however, direct that an application proceed by way of originating summons to a judge in chambers. Such a course would be appropriate where the subject matter of an application is suitable for a private hearing, eg the affairs of a minor or a patient. Where a matter is listed for a hearing in chambers, the judge will nevertheless retain power to adjourn the application into open court if desired.[10] The exercise of the power so to adjourn a matter would be appropriate where the judge wished to deliver a judgment involving a point of law of general importance in open court.

## Divisional Court hearings of civil matters

The Court may also direct that an application in a civil matter proceed by originating motion to a Divisional Court of two or more judges rather than to a single judge. Such a cause would only normally occur where a case of particular public importance arose. In such cases the importance of a case may work both ways, however. It may be argued that an important case deserves the attention of two minds, but since such cases would tend to go to appeal in any event it may be argued that a two- or three-man court at first instance is a waste of manpower and that a single judge will better be able to find any necessary facts and enunciate the issues to be considered on appeal.

## 'Family' cases

Where an application for judicial review involves a family matter which would otherwise be within the normal province of the Family Division then the Court may, and normally should, direct that the application be listed before a judge from the Division: per Woolf J in *R v Dover Magistrates' Court, ex p Kidner*.[11]

## Expedited hearings

In order to alleviate the problems caused by the backlog of cases during the 1970s an 'expedited hearing list' was established in the Crown Office following a Practice Direction of Lord Widgery CJ on 2 October 1974.[12] It is at times tempting to regard this as a list for 'Urgent' cases. This is not, however, its intended purpose. Its main purpose is to secure the early disposal of short and simple cases, particularly those which involve sentences of imprisonment, disqualification for driving or possession of property. A characteristic of such cases is intended to be that counsel can be adequately instructed at comparatively short notice. The List is not, therefore, suitable for cases involving particularly novel or complex issues of law.

An application may be placed in the expedited list by direction of the judge granting leave to apply for judicial review. Otherwise application will have to be made to the Master of the Crown Office or the Head Clerk. When a case

9 Ord 53, r 5(2).
10 Ord 32, r 13. This power is expressly preserved by Ord 53, r 5(2).
11 [1983] 1 All ER 475.
12 [1974] 3 All ER 528, [1974] 1 WLR 1219.

goes into the expedited list it goes into part D of the Crown Office List[13] as a case to be heard as soon as practicable. This differs from a case being treated as urgent. Urgent cases will be heard, if necessary within hours rather than weeks, by abridgment of the time for service of the motion or summons from the ten days required by r 5(4). Where an early hearing is sought an applicant may need to apply to the judge granting leave to abridge time for service of the respondent's affidavit evidence in reply.[14]

## THE EFFECT OF GRANTING LEAVE: INTERIM RELIEF

The granting of leave is simply the Court giving an applicant its permission to bring proceedings and implies no more approval and gives no more relief than that. If interim relief is required it must be applied for specifically. The application may be, and usually is, made at the application for leave. Where an applicant wishes to make an application for interim relief then an oral hearing of the application for leave should be requested. In practice the court requires notice of such applications to be given to the intended respondent in all but the most urgent cases.

Except in the case of the Crown, interim injunctions are available against public authorities. The usual balance of convenience test applies.[15] In weighing the competing factors the Court will take into account the fact that the defendant is a public authority exercising functions in the public interest.[16] Interim relief is available in injunction cases where such relief would be available in an ordinary action.[17]

Interim relief is also available in certiorari and prohibition cases. RSC Ord 53 r 3(10) permits the court to direct a 'stay of the proceedings to which the application relates'. In *R v Secretary of State for Education and Science, ex p Avon County Council*[18] the Court of Appeal held that 'proceedings' included the implementation of the decision being challenged, in that case the approval of a school's decision to opt out of local authority control. However, in *Minister of Foreign Affairs Trade and Industry v Vehicles and Supplies Ltd*[19] the Privy Council took the view that a 'stay' applied only to proceedings pending before a court or tribunal and could have no application to an 'executive decision' already reached.[20] Interim relief against a decision already reached must, according to this view, be by injunction. The case involved the reduction by a minister in Jamaica of the applicant's motor vehicle import allocation and the language of the relevant code was substantially the same as RSC Ord 53 r 3(10).

Interim relief by means of a declaration is not possible in any circumstances.[21]

The question of interim relief against the Crown is an unfortunate muddle. By virtue of the Crown Proceedings Act 1947 s 21, injunctions are not avail-

13 See ch 19, below.
14 Ord 53, r 6(4) and see *Practice Note* 7 March 1989 [1989] 1 All ER 1024, [1989] 1 WLR 358.
15 *American Cyanamid Co v Ethicon Ltd* [1975] AC 396, [1975] 1 All ER 504, HL.
16 *Smith v Inner London Education Authority* [1978] 1 All ER 411, CA; *Re Smith Kline & French Laboratories Ltd*, [1990] 1 AC 64.
17 RSC Ord 53, r 3(1)b.
18 [1991] 1 QB 558, [1991] 1 All ER 282.
19 [1991] 4 All ER 65, [1991] 1 WLR 550, PC.
20 Above, at 71.
21 *R v IRC, ex p Rossminster Ltd* [1980] AC 952.

able either against the Crown itself or an officer of the Crown acting as such.[1] Section 21 applies only to 'civil proceedings' and proceedings on the Crown side of the Queen's Bench Division, which includes applications for judicial review, are not civil proceedings for this purpose.[2] It is therefore arguable and had been accepted by the Court of Appeal in *R v Licensing Authority, ex p Smith Kline French Ltd (No 2)*[3] that interim injunctions could be granted against the Crown. Woolf LJ thought that the reformed Ord 53 procedure should be treated as making a fresh start unfettered by outmoded technicalities. However in *Factortame Ltd v Secretary of State for Transport*[4] the House of Lords held that an interim injunction was not available against the Crown in judicial review proceedings. Their Lordships accepted that judicial review proceedings were not civil proceedings within s 21 of the Crown Proceedings Act 1947 but held that injunctions had never been available against ministers and other Crown servants and that Ord 53 must be construed against the background of the earlier law. This narrow approach to the reform of judicial review confounds earlier hopes for a more flexible approach to the Ord 53 procedure. *Factortame* was an attempt to obtain an interim injunction preventing the implementation of an Act of Parliament that was alleged, correctly as it later transpired, to be contrary to European Community law. In *Factortame v Secretary of State for Transport (No 2)*[5] the European Court held that the absence of an interim remedy was in breach of the overriding duty in European law to give effect to binding European Community provisions. The House of Lords therefore granted the interim injunction on the basis of the ordinary balance of convenience principles.

The result of the *Factortame* litigation is the absurdity that interim injunctions are not available against the Crown in domestic matters but are available against the Crown to protect a right enforceable in English law under European Community provisions. The Law Commission has recently described the Crown's continuing immunity in non-EC cases in these circumstances as 'not sustainable'.[6]

A further anomaly is that interim relief may still be available against the Crown servant in certiorari or prohibition cases. This has long been the case with prohibition.[7] We have already seen that a 'stay' was granted against a minister of the Crown in *R v Secretary of State for Education and Science, ex p Avon County Council*.[8] This possibility was also supported by Woolf LJ and Taylor LJ in *R v Licensing Authority, ex p Smith Kline and French Laboratories Ltd (No 2)*.[9] Glidewell LJ distinguished between a stay and an injunction upon the basis that a certiorari application is not a dispute between parties as such but a

1 See *Merricks v Heathcoat-Amory and Minister of Agriculture, Fisheries and Food* [1955] Ch 567, [1955] 2 All ER 453 assuming that ministers in their official capacity always act on behalf of the Crown. Cf *Town Investments v Department of the Environment* [1978] AC 359, [1977] 1 All ER 813, HL and see above, p 79.

2 S 38(2).

3 [1989] 2 All ER 113 see per Woolf LJ at 122 & 123. See also *R v Secretary of State for the Home Department, ex p Herbage* [1987] QB 872, [1986] 3 All ER 209.

4 [1990] 2 AC 85, [1989] 2 All ER 692 but accepting that judicial review proceedings are not civil proceedings within the Act.

5 [1991] 1 All ER 70; affd sub nom *R v Secretary of State for Transport, ex p Factortame Ltd (No 2)* [1991] 1 AC 603, [1990] 3 WLR 818, HL.

6 Law Commission Consultation Paper No 126 'Administrative Law judicial review and statutory appeals' 1993.

7 Eg *R v Minister of Health, ex p Davis* [1929] 1 KB 619.

8 Above, n 18, p 147.

9 [1989] 2 All ER 113 at 120, 125, 126.

challenge to a decision whereas the purpose of an injunction is to protect specific interests of the parties. However this view has been rejected by the Privy Council. In *Minister of Foreign Affairs Trade and Industry v Vehicles and Supplies Ltd*,[10] Lord Oliver pointed out that in relation to an executive decision the effect of a stay and of an injunction are the same and refused to grant a stay against a minister. Nevertheless the Court of Appeal (obiter) has affirmed the *Avon* decision (which was contemporaneous with the *Vehicles and Supplies* case) in *R v Secretary of State for the Home Department, ex p Muboyayi*.[11]

In principle there is no reason to deny interim relief against the Crown. The main objections to interim relief are the need to give the executive freedom of action in an emergency and also constitutional propriety in relation to clashes between courts and executive. However interim relief is available against the Crown, under the statutory application to quash procedure,[12] against parts of the executive other than the Crown, and in relation to European matters. Moreover their Lordships in *Factortame* may have underestimated the weight of previous authorities in support of granting interim injunctions against ministers and other Crown officers, as opposed to the Crown itself.[13]

Finally in extradition and immigration cases a form of interim relief might be possible by means of habeas corpus or even the ancient prerogative writ of *ne exeat regno*, which prevents its subject from leaving the country.[14] Neither of these remedies is, strictly speaking, available under Ord 53. However Taylor LJ has suggested that in an appropriate case habeas corpus might be granted in aid of certiorari.[15]

## BAIL

The High Court has an inherent jurisdiction to grant bail. In *R v Secretary of State for the Home Department, ex p Turkoglu*[16] the Court of Appeal considered the circumstances in which the power to grant bail should be exercised in judicial review proceedings. The following guidelines were given.

(a) Bail cannot be granted *in vacuo*. It must be granted as ancillary to some other proceedings of which the Court is seized.
(b) Bail may be granted where the Court is seized either of an application for leave to apply for judicial review or of a substantive application for judicial review.
(c) If leave to apply for judicial review is granted then the application for leave merges with the substantive application. The Court is seized of a continuing underlying proceeding and so bail can be granted.
(d) If an application for leave is adjourned (eg to give the proposed respondent an opportunity to be heard) then the Court remains seized of the matter and bail can be granted.
(e) If leave is refused then the Court is no longer seized of the matter and it can no longer grant bail. The application for leave may be renewed to the

10 [1991] 4 All ER 65, [1991] 1 WLR 550, PC.
11 [1991] 4 All ER 72 at 86, 91.
12 Below, p 186.
13 *Ellis v Earl Gray* (1833) 6 Sim 214. See Wade [1992] 142 NLJ 1275. The distinction between the Crown and Crown servants is of constitutional importance and is due to come before the House of Lords in *M v Home Office* [1992] 1 QB 270, [1992] 4 All ER 937.
14 *R v Secretary of State for the Home Department, ex p Muboyayi* [1991] 4 All ER 72 at 89, 90. See *Felton v Collis* [1968] 1 QB 200, [1968] 3 All ER 673.
15 *Ex p Muboyayi* ibid at 91.
16 [1988] QB 398, [1987] 2 All ER 823.

Court of Appeal and that court may grant bail unless and until it refuses leave and is itself functus officio.

(f) If bail is refused by a High Court Judge then that decision is appealable to the Court of Appeal.[17]

(g) Where, as in immigration cases, there are statutory powers available to the Secretary of State or to adjudicators to grant bail or similar relief, then the Court will not usurp those functions by granting bail in the absence of consent[18] by the Secretary of State unless the decision to refuse bail or similar relief can itself be challenged on judicial review grounds.

## DISQUALIFICATION FROM DRIVING

Section 40 of the Road Traffic Offenders Act 1988 gives the High Court power to suspend a period of disqualification from driving pending an application for certiorari to quash either the conviction or sentence leading to the disqualification. A suspension may be granted at any time after an application for leave has been made but the application will normally be dealt with on an oral application for leave to a single judge in open court. Notice of the application for a suspension should be included in Form 86A.

## SUMMARY RELIEF

Where an applicant seeking leave alleges that a decision is vitiated by an error of law appearing on the face of the record (which itself gives the Court jurisdiction to interfere: *R v Northumberland Compensation Appeal Tribunal, ex p Shaw*)[19] then the Court may make an order summarily if and to the extent that the error is admitted. In *R v Newcastle-under-Lyme Justices, ex p Whitehouse*[20] the applicant's affidavit stated that he had been committed for sentence to Quarter Sessions but that through inadvertence it had not been explained to him before he had pleaded that he might be so committed. The effect of the omission was to render the conviction bad in law. Since the applicant's affidavit evidence was confirmed by an affidavit from the clerk to the justices, Goddard CJ made a peremptory order of certiorari to quash the conviction on the hearing of the application for leave. A telegram was sent in order to release the applicant from prison forthwith.

The procedural changes to the rules for granting leave under Ord 53 in 1980 inadvertently limited the availability of such peremptory relief in criminal causes or matters. Since January of 1981 all applications for leave have had to be considered initially by a single judge alone but matters of substantive relief in criminal causes or matters have still been reserved for the Divisional Court. A single judge granting leave in a criminal cause or matter cannot make a peremptory order, therefore, and an applicant has to apply by motion to a Divisional Court. Ironically if a single judge refuses leave and an application is renewed to a Divisional Court then if the Divisional Court grants leave it may also make a peremptory order. In practice, of course, this is unlikely to occur. Since the Divisional Court consists of judges who may each grant leave, one of them could grant leave and then the full court could grant the relief sought.

17 S 16 of the Supreme Court Act 1981.

18 This seemingly unlikely event may occur where the Secretary of State is content for bail to be granted on terms that he has no power to impose, eg as to the provision of sureties.

19 [1952] 1 KB 338, [1952] 1 All ER 122, CA.

20 [1952] 2 All ER 531n, [1952] WN 416.

CHAPTER 14

# The hearing of the application for judicial review

## CIVIL OR CRIMINAL?

Once leave has been obtained, an application for judicial review must be made by originating motion or summons. The manner of the application will depend upon whether the case is criminal or civil in nature. In a criminal cause or matter the application must be by originating motion to the Divisional Court of the Queen's Bench Division. The category of 'Criminal Cause or Matter' is widely interpreted to include any proceedings where the ultimate outcome may result in the punishment of a person for an alleged offence. Thus the review of proceedings for the extradition of a fugitive criminal is a criminal cause or matter. In one such case Lord Esher, having said that the phrase should be interpreted widely said 'I think the (phrase) applies to a decision by way of judicial determination of any question raised or with regard to proceedings, the subject matter of which is criminal, at whatever stage of the proceedings the question arises.'[1] Extradition to a foreign military court is equally a criminal cause or matter.[2] Similarly an objection to the jurisdiction of English criminal courts over Russian subjects removed from a Danish ship whilst in a British port was a criminal cause or matter.[3] Review of the procedure of the Army Council in refusing to hear a petition concerning a court martial sentence has also been held to be a criminal cause or matter.[4] In *R v Secretary of State for the Home Department, ex p Dannenberg*[5] the review of a criminal court's recommendation for deportation was held to be a criminal cause or matter although the review of the Secretary of State's resultant deportation order on the ground that the recommendation was invalid was a non-criminal cause or matter.

Cases which concern trials for criminal offences have been held to be non-criminal causes or matters where the issue in dispute is remote from the end result of punishment.[6] Thus an application to review police policy on prosecution for gaming offences has been held not to be a criminal cause or matter,[7] as has an application for a declaration that exhibits in a criminal case could not be released by the DPP to a foreign (Irish) court without the leave of the Crown Court or High Court.[8] An application for mandamus to oblige the

1 *Ex p Woodhall* (1888) 20 QBD 832, 57 LJMC 71, CA.
2 *Amand v Home Secretary and Minister of Defence of Royal Netherlands Government* [1943] AC 147, sub nom *Amand v Secretary of State for Home Affairs* [1942] 2 All ER 381, HL.
3 *R v Garrett, ex p Sharf* [1917] 2 KB 99, 86 LJKB 894, CA.
4 *R v Army Council, ex p Sandford* [1940] 1 KB 719, [1940] 2 All ER 372, CA.
5 [1954] QB 766, [1984] 2 All ER 481, CA.
6 *R v Southampton Justices, ex p Green* [1976] QB 11, [1975] 2 All ER 1073, CA; review of proceedings to extract a recognisance.
7 *R v Metropolitan Police Comr, ex p Blackburn* [1968] 2 QB 118, [1968] 1 All ER 763, CA.
8 *R v Lambeth Metropolitan Stipendiary Magistrate, ex p McComb* [1983] QB 551, [1983] 1 All ER 321 (the application was refused).

police to assist in the bringing of prosecutions may arguably, however, be a criminal cause or matter,[9] just as review of a direction that a prosecution be brought which was made by a 'profiteering committee' set up under emergency legislation has been held to be a criminal cause or matter.[10] The granting of leave by the High Court for criminal libel proceedings to be brought has similarly been held to be a criminal cause or matter.[11] Eviction proceedings by a local authority under s 11 of the Caravan Sites Act 1968 have been held to be civil in nature even though the stationing of a caravan justifying the eviction amounts to an alleged criminal offence under s 10 of the Act.[12]

In non-criminal causes or matters the application is normally by originating motion to a single judge sitting in open court. The single judge will be one of the judges of the Queen's Bench Division specifically assigned to the Crown Office List. A direction may be made, however, by a judge of the High Court, either upon granting leave or upon later application for the application to be by originating summons to a judge in chambers or by originating motion to a Divisional Court of the Queen's Bench Division.[13]

## SERVICE OF THE NOTICE OF MOTION OR SUMMONS

The notice of motion or summons must be served at least ten days before the hearing date of the application. The Court may, however, abridge or extend this time limit.[14] A motion applying for judicial review must be entered for hearing within fourteen days after the granting of leave.[15] Since an affidavit of service must be filed in the Crown Office before a motion or summons is entered for hearing,[16] service must in practice be effected within fourteen days after the granting of leave.

Time may be abridged or extended under RSC Ord 3, r 5 by application by summons to the Master of the Crown Office who in practice deals with all such applications relating to judicial review which are not dealt with by a judge.

The notice of motion or summons must be served on all persons directly affected by the application. If the applicant is in doubt as to who ought to be served then the directions of a judge of the High Court as to service should be sought. Where the application relates to any proceedings in or before a court and the object of the application is either to compel the court or an officer of the court to do any act in relation to the proceedings, or to quash the proceedings or any order made in them, then the notice of motion or summons must also be served on the clerk or registrar of the court. It is not necessary to serve the judge who sat in an inferior court unless objection is to be made to his personal conduct.[17]

9 *R v Metropolitan Police Comr, ex p Blackburn*, supra per Lord Denning [1968] 2 QB 118 at 134, [1968] 1 All ER 763 at 768.

10 *Provincial Cinematograph Theatres Ltd v Newcastle-upon-Tyne Profiteering Committee* (1921) 90 LJKB 1064, HL.

11 *Ex p Pulbrook* [1892] 1 QB 86, 61 LJMC 91 under s 8 of the Law of Libel Amendment Act 1888.

12 *Stubbings v Beaconsfield Justices and South Buckinghamshire District Council* (1987) 152 JP 17, 85 LGR 821, CA.

13 As to such directions see p 146, above.

14 Ord 53, r 5(4).

15 Ord 53, r 5(5).

16 Ord 53, r 5(6) and see p 154, below.

17 RSC Ord 53, r 6(3).

Sections 83 and 84 of the County Courts Act 1984 make express provision for the control of county court procedure by way of orders or prohibition and certiorari. This power of the High Court is in addition to the jurisdiction of the Court of Appeal to hear appeals under s 77 of the County Courts Act 1984. Section 84(2) of the County Courts Act 1984 provides that where such an application is made, the judge in the county court is not to be served with notice. Further, unless the judge of the High Court dealing with the application for review so orders, the county court judge will not be required to appear or be heard on the application, nor will he be liable to any order for costs. Applications to the High Court are dealt with in the same manner as appeals from the county court save that they are brought in the Divisional Court of the Queen's Bench Division after the grant of leave. Notice of the application must be served on the registrar of the county court[18] and on those parties to the county court matter who are directly affected by the application.[19] Those parties who are not directly affected by the application need not be served unless the High Court makes a direction for service on them, or on any other person whether a party or not.[20]

Since Ord 53, r 5(3) requires that a judge of an inferior court should be served with notice of an application for judicial review where objection to his conduct is to be made, it would seem advisable, having regard to the protection afforded to county court judges by s 84(1) of the County Courts Act 1984, to seek the directions of a judge of the High Court before serving a judge of the county court. Such a direction could be sought when applying for leave but may be sought at any time.

## APPEARANCE OF PERSONS SERVED

It is not necessary for every party served with a notice of application to appear at the hearing. Where, for example, both the tribunal and some other respondent intend to support the tribunal's decision in an application for its review and there is no conflict in their interests they should agree between themselves who is to appear and instruct counsel.[1] Although they will not be prevented from appearing separately, they will do so at their own risk as to costs.[2]

Where an application calls into question a decision by a magistrates' court then there is no need for the justices to appear and be heard unless their character or bona fides is being called into question or there are other special circumstances.[3] The Review of Justices Decisions Act 1872 makes special provision for justices to set out the grounds of their decision, and any material facts, in an affidavit. Such an affidavit may be filed by sending it by post to the Master of the Crown Office and the Court hearing the application will consider its contents even though no counsel appears on behalf of the justices. If the decision was taken by a majority of a justices' bench then the affidavit must be sworn by a member of that majority. Dissenting justices have no right

18 RSC Ord 59, r 19(2).
19 RSC Ord 59, r 3(5).
20 RSC Ord 59, r 8.
1 *R v Industrial Disputes Tribunal, ex p American Express Co Inc* [1954] 2 All ER 764n, [1954] 1 WLR 1118.
2 See p 160, below.
3 *R v Thornton Justices, ex p Lacon & Co* (1898) 67 LJQB 249 at 251.

to file an affidavit[4] nor may they appear as a party to the hearing. The wording and intention of the 1872 Act require that the affidavit be sworn and filed by the justices. It does not allow, therefore, for the filing of affidavits by witnesses on whose evidence the justices made their decision. Thus an affidavit by a police superintendent who had given information to a licensing hearing was held to be inadmissible on the application for review.[5] In practice, however, the Divisional Court does not refuse to consider affidavits prepared and sworn by a Clerk to the Justices under the justices' direction. In one reported case the Divisional Court presided over by Lord Hewart CJ considered an affidavit sworn by a prosecuting rating officer which had been filed by the justices in support of their own affidavits.[6] Once an affidavit has been filed by the justices the applicant is entitled to refer to it and rely on it as part of his case if he so chooses.[7]

If, rather than avail themselves of the procedure of the Act of 1872, justices insist on appearing and being heard at the hearing of the application they stand to be penalised in costs. Even if they are successful in opposing the application they may not recover their costs unless some attack has been made on them such as that they acted improperly by showing bias or misconducting themselves.[8] If the justices appear and fail in their opposition then they will be liable to have an order for costs made against them.[9] See, however, the provisions for costs from central funds and costs generally at p 160, below. Where a claim for damages is included it may be necessary to join liable individuals as parties to the application when they need not otherwise be joined.[10]

If on the hearing of the motion or summons the Court is of the opinion that any person ought to have been served and has not been served then the Court may adjourn the hearing to allow for such service. Any such adjournment may be on such terms as the Court may direct. The scope of this provision is not limited to persons who necessarily fall within the 'all persons directly affected' on whom service is provided for by r 5(3), but extends to any person it appears to the Court ought to be served.

## AFFIDAVIT OF SERVICE

Once the notice or summons has been served an affidavit of service must be filed before the matter is entered for hearing. The affidavit must give the names and addresses of persons served and the places and dates of service on all the persons who have been served with the notice of motion or summons. If any person who ought to be served has not been served the affidavit must state that fact and the reason for it. Though apparently formal in nature, the affidavit of service must, by r 5(6), be before the Court before the hearing of the motion or summons. It should be included in the bundles before the Court hearing the

4 *R v Waddingham, Gloucestershire Justices and Tustin* (1896) 60 JP Jo 372.
5 *R v Sperling Justices* (1873) 21 WR 461, per Cockburn CJ.
6 *R v Kent Justices, ex p Smith* [1928] WN 137.
7 *R v Rotherham Licensing Justices, ex p Chapman* [1939] 2 All ER 710.
8 *R v Thornton Justices*, above, n 3; *R v Marlow (Bucks) Justices, ex p Schiller* [1957] 2 QB 508 at 515, [1957] 2 All ER 783 at 785.
9 *R v Llanidloes Licensing Justices, ex p Davies* [1957] 2 All ER 610, [1957] 1 WLR 809.
10 See ch 8, above.

application at first instance when any party served is not appearing as a respondent.

## SERVICE OF THE STATEMENT

A copy of the statement in Form 86A contained in the notice of application for leave must be served together with the notice of motion or summons. No relief may be sought in the notice of motion or summons, nor may any grounds be relied upon, save those set out in the statement unless leave of the Court is obtained.[11] If an applicant intends to ask to be allowed to amend his statement then he must give notice of his intention and of any proposed amendment to the other party. In particular an applicant can only claim damages in an application for judicial review if the claim is included in the statement.[12] For reasons discussed above at p 141 the Court will be particularly reluctant to allow an applicant to amend his statement in respect of a claim for damages.

## FILING OF AFFIDAVITS

If a respondent to an application intends to use an affidavit at the hearing he must file it in the Crown Office as soon as practicable and in any event within 56 days after service on him of the notice of motion or summons and the accompanying copy of the Form 86A statement. This time limit may be varied by the Court.[13] The time limit was increased to 56 days from 21 days by a *Practice Note* in 1989.[14] The change was intended to introduce a realistic time limit which the court would expect to be adhered to. The time limit will not be extended, therefore, without good reason and the Crown Office will not accept respondents' affidavits outside the 56-day period unless an extension of time has first been obtained. In the 1989 *Practice Note* Watkins LJ warned 'For all practical purposes respondents will be well advised to treat the period of 56 days as absolute'. The Court may allow the applicant to rely on additional affidavit evidence not before the court on the application for leave[15] but where an applicant intends so to ask, he must give notice of his intention to every other party.[16] Each party to an application must supply copies of his affidavits to every other party on demand and upon payment of the proper charges.[17] This includes the applicant's affidavit used in support of the application for leave. In practice all affidavits are normally served on other parties as a matter of course.

Once notice of a respondent's evidence has been received it is desirable for counsel and solicitors instructed by an applicant for judicial review to give further careful consideration to the merits of the application. The Divisional

11 Ord 53, r 6.
12 Ord 53, r 7.
13 Ord 53, r 6(4). Applications for extensions of time should be made to the Master of the Crown Office from whom appeal lies to a judge nominated to hear Crown Office business. Applications to abridge time should be made to the judge granting leave.
14 [1989] 1 All ER 1024, [1989] 1 WLR 358.
15 Ord 53, r 6(2).
16 Ord 53, r 6(3).
17 Ord 53, r 6(5).

Court has encouraged such reassessments in an effort to save the time and expense of hopeless applications.[18]

## LODGING OF ORDERS

Where an applicant seeks an order of certiorari to quash any proceedings then a copy of any order, warrant, commitment, conviction, inquisition or record the validity of which is questioned, must be lodged in the Crown Office before the hearing of the motion or summons.[19] The copy must be verified by affidavit. If a copy cannot or has not been lodged then the Court must be satisfied as to the reason for the failure before it will hear the motion or summons. Although the rules of the Supreme Court do not require such an explanation to be set out in affidavit form it is good practice to verify the relevant facts in a supporting affidavit.

## MODE OF TRIAL

Hearings of applications in criminal causes or matters will ordinarily be listed for hearing before a Divisional Court consisting of two judges. Applications in other causes or matters will be listed for hearing before a single judge. Cases of particular importance may be listed before three-judge Divisional Courts if application is made in advance: see p 145, above. Similarly, appropriate cases may be listed for hearing in chambers and cases involving an issue of family law may be listed for hearing before a judge from the Family Division: see p 146, above. Applications for judicial review under RSC Ord 53 are set down in the Crown Office List. The operation of the Crown Office List is governed by Practice Directions and Notes issued from time to time by judges of the Divisional Court and is considered in ch 19 below. The administrative requirements of the Crown Office List need to be considered carefully by all applicants and respondents alike.

## PARTIES AT TRIAL

At the hearing of an application for judicial review the Court may be moved either by the applicant in person[20] or counsel instructed on his behalf. Normally, the court will only hear one counsel for each party and so junior counsel appearing with leading counsel will have no right to follow on. Where there is more than one applicant, however, leading counsel may appear with junior counsel and be heard on behalf of one applicant, and junior counsel alone may appear and be heard separately on behalf of other applicants. After the respondents or their counsel have been heard, the applicant or his counsel has a right of reply.[1]

Any person who desires to be heard in opposition to a motion or summons for judicial review may appear and be heard with leave of the Court if they can

18 *R v Secretary of State for the Home Department, ex p Brown* (1984) Times, 6 February.
19 Ord 53, r 9(2).
20 *Practice Note* [1947] WN 218 and RSC Ord 5 r 6(1).
1 *R v Dunne, ex p Sinnatt* [1943] KB 516 at 519 per Viscount Caldecote CJ.

satisfy the Court that they are a proper person to be heard. This is so notwithstanding that they have not been served with notice of the motion or summons either as a 'person directly affected' within r 5(3) or by direction of the Court. Such persons appear, however, at their own risk as to costs.

## DELAY

Where an applicant delayed in bringing his application this may be raised as an objection to the granting of relief at the substantive hearing notwithstanding that an extension of the time limit for bringing the application was granted when leave was sought.[2] Indeed, even though an applicant may be able to bring himself within the scope of the remedies of Ord 53, it is always a matter for the discretion of the Court as to whether relief ought to be granted or not. The Court may take account of any relevant circumstances in exercising its discretion, including the practical consequences of making an order and the conduct of the parties. Any lack of candour in the making of the application for leave may weigh with the Court in deciding upon the exercise of its discretion on the substantive hearing.[3] Section 36(6) of the Supreme Court Act 1981 gives the Court an express power to refuse relief in cases of undue delay. The effect of this section and its relationship with the provisions of RSC Ord 53 r 4 relating to late applications for leave to apply for judicial review are considered in chapter 12.

## APPLICATIONS OUTSIDE LONDON

Applications for judicial review should, wherever practical, be commenced in London. Where the urgency makes it necessary for an application in respect of such proceedings to be made outside London, the Crown Office should be consulted prior to making the application, if necessary by telephone,[4] and the application should be made in accordance with any arrangements made by the Crown Office for its hearing outside London. The application should be confined to those matters which have to be dealt with urgently and, as soon as the application is dealt with, the proceedings should be continued in London and further applications should be heard and directions given in London.[5]

## REMITTING DECISIONS

Where an order of certiorari is made to quash any proceedings, the order will direct that the proceedings be quashed forthwith on their removal into the Queen's Bench Division[6] but the Court may, in addition to quashing a

2 *R v British Railways Board, ex p Great Yarmouth Borough Council* (1983) Times, 15 March; *R v Swale Borough Council, ex p Royal Society for the Protection of Birds* [1991] 1 PLR 6, [1991] JPL 39 and *Practice Note* [1983] 2 All ER 1020, [1983] 1 WLR 925.

3 *O'Reilly v Mackman* [1983] 2 AC 237 at 280g–281a, [1982] 3 All ER 1124 at 1130j–1131a per Lord Diplock. As to the discretionary nature of remedies under Ord 53 see ch 11, above.

4 The High Court's telephone number is 071–936 6000. The Crown Office General Office number is 071–936–6653/6205. The Crown Office Listing Office number is 071–936–6297.

5 *Practice Note* [1983] 2 All ER 1020, [1983] 1 WLR 925.

6 Ord 53, r 9(3), (4).

decision, remit the matter to the court, tribunal or authority concerned with a direction to reconsider it and reach a decision in accordance with the findings of the Court.[6] Although facts may be admitted for the purpose of an application under Ord 53, the court will not base a direction on such admissions.[7]

## TRANSFER OF ORD 53 APPLICATIONS TO WRIT ACTIONS

Where the relief sought is other than a prerogative order (ie is for a declaration, an injunction or damages) and the Court considers that it should not be granted on an application for judicial review but might have been granted if it had been sought in an action begun by writ by the applicant at the time of making his application, the Court may order that the proceedings continue as if they had begun by writ instead of refusing the application. Order 53 contains an express power to make such orders in r 9(5). The power applies even if proceedings contain allegations of fraud, notwithstanding that Ord 5, r 2 provides that proceedings alleging fraud be commenced by writ. This is so not only because of the express nature of Ord 53, r 9(5) but because of the protective effect of Ord 2, r 1(3) which provides:

> The Court shall not wholly set aside any proceedings or the writ or other originating process by which they were begun on the ground that the proceedings were required by any of these Rules to be begun by an originating process other than the one employed.[8]

The Courts have held, however, that no order under Ord 53 r 9(5) should be made in cases that do not involve a breach of some public law obligation.[9] Order 53 r 9(5) cannot, therefore, be used to correct cases which are struck out as an abuse of process for being commenced under Ord 53.

Where an order for transfer to a writ action is made the Court may give directions for the further conduct of the matter. It may require pleadings to be served or it may, in accordance with a widespread practice, order that the affidavits stand as pleadings. The parties may be given leave to add to the affidavits standing as pleadings, for example to plead particulars of special damage under Ord 18, r 12. Parties may also apply for further particulars of the matters contained in the affidavits.[10] Where the affidavits are not comprehensive of the issues in the claim and the defence, however, it may in the long term be better to resist the temptation to permit them to stand as pleadings and to require fresh pleadings to be served since costs may ultimately be saved and clearer pleadings ought to result.[11]

## TRANSFER OF WRIT ACTIONS TO ORD 53 APPLICATIONS

There is no express power to convert actions commenced by writ into applications for judicial review under Ord 53. In *O'Reilly v Mackman* Lord Denning MR in the Court of Appeal expressed the view that the Rules of the Supreme

7 *R v Vaccine Damage Tribunal, ex p Loveday* (1985) Times, 20 April, CA.
8 See *Re Deadman, Smith v Garland* [1971] 2 All ER 101 at 103, [1971] 1 WLR 426 at 429.
9 *R v East Berkshire Health Authority, ex p Walsh* [1985] QB 152, [1984] 3 All ER 425, CA and *R v Secretary of State for Home Affairs, ex p Dew* [1987] 2 All ER 1049, [1987] 1 WLR 881.
10 RSC Ord 28, r 8.
11 *R v East Berkshire Health Authority, ex p Walsh* [1984] 3 All ER 425 at 432, 437.

Court did allow for such a power.[12] Having asserted a defendant's option to apply to have proceedings by writ struck out where they ought to have been commenced under Ord 53[13] he continued:

> Alternatively, if he feels that leave would have been granted under RSC Order 53, he can apply for the action to be transferred to the Order 53 List: and the case can then proceed under Order 53 just as if leave had been granted. The High Court has sufficient control over its proceedings to enable this to be done. Just as an action in the ordinary List can be transferred to the commercial List, so it can be transferred to the Order 53 List which I would like to see called the Administrative List. If this be thought to be too venturesome, the Rule Committee might make a Rule to enable it to be done.
>
> So also if it is brought in the Chancery Division, it should be transferred to the Queen's Bench Division under Section 65 of the Supreme Court Act 1981 to be heard as upon an Application for Judicial Review. Likewise if it is brought in the County Court.

When the judgment of the House of Lords was given in *O'Reilly v Mackman*, Lord Diplock disagreed with Lord Denning:[14]

> . . . the court has power under rule 9(5), instead of refusing the application, to order the proceedings to continue, as if they had begun by writ. There is no such converse power under the Rules of the Supreme Court to permit an application begun by writ to continue as if it were an application for judicial review; and I respectfully disagree with that part of the judgment of Lord Denning MR which suggests that such power may exist; nor do I see the need to amend the Rules in order to create one.

Lord Diplock's comments were, however, obiter and appear to have been made without reference to the wide general provisions of Ord 2, r 1(3) mentioned above. The importance of that rule in giving the court a wide power to permit proceedings to continue was pointed out by Stamp J in *Re Deadman, Smith v Garland*.[15] Since such a transfer would require an application to the Court when consideration could be given as to whether leave would have been granted under Ord 53, and since an affidavit may be filed to support the application, the protection granted to administrative bodies by Ord 53 would not be eroded by the use of the Court's power. It would seem, therefore, that an action commenced by writ may be allowed to proceed as an application under Ord 53. As a matter of practice, however, such an order should be sought from one of the Queen's Bench Division judges nominated to deal with Crown Office business.

## UNCONTESTED APPLICATIONS

Where the parties to an application for judicial review are agreed as to the terms on which the application can be dealt with, but require an Order of the Court to give effect to those terms then such order can be obtained without the parties having to attend Court. The procedure to be adopted is set out at p 204, below, together with a consideration of when applications are to be regarded as 'uncontested'.

12 [1983] 2 AC 237 at 258F, [1982] 3 All ER 680 at 695e.
13 See ch 10, above.
14 [1983] 2 AC 237 at 284A, [1982] 3 All ER 1124 at 1133d.
15 Above, n 8.

## COSTS

The Divisional Court has jurisdiction to make such orders as to costs as it feels just. This is a discretionary power and because of the special nature of applications for judicial review the normal rule that costs follow the event is subject to many qualifications.

### Central funds

In a criminal cause or matter the Divisional Court may order the payment of the costs of any party out of central funds. Such an order may cover not only expenses incurred in the proceedings in the Divisional Court but also in the court below. An applicant may, therefore, by order of the Divisional Court recover from central funds the costs of proceedings before, for example, a magistrates' court even though the magistrates would not have had jurisdiction to make such an order. This would apply to proceedings in respect of offences triable only summarily to which objections are raised in the Divisional Court. Section 5 of the Costs in Criminal Cases Act 1973 provides for costs 'out of central funds' to be assessed by the Master of the Crown Office as such sums reasonably sufficient to compensate the party for any expenses properly incurred by him. In practice, however, the assessment is made by taxation in the Supreme Court Taxing Office.

### Justices

As a general principle, costs will not be awarded against justices or a similar tribunal where, although served with the proceedings, they have not appeared or resisted the application. They may be ordered to pay costs, however, if they have behaved badly, either by flouting decisions of the Court or being guilty of some outrageous conduct.[16] A similar principle applies to parties, such as prosecutors, who have not materially contributed to the error giving rise to the application.[17] This policy has received approval from the Divisional Court in *R v West Yorkshire Coroner, ex p Kenyon*[18] where it was said that the general principle was that on an application for judicial review costs would not be granted against a public body where the body had not appeared and was not represented and the error of law was not something that called for strong disapproval by the courts.

Where justices or any other tribunal do choose to appear at the hearing of the application and are unsuccessful in their opposition then the Court may make an order for the applicant's costs to be paid by them.[19]

If justices appear at the hearing of an application unnecessarily then they may not receive their costs even if they are successful in their opposition since they could have filed an affidavit containing their case under the Review of Justices Decisions Act 1872.[20] They will not be so penalised, however, where the application includes an attack on their conduct, character or bona fides or where other special circumstances require their appearance.[1]

16 *R v Amersham Justices, ex p Fanthorne* (1964) 108 Sol Jo 841 per Lord Parker CJ.
17 *R v Liverpool Justices, ex p Roberts* [1960] 2 All ER 384n [1960] 1 WLR 585.
18 (1984) Times, 11 April.
19 *R v Llanidloes Licensing Justices, ex p Davies* [1957] 2 All ER 610n, [1957] 1 WLR 809n.
20 See p 153, above.
1 *R v Thornton Justices, ex p Lacon & Co* (1898) 67 LJQB 249 at 251; *R v Marlow (Bucks) Justices, ex p Schiller* [1957] 2 QB 508 at 515, [1957] 2 All ER 783 at 785.

Where a party has continued to resist an application for judicial review up to the time of the hearing but does not actually seek to do so at the hearing it may nevertheless be ordered to pay the costs on the grounds that by substantially litigating the matter they have put the applicant to cost.[2] In *R v Hastings Licensing Justices, ex p John Lovibond & Sons Ltd*[3] the respondents, who had improperly been granted consent for alterations to a building which had in fact been demolished, resisted an application to quash the consent brought by rival licensees up until three months before the hearing. At that time they gave written notice to the applicants that the application would no longer be contested. The Divisional Court ordered the respondents to pay the applicants' costs to the date of the written notification.

Although the High Court has a general discretion in respect of the costs of any of the parties it has no such power to award costs to strangers to the proceedings.[4] Under Ord 53 the Divisional Court has a wide power to require additional parties to be served[5] or to permit persons who have not been served to be heard in opposition of the application.[6] Notwithstanding these powers costs are not as a matter of practice awarded to persons who appear without having been served and an unsuccessful applicant will not normally be condemned in the costs of more than one appearing party unless there is some conflict between them to justify them both appearing and being separately represented.[7]

## The Crown

Prior to the Crown Proceedings Act 1947 the rule of practice was that the Crown neither paid nor received costs in proceedings.[8] Section 24(2) of that Act abolished that rule and now the ordinary rules of liability for costs apply to proceedings to which the Crown is a party.

## Legal Aid

Legal aid is available for judicial review proceedings from the Legal Aid Board in the ordinary way.[9] Special care must be taken to ensure that the terms of a Legal Aid certificate cover the exact proceedings that are taken. Notice of the issue of a Legal Aid certificate must be given to other parties to the proceedings and a copy of the certificate must be filed in the Crown Office.[10] Where a party (usually the applicant) is an assisted person under the Legal Aid Scheme then the final order made in an application for judicial review must include a direction that the costs of the assisted person be taxed on the Standard basis.[11] Such a direction is in addition to any other direction as to taxation and must be made even though no other order for costs is made. Counsel for the assisted

2 *R v Birmingham Union Guardians* (1874) 44 LJMC 48.
3 [1968] 2 All ER 270, [1968] 1 WLR 735.
4 *Forbes-Smith v Forbes-Smith and Chadwick* [1901] P 258, 70 LJP 61, CA per Collins LJ as to the meaning of 'any of the parties'.
5 Ord 53, r 5(7).
6 Ord 53, r 9(1).
7 *R v Industrial Disputes Tribunal, ex p American Express Co Inc* [1954] 2 All ER 764n, [1954] 1 WLR 1118.
8 *Rowland v Air Council* [1923] WN 72.
9 Neither the Court nor the Crown Office can grant Legal Aid.
10 Regulation 50, Civil Legal Aid (General) Regulations 1989.
11 Regulation 107, Civil Legal Aid (General) Regulations 1989. For the meaning of 'Standard basis' see RSC Ord 62, r 12.

person must ensure that such a direction is included in the final order by application at the close of the case.

The fact that the party is an assisted person is to be disregarded by the Court when exercising any discretion and does not alter the rights or liabilities of other parties. Thus the fact that a party is an assisted person does not disentitle him to an order for costs though any sums recovered under an order for costs must be paid to the Legal Aid Board.[12] An order for costs may be made against an assisted person personally but it must not exceed the amount (if any) which is a reasonable one for him to pay having regard to all the circumstances including the means and conduct of the parties.[13]

Once the court has considered making an order against an assisted person personally it may then consider making an order (or further orders) for costs to be paid out of the legal aid fund in favour of an unassisted person who has succeeded in the proceedings brought by the assisted person.[14] For these purposes judicial review proceedings in relation to an executive decision count as proceedings at first instance[15] but the position remains arguable in relation to judicial review of proceedings by a court or tribunal.[16] No order against the legal aid fund can be made unless the Court would have made an order (or an unrestricted order) against the applicant had they not been an assisted person. The general provisions as to costs mentioned above apply equally in the case of the legal aid fund, therefore. In proceedings at first instance any person seeking costs against the legal aid fund must show that they would suffer severe financial hardship if no order were made. In all cases the court must be satisfied that it would be just and equitable to make an order against the legal aid fund. It may be just and equitable to make such an order even though a party is being supported by an association of which he is a member.[17]

12 Legal Aid Act 1988, s 16 but see reg 106 of the Civil Legal Aid (General) Regulations 1989.

13 Legal Aid Act 1988, s 17 and see regulations under that section viz Civil Legal Aid Regulations 1989, regs 123–133.

14 Legal Aid Act 1988, s 18 and see regs 134–147 of the Civil Legal Aid (General) Regulations 1989 and *Hanning v Maitland (No 2)* [1970] 1 QB 580, [1970] 1 All ER 812.

15 *R v Greenwich London Borough Council, ex p Lovelace (No 2)* [1992] 1 QB 155, [1992] 1 All ER 679, CA, overruling *R v Leeds County Court, ex p Morris* [1990] 1 QB 523, [1990] 1 All ER 550 relying on *R v Greater Manchester Coroner, ex p Tal* [1985] QB 67, [1984] 3 All ER 240.

16 *Ex p Lovelace*, above, per Neill LJ.

17 *Lewis v Averay (No 2)* [1973] 2 All ER 229, [1973] 1 WLR 510, CA.

CHAPTER 15

# Evidence on applications for judicial review

## GENERAL

The High Court may admit evidence in applications for judicial review as long as it is relevant to the issues before it. It is a fundamental principle of administrative law that a public body's power to make a decision includes the power to choose between different options and even to make decisions which on their merits may appear wrong or mistaken to a different body. The purpose of judicial review is not to provide an appeal procedure against decisions of public bodies on their merits but to control the jurisdiction of public bodies by ensuring that they comply with their duties or by keeping them within the limits of their powers. Thus, for example, when reviewing a decision of a public body the High Court will not admit evidence which is relevant to whether the decision is a reasonable one but will permit evidence which is relevant to whether the decision is one which the body had power to make or whether it was made in circumstances in which reasonable body could have made it.

An applicant will need to adduce the evidence necessary to support his application. In an application for mandamus he must prove the facts necessary to show that the body is under a duty to act and that despite a demand it has not done so. He must also prove the facts necessary to establish his locus standi and satisfy the Court on the facts that it should exercise its discretionary powers. In an application for certiorari or prohibition an applicant must prove the various facts necessary to show that the decision complained of is invalid and therefore liable to be quashed or prohibited. Where a declaration is sought the applicant will have to adduce evidence to establish the right to which he lays claim. Declarations will not be granted based on admissions or in default. They will only be granted after the appropriate facts have been proven and the merits have been argued.[1] Thus in an application for judicial review an applicant will prepare his evidence for trial in the same way as any other case where it is necessary to establish facts, remembering however, that the purpose of the evidence is to establish a breach of duty or the invalidity of a decision and not merely that a public body's action is disagreeable or unmeritorious.

## 'FRESH' EVIDENCE

Given the above limits on the powers of the High Court in an application for judicial review it is strictly speaking never open to the Court to re-open an investigation of facts and admit 'fresh' evidence in reviewing the acts and decisions of inferior bodies. Where a Court sits in an appellate capacity (unlike the High Court in applications for judicial review) it may be permitted to consider the merits of a decision. Thus the Court of Appeal hearing an application from

1 *Wallersteiner v Moir* [1974] 3 All ER 217, [1974] 1 WLR 991, CA.

a Court below may admit 'fresh' evidence which was not before that Court where:

(i) the evidence is as to matters occurring after the date of trial and substantially affects a basic assumption made at trial;[2] or

(ii) the evidence is of matters before trial which

 (a) could not have been obtained with reasonable diligence for use at the trial,

 (b) is such that, if given, would probably have an important influence on the result of the case, though it need not be decisive, and

 (c) is apparently credible though not necessarily incontrovertible.[3]

Although Lord Denning, when Master of the Rolls, considered that the High Court ought in principle to have such a power in review proceedings, his view was contained in obiter dicta unsupported by the majority of the Court of Appeal and there remains no authority for any such power and much authority against.[4]

Although the High Court cannot re-open or re-try a decision of a public body it may nevertheless look at evidence of matters surrounding the decision since such matters may affect the validity of that decision. Such evidence may include evidence not before the body at the time of the decision. For example, where complaint is made that a decision was made without consideration of a relevant matter then the evidence may, ex hypothesi, be of matters not before the body when purporting to make a decision.

In *R v Boycott, ex p Keasley*[5] the Court was asked to review a certificate by a doctor that a boy was an ineducable imbecile. The doctor was permitted by statute to issue such a certificate unless it was a case of doubt in which event the matter fell to be determined by the Board of Education. The Court admitted evidence to show that the case was very much one of doubt and ought therefore to have been referred to the Board. It thus found that the doctor had lacked jurisdiction to issue the certificate which was invalid. The Court quashed the certificate by certiorari. The evidence was admitted because it went to the jurisdiction of the doctor to issue the certificate not because it showed that the boy was educable. The certificate was quashed because it was invalid, not because it was wrong.

It is when considering applications for certiorari that the High Court most resembles an appellate body and that the scope of the evidence to which it may pay heed tends to be most in dispute. In practice the courts have distinguished three functions which may be performed by evidence in the High Court:

1. to inform the Court of the factual material upon which a tribunal or public body purported to act;
2. where jurisdiction of the tribunal or body depended on a question of fact or where the question is whether essential procedural requirements were observed, to determine the jurisdictional fact or procedural error; and
3. to explore allegations that the proceedings were tainted by misconduct such as bias, fraud or perjury.[6]

The matters which may go to the jurisdiction of a body to reach a decision are now well developed and include misdirections as to law and decisions

2 *Mulholland v Mitchell* [1971] AC 666, [1971] 1 All ER 307, HL.

3 *Ladd v Marshall* [1954] 3 All ER 745, [1954] 1 WLR 1489, CA. See also *Ali v Secretary of State for the Home Department* [1984] 1 All ER 1009 sub nom *R v Secretary of State for the Home Department, ex p Monin Ali* [1984] 1 WLR 663.

4 *R v West Sussex Quarter Sessions, ex p Albert and Maud Johnson Trust Ltd* [1974] QB 24, [1973] 3 All ER 289, CA.

5 [1939] 2 KB 651, [1939] 2 All ER 626.

6 *R v Secretary of State for the Environment, ex p Powis* [1981] 1 All ER 788, [1981] 1 WLR 584, CA.

which no reasonable authority could have come to.[7] The High Court may even consider the facts upon which a body purported to act and interfere if it appears that a decision was taken with no evidence to support it[8] although not if it simply disagrees with the decision on the evidence available. If a body ought by investigation to have known of a matter, the High Court may look at evidence of it even though the body was in fact ignorant of it.[9]

If a tribunal or body produces its own record of the facts before it then the Court will place heavy reliance upon that record. An inferior tribunal or body's power to reach a decision includes a right to determine material facts. The Court will, in general, not interfere with such determinations unless the fact is jurisdictional in nature. Thus where the report of an inspector in relation to a hearing conducted by him includes the material findings of fact the Court will not allow an applicant to refer to additional evidence merely to re-argue the matter afresh.[10] The Court may admit evidence to establish that the record produced by a tribunal or body omits or distorts matters of real importance, however, and may intervene accordingly. Such intervention is of particular importance where the fact-finding and decision-making processes are separated. Thus if an inspector reporting his findings to a minister omits or misinterprets a material fact then the minister's decision will be taken on a false basis and the Court will interfere.[11] Such judicial review is consistent with the classic decision of *Associated Provincial Picture Houses Ltd v Wednesbury Corpn*[12] in that the minister is failing to take into account matters which ought to be taken into account.[13] The same reasoning would apply to a local government committee taking a decision based on reports from its officials or even to any body misdirecting itself by ignoring or misunderstanding material facts. The problem for the Court comes in distinguishing between a body misunderstanding facts or ignoring them and a body taking a view of facts as part of its decision or deciding not to give much weight to various facts. It is this distinction which gives rise to much argument in cases before the High Court under Ord 53.

Where a tribunal or body does not disclose its findings of fact, or does so inadequately, then the Court will have to determine those findings by affidavit, and if necessary, oral evidence. The proper enquiry is into the facts before an inferior body to justify its purported findings. The Court is not enquiring whether it would have reached the same findings on facts disclosed by the evidence.

When the court considers evidence to determine a jurisdictional fact it is exercising its own de novo power and not re-trying the decision reached below. In *Re Ripon (Highfield) Housing Confirmation Order 1938, White and Collins v Minister of Health*[14] the Court quashed a compulsory purchase order which had been

7 See ch 2, above.

8 *Edwards (Inspector of Taxes) v Bairstow and Harrison* [1956] AC 14, [1955] 3 All ER 48, HL; *Ashbridge Investments Ltd v Minister of Housing and Local Government* [1965] 3 All ER 371, sub nom *Re Stalybridge (Castle Hall No 7) and (Acres Lane and Lawton Street) Compulsory Purchase Order 1963, Ashbridge Investments Ltd v Minister of Housing and Local Government* [1965] 1 WLR 1320, CA.

9 *Secretary of State for Education and Science v Tameside Metropolitan Borough Council* [1977] AC 1014 at 1030, [1976] 3 All ER 665 at 674–675.

10 *Ashbridge Investments Ltd v Minister of Housing and Local Government* [1965] 3 All ER 371, sub nom *Re Stalybridge (Castle Hall No 7) and (Acres Lane and Lawton Street) Compulsory Purchase Order 1963, Ashbridge Investments Ltd v Minister of Housing and Local Government* [1965] 1 WLR 1320, CA.

11 *East Hampshire District Council v Secretary of State for the Environment, ex p Josephi* (1979) 251 Estates Gazette 763, [1979] JPL 533, CA.

12 [1948] 1 KB 223, [1947] 2 All ER 680, CA.

13 *R v Secretary of State for the Environment, ex p Powis* [1981] 1 All ER 788, [1981] 1 WLR 584, CA.

14 [1939] 2 KB 838, [1939] 3 All ER 548.

confirmed by the minister. The statutory provisions under which the order was purportedly made and confirmed specifically excluded from its scope land forming part of a park.[15] The Court admitted evidence which showed that the land was in fact part of a park and thus that there was no jurisdiction to make or confirm the order and that it was invalid. The evidence had not been available to the minister but was admitted since it went to jurisdiction and therefore to the validity of the order.

Where the admissibility of any evidence is in dispute the Court will admit it de bene esse before ruling on whether or not it can take it into account and consider it without prejudice to the eventual outcome. It is quite usual, however, for the Court simply to consider the evidence and then decide that because of its nature it does not entitle the applicant to any remedy rather than decide on the narrower ground that the evidence is inadmissible.

## EVIDENCE BY AFFIDAVIT

In all applications for judicial review the principal source of evidence is from affidavits. The basis of the applicant's case will be set out in the affidavit sworn in support of the application for leave.[16] A copy of that affidavit must be served with the notice of motion or summons.[17] Affidavit evidence in reply from a respondent to the application must be filed in the Crown Office as soon as is practicable and in any event within 21 days of service of the notice of motion or summons and accompanying documents.[18] The Court may allow a respondent to file evidence outside the time limit.[18] It may also allow an applicant to use further affidavits in support of his case[19] and in practice the courts will readily give leave for additional evidence to be referred to. Where an applicant intends to seek leave to refer to additional affidavits he is required by RSC Ord 53, r 6(3) to give notice of his intention to every other party in the application. In practice the same requirement applies to any respondent who intends to refer to further evidence.

The general formal requirements for the preparation of affidavits in the High Court apply equally to affidavits in applications for judicial review.[20] The most important of these requirements are as follows:

1. Affidavits must be marked at the top right-hand corner of the first page and the back sheet in clear permanent dark blue or black marking with:
   (i) the party on whose behalf it is filed;
   (ii) the initials and surname of the deponent;
   (iii) the number of the affidavit in relation to the deponent; and
   (iv) the date when sworn.
   eg 'Appnt J.J. JONES: 1st; 14.6.84.'
2. Documentary exhibits should, whenever possible, be similarly marked. Non-documentary exhibits must display the same information clearly in a manner that is securely attached.
3. Affidavits must not be bound with thick plastic strips or anything else which would hamper binding.

15 S 75 of the Housing Act 1936.
16 See p 141, above.
17 RSC Ord 53, r 6(1).
18 RSC Ord 53, r 6(4).
19 RSC Ord 53, r 6(2)—as amended in 1992 by SI 1907/92, r 11 to reverse the decision in *R v Secretary of State for the Environment, ex p ARC Properties Ltd* [1991] TLR 560, (1991) Times, 5 December, EAT. Previously further affidavits were meant to deal only with matters raised in a respondent's affidavit although this was rarely applied in practice.
20 *Practice Note* [1983] 3 All ER 33, sub nom *Practice Direction* [1983] 1 WLR 922.

4. Legible copies of documents may be exhibited instead of originals as long as the originals are made available for inspection by other parties and also by the Court at the hearing. Copies of letters should be exhibited in bundles rather than individually. Where a sequence of correspondence is exhibited it must be in correct date order with the earliest at the top. Where documents are exhibited in bundles, a front page must be attached listing the contents and, where letters are enclosed, the number of original letters and the number of copy letters must be specified.

5. All bundles must be securely fastened so that they cannot be readily undone. Staples are an inadequate method of fastening.

6. Where it is not possible to provide an easily legible copy of a document then a typed transcript should be included as the following page.

7. All bundles should be paginated consecutively at centre bottom with transcripts appearing as 'a' numbers. Hence the transcript of a document appearing as page 6 will appear as the next document but paginated as page 6a.

8. Court documents such as probates, orders, affidavits or pleadings need not be exhibited. Office copies of such documents prove themselves.

9. Exhibits must not be bound up with, or otherwise attached to, the affidavit itself.

10. Where a deponent deposes to more than one affidavit in an application then the numbering of any exhibits should run consecutively throughout and not begin again with each affidavit.

11. Where a document to which reference is made has already been exhibited to any other affidavit in the application then it need not be exhibited again.

12. If, by the time of the hearing, the affidavits or exhibits have become numerous, they should be put in a consolidated bundle, or file or files, and be paged consecutively throughout in the top right-hand corner. Affidavits and exhibits should be put in separate bundles or files. Transcripts of judgments or evidence must not be bound up with any other documents but must be kept separate.

The applicant is required by RSC Ord 53, r 5(6) to file an affidavit of service of the notice of motion or summons before the matter is entered for hearing. The affidavit must give the names and addresses of, and the places and dates of service on, all persons who have been served. If any person who ought to have been served has not been served then they must be identified in the affidavit and the reason for non-service given.

The rule requires that the affidavit of service be before the Court at the hearing. It should be included in the bundle prepared for the Court when any party served is not appearing as a respondent and be available in court in all other cases.

## ORAL EVIDENCE AND CROSS-EXAMINATION

In the ordinary course of events affidavit evidence will be the only form of evidence before the Court on applications for judicial review. The Court has power, however, to order that a deponent attend to give oral evidence and to be cross-examined.[1] Such an order will be made wherever the justice of the

1 RSC Ord 53, r 8 and Ord 38, r 2.

particular case so requires.[2] Applications for such orders may be made by summons at any stage of the proceedings to any judge or master of the Queen's Bench Division even where the substantive motion for relief is to be heard by a full Divisional Court. In such cases, though, any appeal from a decision of a master will lie to a Divisional Court rather than to a single judge in chambers.[3] Although any master may deal with applications they are normally dealt with by the Master of the Crown Office. Applications of substance are normally referred to a judge by the master under RSC Ord 32, r 11 in any event. They should therefore be made by summons to the judge rather than the master.

Although Ord 53 has contained an express provision for cross-examination only since 1977, the power of the Court to order the attendance of deponents for cross-examination is of long standing. It has, however, been little used in the past. In 1928 Lord Hewart CJ, when refusing an application, commented:

> For something like 50 or 60 years no order has been made on the Crown's side [ie in what are now called applications for judicial review] for the cross-examination of a deponent. It is enough to add that such an order was not likely to be made except in very special circumstances.[4]

Twenty-eight years later, in 1956, the Divisional Court allowed an application for cross-examination in a 'remarkable case' in which it was alleged that a false order had been put before the Court. Having referred to the comments of Lord Hewart CJ 28 years earlier, Lord Goddard CJ commented:

> It is the first time in my experience and, I think, in anyone else's experience in Crown practice matters, vis. applications for prerogative orders or writs, that cross-examination has ever taken place. I do not want this to be thought to be an easy precedent. We allowed cross-examination in this case because it is one of a very remarkable character.[5]

The reluctance of the courts to order cross-examination in applications for judicial review has remained to date. In continuing to adhere to such an attitude the courts clearly distinguish between applications for judicial review and other proceedings where affidavit evidence is normally regarded as an unsatisfactory means of achieving justice where facts are in dispute. The more open attitude of the courts to cross-examination of affidavits in other proceedings is exemplified by the comments of Lord Greene MR in a case where the plaintiffs sought to have their names inserted in a company's register of shareholders on the ground that the refusal of the directors of the company to do so was not in good faith:

> I strongly dislike being asked on affidavit evidence alone to draw inferences as to the bona fides or mala fides of the actors. If it is desired to charge a deponent with having given an account of his motives and his reasons which is not the true account, then the person on whom the burden of proof lies should take the ordinary and obvious course of requiring the deponent to submit himself to cross-examination.[6]

2 *O'Reilly v Mackman* [1983] 2 AC 237, [1982] 3 All ER 1124, HL.
3 RSC Ord 58, r 1 and Ord 53, r 8(2).
4 *R v Kent Justices, ex p Smith* [1928] WN 137 at 138.
5 *R v Stokesley (Yorkshire) Justices, ex p Bartram* [1956] 1 All ER 563n at 565.
6 *Re Smith & Fawcett Ltd* [1942] Ch 304 at 308, CA.

Lord Denning, when Master of the Rolls, in a case concerning the validity of a compulsory purchase order gave three reasons for this judicial reluctance to order cross-examination in cases of judicial review:

(i) that because the affidavits will usually speak as to what took place before a judicial or quasi-judicial body they may have to be sworn by a planning inspector or a magistrate, or someone of that kind. Since it is undesirable that such a person should be subjected to cross-examination, the applicant should not be liable to cross-examination either;

(ii) experience shows that on procedural questions arising on judicial review there is very little conflict on the affidavits; and

(iii) if cross-examination is permitted there will be a temptation to try and undermine the actual findings of the inferior body.[7]

In that case the judge at first instance[8] had permitted cross-examination of the applicant de bene esse since the applicant was about to leave the country. Then, on the substantive hearing, he had determined that the evidence given on cross-examination should not be admitted. The Court of Appeal concluded that cross-examination should only be allowed in exceptional cases where it was necessary to do justice between the parties. They would not have permitted cross-examination on the basis that the applicant's case failed on the face of the affidavits and so cross-examination was unnecessary. Had the affidavit evidence been merely unsatisfactory standing alone and without being tested by cross-examination, rather than being considered as worthless, then cross-examination may have been permissible.

In *R v Secretary of State for the Home Department, ex p Manuel*,[9] cross-examination of an applicant was allowed where fraud was alleged against him by the respondent. The applicant sought review of detention and removal orders made by the Home Secretary in the belief that the applicant was an illegal immigrant. The applicant had obtained clearance to enter the United Kingdom but it was alleged that he had done so by tendering false documents. Cross-examination was ordered after an application by the Secretary of State. Although the applicant had previously tendered himself for cross-examination voluntarily McNeill J had doubted whether an applicant was entitled to do so without a request by the respondent. Although Ord 38, r 2(3) refers to an application to cross-examine by 'any party' the context presupposes that it will be an opposing party.

## Non-attendance of deponent

An order of the Court for the attendance of a deponent for cross-examination is made under RSC Ord 38, r 2(3) which provides expressly that if a person fails to attend having been ordered so to do, his affidavit shall not be used as evidence without the leave of the Court. In appropriate cases the court may refuse such leave, or it may permit the affidavit to be read though attaching only such weight to its contents as the circumstances warrant.

The fact that a deponent is to be cross-examined does not prevent his affidavit being used in the proceedings until that has happened.[10] Nor does the

7 *George v Secretary of State for the Environment* (1979) 38 P & CR 609 at 615, CA. See also *O'Reilly v Mackman* [1983] 2 AC 237 at 282, [1982] 3 All ER 1124 at 1132 per Lord Diplock.
8 Sir Douglas Frank QC sitting as a deputy judge of the Queen's Bench Division.
9 (1984) Times, 21 March.
10 *Lewis v James* (1886) 32 Ch D 326, 56 LJ Ch 163, CA.

fact that an affidavit has already been used prevent the Court from ordering the deponent to attend for cross-examination.[11]

## DISCOVERY AND INTERROGATORIES

Before the rule changes in 1977 there was no provision for discovery or interrogatories to be ordered in applications for judicial reviews. In actions begun by writ discovery was automatic and the Court had power to order the administration of interrogatories. This procedural deficiency in applications for judicial review was one of the major reasons for permitting plaintiffs to proceed by writ in a matter where they might also have sought relief under Ord 53. The potential importance of discovery in applications for judicial review has been stressed by Lord Diplock in *O'Reilly v Mackman*[12] when he pointed out that had the plaintiffs in *Anisminic Ltd v Foreign Compensation Commission*,[13] a landmark case in the development of judicial review, not been able to proceed by writ and so obtain discovery then they would never have obtained the minutes giving the reasons for the Commission's decision which led to a successful challenge.

Discovery is still not automatic in applications for judicial review but requires an application to be made to the Court by summons. Discovery and or interrogatories will be ordered whenever, and to the extent that, the justice of the case requires it.[14] As with any other interlocutory applications, discovery or interrogatories may be obtained by application by summons to any judge or master of the Queen's Bench Division even where the substantive motion for relief is to be heard by a full Divisional Court. In such cases any appeal from a decision by a master will lie to a Divisional Court rather than to a single judge in chambers.[15] Although any master may deal with applications they are normally dealt with by the Master of the Crown Office. Applications of substance are normally referred to a judge by the master under RSC Ord 32, r 11 in any event. They should therefore be made by summons to the judge rather than the master.

Applications for discovery are made under RSC Ord 24, r 3 and may extend to any documents which are or have been in the possession of another party relating to any matter in question in the application for judicial review. The Court may order the party to make a further list of such documents and may require it to be verified by an affidavit. In these matters the general law and procedure relating to discovery applies equally to applications for judicial review. Applications for interrogatories are made under RSC Ord 26 which now allows two attempts at interrogatories without leave, although no interrogatories may be served on the Crown without leave. A party may require any other party to answer questions as to facts in issue in the application for judicial review where to do so is necessary either for disposing fairly of the cause or matter or for saving costs. Where the party in question is a body of persons, eg a local authority, then the Court may allow interrogatories to be served on specified officers or members of the body. Interrogatories will not be permitted if the questions go merely as to matters of evidence to be adduced at

11 *Strauss v Goldschmidt* (1892) 8 TLR 239.
12 *O'Reilly v Mackman* [1983] 2 AC 237 at 280b, [1982] 3 All ER 1124 at 1130e, HL.
13 [1969] 2 AC 147, [1969] 1 All ER 208, HL.
14 Eg *R v Secretary of State for the Home Department, ex p Herbage (No 2)* [1987] QB 1077, [1987] 1 All ER 324, CA.
15 Ord 53, r 8(2).

the hearing, as to matters of credit or as to matters of opinion. If a party wishes to claim public interest immunity (or any other form of privilege) against answering the interrogatories then he should do so in his affidavit in answer and not as a means of objecting to the service of the interrogatories.[16] In these matters the general law and procedure relating to interrogatories apply equally to applications for judicial review.

## PUBLIC INTEREST IMMUNITY

Applications for judicial review may involve investigation of very delicate areas of government operations. The documentation which would ordinarily be relevant and discoverable may be so sensitive that objection will be taken to its production. Gone are the days, however, when a minister could prevent the disclosure of information simply by swearing an affidavit stating that disclosure was against the public interest. From 1942 to 1968 the authority of a decision of the House of Lords[17] supported such a sweeping power to deprive a litigant of access to justice. During that period the right to refuse to disclose information was thought to attach to the Crown by virtue of its constitutional position and for that reason was called 'Crown privilege'. It was a privilege which had only to be claimed and did not need to be justified upon enquiry.

In 1968 the House of Lords performed a judicial reversal and opened up the files of government to judicial review. In *Conway v Rimmer*[18] a young police constable sought damages for malicious prosecution. He had been unsuccessfully prosecuted for the theft of a torch and sought discovery of the police records as evidence in his claim of malice. The Chief Constable sought to prevent discovery of the records. His resistance was rooted in the British obsession with closed government. It was argued that good government depended upon freedom of communication with and within government bodies. Such freedom was thought to be threatened if informants were to be open to disclosure and question on the information they gave. That argument was unanimously rejected by the House of Lords. Although government bodies may ask for confidences to be respected they now have to justify their request to the Court.

Judges should now inspect disputed documents and themselves decide whether or not they should be disclosed. In doing so the Court will weigh the public interest which the government body claims to be protecting against the public interest in open justice being done. However, the courts do not encourage 'fishing expeditions' and an applicant will need to establish a strong likelihood that the document in question is material to the issues before the Court. The Court will be more likely to venture a 'judicial peep'[19] and inspect the documents itself before ordering discovery if there is doubt about their content and whether they fall into a protected category than where the doubt is as to the balance of the public interest. The considerations in favour of disclosure include not only the private rights of a litigant to a remedy for wrong done to him but also the public interest in quieting grievances and adding to public confidence in the administration of justice. In particular the courts will

16 RSC Ord 26, r 4.
17 *Duncan v Cammell, Laird & Co Ltd* [1942] AC 624, [1942] 1 All ER 587, HL.
18 [1968] AC 910, [1968] 1 All ER 874, HL; *Burmah Oil Co Ltd v Bank of England* [1980] AC 1090, [1979] 3 All ER 700, HL.
19 *Air Canada v Secretary of State for Trade (No 2)* [1983] 2 AC 394, [1983] 1 All ER 910, HL.

consider the context of any statutory provisions under which information may have been collected by a government body.[20] Moreover, where the Court concludes that the limitations on judicial experience render an assessment of the public interest by the Court inappropriate then it will defer to a governmental assessment.[1]

In the wake of the *Matrix Churchill* arms to Iraq case the Attorney General wrote to *The Times*[2] setting out his understanding of public interest immunity and confirming the limited role of ministers when signing certificates 'claiming' public interest immunity. He wrote:

> Public interest immunity is not—to quote a judgment of Lord Justice Bingham, now the Master of the Rolls—a trump card vouchsafed to certain privileged players[3a]. It is an exclusionary rule, applying equally to all parties to litigation and irrespective of whether it helps or hinders them, whereby certain classes of documents are immune from production if harm may thereby be done to the operation of the public service.
>
> Such a claim cannot be waived by the minister. In the Matrix Churchill case, ministers had been advised that there were certain well recognised classes of documents capable of attracting public interest immunity. They saw the documents and concluded they fell within those classes. On that basis, they were advised by counsel and myself that they were required by law to claim public interest immunity on behalf of the Crown. Counsel did not advise the case was one where the court would inevitably order disclosure and accordingly certificates saying that the documents fell within a category where their disclosure would in principle be contrary to the public interest were signed on our advice. I should add that if, at that stage, any of the documents had shown that it was unfair to continue this case it would have been withdrawn forthwith.
>
> Such certificates are not conclusive. Each claim is considered by the court which may inspect the documents before determining its validity. Where the claim is upheld, as in the present case, the court must go on to consider whether the interests of justice in the particular case require that the public interest in confidentiality be overridden. It is not open to ministers to second guess the court on this issue. The decision is for the court to make, *not* for the minister. This applies equally whether the document may be helpful to the prosecution or to the defence.

Where discovery is ordered the party objecting to the order should be given an opportunity to appeal before the document is produced.[3b] A similar opportunity should be given where a Court decides to inspect documents prior to deciding whether to order discovery or not.[4]

The protection now afforded against discovery is, therefore, not a true privilege but is an immunity granted where the public interest so requires. The immunity attaches to the information in question and not to the Crown as its holder. It is, therefore, open to any party to assert that the public interest requires that information be withheld. Thus in 1977 the House of Lords upheld a claim for immunity from disclosure of information which the Gaming Board

20 *Alfred Crompton Amusement Machines Ltd v Customs and Excise Comrs (No 2)* [1974] AC 405 at 434, [1973] 2 All ER 1169 at 1185, HL. Cf *Norwich Pharmacal Co v Customs and Excise Comrs* [1974] AC 133, [1973] 2 All ER 943, HL.

1 *Conway v Rimmer* [1968] AC 910 at 952, 971–972, [1968] 1 All ER 874 at 888, 900, HL.

2 Published in *The Times*, 13 November 1992.

3a *Makanjvola v the Metropolitan Police Comr* [1992] 3 All ER 617 at 623f.

3b *Conway v Rimmer* [1968] AC 910 at 953 per Lord Reid and [1968] 1 All ER 874 at 888, HL; *Burmah Oil Co Ltd v Bank of England* [1980] AC 1090 at 1147, [1979] 3 All ER 700 at 735.

4 *Williams v Home Office* [1981] 1 All ER 1151 at 1154a per McNeill J.

had made independently of a similar claim by the Home Secretary.[5] The existence of a public interest immunity may not prevent the holder of the documentation from using it in the preparation or defence of litigation but it does limit the use of the documentation by the process of discovery or in the course of a trial.[6]

The ingredients of the public interest have been kept deliberately vague by the courts. Instead of laying down hard and fast criteria the courts approach the facts of each case afresh. There are areas, however, in which the courts have been prepared to accept that the public interest will generally require non-disclosure. These include national security[7] and defence, cabinet papers though not mere high level policy documents,[8] law enforcement, the protection of children's interests[9] and the conduct of diplomatic relations.[10] The public interest with which the English courts will concern themselves is that of the United Kingdom. They will, however, recognise that there may be an English public interest in supporting the interests of foreign states.[11] Although the openness of justice weighs in the balance of the public interest, so too does the prevention of 'ill-informed criticism' of government activities.[12] Stress is still placed upon the need to protect sources of information and reference is still made to the 'candour within government' argument which was rejected in *Conway v Rimmer*. A better view appears to be that the candour argument as such now carries little weight.[13]

Since discovery is a relatively new feature of applications for judicial review, the decided cases relate primarily to actions commenced by writ. However, the immunity is of general application and may be relied upon in proceedings for judicial review. This was confirmed by Lord Diplock in *R v IRC, ex p Rossminster*:[14]

> . . . it will not in my view be open to a person claiming to have been injured by the purported but unlawful exercise by a police officer of statutory powers to circumvent the public interest immunity against premature disclosure of the grounds on which the officer's exercise of the power was based, by applying under RSC Ord 53 for judicial review instead of bringing an ordinary action.

In that case the House of Lords recognised that the grounds for an officer's belief that a document that he seized may be required as evidence in a future

5 *Rogers v Secretary of State for the Home Department* [1973] AC 388, [1972] 2 All ER 1057.

6 *R v Metropolitan Police Comr, ex p Hart-Leverton* [1990] TLR 93, (1990) Times, 8 February. A decision of a two judge Divisional Court which was not followed by Popplewell J in *R v Chief Constable of the West Midlands, ex p, Wiley* CO, (16 December 1992, unreported) and proceeding to appeal at the time of writing.

7 *Conway v Rimmer* [1968] AC 910 at 952–953, 955, 956–957, 971, 993, [1968] 1 All ER 874 at 888, 890; *Burmah Oil Co Ltd v Bank of England* [1980] AC 1090 at 1134–1135, 1143–1144, [1979] 3 All ER 700 at 725–726, 732–733; *Air Canada v Secretary of State for Trade (No 2)* [1983] 2 AC 394, [1983] 1 All ER 910, HL.

8 *Conway v Rimmer* [1968] AC 910 at 952, [1968] 1 All ER 874 at 888.

9 *D v National Society for the Prevention of Cruelty to Children* [1978] AC 171, [1977] 1 All ER 589.

10 *Rogers v Secretary of State for the Home Department* [1973] AC 388 at 412, [1972] 2 All ER 1057 at 1070.

11 *Buttes Gas and Oil Co v Hammer (No 2)* [1981] QB 223, [1980] 3 All ER 475, CA; on appeal [1982] AC 888, [1981] 3 All ER 616, HL.

12 *Burmah Oil Co Ltd v Bank of England* [1980] AC 1090 at 1134, 1145–1147, [1979] 3 All ER 700 at 725, 734, 735.

13 See *Conway v Rimmer* [1968] AC 910 at 952, [1968] 1 All ER 874 at 888; *Burmah Oil Co Ltd v Bank of England* [1980] AC 1090 at 1112, 1145, [1979] 3 All ER 700 at 707, 733; *Williams v Home Office* [1981] 1 All ER 1151.

14 [1980] AC 952 at 1013, [1980] 1 All ER 80 at 94.

prosecution for an offence involving tax fraud may benefit from a temporary immunity from disclosure. Since the immunity would only last until the trial for the offence in question or until a decision not to proceed with the prosecution had been taken the public interest could be protected by adjourning any application for judicial review. Even the step of adjourning an application may diminish the force of judicial intervention to correct an abuse since the grant of a remedy will be delayed.

Judicial interest in obtaining access to government files extends only for the purposes of litigation. It is an interest in enabling a litigant to present information to the Court rather than enabling a litigant to obtain information for its own sake or to make it known publicly. Thus where discovery is permitted it is limited to use in the proceedings in question and a party or his advisers may be liable to proceedings for contempt if he or she distributes the information for other purposes even though it may have been disclosed publicly in open court.[15] A general right of access to information will, it appears, require parliamentary rather than judicial intervention.

15 *Harman v Secretary of State for the Home Department* [1983] 1 AC 280, sub nom *Home Office v Harman* [1982] 1 All ER 532, HL.

CHAPTER 16

# Appeals in judicial review proceedings

## POWERS AND EVIDENCE ON APPEAL

Decisions of the Divisional Court or of a single judge in applications for judicial review are appealable in the ordinary way as decisions of the High Court. It is important to note, however, that such appeals are against the refusal or grant of the application for review and are not a method of appeal against the decision of the inferior body which is the subject of the application for judicial review. The Court of Appeal and the House of Lords have no greater power to review decisions of inferior bodies than has the Divisional Court.[1] Similarly the appeal courts have no power to admit evidence for consideration which would not have been admissible in the Divisional Court.[2] 'Fresh' evidence will only be admitted on appeal if it would have been admissible at first instance and where:

(i) The evidence is as to matters occurring after the date of trial and substantially affects a basic assumption made at trial;[3] or

(ii) The evidence is of matters before trial which
 (a) could not have been obtained with reasonable diligence for use at the trial,
 (b) is such that, if given, would probably have an important influence on the result of the case, although it need not be decisive, and
 (c) is apparently credible though not necessarily incontrovertible.[4]

In cases where liberty is at stake, however, a more flexible attitude tends to be shown.[5]

Where a party wishes to rely on fresh evidence on appeal its contents should be set out in affidavit form for the consideration of the Court. If any other party objects to the admission of the evidence then they should nevertheless file any evidence in reply upon which they would wish to rely should the fresh evidence be considered. Such evidence in reply may be filed without prejudice to the contention that the fresh evidence is inadmissible. The appeal court will then consider the new evidence de bene esse before deciding whether or not it should be admitted.[6]

1 See RSC Ord 59, r 10.
2 See ch 15, above.
3 *Mulholland v Mitchell* [1971] AC 666, [1971] 1 All ER 307, HL.
4 *Ladd v Marshall* [1954] 3 All ER 745, [1954] 1 WLR 1489, CA. See also *Ali v Secretary of State for the Home Department* [1984] 1 All ER 1009, sub nom *R v Secretary of State for the Home Department, ex p Momin Ali* [1984] 1 WLR 663.
5 See eg *Irtelli v Squatriti* [1992] 3 All ER 294, [1992] 3 WLR 218, CA.
6 *Langdale v Danby* [1982] 3 All ER 129, [1982] 1 WLR 1123, HL.

## APPEALS AGAINST GRANT OR REFUSAL OF LEAVE

No appeal can be made against the refusal of leave to apply for judicial review, or against the terms upon which it has been granted, if the applications can be renewed. Where in a criminal cause or matter a single judge of the High Court refuses leave or grants it on terms either with or without a hearing under Ord 53, r 3(3) then the application may be renewed to a Divisional Court of the Queen's Bench Division under Ord 53, r 3(4). If, in a civil case, a single judge refuses leave or grants it on terms after considering the papers in private and without a hearing then the application may be renewed to a single judge sitting in open court, or, if the Court directs, to a Divisional Court of the Queen's Bench Division. Such a direction would be unusual.[7] Once leave in a civil case has been refused or granted on terms by a single judge sitting in open court then it may not be renewed either before a different single judge or before a Divisional Court. As to renewal generally see p 143, above, and for the distinction between criminal causes or matters and civil matters see p 151.

Once all opportunities for renewal of an application have been used then appeal will lie to the Court of Appeal without leave in civil proceedings.[8] In *Re Poh*[9] the House of Lords held that it had no jurisdiction to entertain an appeal from the Court of Appeal against the refusal of leave to bring an application for judicial review in a civil matter. The decision was based on the wording of the Appellate Jurisdiction Act 1876, s 3 which provides for appeals against orders or judgments of the Court of Appeal. Their Lordships followed an earlier decision of the House in *Lane v Esdaile*[10] that a refusal of leave was not an order or judgment. They did so even though the House had earlier entertained such an appeal when the jurisdiction had not been challenged.[11] The reasoning of *Re Poh* can be applied equally to the jurisdiction of the Court of Appeal under the Supreme Court Act 1981, s 16. It is submitted, however, that the practice of the Court of Appeal in considering appeals against the refusal of leave is too well established for it to be successfully challenged now. Indeed in *Chief Adjudication Officer v Foster*[12] the Court of Appeal held that it had wide powers to deal with judicial review issues even on a direct appeal from a statutory body that could not itself have dealt with issues of judicial review. The breadth of such powers was said to come from the fact that under s 9 of the Supreme Court Act 1981 a Lord Justice of Appeal can sit as a High Court judge to deal with judicial review matters where necessary.

Where an application for leave to apply for judicial review has been made to and refused by, the Court of Appeal, any further applications for such leave should be made to the Court of Appeal[13] except where the renewed application is made after a considerable delay and the Court of Appeal is no longer

7 See p 143, above.

8 It was proposed in clause 43 of the Administration of Justice Bill that s 31 of the Supreme Court Act 1981 should be amended to remove the right of appeal to the Court of Appeal against refusals of leave in civil cases. The proposal was the subject of adverse judicial comment; see *R v IT Acts Special Purposes Comr, ex p Stipplechoice Ltd* [1985] 2 All ER 465 and *R v Beverly County Court, ex p Brown* (1985) Times, 25 January, and was defeated.

9 [1983] 1 All ER 287, [1983] 1 WLR 2, HL.

10 [1981] AC 210, sub nom *Payne v Esdaile* 60 LJ Ch 644, HL.

11 *Suthendran v Immigration Appeal Tribunal* [1977] AC 359, [1976] 3 All ER 611, HL.

12 [1992] 1 QB 31, [1991] 3 All ER 846, an appeal to the Court of Appeal from the Social Security Commissioners under the Social Security Act 1975.

13 *M v Home Office* [1992] 2 WLR 73, 83, CA.

constituted by the same judges in which case a fresh application for judicial review in the normal way is more appropriate.[14]

The Court of Appeal has no jurisdiction to entertain appeals against the grant or refusal of leave in criminal causes or matters.[15] Any appeal must, therefore, be to the House of Lords under the Administration of Justice Act 1960, s 1. That section provides for appeals to the House of Lords 'from any decision of a Divisional Court of the Queen's Bench Division in a criminal cause or matter'. The reasoning of *Re Poh* which relates to 'orders or judgments' rather than 'decisions' is, therefore, distinguishable.[16] No appeal will lie, however, without the leave of the Divisional Court or the House of Lords. Such leave will not be granted unless the Divisional Court certifies that a point of law of general public importance is involved in the decision and it appears to the Court or to the House of Lords that the point is one which ought to be considered by the House of Lords.[17] For this reason no appeal will lie in matters of leave to apply for judicial review in practice. If leave to apply is granted then objections should be taken at the substantive hearing rather than on appeal and if a point of law of general public importance is involved it is hardly likely that leave would be refused.

If leave is granted to an applicant upon an ex parte application then an aggrieved respondent should apply to set the leave aside a tan inter partes hearing rather than appeal to the Court of Appeal. Although the Court of Appeal has jurisdiction under s 16(1) of the Supreme Court Act 1981 to entertain appeals from orders made on ex parte application, such appeals will normally be dismissed as an abuse of the process of the Court.[18] Since the granting of leave raises no presumptions in an applicant's favour, the objections which may be raised to the granting of leave on an application to set aside may also be raised at the substantive hearing. In many cases this will be the more appropriate course since then the court will have all the available information before it to consider.[19] The Court of Appeal may be more willing to consider an appeal against an order made upon inter partes hearing concerning the granting or setting aside of leave,[20] but since the granting of leave is largely a matter of discretion the Court of Appeal may be loath to interfere.

Where the Court of Appeal in a civil matter granted leave on an appeal against a refusal of leave, or against the terms upon which leave was granted, the practice used to be for the Court of Appeal to hear the substantive application.[1] Since 1982, however, that practice has ended. Now if the Court of Appeal grants leave on appeal the substantive application will be made to the Queen's Bench Division unless the Court otherwise directs. The Court of Appeal will only hear the substantive application when granting leave if the

14 *Miah v Secretary of State for the Home Department* [1992] Imm AR 581, CA.
15 Supreme Court Act 1981, s 18(1)(a). See p 151 above for meaning of 'Criminal Cause or Matter'.
16 But see *Podbery v Peak* [1981] Ch 344, [1981] 1 All ER 699, CA.
17 Administration of Justice Act 1960, s 1(2). It is to be noted that no such certificate is required in cases of Habeas Corpus, see ch 18 below.
18 *WEA Records Ltd v Visions Channel 4 Ltd* [1983] 2 All ER 589, [1983] 1 WLR 721, CA.
19 *IRC v National Federation of Self-Employed and Small Businesses Ltd* [1982] AC 617, [1981] 2 All ER 93, HL.
20 *R v East Berkshire Health Authority, ex p Walsh* [1985] QB 152, [1984] 3 All ER 425, CA.
1 *R v Industrial Injuries Comr, ex p AEU (No 2)* [1966] 2 QB 31, [1966] 1 All ER 97, CA.

Divisional Court would be bound by existing authority or where an appeal to the Court of Appeal is for some other reason inevitable.[2]

## APPEALS AGAINST GRANT OR REFUSAL OF RELIEF

Appeals against the grant or refusal of an order of judicial review in non-criminal (ie civil) causes or matters lie without leave to the Court of Appeal. The procedure for such appeal is provided for by RSC Ord 59 and is in common with all civil appeals from the High Court. By RSC Ord 59 r 1A(5)(b) an order granting any relief made at the hearing of an application for judicial review is to be treated as final rather than interlocutory for the purposes of appeals to the Court of Appeal. For the distinction between criminal and non-criminal causes or matters see p 151, above.

Appeals against orders made on applications for leave or on substantive applications for judicial review in criminal causes or matters lie direct to the House of Lords and not to the Court of Appeal.[3] Such appeals lie at the instance of either a defendant or the prosecution but require the leave of the Divisional Court or of the House of Lords. Such leave will not be granted unless the Divisional Court certifies that a point of law of general public importance is involved in the decision and it appears to the Court or to the House of Lords that the point is one which ought to be considered by the House of Lords.[4]

## INTERLOCUTORY APPEALS

RSC Ord 53, r 8 now makes express provision in judicial review proceedings for interlocutory applications including applications for discovery, interrogatories and cross-examination of deponents. Interlocutory applications may be made to any judge or any master of the Queen's Bench Division even where the substantive hearing is to be heard by the Divisional Court. In practice applications to a master are dealt with by the Master of the Crown Office but any applications of substance are either made to a judge or referred to a judge by the master under RSC Ord 32, r 11. If the substantive hearing is to be heard by a Divisional Court then any appeal from a master would be to that Court rather than to a single judge in chambers. A notice of appeal must be issued within five days of the master's orders and served not less than two clear days before the day fixed for the hearing of the appeal. Such an appeal from a master does not require leave. Appeals from interlocutory decisions of the Divisional Court or of a single judge lie to the Court of Appeal in civil matters and to the House of Lords in criminal matters. Leave is required in each case and the restricted circumstances in which leave may be granted to the House of Lords set out above will apply.

2 *Practice Direction* [1982] 3 All ER 800, [1982] 1 WLR 1375. Eg *R v Independent Television Commission, ex p TSW Broadcasting Ltd* (1992) Times, 30 March, HL.

3 S 18(1)(a) of the Supreme Court Act 1981.

4 S 1 of the Administration of Justice Act 1960. Cf Habeas Corpus; n 17 above.

## DISAGREEMENT BY THE DIVISIONAL COURT

If an application for judicial review is considered by a Divisional Court comprising an even number of judges there is a risk of them being unable to agree. Where this risk is foreseeable an application should be made in advance for the case to be listed before a three-judge court.[5] If the court is unable to agree then it may dismiss the application and allow it to proceed for a decision to the Court of Appeal.[6]

## COSTS

Costs are a matter for the discretion of the Court but the discretion must be exercised judicially. Costs will normally follow the outcome of an appeal subject to the considerations set out on p 160, above. On appeal to the House of Lords in a criminal cause or matter the costs of the accused or the prosecutor may be met by payment out of central funds.[7] Such an order may include the costs of proceedings in the courts below.

## LEGAL AID

Where an applicant is legally aided the Court must order that his costs be taxed on the standard basis.[8] Such a direction is in addition to any other direction as to taxation and must be made even though no other order for costs is made. Counsel for the assisted person must ensure that such a direction is included in the final order by applying at the close of the case.

Where a legally aided party is unsuccessful on appeal costs may be awarded in favour of the successful party against the legal aid fund. The considerations set out on p 161, above, apply in such cases save that on appeal the party seeking an order for costs need not satisfy the Court that he would suffer severe financial hardship if no order were made.

5 See p 145, above.
6 *Findlay v Secretary of State for the Home Department*, [1984] 3 All ER 801.
7 S 6 of the Costs in Criminal Cases Act 1973.
8 Reg 107, Civil Legal Aid (General) Regulations 1989. For the meaning of 'standard basis' see RSC Ord 62, r 12.

CHAPTER 17

# Case stated, statutory rights of challenge and statutory appeals

## CASE STATED

In applications for judicial review or habeas corpus the High Court is exercising its inherent powers through the prerogative writs. In addition to these inherent powers of supervision the High Court has a limited number of appellate functions expressly conferred on it by statute. Some statutes give a straightforward right of appeal to the High Court, normally limited to appeals on points of law. Such appeals are normally subject to tight time limits. A more complex, and also more historic, statutory appeal procedure is appeal by way of case stated. The idea of a case stated is that an inferior tribunal can be required to state a case for the opinion of the High Court on a question of law or jurisdiction. Among the inferior tribunals that can be required to state cases for the Divisional Court of the Queen's Bench Division are magistrates' courts, Crown Courts, and ministers and statutory tribunals exercising judicial functions, although not all of the functions of these courts and other bodies may be the subject of case stated. No power to state a case exists in the absence of statutory provision.

### Case stated from magistrates' courts

By the Magistrates' Courts Act 1980, s 111, any person who was a party to any proceedings before a magistrates' court or is aggrieved by their order, determination or other proceeding may request that a case be stated on the grounds that the justices were wrong in law or acting in excess of jurisdiction.

The definition of 'magistrates' court' in s 148(1) of the Magistrates' Courts Act 1980—'justices of the peace acting under any enactment'—is wide enough to include licensing justices, so that, although the definition is for the purposes of the Magistrates' Courts Act, its effect is to apply to justices acting as licensing justices under the Licensing Acts the provisions of s 111 of the Magistrates' Courts Act relating to the stating of a case.[1] The same argument can be applied to justices sitting as examining magistrates (eg dealing with committals and extradition proceedings) and the pre-1980 authorities[2] that suggest that examining magistrates have no jurisdiction to state a case are possibly no longer good law. In relation to extradition, special statutory rights of appeal by way of case stated exist under s 7 of the Criminal Justice Act 1988, s 7A of the Fugitive Offenders Act 1967 and s 2A of the Backing of Warrants (Republic of Ireland)

1 *Jeffrey v Evans* [1964] 1 All ER 536, [1964] 1 WLR 505; *R v East Riding of Yorkshire Quarter Sessions, ex p Newton* [1968] 1 QB 32, 53, [1967] 3 All ER 118, 121, CA.

2 *Card v Salmon* [1953] 1 QB 392, [1953] 1 All ER 324; *Atkinson v United States of America Government* [1971] AC 197. In *Neill v North Antrim Magistrates' Court* [1992] 4 All ER 846, [1992] 1 WLR 1220 the House of Lords held that the power of the Divisional Court to give leave to move for judicial review to quash committal proceedings should only be used where there was a really substantial error leading to a demonstrable injustice.

Act 1965, and Ord 56 r 12(a) of the Rules of the Supreme Court makes special provision for such appeals.

A stipendiary magistrate can be asked to state a case in just the same way as justices since they are, by virtue of their office, justices of the peace.[3]

The wording of s 111 is wide enough to include not only final determinations but also 'interlocutory' determinations made in the course of proceedings before magistrates, but before they have made a final determination of the matter before them. In practice, however, a distinction has been drawn between cases stated on interlocutory matters in civil and criminal cases.[4] In practice justices cannot state a case in criminal cases until they have reached the final determination of the matter before them[5] but in civil cases they have a discretion to state an 'interlocutory' case which should only be used in exceptional cases.[6] Thus, where objection is taken to any 'interlocutory' decision of the justices the proper procedure will normally be for the justices to continue to hear and determine the matter before them and then to state a case if so required.[7] Where, however, justices decline to exercise jurisdiction then a case stated may be sought,[8] even in criminal cases, and the Divisional Court has indicated that such a procedure is normally preferable to seeking judicial review.[9] The same preference was expressed by the Court of Appeal in relation to challenges to proceedings under s 11 of the Caravan Sites Act 1968 in *Stubbings v Beaconsfield Justices and South Buckinghamshire District Council*[10] where proceedings had been commenced by way of judicial review. In *Bone v Mental Health Review Tribunal*[11] Nolan J expressed the view that judicial review was

3 See eg s 31 of the Justices of the Peace Act 1979.
4 For the distinction between civil and criminal see p 151.
5 *Streames v Copping* [1985] QB 920, [1985] 2 All ER 122 and *Loade v DPP* [1990] 1 QB 1052, [1990] 1 All ER 36, but see n 6, below.
6 See *R v Chesterfield Justices, ex p Kovacs* [1992] 2 All ER 325 and the cases there referred to. A clear exceptional case would be where the interlocutory issue would dispose of the matter finally (see *Norwich Rating Authority v Norwich Assessment Committee* [1941] 2 KB 326 at 330–332, [1941] 3 All ER 225 at 228–229) and this one exception may even apply to criminal cases (see Roch J, obiter, in *R v Chesterfield Justices, ex p Kovacs* above at 333e).
7 Even where there is no power to state a case or a case stated is refused, an application for judicial review is theoretically possible but relief is likely to be refused as premature where the application relates to an interlocutory decision and it will normally be preferable for justices to continue to hear a case even though objection has been taken to a ruling, eg as to admissibility of evidence, and then state a case, if requested to do so, having heard and determined the full matter—see *R v South East London Licensing Justices, ex p Kelly* (14 March 1985, unreported) QBD, Crown Office number 205/85, Lexis per Glidewell J. See also McCullough J in *R v Association of Futures Brokers and Dealers Ltd, ex p Mordens Ltd* [1991] COD 40, [1991] 3 Admin LR 254 re an 'interlocutory' decision by a regulatory commissioner appointed by the Bank of England pursuant to the Financial Services Act 1986 to refuse an order for discovery.
8 *R v Clerkenwell Metropolitan Stipendiary Magistrate, ex p DPP* [1984] QB 821, [1983] 2 All ER 193 following *R v Wisbech Justices* (1890) 54 JP 743 and not following *Pratt v AA Sites Ltd* [1983] 2 KB 459, [1938] 2 All ER 371.
9 *R v Clerkenwell Metropolitan Stipendiary Magistrate, ex p DPP*, above, n 8, and *R v Crown Court at Ipswich, ex p Baldwin* [1981] 1 All ER 596; in *Re Harrington* [1984] AC 473, sub nom *Harrington v Roots* [1984] 2 All ER 474 the House of Lords granted judicial review in such a case but the point was not taken and although contrary statements were made by the Divisional Court in *Streames v Copping*, above, n 5, they were obiter and also per incuriam since they followed *Pratt v AA Sites Ltd*, above, n 8, but neither *R v Wisbech Justices*, above, n 8, nor *R v Clerkenwell Metropolitan Stipendiary Magistrate, ex p DPP*, above, n 8, were cited to the Court. But see *R v Wimbledon Justices, ex p Derwent* [1953] 1 QB 380, [1953] 1 All ER 390 re prohibition.
10 (1987) 152 JP 17, 85 LGR 821.
11 [1985] 3 All ER 330.

preferable to case stated under s 78(8) of the Mental Health Act 1983 where a detained patient was dissatisfied with the reasons given by a tribunal in refusing to direct his discharge since judicial review allowed a broader consideration of the issues and offered a more comprehensive range of reliefs.

An application to justices to state a case must be made within 21 days after the day on which the decision of the court was given.[12] There is no power to extend this period.[13] When a court adjourns a case for sentence after conviction then time for applying for a case stated does not begin to run until sentence has been dealt with.[14]

Applying for a case to be stated involves making a decision about which form of appeal to pursue where there is also a right of appeal to the Crown Court. An appeal to the Crown Court is not limited to points of law and jurisdiction and involves a complete rehearing of the case on its merits. But once an application has been made for a case to be stated then any right to appeal to the Crown Court ceases.[15] The bar remains even if the appeal by way of case stated is subsequently withdrawn.[16] If an application for a case stated is a nullity,[17] however, then it does not operate to prevent an appeal to the Crown Court. If a party is aggrieved by the decision of the Crown Court on appeal then the Crown Court may be asked to state a case except in relation to licensing matters (see below).

The procedure for requesting and obtaining a case stated from justices is provided for by rules 76–81 of the Magistrates' Courts Rules 1981. The requirements of the rules are, however, directory rather than mandatory and do not affect the jurisdiction of the High Court to determine a case stated.[18] Rule 76 requires that the application for justices to state a case must be in writing and signed by or on behalf of the applicant. The application, which should be sent to the clerk to the magistrates, must identify the question or questions of law or jurisdiction on which the opinion of the High Court is sought. The rules then provide for the justices' clerk to produce a draft case within 21 days and submit it to the parties. The parties then have 21 days in which to make representations as to the contents of the case, and within a further 21 days the justices should consider the draft and the representations and sign the final case. The case may be signed by two of the justices or even by the clerk if the justices have so directed. These time limits can be extended under r 79 but, if they are, the clerk must attach a statement of the extension and the reasons for it with the case. Service of these various documents can be done by post but in a registered letter or by recorded delivery service. If they are sent by post to the parties then they should be addressed to their last known or usual place of abode.

The case stated must contain the facts found by the court and the question or questions of law or jurisdiction on which the opinion of the High Court is sought. Although the findings of fact should be stated, the evidence should not be set out unless one of the grounds of challenge is that the decision or a finding of fact cannot be justified on the evidence in which case the particular finding

12 MCA 1980, s 111(2)
13 *Michael v Gowland* [1977] 2 All ER 328, [1977] 1 WLR 296.
14 MCA 1980, s 111(3)
15 MCA 1980, s 111(4)
16 *R v Crown Court at Winchester, ex p Lewington* [1982] 1 WLR 1277, [1982] Crim LR 664.
17 Eg by being out of time; see *P and M Supplies (Essex) Ltd v Hackney London Borough Council* (1990) 154 JP 814, [1990] Crim LR 569.
18 *R v Croydon Justices, ex p Lefore Holdings Ltd* [1981] 1 All ER 520, [1980] 1 WLR 1465, CA.

of fact in question must have been identified in the application and must be specified in the case stated. If need be, the High Court may send the case back to the justices for amendment, either upon application prior to the hearing, or upon consideration of the case at the hearing.[19]

The justices may refuse to state a case if they consider the request to be frivolous, unless the request is made by or at the direction of the Attorney General.[20] If they do refuse a request then they must certify that they have done so if the applicant so requires. If the applicant considers that the case ought to be stated notwithstanding the refusal then he may apply to the High Court[1] for an order requiring the justices to state a case.[2] The clerk to the justices is not required to deliver the case to the applicant until the fees for the case and any required recognisances have been paid.[3]

Once the case has been stated it is up to the appellant to lodge it at the High Court. In the High Court the procedure is contained in Ords 56 and 57 of the Rules of the Supreme Court. The appellant must lodge the case stated in the Crown Office within ten days of receiving it from the clerk to the justices. A fee is payable on lodging. In practice the Crown Office requires three copies of any document to be lodged. Within four days of lodging the case the appellant must serve on the respondent a notice of the entry of the appeal together with a copy of the case.[4]

Once the case has been lodged the matter will be put in the Crown Office List for hearing. The operation of the List is governed by the *Practice Note* handed down by the Lord Chief Justice on 3 February 1987 reported at [1987] 1 All ER 368, [1987] 1 WLR 232 and dealt with in chapter 19. Appeals in criminal cases will be dealt with by the Divisional Court of the Queen's Bench Division. Civil cases may be dealt with by the Divisional Court if the Court so directs but normally they will be dealt with by a single judge sitting in open court.[5] If an appeal concerns an order relating to the custody or care of minors or to maintenance payments then it will be heard by a judge of the Family Division.[6]

On the hearing of an appeal by case stated the justices should not normally appear or be represented.[7] Costs may be awarded against unsuccessful respondents to an appeal by case stated but will not normally be awarded against respondents who do not appear and contest the application. Costs cannot be awarded against the justices who stated the case even if they are found to have been wrong.[8]

19 Summary Jurisdiction Act 1857, s 7; *Spicer v Warbey* [1953] 1 All ER 284, [1953] 1 WLR 334, *Practice Note* [1953] 1 WLR 334.

20 MCA 1980, s 111(5).

1 By originating motion, entered for hearing in the Crown Office or the Principal Registry of the Family Division as appropriate (RSC Ord 56, r 8 and Ord 57, r 2), or by mandamus obtained in judicial review proceedings.

2 MCA 1980, s 111(6); the application may be by originating motion entered in the Crown Office or the Principal Registry of the Family Division as appropriate (RSC Ord 56, r 8 and Ord 57, r 2) or by way of judicial review for an order of mandamus.

3 MCA 1980, s 114.

4 Ord 56, r 6 RSC these time limits may be extended on a summons to the Master of the Crown Office on at least two days' notice to the respondent; see RSC Ord 3, r 5 and Ord 56, r 13.

5 Ord 56, r 5.

6 RSC Ord 56, r 5(2).

7 *Smith v Butler* (1885) 16 QBD 349.

8 The Summary Jurisdiction Act 1857 s 6, as amended by the Magistrates' Courts Act 1952, Sch 5, Administration of Justices Act 1960, Sch 3 and the Magistrates' Courts Act 1980, Sch 7.

## Case stated from Crown Court

Section 28 of the Supreme Court Act 1981 provides that any order, judgment or other decision of the Crown Court may be questioned by any party to the proceedings, on the ground that it is wrong in law or is in excess of jurisdiction, by applying to the Crown Court to have a case stated for the opinion of the High Court except for judgments or other decisions relating to trial on indictment[9] and decisions on licensing matters.[10] It is to be noted that the provision of this right to parties to the proceedings is narrower than the right that is given to parties or 'persons aggrieved' in the case of justices. The power of the Crown Court to state a case relating to an interlocutory determination before a final disposal of the case before it is the same as that of justices,[11] as to which see p 181, above.

The procedure for obtaining a case stated from the Crown Court is governed by r 26 of the Crown Court Rules 1982. There are subtle differences in procedure between case stated from the Crown Court and from justices. As with justices, an application to state a case must be made in writing within 21 days of the decision in question. Unlike the time limit for case stated from justices this time limit can be extended by the Crown Court either before or after it expires, as indeed can any of the time limits in r 26 of the Crown Court Rules. The application, which must state the grounds on which the decision is being questioned, must be sent to the Crown Court and to the other parties to the proceedings. The Crown Court will then forward the application to the judge who will decide whether to state a case or not. He can decide not to state a case if he considers that the application is frivolous. The judge informs the officer at the Crown Court of his decision and that officer then informs the applicant as to whether the judge has decided to state a case or not. If the judge decides not to state a case then the applicant can require the judge to give a certificate giving reasons for his decision. The High Court may order the judge to state a case by mandamus.[12]

If the judge decides to state a case then the main difference in procedure between the Crown Court and justices takes effect for it is then for the *applicant* to prepare a draft case. The applicant must send his draft case to the court and to the other parties within 21 days of being told that the judge will state a case. Within 21 days of receiving their copy of the applicant's draft the parties must either:

(a) notify the court in writing that they intend to take no part in the proceedings before the High Court;
(b) indorse on the draft case that they agree with it and return it to the court; or
(c) draft an alternative draft case and return it to the court together with the copy of applicant's draft.

9 S 28(2)a of the Supreme Court Act 1981. For the meaning of 'relating to trial on indictment' see p 41, above.
10 Ie decisions under the Betting, Gaming and Lotteries Act 1963, the Licensing Act 1964, the Gaming Act 1968 or the Local Government Act (Miscellaneous Provisions) Act 1982; see s 28(2)b of the Supreme Court Act 1981 as amended.
11 *R v Chesterfield Justices, ex p Kovacs* [1992] 2 All ER 325 per Roch J.
12 Rule 26(15) of the Crown Court Rules. An order may be obtained by originating motion, entered for hearing in the Crown Office or the Principal Registry of the Family Division as appropriate (RSC Ord 56, r 8 and Ord 57, r 2) or by application for mandamus in judicial review proceedings.

The drafts cannot be referred to at the hearing before the High Court.[13]

The judge then considers the various draft cases that have been produced and must state and sign a case within 14 days of receiving the drafts or the expiry of the 21 day limit for submitting them, whichever is the sooner. The case must state the facts found by the court, the submissions of the parties (including any authorities relied upon), the decision that the court made and the question for the opinion of the High Court. As with justices, the Crown Court can require an applicant for a case stated to enter into recognisances before the case is stated and delivered.

Once the case has been delivered the procedure is governed by the Rules of the Supreme Court and in particular RSC Ord 56, r 1. The applicant has 10 days from receipt of the case within which to lodge the case at the High Court together with a copy of both the order, judgment or decision of the Crown Court being appealed against and any order, decision or judgment made earlier by justices before appeal to the Crown Court. Having lodged these documents the applicant must then enter the case for hearing within the same 10 day period. This period can only be extended if the delay is 'accounted for to the satisfaction of the Divisional Court' (RSC Ord 56, r 1(4)). Notice of intention to apply for an extension of time for entry of the appeal must be served on the respondent at least two clear days before the hearing of the application for extension. If an appeal is not entered in time and no extension is obtained then the case stated becomes a nullity and the Crown Court can proceed as if no case had been stated. Criminal causes or matters are entered in the Crown Office and are heard by a Divisional Court of the Queen's Bench Division. Civil matters (other than family matters) are also entered in the Crown Office but are heard by a single judge in open court unless the court refers them to the Divisional Court. Family cases are entered in the principal Registry of the Family Division and are heard by a single judge of the Family Division unless they are referred to a Divisional Court of the Family Division.[14]

Section 28 of the Supreme Court Act 1981 is couched in permissive rather than mandatory terms. Thus the section provides that decisions of the Crown Court may be questioned by case stated without providing that that is the only method by which they can be challenged. Even the section's predecessor, s 10 of the Courts Act 1971, which provided that decisions of the Crown Court *shall* be questioned by case stated was held to be permissive rather than mandatory.[15] Thus there is no statutory bar to challenging decisions of the Crown Court by judicial review where case stated is available. However where statute provides a method of appeal by way of case stated, that will normally be the preferable method of seeking review by the High Court and judicial review may be refused as a matter of discretion if case stated would have been more appropriate.[16]

## Case stated from ministers and tribunals

A large number and variety of statutes give specific powers to ministers, tribunals, arbitrators and other persons to state cases for determination by the

13 *Tesco Stores Ltd v Seabridge* (1985) Times, 29 April.
14 RSC Ord 56, r 4A.
15 *R v Crown Court at Ipswich, ex p Baldwin* [1981] 1 All ER 596.
16 See *ex p Baldwin*, above.

High Court. The jurisdiction to state such a case may even extend to challenges to interlocutory rulings,[17] although such jurisdiction will depend on the precise wording of the particular statutory provision.[18] Depending on the particular statutory provision and the circumstances in which the need to state a case arises, the case may be stated at the tribunal or other body's own volition, or at the request of an interested party or pursuant to an order of the Court.[19] Where such a case is stated it is determined on originating motion, heard (unless there is some specific provision to the contrary[20]) by a single judge of the Queen's Bench Division. The general provisions for the procedure in such cases are to be found in Ord 56, rr 7 and 9–12 of the Rules of the Supreme Court.[1]

## STATUTORY RIGHTS OF CHALLENGE: APPLICATIONS TO QUASH

Known as the six weeks' time limit procedure this statutory remedy is a form of judicial review rather than an appeal. It is standard form in statutes conferring powers on central government in relation to land use and compulsory purchase matters. It does not apply to planning enforcement decisions where there is an appeal proper, nor to local authority decisions to refuse or impose conditions upon planning permission—here judicial review may be appropriate[2]—nor does it apply to challenges before the final decision is made.

The normal locus standi requirement is 'a person aggrieved' and is if anything, more limited than that for judicial review.[3] The grounds of challenge correspond to the normal judicial review grounds.[4] The differences are, first no leave is required; second, the court's power, (apart from an interim power to suspend the decision challenged) is limited to quashing the decision, thus leaving the decision-maker free to make another decision in the light of changed circumstances;[5] third, there is a strict six weeks' time limit running from the date the decision was made,[6] after which no challenge is possible at

17 See eg *R v Secretary of State for the Environment, ex p The Royal Borough of Kensington and Chelsea* (1987) 19 HLR 161, [1987] JPL 567 and *R v Chesterfield Justices, ex p Kovacs* [1992] 2 All ER 325 and the cases there referred to.

18 In *R v Lands Tribunal, ex p City of London Corpn* [1982] 1 All ER 892, [1982] 1 WLR 258, the word 'decision' in s 3(4) of the Lands Tribunal Act 1949 was held to mean only final decisions and thus no jurisdiction existed to state a case in relation to an interlocutory ruling.

19 An application may be made by originating motion for an order requiring that a case be stated under r 8 RSC, Ord 56.

20 In particular certain matters are assigned to the Chancery Division by RSC Ord 91 (revenue proceedings) and RSC Ord 93, especially r 10 (a miscellany of statutory provisions).

1 Specific provisions for case stated are to be found in, inter alia, RSC Ord 94, r 7 (The Agricultural Land Tribunal), Ord 94, r 8 (cases stated by tribunals covered by s 13(1) of the Tribunals and Enquiries Act 1971), Ord 94, r 11 (The Mental Health Review Tribunal) and Ord 111 (The Social Securities Acts 1975 to 1986).

2 See *R v Hillingdon Borough Council, ex p Royco Homes Ltd* [1974] QB 720, [1974] 2 All ER 643—where issues of fact are involved a right of appeal must be exercised to the Secretary of State.

3 Above p 105.

4 *Ashbridge Investments Ltd v Minister of Housing and Local Government* [1965] 3 All ER 371, sub nom *Re Stalybridge (Castle Hall No 7) and (Acres Lane and Lawton Street) Compulsory Purchase Order 1963, Ashbridge Investments Ltd v Minister of Housing and Local Government* [1965] 1 WLR 1320, CA; *Seddon Properties v Secretary of State for the Environment* (1981) 42 P & CR 26n.

5 *Kingswood District Council v Secretary of State for the Environment* [1988] JPL 248. See Town and Country Planning (Inquiries Procedure) Rules 1988, SI 1988, No 944 r 18; Town and Country Planning Appeals (Determination by Impertas) (Inquiries Procedure) Rules 1988, SI 1988, No 945 r 19.

6 See above pp 34–35.

all. The ordinary judicial review procedure is completely excluded both within and without the six weeks' period.[7] The court's power to quash is discretionary but there is perhaps a stronger presumption in favour of quashing than under Ord 53.[8]

The court is as reluctant under this procedure as under Ord 53 to consider questions of fact. The court will normally confine itself to the Secretary of State's formal decision letter and the inspector's report at any public inquiry. However evidence can be taken by affidavit and there is a power to call for further evidence.[9] This might be used in exceptional cases where, for example, it has been alleged that the inspector's report misrepresented what happened at the inquiry.[10]

The procedure for these applications to quash is subject to any specific provisions in the relevent statute but generally application is by originating motion.[11] The originating motion must state the grounds of the application and must do so with clarity.[12] The motion will be set down in the Crown Office List for hearing by a single judge. Increasing use is being made of deputy judges for these applications.

## STATUTORY APPEALS

Particular statutes may give a right of appeal to the High Court instead of, or in addition to, a right of appeal by way of case stated. Statutory appeals are normally limited to points of law rather than by way of complete rehearing and often provide that there shall be no appeal from the High Court decision. For these purposes a 'point of law' is normally construed narrowly as an appellate rather than a supervisory review matter. Normally statutory rights of appeal are subject to short time limits. Certain appeals are assigned to the Chancery Division by RSC Ord 91 (revenue proceedings) and RSC Ord 93 (miscellaneous statutory appeals) and arbitration proceedings are assigned to Commercial Court judges (see RSC Ord 73) but, unless there is some specific provision to the contrary, appeals are brought by originating motion entered in the Crown Office of the Queen's Bench Division. Such appeals are heard by the Divisional Court where the decision of the High Court is final but otherwise by a single judge. The general provisions for the procedure in such cases are to be found in RSC Ord 55.[13] The Court has power to allow grounds of appeal to be amended,[14] to hear interlocutory applications[15] and to receive

7 *R v Secretary of State for the Environment, ex p Ostler* [1977] QB 122, [1976] 3 All ER 90, CA. There appear to be no exceptions to this; see *R v Secretary of State for the Environment, ex p Kent* [1988] 3 PLR 17. *R v Cornwall County Council, ex p Huntingdon* [1992] 3 All ER 566. The precise scope of the ouster clause must therefore be carefully examined. See eg Town and Country Planning Act 1990 ss 284 and 287.

8 *Miller v Weymouth and Melecombe Regis Corpn* (1974) 118 Sol Jo 421; *Peak Park Joint Planning Board v Secretary of State for the Environment* (1979) 39 P & CR 361, 385.

9 RSC Ord 94, r 3. See *Burton v Secretary of State for Transport* [1988] 2 EGLR 35, [1985] 31 EG 50, CA; *George v Secretary of State for the Environment* (1979) 77 LGR 689 at 693, CA.

10 *East Hampshire District Council v Secretary of State for the Environment* (1978) JPL 182.

11 See RSC Ord 94.

12 See *Burton v Secretary of State for Transport* [1988] 2 EGLR 35, [1988] 31 EG 50.

13 Specific provisions for appeals are to be found in, inter alia, RSC Ord 98 (appeals against district auditor's decisions under the Local Government Finance Act 1982), RSC Ord 101 (appeals under the Pensions Appeal Tribunals Act 1943) and the orders noted in n 1, above.

14 Ord 55, r 6.

15 Ord 55, r 6A, as to interim relief see p 147, above.

further evidence as to questions of fact, although a restrictive view has been taken of this latter power.[16]

The attitude of the Divisional Court to precedent in the exercise of its appellate jurisdiction differs from its attitude when exercising its supervisory jurisdiction of judicial review. In *Huddersfield Police Authority v Watson*[17] the Divisional Court, when exercising its appellate jurisdiction, held that it was subject to the principles followed by the Court of Appeal in civil cases as set out in *Young v Bristol Aeroplane Co Ltd.*[18] The court is therefore bound to follow its own decisions unless they are per incuriam or in conflict with each other or with higher authority.[19]

A substantial change in procedure for challenging planning enforcement notices by statutory appeal has been brought about by s 289 of the Town and Country Planning Act 1990 and s 65 of the Planning (Listed Buildings and Conservation Areas) Act 1990 which introduced a requirement to obtain leave to appeal. Leave is obtained by application to the High Court and the procedure for such applications is now contained in RSC Ord 94, rr 12 and 13 as amended.[20] In particular the procedure requires notice of the application for leave to be given to various interested parties who are entitled to be heard on the application for leave.

Where proceedings are brought by way of a statutory appeal the court may be willing where it thinks judicial review is more appropriate to treat the case as if leave had been given for judicial review.[21]

16 See eg *London Parachuting v Secretary of State for the Environment* [1986] JPL 4282.
17 [1947] KB 842, [1947] 2 All ER 193.
18 [1944] KB 718, [1944] 2 All ER 293.
19 As to precedent in judicial review see *R v Greater Manchester Coroner, ex p Tal* [1985] QB 67, [1984] 3 All ER 240, but also see *Hornigold v Chief Constable of Lancashire* [1985] Crim LR 792. For a discussion of precedent in the Divisional Court see Ian McLeod *The Law Society's Gazette*, 9 May 1990, p 24.
20 By RSC (Amendment) Ord 1992 (SI 638/92) with effect from 1 April 1992.
21 Rhymney Valley District Council v Secretary of State for the Environment [1985] JPL 27.

CHAPTER 18

# Habeas corpus

## 'THE GREATEST AND OLDEST OF ALL PREROGATIVE WRITS'

There are three forms of the writ of habeas corpus left in use but it is the writ of habeas corpus ad subjiciendum that is known popularly simply as habeas corpus. It is a prerogative writ available in the High Court to require those in authority to produce a person[1] being detained by them and to justify the detention. The effect of service of the writ is to make the 'gaoler' responsible to the court in place of the authority which ordered the detention, leaving it to the court to determine on the return of the writ whether the detention should continue or not. As with applications for judicial review, the Court is concerned with the legality of the action that has been taken rather than with the merits. Since the days of the Star Chamber habeas corpus has become an important part of British constitutional mythology, but it is the right not to be detained without lawful justification that is important rather than the writ itself. The right stems from Magna Carta which declared:

> No freeman shall be arrested or imprisoned or disseised or outlawed or exiled or in any way destroyed, neither will we set forth against him or send against him, except by the lawful judgment of his peers and by the law of the land. To no one will we sell, to no one will we refuse or delay right or justice.

The duty of the courts, as recently reaffirmed by the Master of the Rolls, is to uphold this classic statement of the rule of law and, in the armoury of the courts, habeas corpus, 'the greatest and oldest of all prerogative writs', is quite capable of adapting itself to the circumstances of the times.[2]

The other forms of the writ of habeas corpus left in practical use are also commands to produce prisoners but deal with the more humdrum work of the courts and are rarely matters of controversy except when a prison governor is so short-staffed that his deliveries to court are delayed. The forms of writ are as follows:

(a) The writ of habeas corpus ad testificandum is a command to bring a prisoner up to give evidence. The work of this writ is largely superseded now by the power of the Home Office under s 29 of the Criminal Justice Act 1961 to produce prisoners where necessary to give evidence.

1 The writ can apply to any person within the jurisdiction and not just to British citizens (*Khawaja v Secretary of State for the Home Department* [1984] AC 74, 111) but it will not issue in relation to detention outside the jurisdiction or in 'foreign dominions' (see Habeas Corpus Act 1862 and *R v Pinckney* [1904] 2 KB 84, CA). Thus habeas corpus will not issue from English courts to Scotland (*R v Cowle* (1759) 2 Burr 834), Northern Ireland (*Re Keenan* [1972] 1 QB 533; [1971] 3 All ER 883, CA) or the Channel Islands (which are historically foreign dominions with their own jurisdictions), but will issue to the Isle of Man (*ex p Brown* (1864) 33 LJQB 193) its being a dominion but not a 'foreign' dominion.

2 *R v Secretary of State for the Home Department, ex p Muboyayi* [1991] 3 WLR 442, 453.

(b) The writ of habeas corpus ad respondendum is a command to bring up a prisoner to answer criminal charges.

Applications for these writs are made to a judge in chambers supported by affidavit (Ord 54, r 9) and are not dealt with further in this work.

## HABEAS CORPUS OR JUDICIAL REVIEW?

The remedies of habeas corpus and judicial review can overlap and at times the courts have failed to make clear distinctions between them. Habeas corpus is appropriate where someone is detained without any authority or where the purported authority was beyond the powers of the person authorising the detention and so was unlawful. Judicial review under RSC Ord 53 is appropriate where the decision sought to be impugned with within the powers of the person taking it but is invalidated by a procedural error, a misappreciation of the law, a failure to take account of relevant matters, taking account of irrelevant matters or the fundamental unreasonableness of the decision.[3] It is in relation to the investigation of facts that the distinction between habeas corpus and judicial review is at its most apparent and this aspect is considered further below.

Habeas corpus is solely concerned with the detention or release of the applicant. It is not concerned with compensation. An application for judicial review may now include a claim for damages, although this is still unusual. Since the inclusion of a claim for damages in an application for judicial review contains no magic to create a right to damages in 'public law' where none existed in the 'private law' of tort, there is little to be gained from seeking compensation at the same time as trying to obtain release. Since an applicant normally wishes to be released as soon as possible, and a claim for damages inevitably delays matters, there is every reason to use habeas corpus to obtain release with a separate writ action thereafter to enforce such right to damages as may exist.

## THE INVESTIGATION OF FACTS IN HABEAS CORPUS PROCEEDINGS

The power of the court to investigate underlying facts is wider in proceedings for habeas corpus than in proceedings by way of judicial review but it is not so wide as to create a general right of appeal. At common law the enquiry on a return of a writ of habeas corpus was limited to asking whether the reason for detention given on the return of the writ was valid on its face. This limitation was similar to the 'error on the face of the record' limitation in the history of judicial review that the courts have now all but abolished by judicial creativity.[4] In the case of habeas corpus, Parliament intervened by way of the Habeas Corpus Act 1816.[5] Section 3 conferred upon judges the power in non-criminal cases to 'proceed to examine into the truth of the facts set forth' in the return, even though 'the return to any writ of habeas corpus shall be good and sufficient in

3 *R v Secretary of State for the Home Department, ex p Cheblak* [1991] 1 WLR 890, 894, CA endorsed on this point in *ex p Muboyayi*, see n 2, above. See also *R v Secretary of State for the Home Department, ex p Phansopkar* [1976] QB 606, [1975] 3 All ER 487.

4 See p 55, above.

5 'The great statute of 1816' as Lord Scarman called it in *Khawaja v Secretary of State for the Home Department,* [1984] AC 74, 110.

law', and to do 'as to justice shall appertain'. This section founded the modern practice of looking behind the mere wording of a return endorsed on a writ of habeas corpus as the justification for detention. Thus in a case where the exercise of executive power depends upon the precedent establishment of an objective fact (of the sort considered below as 'precedent facts'), the courts will decide whether the fact has indeed been established on the evidence.[6]

## Precedent facts

The distinction between habeas corpus and judicial review is highlighted by what the courts still refer to in this context as the question of 'precedent' facts. These are also referred to as 'jurisdictional' facts. Where the power to detain depends upon the existence of a particular state of affairs ('a precedent fact') and the existence of that fact is challenged, then the detention can be challenged by an application for habeas corpus or judicial review even if there are alternative procedures available including specific statutory rights of appeal.[7] Habeas corpus will not be available, however, where it is not the existence of a precedent fact, upon which valid detention depends, that is being challenged but only an underlying administrative decision which has led to detention. This is because there will be no grounds for impugning the legality of the detention itself until the administrative decision has been set aside. Thus the underlying administrative decision will have to be challenged first by way of an application for judicial review. Then, if the underlying decision is set aside, the lawful reason for the detention may go. So if a detention depends, for example, on a person being an illegal immigrant then that precedent fact is susceptible to challenge in habeas corpus proceedings. If, however, the fact that the person detained is an illegal immigrant is undisputed but it is alleged that a decision should have been taken to allow legal entry and thus remove the illegal immigrant status, then that allegation cannot be made in habeas corpus proceedings but must be made by way of judicial review of the decision.[8]

## The nature of a precedent fact

It is important to identify the nature of a precedent fact properly since the level of challenge required may differ. Thus a right to detain depending on status as an illegal immigrant has to be contrasted with a right to detain because a minister, or some proper officer, is of the opinion, for example, that an illegal immigrant is not a refugee. Where the relevant fact is the opinion of a particular person then the court has to consider whether there were reasonable grounds on which to hold that opinion. It is an inquiry along 'Wednesbury' reasonableness lines in judicial review proceedings.[9] Where a primary fact is in issue, rather than someone's opinion as to that fact, then the court can inquire deeper. Although in such cases the court's function remains supervisory rather than appellate, the court can look at the evidence to decide whether it is satisfied as to the existence of the primary fact being alleged. In cases involving the liberty of the subject it has often been said that the courts will be astute to prevent that liberty being taken away lightly and without good cause and the courts will be astute to prevent their inquiries being blocked by attempts to

6 Per Lord Scarman in *ex p Khawaja* at 110 (above, n 5).
7 *Ex p Muboyayi*, see above, at 449 and 460 and *ex p Khawaja*, see above, n 1.
8 See eg *ex p Muboyayi*, above, n 2.
9 See eg *Bugdaycay v Secretary of State for the Home Department* [1987] AC 514, [1987] 1 All ER 940, HL.

categorise cases as involving investigation of the grounds for an opinion rather than the existence of a primary fact.[10]

## HABEAS CORPUS IN SUPPORT OF JUDICIAL REVIEW AGAINST THE CROWN

There is no doubt that habeas corpus issues against officers of the Crown[11] even though the practical effect may be the same as issuing an injunction against the Crown. In exceptional circumstances, therefore, where there is a real risk that a person may be removed from the jurisdiction before the court has had an opportunity to consider the case properly unless urgent action is taken, a writ of habeas corpus may be issued to prevent removal in support of an application for judicial review.[12] This jurisdiction is an example of the writ of habeas corpus changing to meet the circumstances of the times.

## ONUS AND BURDEN OF PROOF

In order to obtain a writ of habeas corpus an applicant must show a prima facie case that he is being unlawfully detained. If he does so then he is entitled to a writ of habeas corpus as of right. It is then for the detaining authority to make a return justifying the detention. If, however, the return indorsed on the writ is on its face a good and valid reason for detention then the onus moves back to the applicant to show that the detention is in fact unlawful.[13] The courts do not trouble themselves unduly about questions of burden of proof in habeas corpus proceedings. Neither the formula of 'reasonable doubt' nor that of 'balance of probabilities' is satisfactory to reflect the supervisory nature of the jurisdiction. In so far as the approach of the courts can be reduced to a formula it is the 'flexible civil standard', ie sufficient proof to establish the degree of probability appropriate to the issue in question.[14] Where the issue in question is an applicant's personal liberty then a high degree of probability will be required.

## PROCEDURE

The rules governing applications for habeas corpus are contained in Ord 54 of the Rules of the Supreme Court. Although the language used is of an 'application for a writ' followed by a hearing on the 'return of the writ', the practical effect of the rules is to produce a two-stage procedure similar to that for applications for judicial review under Ord 53. An application is made (normally ex parte) to a judge supported by affidavit and, if successful, that is

10 *Ex p Khawaja* at 104–5 and 109.

11 *Ex p Muboyayi* at 449.

12 *Ex p Muboyayi* at 451g. In such exceptional cases habeas corpus may be more appropriate than a stay under Ord 53, r 3(10) for the reasons given in *Muboyayi* at 452.

13 *R v Governor of Pentonville Prison, ex p Azam* [1974] AC 18, 31–32, [1973] 2 All ER 741, CA. *Re Wajid Hassan* [1976] 2 All ER 123, 130; *R v Secretary of State for the Home Department, ex p Hussain* [1978] 2 All ER 423, 426g and 429e.

14 *Ex p Khawaja* at 113 per Lord Scarman, and *Hornal v Neuberger Products Ltd* [1957] 1 QB 247, [1956] 3 All ER 970, CA.

followed by a full hearing argued inter partes if the relief is resisted. In urgent cases then, the procedure can be concertinaed into a single hearing for either habeas corpus or judicial review.

## APPLYING FOR A WRIT

The process of habeas corpus is started by an application to a judge of the High Court sitting in open court. Although in theory any judge of the High Court has power to issue a writ of habeas corpus, applications are in practice dealt with by the Queen's Bench Division as part of the Crown Office List work. If no judge is sitting in open court then an application may be made in any other way that can be found. In practice this means either an application to a judge in chambers in vacation or out of normal hours or, in emergencies, an application in person or by telephone to the duty judge at home arranged through the duty officer at the High Court.[15]

An application for a writ can be made on notice by motion where there is no urgency but normally the application is made ex parte. The application must be supported by an affidavit unless in cases of extreme urgency the judge can be persuaded to accept an undertaking to set out the matters he is told in an affidavit and swear the affidavit forthwith. Order 54, r 1(2) requires that the affidavit sets out the nature of the restraint complained of but in practice the affidavit should set out as much of the background as possible and state why it is alleged that the restraint is unlawful. Where an application is made ex parte, full and frank disclosure of any matters that may influence the court is required just as with ex parte applications for injunctions or for leave to apply for judicial review. Full disclosure of the whole of the case fairly available to the applicant should also be made since the doctrine of res judicata may operate to prevent any such matters being raised at a later date.[16] On appeal fresh evidence will normally only be admitted where the *Ladd v Marshall* criteria are satisfied[17] but in cases where liberty is at stake a more flexible attitude is shown.[18]

The affidavit must also state that the application is being made 'at the instance of'[19] the person detained which imposes a theoretical procedural limitation on applications by third parties. This requirement is, however, procedural only and does not affect the substantive right to apply on behalf of third parties in detention either as a matter of law or in practice.

The affidavit should be sworn by the person restrained unless that person is unable to do so by reason either of the imprisonment or some other reason. If sworn by a person other than the prisoner then the affidavit must state the reason why the prisoner was unable to do so (Ord 54, r 1(3)). For an ex parte application the affidavit should be accompanied by a draft writ of habeas corpus setting out the order that is sought. Where an application is made on notice every party must supply to every other party copies of the affidavits which they propose to use at the hearing of the application (Ord 54, r 3). Strictly this obligation to supply copies only arises on demand by the other

15 The normal telephone number of the High Court is 071–936 6000 but out of normal hours the direct line emergency number is 071–936 6199. The Crown Office general office number is 071–936–6653/6205.

16 *Re Tarling* [1979] 1 All ER 981.

17 See p 175, above.

18 See eg *Irtelli v Squatriti* [1992] 3 All ER 294, [1992] 3 WLR 218, CA.

19 RSC Ord 54, r 1(2).

parties for copies and on payment of proper copying charges but, since other parties will need copies, the demand can in practice be taken for granted.

## THE POWERS OF THE COURT ON AN APPLICATION FOR A WRIT

An application for the issue of a writ of habeas corpus ad subjiciendum is the first step of the two stage process. If the writ is issued then the final determination will be on the hearing into the return endorsed on the writ by the detainor as the justification for detention.

At the first stage of an application for a writ of habeas corpus ad subjiciendum to issue the court has a number of powers:

(a) It may issue the writ of habeas corpus commanding that the prisoner be brought up and the cause of detention examined, in which case directions must be given as to the court or judge before whom, and the date on which, the writ is to be returnable (ie before whom, and when, the case in full is to be heard) (Ord 54, r 5).

(b) It may order that the prisoner be released regardless of what other procedural order is made (Ord 54, r 4). Such an order is of itself sufficient warrant to any prison governor, constable or other person for the release of the prisoner. Such an order can be made whether a writ of habeas corpus is issued forthwith or some other order is made. The modern practice where release is ordered is for the Crown Office to write to the person holding the prisoner directing that the prisoner be released and not to issue a formal writ which would then be superfluous. The imprisoning authority then confirms the fact of release under the direction for release instead of producing the prisoner and the 'return' hearing deals with the challenge to the detention as if it were continuing.[20]

(c) In a criminal cause or matter[1] a judge who does not order the immediate release of a prisoner must direct that the application for the writ of habeas corpus be made by originating motion to a Divisional Court of the Queen's Bench Division (Ord 54, r 4(2)) since in such cases s 14 of the Administration of Justice Act 1960 provides that only a Divisional Court can refuse an application for habeas corpus. A Divisional Court of the Queen's Bench Division is a court of two or more judges.[2] In recent years a two-judge court including one Lord Justice of Appeal has been the norm. Since this automatic reference to a Divisional Court exists, no appeal lies from a decision of a single judge to refuse an application for habeas corpus in a criminal cause or matter,[3] no such right of appeal being necessary. When an application for a writ to issue is referred to a Divisional Court the prisoner will not be brought up on the hearing of the motion (unlike on the return date when a writ is issued) unless the judge so directs. From the Divisional Court appeal lies in criminal causes or matters direct to the House of Lords with leave under s 1 of the Administration of Justice Act 1960. Unlike in judicial review, the granting of leave to appeal to the House of Lords in cases of habeas corpus is not conditional upon the

20 *Re Amand* [1941] 2 KB 239, 249.
1 For the meaning of criminal cause or matter, see p 151.
2 S 66 of the Supreme Court Act 1981.
3 S 15(2) of the Administration of Justice Act 1960.

Divisional Court certifying that the matter involves a point of law of general public importance.[4]

(d) If no writ is issued forthwith then a judge hearing an application for a writ may direct that the application for a writ be made to a Divisional Court of the Queen's Bench Division (Ord 54, r 1(a)). The Divisional Court may in turn order that notice be given to the person against whom the writ is sought or to such other person as the Court directs (Ord 54, r 2(c)).

(e) If the application is made in chambers then the judge may direct that an originating summons claiming a writ of habeas corpus be issued (Ord 54, r 2(a)), in which case the summons will give notice to the person against whom the writ is sought and any other person that the court may direct but the matter will continue to be dealt with in chambers.

(f) Alternatively, a judge hearing an application in chambers may direct that the application be made by originating motion either to a judge in open court or to a Divisional Court of the Queen's Bench Division (Ord 54, r 2(a)).

(g) If an application is made to a judge in open court then the judge may direct that the application be made by originating motion to a Divisional Court of the Queen's Bench Division (Ord 54, r 2(b)).[5]

(h) On an application to a Divisional Court or to a judge in open court the court or judge may adjourn the application so that notice can be given to the person against whom the writ is sought or to such other person as may be directed (Ord 54, r 2(b) and (c)).

(i) The court may grant bail. The High Court has an inherent jurisdiction to grant bail ancillary to proceedings of which it is seized, but it cannot do so *in vacuo*. The subject of bail is considered further in this work at p 149.

(j) The court may grant leave to proceed by way of judicial review if it considers that to be the more appropriate procedure.[6] Where habeas corpus is issued only in support of judicial review then an application for leave to issue judicial review proceedings must be made at the same time.[7]

## RENEWAL OF APPLICATIONS

Once an application has been made and refused no further application can be made unless there are fresh grounds for doing so.[8] To provide a basis for a new application the new grounds must raise new issues or rely on new evidence that could not have been put forward in the earlier application. It is not enough that they were not put forward, even though they could have been.[9]

Although appeal lies to the Court of Appeal (and from there to the House of Lords) against the refusal or grant of habeas corpus in civil matters and to the

4 S 15(3) of the Administration of Justice Act 1960.
5 See (c) above for circumstances where such an order *must* be made.
6 See 'Habeas corpus or judicial review?' above, p 190.
7 *R v Secretary of State for the Home Department, ex p Muboyayi* [1991] 3 WLR 442, 451g.
8 See s 14(2) of the Administration of Justice Act 1960 and *Re Kray* [1965] Ch 736, [1965] 1 All ER 710 in which the Kray brothers tried, unsuccessfully, to get bail from the Lord Chancellor.
9 *Re Tarling* [1979] 1 All ER 981.

House of Lords direct in criminal causes or matters,[10] neither court has an original jurisdiction to hear applications for the issue of a writ. The historic anomaly whereby the Court of Appeal claims original jurisdiction to consider renewed applications for leave to apply for judicial review[11] does not appear to extend to habeas corpus. This is, no doubt, because the 'historic anomaly' is not required as a legal fiction to get round the absence of a right of appeal.[12] The Court of Appeal has held that where an application for leave to apply for judicial review has been made to, and refused by, the Court of Appeal then any further application for such leave should be made to the Court of Appeal.[13] A further application to a single judge in such circumstances was held to be an abuse. It would seem sensible for a similar rule to apply where the Court of Appeal has already dealt on appeal with an application for habeas corpus but, in the absence of the Court of Appeal having any original jurisdiction to hear applications for habeas corpus, it would appear to be an abuse to reapply to the Court of Appeal rather than go back to a judge of the Divisional Court. It is now certain that the Lord Chancellor has no greater powers in respect of habeas corpus than any other judge of the High Court.[14]

## PROCEEDINGS BY SUMMONS OR MOTION

In proceedings for habeas corpus, originating summons[15] are issued out of, and originating motions[16] are entered in, the Crown Office of the Queen's Bench Division or in the Principal Registry of the Family Division for proceedings in the Family Division. Cases must be commenced in the Family Division if they involve a minor (see below). The forms are as for judicial review with the headings as for the writ above. Affidavits sworn in habeas corpus proceedings must be filed in the Crown Office[17] or the Principal Registry of the Family Division[18] as appropriate. In practice the Crown Office will require three copies of affidavits to be filed.

## APPLICATIONS RELATING TO MINORS

Any application by a parent or guardian of a minor for a writ of habeas corpus ad subjiciendum relating to the custody, care or control of a minor must be made in the Family Division (Ord 54, r 11) and any application on behalf of a minor must be made in the first instance to a judge in chambers (Ord 54, r 1(3)).

10 Appeals are dealt with at p 199 at the end of this chapter. It is to be noted that the right of appeal to the House of Lords against a refusal of habeas corpus compares favourably with the exclusion of such a right of appeal against a refusal of leave to apply for judicial review (see p 176, above).
11 *Re Dhillon v Secretary of State for the Home Department* [1987] Imm AR 222, CA and *R v Secretary of State for the Home Department, ex p Turkoglu* [1987] 2 All ER 823, 825, CA.
12 See *Re Poh* [1983] 1 All ER 287, [1983] 1 WLR 2, HL.
13 *M v Home Office and Baker* [1992] 2 WLR 73, 83, CA. But see p 176.
14 See n 8, above.
15 RSC Ord 54, r 3.
16 RSC Ord 57, r 2.
17 RSC Ord 57, r 4.
18 RSC Ord 41, r 9(3).

## THE WRIT

Where the court orders the issue of a writ of habeas corpus it is issued out of the Crown Office or Family Division as appropriate and must be prepared by the party seeking to issue the writ.[19]

A writ of habeas corpus ad subjiciendum must be in the following archaic form:

In the High Court of Justice
Queen's Bench [Family] Division
A.B. APPLICANT
AND
[The Governor of ] RESPONDENT
Writ of Habeas Corpus

ELIZABETH THE SECOND, by the Grace of God, of the United Kingdom of Great Britain and Northern Ireland and of Our other realms and territories Queen, Head of the Commonwealth, Defender of the Faith.

To the Governor of Our prison at greeting:

We command you that you have in the Queen's Bench [or Family] Division of our High Court of Justice [before a judge in chambers or appropriate] at the Royal Courts of Justice, Strand, London, on the day and at the time specified in the notice served with this writ, the body of [the applicant] being taken and detained under your custody as is said, together with the day and cause of his being taken and detained, by whatsoever name he may be called therein, that Our Court [or Judge] may then and there examine and determine whether such cause is legal, and have you there then this writ.

Witness Lord High Chancellor of Great Britain the day of 199 .

*Endorsement*

By order of Court [or Mr Justice ].
This writ was issued by solicitor for .

The Writ must be accompanied by a notice in the following, equally archaic, form:

In the High Court of Justice
Queen's Bench [Family] Division
A.B. APPLICANT
AND
[The Governor of ] RESPONDENT

Whereas this Court [or the Honourable Mr Justice ] has granted a writ of habeas corpus directed to commanding him to have the body of before the said Court [or before a judge in chambers] at the Royal Courts of Justice, Strand, London, on the day and at the time specified in the notice together with the day and cause of his being taken and detained.

Take notice that you are required by the said writ to have the body of the said before this Court [or before judge aforesaid] on the day of

19 RSC Ord 57, r 5.

199 at o'clock and to make a return to the said writ. In default thereof the said Court will then, or so soon thereafter as counsel can be heard, be moved to commit you to prison for your contempt in not obeying the said writ [or if in vacation application will then be made to one of the judges of the said Court for a warrant for your arrest in order that you may be held to bail to answer for your contempt in not obeying the said writ].

Dated the day of 199 .

signed solicitor for the plaintiff

To .

## SERVICE OF THE WRIT

Where, on an application for a writ of habeas corpus to issue, the court makes an order for the immediate release of the applicant from prison under Ord 54, r 4 then the Crown Office normally secures the release informally without it being necessary to serve the writ. Where service is necessary, however, then it must be in accordance with the special service provisions in Ord 54, r 6. Most writs of habeas corpus are addressed to prison governors or a relevant public official and they are served at the prison or place where the person is held and are served on a member of the prison governor's staff or a servant or agent of such other public official as the writ be addressed to (Ord 54, r 6(2)).

In the rare cases where a writ is addressed to a person other than a prison governor or public official, service must be effected personally on the person to whom it is directed. If personal service cannot be effected then the writ must be served by leaving it with a servant or agent of the person to whom it is directed at the place of detention in question (Ord 54, r 6(1) and (2)).

If a writ is directed to more than one person, it must be served on the first named person, with copies served on the others (Ord 54, r 6(3)).

## THE SUBSTANTIVE HEARING OR 'THE RETURN TO THE WRIT'

Where the substantive issues have not already been dealt with in the application for a writ and the prisoner remains in custody then the writ of habeas corpus ad subjiciendum must be endorsed by the addressee (either on or annexed to the writ) with the justification of the detention. The 'return' must state all the causes of the detention but the court may grant leave to amend the return at the hearing (Ord 54, r 7). A statement of 'all the causes of detention' requires more than mere reference to the statutory provision under which a person is held. It must contain particulars of the material facts relied upon as justifying the detention.[20] The return is then filed at the Crown Office or the Principal Registry of the Family Division (depending on where the writ was issued) with the original writ filed at the time of issue. In due course a copy of any order made on the writ will also be filed in the same place.[1]

Habeas corpus proceedings issued out of the Crown Office are put in the

20 *R v Secretary of State for the Home Department, ex p Iqbal* [1979] 1 All ER 675, 679b and 683c per Boreham and Drake JJ.

1 RSC Ord 57, r 5(2).

Crown Office List for hearing.[2] In either the Crown Office List or the Family Division, habeas corpus proceedings are given precedence over other business since the liberty of the subject is at stake.

The endorsement on the writ is the starting point for the hearing on the return of the writ. The return is read and if it discloses on its face a valid authority for detention then the applicant has the onus of rebutting it. The applicant should appear by counsel despite the fact that RSC Ord 5, r 6(1) allows any person to bring and carry on proceedings in the High Court in person. Peculiarly, and purely out of policy reasons to prevent abuse of a procedure that is given priority over all other court business, habeas corpus is an exception to the rule that applications may be made in person.[3] An applicant for a writ of habeas corpus will not be heard in person unless there is some sufficient reason for doing so. The wish of the applicant to act as his own advocate is not in itself a sufficient ground. If an application is submitted in writing by an unrepresented person who believes that they have been unlawfully imprisoned then the application will be considered by a single judge who, if he thinks that it discloses an arguable case, may refer the papers to the Official Solicitor.[4] The courts have no power to compel the attendance before them of a prisoner in order for him to act as his own advocate.[5] There is no such thing as a writ of habeas corpus ad arguendum.

Once the return has been read the court is addressed by counsel for the applicant and then by counsel for the Crown or detaining authority. Counsel for the applicant then has a right of reply (Ord 54, r 8).

If the writ is not complied with and no return is made and the prisoner not produced then the remedy is to move the court to commit the addressee of the writ for contempt. It is for this reason that the writ must have contained the penal notice referred to above. An application to commit must be supported by an affidavit of service and it must show that the provisions for service have been strictly complied with. The court may issue a bench warrant for the arrest and production of the detainor in support of the committal process.

## APPEALS

The procedure for appealing against a decision on habeas corpus depends on the distinction between civil and criminal cases.[6]

### Civil cases

In civil cases either party may appeal to the Court of Appeal without leave. Such an appeal lies even against the refusal of an application for the issue of a writ of habeas corpus and it is not necessary to invoke any 'historic right' to renew an application to the Court of Appeal as in the case of a refusal of leave

2 For the operation of the Crown Office List see *Practice Direction* [1987] 1 WLR 232 and ch 19, below.

3 *Re Greene* (1941) 57 TLR 533, confirmed in *R v Secretary of State for the Home Department, ex p Wynne, DC* 23 July 1991; considered on appeal on different grounds before the Court of Appeal at [1992] 1 QB 406, [1992] 2 All ER 301, CA and followed in relation to appeals to the House of Lords, by *Practice Direction* [1962] 1 All ER 501 [1962] 1 WLR 270.

4 *Re Wring* [1960] 1 All ER 536n, [1960] 1 WLR 138.

5 *Benns v Mosely and Corbett* (1857) 2 CBNS 116, 117; *Weldon v Neal* (1885) 15 QBD 471.

6 See p 151, above.

to apply for judicial review.[7] An appeal to the Court of Appeal must be made within four weeks of the decision being made unless an application to extend time is made.[8] From the Court of Appeal appeal lies for either party to the House of Lords with leave.

If an applicant succeeds on his application for habeas corpus in obtaining his release (otherwise than merely on bail) and the detaining authority appeals, then the appeal will not limit the applicant's right to be released. Nor will the applicant be liable to be taken back into detention if the detaining authority's appeal is allowed.[9] Having won on appeal, however, the detaining authority may be able to obtain a fresh authority to detain to replace the one that was the subject of the appeal.

## Criminal cases

In criminal cases no appeal lies from a decision of a judge to refuse an application for habeas corpus by reason of s 15(2) of the Administration of Justice Act 1960. This is because in such cases a judge has to refer the matter to the Divisional Court automatically[10] as only a Divisional Court can refuse habeas corpus in a criminal case.[11] From the Divisional Court no appeal lies for any party to the Court of Appeal in criminal cases[12] but either party may appeal direct to the House of Lords. Although leave to appeal to the House of Lords must be obtained from either the Divisional Court or the House of Lords, such leave is not dependent, in habeas corpus proceedings, on the Divisional Court certifying that a point of law of general public importance is involved.[13] Leave must be applied for from the Divisional Court within 14 days of its decision and if it refuses leave, any application to the House of Lords for leave must be made within a further 14 days thereafter. In either case the time may be extended by the Court.[14] If leave is granted to, or applied for by, the person detained then the Court may grant bail pending appeal.[15] Equally, however, if leave is granted to, or applied for by, the prosecutor in a criminal case then the Court may stay any order for release pending appeal, but may then grant bail pending the appeal.[16] If no stay is granted to a prosecutor then an applicant who has succeeded in the Divisional Court will be entitled to be released even if there is an appeal and, having been released, will not be liable to be taken back into detention even if the prosecutor wins on appeal.[17] For that reason the House of Lords has said that a stay should be granted to a prosecutor if there is an appeal and the applicant should not be released save on bail until the House of Lords has disposed of the matter.[18] If the period for which the applicant was liable to be detained in any event expires pending appeal then a stay on release pending appeal will not prevent his release in the ordinary way.[19]

7 See p 176, above.
8 See as to this, and generally on appeals to the Court of Appeal, RSC Ord 59.
9 S 15(4) of the Administration of Justice Act 1960.
10 RSC Ord 54, r 4(2).
11 S 14 of the Administration of Justice Act 1960.
12 S 18(1)(a) of the Supreme Court Act 1981.
13 Ss 1(2) and 15(3) of the Administration of Justice Act 1960.
14 S 2 of the Administration of Justice Act 1960, but not in favour of a prosecutor.
15 S 4 of the Administration of Justice Act 1960.
16 S 5 of the Administration of Justice Act 1960.
17 S 15(4) of the Administration of Justice Act 1960.
18 *United States Government v McCaffery* [1984] 2 All ER 570, 575–6.
19 S 5(3) of the Administration of Justice Act 1960.

CHAPTER 19

# The Crown Office List

The Crown Office has a long and distinguished history, originally acting under its own set of rules before being brought within the Rules of the Supreme Court. The proceedings that are considered in this book are administered at the High Court by the Crown Office. Such proceedings are set down in the Crown Office List. The existence of the Crown Office List is now provided for by the practice direction of Lord Chief Justice Lane in 1981.[1] The Crown Office List is similar in many ways to the Commercial List of the Commercial Court although the Commercial List has a statutory basis in s 6 of the Supreme Court Act 1981. The Crown Office List includes:

(a) proceedings required to be heard by or applications required to be made to a Divisional Court of the Queen's Bench Division;
(b) proceedings pursuant to RSC Ord 53, Ord 54 and Ord 56 which may be heard by a single judge;
(c) actions directed to be set down in the Crown Office List;
(d) proceedings pursuant to RSC Ord 55, Ord 94 and Ord 111;[2] and
(e) save as is otherwise expressly provided, any other special case or case stated under any statute or order.

The Crown Office List is administered by the Crown Office under the direction of the Master of the Crown Office who may refer any matter to a judge nominated to hear Crown Office business. Cases in the Crown Office List are assigned to various different parts of the List depending on their state of readiness. The parts of the List are detailed in a practice note issued by Lord Chief Justice Lane in 1987.[3] The various parts of the Crown Office List are as follows.

**Part A: Cases not Ready to be Heard**
This part includes cases where leave has yet to be obtained, or the time limits for the filing or lodging of notices, affidavits or other documents have not expired and where, in consequence, a case is not yet ready to be heard.

**Part B: Cases Ready to be Heard**
In cases where the time limits for the filing or lodging of notices, affidavits or other documents have expired the Crown Office assumes that all parties are ready to be heard. The case then enters Part B of the Crown Office List. The applicant or his solicitors will be informed that the case has entered Part B of the Crown Office List by a letter in the form set out in Appendix 8, p 238, below. It is the responsibility of the applicant or his solicitors to forward a copy of that letter to both the clerk to counsel

1 [1981] 3 All ER 61, [1981] 1 WLR 1296.
2 Proceedings under the Social Security Acts 1975 to 1986.
3 [1987] 1 All ER 368.

instructed by the applicant and to any respondent to the case or his solicitor. It is then the duty of the respondent or his solicitor to inform the clerk to counsel instructed by him. It is the responsibility of counsel's clerks to inform the Head Clerk of the Crown Office, in writing, of counsel's time estimate for the case and of any alteration thereto.[4]

When a case is in Part B of the Crown Office List, the Head Clerk of the Crown Office will make arrangements for hearing dates to be fixed, drawing cases from Part B in order of entry so far as is practicable. Notice of the hearing will normally be given in writing by a letter in the form set out in Appendix 11, p 243, below. While the Head Clerk will give as much notice as possible of the date fixed for the hearing, he cannot undertake to accommodate the wishes of applicants, respondents, their solicitors or counsel. The occasional need to list cases at short notice may mean that parties are unable to be represented by the counsel of their first choice. In particular it should be remembered that the cases listed in the Crown Office List take precedence, as far as the attendance of counsel is concerned, over cases listed for hearing in the Crown Court unless a Divisional Court or a High Court judge directs otherwise.

As a case approaches the top of Part B of the Crown Office List, the Crown Office will send a letter, known as an 'active case' letter, to the applicant. The applicant must then confirm in writing within two weeks that the case is still active. If such confirmation is not received then the Crown Office will list the case before the Court for the applicant to show cause why it should not be struck out for want of prosecution.[5]

The 'active case' letter requires the applicant to lodge a bundle of documents in the Crown Office in readiness for the hearing. The bundle should be lodged at least three clear working days in advance of the hearing and preferably at least two weeks before the hearing date. The bundle[6] should include the following:

(a) a list of issues;
(b) a list of propositions of law to be advanced, together with the authorities relied upon in support of each, with page references to be relied on;
(c) a chronology of events, with reference to a properly paginated and indexed bundle of documents; and
(d) a list of dramatis personae, where the number of people who feature in the documents warrants it.

The form of 'active case' letter sent out by the Crown Office is set out in Appendix 9, p 239 below.

### Part C: Cases Stood Out

Where a case appears in Part B, or Part E (see below), and any party to the case is of the opinion that he (or it) is not ready to be heard, he may apply to the Master of the Crown Office to have the matter stood out into Part C. Where the Master of the Crown Office grants such an application he may do so on such terms as he thinks fit. If the Master of the Crown Office refuses to stand a case out into Part C then the application can be renewed

4 See *Practice Note* [1987] 1 All ER 1184.
5 *Practice Note* [1991] 1 All ER 1055.
6 As to the general provisions for the preparation of court bundles and the possible cost penalties for non-compliance see the Lord Chief Justice's practice direction, *Practice Note* [1983] 3 All ER 33.

to a Divisional Court or to a single judge by way of an interlocutory notice of motion.[7]

**Part D: The Expedited List**

The expedited list was established in 1974[8] in order to alleviate the problems caused by the backlog of cases that built up during the 1970s. It is at times tempting to regard this as a list for 'urgent' cases. This is not, however, its intended purpose. Its main purpose is to secure the early disposal of short and simple cases, particularly those which involve sentences of imprisonment, disqualification from driving or possession of property. A characteristic of such cases is intended to be that counsel can be adequately instructed at comparatively short notice. The list is not, therefore, suitable for cases involving particularly novel or complex issues of law.

An application or appeal may be placed in the expedited hearing list by direction of a judge when granting leave. Otherwise an application for inclusion in the expedited list should be made in the first instance to the Master of the Crown Office. If the Master refuses the application then it may be renewed to a Divisional Court or a single judge by way of an interlocutory notice of motion.[9]

When a case has been entered into the expedited list the Crown Office will give the applicant written notice of the fact by letter in the form set out at Appendix 10, p 241, below. The applicant must then take the same steps as are required on notice of entry into Part B (see above). The notice of entry into Part D, however, also has the same effect as the 'active case' letter for cases in Part B in that it requires the applicant to deal with bundles (see above).

**Part E: Cases Listed for Hearing**

This part of the List contains cases where a date for hearing has been fixed. It remains the duty of an applicant and his solicitors and counsel to inform the court in writing of any circumstances that may alter the time estimate for a case in Part E.

## WITHDRAWAL OF SOLICITORS

Where a solicitor ceases to act for a party to proceedings in the Crown Office List, and the party has not given notice of change of solicitors in accordance with RSC Ord 67, r 1, then the solicitor may apply to the Court, by way of Summons to the Master of the Crown Office, for an order declaring that the solicitor has ceased to act for that party.[10] If a solicitor fails to obtain such an order then he will be regarded as continuing to act and notice of listing dates and so forth will be given to that solicitor whose responsibility it will be to brief counsel to appear before the court.

7 RSC Ord 8.
8 *Practice Note* of Lord Widgery CJ [1974] 3 All ER 528, sub nom *Practice Direction* [1974] 1 WLR 1219.
9 RSC Ord 8.
10 RSC Ord 67, r 6 and *Practice Note* [1991] 1 All ER 1055.

## UNCONTESTED APPLICATIONS

Where the parties to a matter in the Crown Office List are agreed as to the terms on which the matter can be dealt with, but require an order of the court to give effect to those terms, then an order can be obtained without the parties having to attend court. The parties should hand in to the Crown Office a memorandum signed by the parties setting out the terms of the proposed agreed order and a short statement of the matters relied on as justifying the making of the order. All relevant authorities and statutory provisions relied upon should also be quoted. Where practicable, copies of statutory instruments which are relevant should be annexed to the documents. Two copies of the documents should also be handed in to the Crown Office. The Crown Office will then submit the documents to a judge and, if he is satisfied that an order can be made, he will cause the proceedings to be listed for hearing and the order will be announced in open court without the parties or their representatives having to attend. In a criminal cause or matter the order will be announced at the sitting of a Divisional Court rather than by a single judge. If the judge is not satisfied that it is proper for the order to be made, he may request that further information be provided and if that does not satisfy him, then he will cause the matter to be listed for hearing in the normal way. This procedure applies equally to any matter entered in to the Crown Office and, therefore, includes appeals by way of case stated and statutory appeals as well as applications for judicial review. This procedure was introduced for civil proceedings by a practice direction in 1982 and for criminal causes or matters by a practice note in 1983[11] and is designed to save costs to parties and the time of the court.

Where the parties agree that an application should be dismissed then they may apply by virtue of Ord 53, r 8(1) to the Master of the Crown Office for such an order by consent.

If, after leave has been granted, but before the applicant has served the notice of motion, the respondent performs the act for which an order is sought, or otherwise renders the application unnecessary, then the costs of the application for leave may be obtained by serving an interlocutory notice of motion on two days' notice, seeking costs alone rather than serving the full notice of motion and having it listed for hearing which would cause delay and incur additional cost. The motion for costs should be supported by an affidavit verifying the matters relied on in seeking costs. It does not follow that an application for mandamus or similar relief need or should not be pursued merely because a respondent body finally admits its breach and purports to fulfil its duty (whether before or after the service of the notice of motion). The court may still grant relief if the applicant is left in a position of doubt. Such was the position in *Parr v Wyre Borough Council*[12] where a housing authority 'relented' and purported to offer a homeless family in Fleetwood accommodation in Birmingham. Lord Justice Donaldson said:

> I cannot believe that it was right, faced with an authority which was admittedly in gross breach of their statutory duty, that the learned Judge should have refused the relief for which the Parrs had asked merely because at the eleventh hour the authority had done something which might be, but was not necessarily, a compliance with their duty.

11 [1983] 2 All ER 1020, sub nom *Practice Direction* [1983] 1 WLR 925.
12 (1982) 2 HLR 71, CA.

The Court has a distaste for dealing with substantive motions for judicial review where the only issue is one of costs but where necessary it will do so.[13] Parties pursuing matters for costs alone would be wise to remember, however, that the Court retains a discretion in awarding or withholding costs.

Where an applicant abandons a motion, eg by failing to appear, and the abandonment is not the subject of agreement between the parties, then the respondent may ask for his costs. It is not necessary, although it is usual, to give notice of intention of such an application.[14]

13 *Meade v London Borough of Haringey* [1979] 1 WLR 637 at 645, CA; *Westminster City Council v Croyalgrange Ltd* [1986] 1 WLR 674 at 678, HL; *Ainsbury v Millington* [1987] 1 WLR 379n at 381, HL; and *R v Holderness Borough Council ex p James Roberts Developments Ltd* Co 91/1577/D (1992) Times, 22 December, CA (despite a strong minority judgment by Simon Brown LJ).

14 *Hinde v Power* [1913] WN 184 per Eve J relying on Seton's *Judgments and Orders* (7th edn) p 380.

APPENDIX

# The precedents

# 1 Supreme Court Act 1981, section 31

## Application for judicial review

31.—(1) An application to the High Court for one or more of the following forms of relief, namely—
(a) an order of mandamus, prohibition or certiorari,
(b) a declaration or injunction under subsection (2), or
(c) an injunction under section 30 restraining a person not entitled to do so from acting in an office to which that section applies,
shall be made in accordance with rules of court by a procedure to be known as an application for judicial review.

(2) A declaration may be made or an injunction granted under this subsection in any case where an application for judicial review, seeking that relief, has been made and the High Court considers that, having regard to—
(a) the nature of the matters in respect of which relief may be granted by orders of mandamus, prohibition or certiorari,
(b) the nature of the persons and bodies against whom relief may be granted by such orders, and
(c) all the circumstances of the case,
it would be just and convenient for the declaration to be made or the injunction to be granted, as the case may be.

(3) No application for judicial review shall be made unless the leave of the High Court has been obtained in accordance with rules of court; and the court shall not grant leave to make such an application unless it considers that the applicant has a sufficient interest in the matter to which the application relates.

(4) On an application for judicial review the High Court may award damages to the applicant if—
(a) he has joined with his application a claim for damages arising from any matter to which the application relates, and
(b) the court is satisfied that, if the claim had been made in an action begun by the applicant at the time of making his application, he would have been awarded damages.

(5) If, on an application for judicial review seeking an order of certiorari, the High Court quashes the decision to which the application relates, the High Court may remit the matter to the court, tribunal or authority concerned, with a direction to reconsider it and reach a decision in accordance with the findings of the High Court.

(6) Where the High Court considers that there has been undue delay in making an application for judicial review, the court may refuse to grant—
(a) leave for the making of the application, or
(b) any relief sought on the application,
if it considers that the granting of the relief sought would be likely to cause substantial hardship to, or substantially prejudice the rights of, any person or would be detrimental to good administration.

(7) Subsection (6) is without prejudice to any enactment or rule of court which has the effect of limiting the time within which an application for judicial review may be made.

# 2 Rules of the Supreme Court, Orders 53, 54, 55, 56 and 94

## Order 53 Applications for judicial review

### Ord 53, r 1 Cases appropriate for application for judicial review

1.—(1) An application for—
(a) an order of mandamus, prohibition or certiorari, or
(b) an injunction under section 30 of the Act restraining a person from acting in any office in which he is not entitled to act,
shall be made by way of an application for judicial review in accordance with the provisions of this Order.

(2) An application for a declaration or an injunction (not being an injunction mentioned in paragraph (1)(b)) may be made by way of an application for judicial review, and on such an application the Court may grant the declaration or injunction claimed if it considers that, having regard to—
(a) the nature of the matters in respect of which relief may be granted by way of an order of mandamus, prohibition or certiorari,
(b) the nature of the persons and bodies against whom relief may be granted by way of such an order, and
(c) all the circumstances of the case,
it would be just and convenient for the declaration or injunction to be granted on an application for judicial review.

### Ord 53, r 2 Joinder of claims for relief

2. On an application for judicial review any relief mentioned in rule 1(1) or (2) may be claimed as an alternative or in addition to any other relief so mentioned if it arises out of or relates to or is connected with the same matter.

### Ord 53, r 3 Grant of leave to apply for judicial review

3.—(1) No application for judicial review shall be made unless the leave of the Court has been obtained in accordance with this rule.

(2) An application for leave must be made ex parte to a judge by filing in the Crown Office—
(a) a notice in Form No 86A containing a statement of
 (i) the name and description of the applicant,
 (ii) the relief sought and the grounds upon which it is sought,
 (iii) the name and address of the applicant's solicitors (if any) and
 (iv) the applicant's address for service; and
(b) an affidavit which verifies the facts relied on.

(3) The judge may determine the application without a hearing, unless a hearing is requested in the notice of application, and need not sit in open court; in any case, the Crown Office shall serve a copy of the judge's order on the applicant.

(4) Where the application for leave is refused by the judge, or is granted on terms, the applicant may renew it by applying—
(a) in any criminal cause or matter, to a Divisional Court of the Queen's Bench Division;
(b) in any other case, to a single judge sitting in open court or, if the Court so directs, to a Divisional Court of the Queen's Bench Division:
Provided that no application for leave may be renewed in any non-criminal cause or matter in which the judge has refused leave under paragraph (3) after a hearing.

(5) In order to renew his application for leave the applicant must, within 10 days of

being served with notice of the judge's refusal, lodge in the Crown Office notice of his intention in Form No 86B.

(6) Without prejudice to its powers under Order 20, rule 8, the Court hearing an application for leave may allow the applicant's statement to be amended, whether by specifying different or additional grounds or relief or otherwise, on such terms, if any, as it thinks fit.

(7) The Court shall not grant leave unless it considers that the applicant has a sufficient interest in the matter to which the application relates.

(8) Where leave is sought to apply for an order of certiorari to remove for the purpose of its being quashed any judgment, order, conviction or other proceedings which is subject to appeal and time is limited for the bringing of the appeal, the Court may adjourn the application for leave until the appeal is determined or the time for appealing has expired.

(9) If the Court grants leave, it may impose such terms as to costs and as to giving security as it thinks fit.

(10) Where leave to apply for judicial review is granted, then—

(a) if the relief sought is an order of prohibition or certiorari and the Court so directs, the grant shall operate as a stay of the proceedings to which the application relates until the determination of the application or until the Court otherwise orders;

(b) if any other relief is sought, the Court may at any time grant in the proceedings such interim relief as could be granted in an action begun by writ.

### Ord 53, r 4 Delay in applying for relief

4.—(1) An application for judicial review shall be made promptly and in any event within three months from the date when grounds for the application first arose unless the Court considers that there is good reason for extending the period within which the application shall be made.

(2) Where the relief sought is an order of certiorari in respect of any judgment, order, conviction or other proceeding, the date when grounds for the application first arose shall be taken to be the date of that judgment, order, conviction or proceeding.

(3) The preceding paragraphs are without prejudice to any statutory provision which has the effect of limiting the time within which an application for judicial review may be made.

### Ord 53, r 5 Mode of applying for judicial review

5.—(1) In any criminal cause or matter, where leave has been granted to make an application for judicial review, the application shall be made by originating motion to a Divisional Court of the Queen's Bench Division.

(2) In any other such cause or matter, the application shall be made by originating motion to a judge sitting in open court, unless the Court directs that it shall be made—

(a) by originating summons to a Judge in Chambers; or

(b) by originating motion to a Divisional Court of the Queen's Bench Division.

Any direction under sub-paragraph (a) shall be without prejudice to the judge's powers under Order 32, rule 13.

(3) The notice of motion or summons must be served on all persons directly affected and where it relates to any proceedings in or before a Court and the object of the application is either to compel the Court or an officer of the Court to do any act in relation to the proceedings or to quash them or any order made therein, the notice or summons must also be served on the Clerk or Registrar of the Court and, where any objection to the conduct of the judge is to be made, on the judge.

(4) Unless the Court granting leave has otherwise directed, there must be at least 10 days between the service of the notice of motion or summons and the hearing.

(5) A motion must be entered for hearing within 14 days after the grant of leave.

(6) An affidavit giving the names and addresses of, and the places and dates of service on, all persons who have been served with the notice of motion or summons

must be filed before the motion or summons is entered for hearing and, if any person who ought to be served under this rule has not been served, the affidavit must state that fact and the reason for it; and the affidavit shall be before the Court on the hearing of the motion or summons.

(7) If on the hearing of the motion or summons the Court is of opinion that any person who ought, whether under this rule or otherwise, to have been served has not been served, the Court may adjourn the hearing on such terms (if any) as it may direct in order that the notice or summons may be served on that person.

**Ord 53, r 6 Statements and affidavits**

6.—(1) Copies of the statement in support of an application for leave under rule 3 must be served with the notice of motion or summons and, subject to paragraph (2), no grounds shall be relied upon or any relief sought at the hearing except the grounds and relief set out in the statement.

(2) The Court may on the hearing of the motion or summons allow the applicant to amend his statement, whether by specifying different or additional grounds or relief or otherwise, on such terms, if any, as it thinks fit and may allow further affidavits to be used *by him* (amended 1 October 1992).

(3) Where the applicant intends to ask to be allowed to amend his statement or to use further affidavits, he shall give notice of his intention and of any proposed amendment to every other party.

(4) Any respondent who intends to use an affidavit at the hearing shall file it in the Crown Office as soon as practicable and in any event, unless the Court otherwise directs, within 56 days after service upon him of the documents required to be served by paragraph (1).

(5) Each party to the application must supply to every other party on demand and on payment of the proper charges copies of every affidavit which he proposes to use at the hearing, including, in the case of the applicant, the affidavit in support of the application for leave under rule 3.

**Ord 53, r 7 Claim for damages**

7.—(1) On an application for judicial review the Court may, subject to paragraph (2) award damages to the applicant if—

(a) he has included in the statement in support of his application for leave under rule 3 a claim for damages arising from any matter to which the application relates, and
(b) the Court is satisfied that, if the claim had been made in an action begun by the applicant at the time of making his application, he could have been awarded damages.

(2) Order 18, rule 12, shall apply to a statement relating to a claim for damages as it applies to a pleading.

**Ord 53, r 8 Application for discovery, interrogatories, cross-examination, etc**

8.—(1) Unless the Court otherwise directs, any interlocutory application in proceedings on an application for judicial review may be made to any judge or a master of the Queen's Bench Division, notwithstanding that the application for judicial review has been made by motion and is to be heard by a Divisional Court.

In this paragraph 'interlocutory application' includes an application for an order under Order 24 or 26 or Order 38, rule 2(3) or for an order dismissing the proceedings by consent of the parties.

(2) In relation to an order made by a Master pursuant to paragraph (1) Order 58, rule 1, shall, where the application for judicial review is to be heard by a Divisional Court, have effect as if a reference to that Court were substituted for the reference to a judge in chambers.

(3) This rule is without prejudice to any statutory provision or rule of law restricting the making of an order against the Crown.

### Ord 53, r 9 Hearing of application for judicial review

9.—(1) On the hearing of any motion or summons under rule 5, any person who desires to be heard in opposition to the motion or summons, and appears to the Court to be a proper person to be heard, shall be heard, notwithstanding that he has not been served with notice of the motion or the summons.

(2) Where the relief sought is or includes an order of certiorari to remove any proceedings for the purpose of quashing them, the applicant may not question the validity of any order, warrant, commitment, conviction, inquisition or record unless before the hearing of the motion or summons he has lodged in the Crown Office a copy thereof verified by affidavit or accounts for his failure to do so to the satisfaction of the Court hearing the motion or summons.

(3) Where an order for certiorari is made in any such case as is referred to in paragraph (2) the order shall, subject to paragraph (4) direct that the proceedings shall be quashed forthwith on their removal into the Queen's Bench Division.

(4) Where the relief sought is an order of certiorari and the Court is satisfied that there are grounds for quashing the decision to which the application relates, the Court may, in addition to quashing it, remit the matter to the Court, tribunal or authority concerned with a direction to reconsider it and reach a decision in accordance with the findings of the Court.

(5) Where the relief sought is a declaration, an injunction or damages and the Court considers that it should not be granted on an application for judicial review but might have been granted if it had been sought in an action begun by writ by the applicant at the time of making his application, the Court may, instead of refusing the application, order the proceedings to continue as if they had been begun by writ; and Order 28, rule 8, shall apply as if, in the case of an application made by motion, it had been made by summons.

### Ord 53, r 10 Saving for person acting in obedience to mandamus

10. No action or proceeding shall be begun or prosecuted against any person in respect of anything done in obedience to an order of mandamus.

### Ord 53, r 11 Proceedings for disqualification of member of local authority

11.—(1) Proceedings under section 92 of the Local Government Act 1972 must be begun by originating motion to a Divisional Court of the Queen's Bench Division, and, unless otherwise directed, there must be at least 10 days between the service of the notice of motion and the hearing.

(2) Without prejudice to Order 8, rule 3, the notice of motion must set out the name and description of the applicant, the relief sought and the grounds on which it is sought, and must be supported by affidavit verifying the facts relied on.

(3) Copies of every supporting affidavit must be lodged in the Crown Office before the motion is entered for hearing and must be supplied to any other party on demand and on payment of the proper charges.

(4) The provisions of rules 5, 6 and 9(1) as to the persons on whom the notice is to be served and as to the proceedings at the hearing shall apply, with the necessary modifications, to proceedings under the said section 92 as they apply to an application for judicial review.

### Ord 53, r 12 Consolidation of applications

12. Where there is more than one application pending under section 30 of the Act, or section 92 of the Local Government Act 1972, against several persons in respect of the

same office, and on the same grounds, the Court may order the applications to be consolidated.

### Ord 53, r 13 Appeal from judge's order

13. No appeal shall lie from an order made under paragraph (3) of rule 3 on an application for leave which may be renewed under paragraph (4) of that rule.

### Ord 53, r 14 Meaning of 'Court'

14. In relation to the hearing by a judge of an application for leave under rule 3 or of an application for judicial review, any reference in this Order to 'the Court' shall, unless the context otherwise requires, be construed as a reference to the judge.

## Order 54 Applications for writ of habeas corpus

### Ord 54, r 1 Application for writ of habeas corpus ad subjiciendum

1.—(1) Subject to rule 11, an application for a writ of habeas corpus ad subjiciendum shall be made to a judge in Court, except that—

(a) it shall be made to a Divisional Court of the Queen's Bench Division if the Court so directs;
(b) it may be made to a judge otherwise than in court at any time when no judge is sitting in court; and
(c) any application on behalf of a minor must be made in the first instance to a judge otherwise than in court.

(2) An application for such writ may be made ex parte and, subject to paragraph (3) must be supported by an affidavit by the person restrained showing that it is made at his instance and setting out the nature of the restraint.

(3) Where the person restrained is unable for any reason to make the affidavit required by paragraph (2) the affidavit may be made by some other person on his behalf and that affidavit must state that the person restrained is unable to make the affidavit himself and for what reason.

### Ord 54, r 2 Power of Court to whom ex parte application made

2.—(1) The Court or judge to whom an application under rule 1 is made ex parte may make an order forthwith for the writ to issue, or may—

(a) where the application is made to a judge otherwise than in court, direct that an originating summons for the writ be issued, or that an application therefor be made by originating motion to a Divisional Court or to a judge in court;
(b) where the application is made to a judge in court, adjourn the application so that notice thereof may be given, or direct that an application be made by originating motion to a Divisional Court;
(c) where the application is made to a Divisional Court, adjourn the application so that notice thereof may be given.

(2) The summons or notice of the motion must be served on the person against whom the issue of the writ is sought and on such other persons as the Court or judge may direct, and, unless the Court or judge otherwise directs, there must be at least 8 clear days between the service of the summons or notice and the date named therein for the hearing of the application.

### Ord 54, r 3 Copies of affidavits to be supplied

3. Every party to an application under rule 1 must supply to every other party on demand and on payment of the proper charges copies of the affidavits which he proposes to use at the hearing of the application.

**Ord 54, r 4 Power to order release of person restrained**

4.—(1) Without prejudice to rule 2(1) the Court or judge hearing an application for a writ of habeas corpus ad subjiciendum may in its or his discretion order that the person restrained be released, and such order shall be sufficient warrant to any governor or a prison, constable or other person for the release of the person under restraint.

(2) Where such an application in a criminal cause or matter is heard by a judge and the judge does not order the release of the person restrained, he shall direct that the application be made by originating motion to the Divisional Court of the Queen's Bench Division.

**Ord 54, r 5 Directions as to return to writ**

5. Where a writ of habeas corpus ad subjiciendum is ordered to issue, the Court or judge by whom the order is made shall give directions as to the Court or judge before whom, and the date on which, the writ is returnable.

**Ord 54, r 6 Service of writ and notice**

6.—(1) Subject to paragraphs (2) and (3) a writ of habeas corpus ad subjiciendum must be served personally on the person to whom it is directed.

(2) If it is not possible to serve such a writ personally, or if it is directed to a governor of a prison or other public official, it must be served by leaving it with a servant or agent of the person to whom the writ is directed at the place where the person restrained is confined or restrained.

(3) If the writ is directed to more than one person, the writ must be served in manner provided by this rule on the person first named in the writ, and copies must be served on each of the other persons in the same manner as the writ.

(4) There must be served with the writ a notice (in Form No 90 in Appendix A) stating the Court or judge before whom and the date on which the person restrained is to be brought and that in default of obedience proceedings for committal of the party disobeying will be taken.

**Ord 54, r 7 Return to the writ**

7.—(1) The return to a writ of habeas corpus ad subjiciendum must be endorsed on or annexed to the writ and must state all the causes of the detainer of the person restrained.

(2) The return may be amended, or another return substituted therefor, by leave of the Court or judge before whom the writ is returnable.

**Ord 54, r 8 Procedure at hearing of writ**

8. When a return to a writ of habeas corpus ad subjiciendum is made, the return shall first be read, and motion then made for discharging or remanding the person restrained or amending or quashing the return, and where that person is brought up in accordance with the writ, his counsel shall be heard first, then the counsel for the Crown, and then one counsel for the person restrained in reply.

**Ord 54, r 9 Bringing up prisoner to give evidence, etc**

9.—(1) An application for a writ of habeas corpus ad testificandum or of habeas corpus ad respondendum must be made on affidavit to a judge in chambers.

(2) An application for an order to bring up a prisoner, otherwise than by writ of habeas corpus, to give evidence in any cause or matter, civil or criminal, before any Court, tribunal or justice, must be made on affidavit to a judge in chambers.

**Ord 54, r 10 Form of writ**

10. A writ of habeas corpus must be in Form No 89, 91 or 92 in Appendix A, whichever is appropriate.

**Ord 54, r 11 Applications relative to the custody, etc, of minors**

11. An application by a parent or guardian of a minor for a writ of habeas corpus ad subjiciendum relative to the custody, care or control of the minor must be made in the Family Division, and this Order shall accordingly apply to such applications with the appropriate modifications.

**Order 55 Appeals to High Court from court, tribunal or person: general**

**Ord 55, r 1 Application**

1.—(1) Subject to paragraphs (2) (3) and (4) this Order shall apply to every appeal which by or under any enactment lies to the High Court from any court, tribunal or person.

(2) This Order shall not apply to an appeal by case stated or to any appeal to which Order 73 applies.

(3) The following rules of this Order shall not apply to an appeal from a county court to a single judge under section 375 of the Insolvency Act 1986, but subject to the Insolvency Rules 1986, as amended, Order 59 shall, with the necessary modifications, apply to such an appeal as it applies to an appeal from a county court to the Court of Appeal.

(4) The following rules of this Order shall, in relation to an appeal to which this Order applies, have effect subject to any provision made in relation to that appeal by any other provision of these rules or by or under any enactment.

(5) In this Order references to a tribunal shall be construed as references to any tribunal constituted by or under any enactment other than any of the ordinary courts of law.

**Ord 55, r 2 Court to hear appeal**

2. Except where it is otherwise provided by these rules or by or under any enactment, an appeal to which this Order applies shall be assigned to the Queen's Bench Division and shall be heard and determined—

(a) where the decision of the High Court on the appeal is final, by a Divisional Court, and

(b) in any other case, by a single judge.

**Ord 55, r 3 Bringing of appeal**

3.—(1) An appeal to which this Order applies shall be by way of rehearing and must be brought by originating motion.

(2) Every notice of the motion by which such an appeal is brought must state the grounds of the appeal and, if the appeal is against a judgment, order or other decision of a court, must state whether the appeal is against the whole or a part of that decision and, if against part only, must specify the part.

(3) The bringing of such an appeal shall not operate as a stay of proceedings on the judgment, determination or other decisions against which the appeal is brought unless the Court by which the appeal is to be heard or the court, tribunal or person by which or by whom the decision was given so orders.

**Ord 55, r 4 Service of notice of motion and entry of appeal**

4.—(1) The persons to be served with notice of the motion by which an appeal to which this Order applies is brought are the following:—

(a) if the appeal is against a judgment, order or other decision of a court, the registrar or clerk of the court and any party to the proceedings in which the decision was given is directly affected by the appeal;
(b) if the appeal is against an order, determination, award or other decision of a tribunal, Minister of the Crown, government department or other person, the chairman of the tribunal, Minister, government department or person, as the case may be, and every party to the proceedings (other than the appellant) in which the decision appealed against was given.

(2) The notice must be served, and the appeal entered, within 28 days after the date of the judgment, order, determination or other decision against which the appeal is brought.

(3) In the case of an appeal against a judgment, order or decision of a court, the period specified in paragraph (2) shall be calculated from the date on which the decision was given.

(4) In the case of an appeal against an order, determination, award or other decision of a tribunal, Minister, government department or other person, the period specified in paragraph (2) shall be calculated from the date on which notice of the decision, or, in a case where a statement of the reasons for a decision was given later than such notice, on which such a statement was given to the appellant by the person who made the decision or by a person authorised in that behalf to do so.

### Ord 55, r 5 Date of hearing of appeal

5. Unless the Court having jurisdiction to determine the appeal otherwise directs, an appeal to which this Order applies shall not be heard sooner than 21 days after service of notice of the motion by which the appeal is brought.

### Ord 55, r 6 Amendment of grounds of appeal, etc

6.—(1) The notice of the motion by which an appeal to which this Order applies is brought may be amended by the appellant, without leave, by supplementary notice served not less than 7 days before the day appointed for the hearing of the appeal, on each of the persons on whom the notice to be amended was served.

(2) Within 2 days after service of a supplementary notice under paragraph (1) the appellant must lodge two copies of the notice in the office in which the appeal is entered.

(3) Except with the leave of the Court hearing any such appeal, no grounds other than those stated in the notice of the motion by which the appeal is brought or any supplementary notice under paragraph (1) may be relied upon by the appellant at the hearing; but that Court may amend the grounds so stated or make any other order, on such terms as it thinks just, to ensure the determination on the merits of the real question in controversy between the parties.

(4) The foregoing provisions of this rule are without prejudice to the powers of the Court under Order 20.

### Ord 55, r 6A Interlocutory applications

6A.—(1) Unless the Court otherwise directs, any interlocutory application in proceedings to which this Order applies may be made to any judge or a Master of the Queen's Bench Division or, as the case may be, any judge or a Registrar of the Family Division, notwithstanding that the appeal had been brought by motion and is to be heard by a Divisional Court.

In this paragraph 'interlocutory application' includes an application for the extension of time for the service of the notice of motion or the entry of the appeal or for the amendment of the notice of motion.

(2) In relation to an order made by a Master or Registrar pursuant to paragraph (1), Order 58, rule 1 shall, where the appeal is to be heard by a Divisional Court, have effect as if a reference to that Court were substituted for the reference to a judge in chambers.

(3) This rule is without prejudice to any statutory provision or rule of law restricting the making of an order against the Crown.

## Ord 55, r 7 Powers of Court hearing appeal

7.—(1) In addition to the power conferred by rule 6(3) the Court hearing an appeal to which this Order applies shall have the powers conferred by the following provisions of this rule.

(2) The Court shall have power to receive further evidence on questions of fact, and the evidence may be given in such manner as the Court may direct either by oral examination in Court, by affidavit, by deposition taken before an examiner or in some other manner.

(3) The Court shall have power to draw any inferences of fact which might have been drawn in the proceedings out of which the appeal arose.

(4) It shall be the duty of the appellant to apply to the judge or other person presiding at the proceedings in which the decision appealed against was given for a signed copy of any note made by him of the proceedings and to furnish that copy for the use of the Court; and in default of production of such a note, or if such note is incomplete, in addition to such note, the Court may hear and determine the appeal on any other evidence or statement of what occurred in those proceedings as appears to the Court to be sufficient.

Except where the Court otherwise directs, an affidavit or note by a person present at the proceedings shall not be used in evidence under this paragraph unless it was previously submitted to the person presiding at the proceedings for his comments.

(5) The Court may give any judgment or decision or make any order which ought to have been given or made by the Court, tribunal or person and make such further or other order as the case may require or may remit the matter with the opinion of the Court for rehearing and determination by it or him.

(6) The Court may, in special circumstances, order that such security shall be given for the cost of the appeal as may be just.

(7) The Court shall not be bound to allow the appeal on the ground merely of misdirection, or of the improper admission or rejection or evidence, unless in the opinion of the Court substantial wrong or miscarriage has been thereby occasioned.

## Ord 55, r 8 Right of Minister, etc, to appear and be heard

8. Where an appeal to which this Order applies is against an order, determination or other decision of a Minister of the Crown or government department, the Minister or department, as the case may be, shall be entitled to appear and be heard in the proceedings on the appeal.

## Order 56 Appeals to High Court by case stated: general

## Ord 56, r 1 Appeals from the Crown Court by case stated

1.—(1) Except where they relate to affiliation proceedings or to care proceedings under the Children and Young Persons Act 1969 all appeals from the Crown Court by case stated shall be heard and determined—

(a) in any criminal cause or matter, by a Divisional Court of the Queen's Bench Division;

(b) in any other cause or matter, by a single judge sitting in Court, or if the Court so directs, by a Divisional Court of the Queen's Bench Division.

(2) [*Revoked by RSC (Amendment No 5) 1971 (SI 1971 No 1955).*]

(3) An appeal from the Crown Court by case stated shall not be entered for hearing unless and until the case and a copy of the judgment, order or decision in respect of which the case has been stated and, if that judgment, order or decision was given or

made on an appeal to the Crown Court, a copy of the judgment, order or decision appealed from, have been lodged in the Crown Office.

(4) No such appeal shall be entered after the expiration of 10 days from the receipt by the appellant of the case unless the delay is accounted for to the satisfaction of the Divisional Court.

Notice of intention to apply for an extension of time for entry of the appeal must be served on the respondent at least 2 clear days before the day named in the notice for the hearing of the application.

(5) Where any such appeal has not been entered by reason of a default in complying with the provisions of this rule, the Crown Court may proceed as if no case had been stated.

### Ord 56, r 2 Form of case

2. [*Revoked by RSC (Amendment No 2) 1978 (SI 1978 No 359)*.]

### Ord 56, r 3 Application for direction to clerk of the peace

3. [*Revoked by RSC (Amendment No 5) 1971 (SI 1971 No 1955)*.]

### Ord 56, r 4 Notice of entry of appeal

4. Within 4 days after an appeal from the Crown Court by case stated is entered for hearing, the appellant must serve notice of the entry of the appeal on the respondent.

### Ord 56, r 4A Appeals relating to affiliation proceedings and care proceedings

4A. Appeals from the Crown Court by case stated which relate to affiliation proceedings or to care proceedings under the Children and Young Persons Act 1969 shall be heard and determined by a single judge, or if the Court so directs, a Divisional Court of the Family Division, and the foregoing provisions of this Order shall accordingly apply to such appeals with the substitution of references to the principal registry of the Family Division for references to the Crown Office and such other modifications as may be appropriate.

### Ord 56, r 5 Appeal from Magistrates' Court by case stated

5.—(1) Except as provided by paragraph (2) all appeals from a Magistrates' Court shall be heard and determined—

(a) in any criminal cause or matter, by a Divisional Court of the Queen's Bench Division;

(b) in any other matter, by a single judge sitting in Court or, if the Court so directs, by a Divisional Court of the Queen's Bench Division.

(2) An appeal by way of case stated against an order or determination of a Magistrates' Court shall be heard and determined by a single judge or, if the Court so directs, by a Divisional Court of the Family Division if the order or determination appealed against was made or given in affiliation proceedings, or in care proceedings under the Children and Young Persons Act 1969, or on an application under section 35 of the Matrimonial Causes Act 1973, or if it relates to the enforcement of—

(a) an order for the payment of money made by virtue of the Matrimonial Proceedings (Magistrates' Courts) Act 1960, the Guardianship of Minors Act 1971 or the Domestic Proceedings and Magistrates' Courts Act 1978, or

(b) an order for the payment of money to a wife for her maintenance or for her maintenance and that of any child or children of hers, registered in a Court in England or Wales under Part II of the Maintenance Orders Act 1950 or the Maintenance Orders (Facilities for Enforcement) Act 1920 or the Maintenance Orders (Reciprocal

Enforcement) Act 1972 or confirmed by such a Court under either of the two last-mentioned Acts or registered in such a Court under the Civil Jurisdiction and Judgments Act 1982, or

(c) an order for periodical or other payments made, or having effect as if made, under Part II of the Matrimonial Causes Act 1973 and registered in a Magistrates' Court under the Maintenance Orders Act 1958.

**Ord 56, r 6 Case stated by Magistrates' Court: lodging case, etc**

6.—(1) Where a case has been stated by a Magistrates' Court the appellant must—

(a) within 10 days after receiving the case, lodge it in the Crown Office or, if the appeal falls to be heard by a Divisional Court of the Family Division, the principal registry of the Family Division, and

(b) within 4 days after lodging the case as aforesaid serve on the respondent a notice of the entry of appeal together with a copy of the case.

(2) Unless the Court having jurisdiction to determine the appeal otherwise directs, the appeal shall not be heard sooner than 8 clear days after service of notice of the entry of the appeal.

**Ord 56, r 7 Case stated by Ministers, tribunal, etc**

7.—(1) The jurisdiction of the High Court under any enactment to hear and determine a case stated by a Minister of the Crown, government department, tribunal or other person, or question of law referred to that Court by such a Minister or department or a tribunal or other person by way of case stated, shall be exercised by a single judge of the Queen's Bench Division, except where it is otherwise provided by these rules or by or under any enactment.

(2) The jurisdiction of the High Court under any enactment to hear and determine an application for an order directing such a Minister or department or a tribunal or other person to state a case for determination by the High Court, or to refer a question of law to that Court by way of case stated, shall be exercised by the Court or judge having jurisdiction to hear and determine that case or question except where by some other provision of these rules or by or under any enactment it is otherwise provided.

(3) This rule and rules 8 to 12 of this Order shall apply to proceedings for the determination of such a case, question or application and, in relation to any such proceedings, shall have effect subject to any provision made in relation to those proceedings by any other provision of these rules by or under any enactment.

(4) In this Order references to a tribunal shall be construed as references to any tribunal constituted by or under any enactment other than any of the ordinary Courts of law.

(5) In the following rules references to a Minister shall be construed as including references to a government department, and in those rules and this rule 'case' includes a special case.

**Ord 56, r 8 Application for order to state a case**

8.—(1) An application to the Court for an order directing a Minister, tribunal or other person to state a case for determination by the Court or to refer a question of law to the Court by way of case stated must be made by originating motion; and the persons to be served with notice thereof are the Minister, secretary of the tribunal or other person, as the case may be, and every party (other than the applicant) to the proceedings to which the application relates.

(2) The notice of such motion must state the grounds of the application, the question of law on which it is sought to have the case stated and any reasons given by the Minister, tribunal or other person for his or its refusal to state a case.

(3) The motion must be entered for hearing, and the notice thereof served, within 14 days after receipt by the applicant of notice of the refusal of his request to state a case.

**Ord 56, r 9 Signing and service of case**

9.—(1) A case stated by a tribunal must be signed by the chairman or president of the tribunal, and a case stated by any other person must be signed by him or by a person authorised in that behalf to do so.

(2) The case must be served on the party at whose request, or as a result of whose application to the Court, the case was stated; and if a Minister, tribunal, arbitrator or other person is entitled by virtue of any enactment to state a case, or to refer a question of law by way of case stated, for determination by the High Court without request being made by any party to the proceedings before that person, the case must be served on such party to those proceedings as the Minister, tribunal, arbitrator or other person, as the case may be, thinks appropriate.

(3) When a case is served on any party under paragraph (2) notice must be given to every other party to the proceedings in question that the case has been served on the party named, and on the date specified, in the notice.

**Ord 56, r 10 Proceedings for determination of case**

10.—(1) Proceedings for the determination by the High Court of a case stated, or a question of law referred by way of case stated, by a Minister, tribunal, arbitrator or other person must be begun by originating motion by the person on whom the case was served in accordance with rule 9(2) or, when the case is stated without a request being made, by the Minister, secretary of the tribunal, arbitrator or other person by whom the case is stated.

(2) The applicant shall serve the notice of a motion under paragraph (1), together with a copy of the case, on—

(a) the Minister, secretary of the tribunal, arbitrator or other person by whom the case was stated, unless that Minister, tribunal, arbitrator or other person is the applicant,

(b) every party (other than the applicant) to the proceedings in which the question of law to which the case relates arose, and

(c) any other person (other than the applicant) served with the case under rule 9(2).

(3) The notice of such motion must set out the applicant's contentions on the question of law to which the case stated relates.

(4) The motion must be entered for hearing, and the notice thereof served, within 14 days after the case stated was served on the applicant.

(5) If the applicant fails to enter the motion within the period specified in paragraph (4) then, after obtaining a copy of the case from the Minister, tribunal, arbitrator or other person by whom the case was stated, any other party to the proceedings in which the question of law to which the case relates arose may, within 14 days after the expiration of the period so specified, begin proceedings for the determination of the case, and paragraphs (1) to (4) shall have effect accordingly with the necessary modifications.

The references in this paragraph to the period specified in paragraph (4) shall be construed as including references to that period as extended by any order of the Court.

(6) The documents required to be lodged in accordance with Order 57, rule 2, before entry of the motion include a copy of the case stated.

(7) Unless the Court having jurisdiction to determine the case otherwise directs, the motion shall not be heard sooner than 7 days after service of notice of the motion.

**Ord 56, r 11 Amendment of case**

11. The Court hearing a case stated by a Minister, tribunal, arbitrator or other person may amend the case or order it to be returned to that person for amendment, and may draw inferences of the fact from the facts stated in the case.

**Ord 56, r 12 Right of Minister to appear and be heard**

12. In proceedings for the determination of a case stated, or of a question of law referred by way of case stated, the Minister, chairman or president of the tribunal, arbitrator or other person by whom the case was stated shall be entitled to appear and be heard.

**Ord 56, r 12A Extradition**

12A.—(1) Rules 5 and 6 of this Order shall apply to appeals by case stated under—
(a) section 7 of the Criminal Justice Act 1988, and
(b) section 10 of the Extradition Act 1989, as they apply to appeals by case stated from a Magistrates' Court and references in those rules to appellant and respondent shall be construed as references to the requesting state and the person whose surrender is sought respectively.

(2) An application for an order under either of the sections mentioned in paragraph (1) or under Section 2A of the Backing of Warrants (Republic of Ireland) Act 1965 requiring a Court to state a case shall be made in accordance with rule 8 of this Order the references in that rule to a tribunal and the secretary of a tribunal being construed for this puprpose as references to the Court and the Clerk of the Court respectively.

**Ord 56, r 13 Interlocutory applications**

13.—(1) Unless the Court otherwise directs, any interlocutory application in proceedings to which this Order applies may be made to any judge or a Master of the Queen's Bench Division or, as the case may be, any judge or a Registrar of the Family Division, notwithstanding that the appeal has been brought by a case stated and is to be heard by a Divisional Court.

In this paragraph 'interlocutory application' includes an application for an order extending the time for entry of the appeal or for service of notice of entry of the appeal.

(2) In relation to an order made by a Master or Registrar pursuant to paragraph (1), Order 58, rule 1 shall, where the application is to be heard by a Divisional Court, have effect as if a reference to that Court were substituted for the reference to a judge in chambers.

(3) This rule is without prejudice to any statutory provision or rule of law restricting the making of an order against the Crown.

**Order 94 Applications and appeals to High Court under various Acts: Queen's Bench Division**

**Ord 94, r 1 Jurisdiction of High Court to quash certain orders, schemes, etc**

1.—(1) Where by virtue of any enactment the High Court has jurisdiction, on the application of any person, to quash or prohibit any order, scheme, certificate or plan, any amendment or approval of a plan, any decision of a Minister or government department or any action on the part of a Minister or government department, the jurisdiction shall be exercisable by a single judge of the Queen's Bench Division.

(2) The application must be made by originating motion and, without prejudice to Order 8, rule 3(2) the notice of such motion must state the grounds of the application.

**Ord 94, r 2 Entry and service of notice of motion**

2.—(1) Notice of a motion under rule 1 must be entered at the Crown Office, and served, within the time limited by the relevant enactment for making the application made by the motion.

(2) Subject to paragraph (4) notice of motion must be served on the appropriate Minister or government department, and—

(a) if the application relates to a compulsory purchase order made by an authority other than the appropriate Minister or government department, or to a clearance order under the Housing Act 1957, on the authority by whom the order was made;

(b) if the application relates to a scheme or order to which Schedule 2 to the Highways Act 1959, applies made by an authority other than the Secretary of State, on that authority;

(c) if the application relates to a structure plan, local plan or other development plan within the meaning of the Town and Country Planning Act 1971, on the local planning authority who prepared the plan;

(d) if the application relates to any decision or order, or any action on the part of a Minister of the Crown to which section 21 of the Land Compensation Act 1961, or section 245 of the Town and Country Planning Act 1971, applies, on the authority directly concerned with such decision, order or action or, if that authority is the applicant, on every person who would, if he were aggrieved by the decision, order or action, be entitled to apply to the High Court under the said section 21 or the said section 245, as the case may be;

(e) if the application relates to a scheme to which Schedule 32 to the Local Government, Planning and Land Act 1980 applies, on the body which adopted the scheme.

(3) In paragraph (2) 'the appropriate Minister or government department' means the Minister of the Crown or government department by whom the order, scheme, certificate, plan, amendment, approval or decision in question was or may be made, authorised, confirmed, approved or given or on whose part the action in question was or may be taken.

(4) Where the application relates to an order made under the Road Traffic Regulation Act 1967, notice of the motion must be served—

(a) if the order was made by a Minister of the Crown, on that Minister;

(b) if the order was made by a local authority with the consent, or in pursuance of a direction, of a Minister of the Crown, on that authority and also on that Minister;

(c) in any other case, on the local authority by whom the order was made.

In this paragraph 'local authority' includes the Greater London Council.

## Ord 94, r 3 Filing of affidavits, etc

3.—(1) Without prejudice to the powers of the Court under Order 38, rule 2(3) evidence at the hearing of a motion under rule 1 shall be by affidavit.

(2) Any affidavit in support of the application made by such motion must be filed by the applicant in the Crown Office within 14 days after service of the notice of motion and the applicant must, at the time of filing, serve a copy of the affidavit and of any exhibit thereto on the respondent.

(3) Any affidavit in opposition to the application must be filed by the respondent in the Crown Office within 21 days after the service on him under paragraph (2) of the applicant's affidavit and the respondent must, at the time of filing, serve a copy of his affidavit and of any exhibit thereto on the applicant.

(4) When filing an affidavit under this rule a party must leave a copy thereof and of any exhibit thereto at the Crown Office for the use of the Court.

(5) Unless the Court otherwise orders, a motion under rule 1 shall not be heard earlier than 14 days after the time for filing an affidavit by the respondent has expired.

**Ord 94, r 4 Rectification of register deeds of arrangement**

4.—(1) Every application to the Court under section 7 of the Deeds of Arrangement Act, 1914, for an order—
(a) that any omission to register a deed of arrangement within the time prescribed by that Act be rectified by extending the time for such registration, or
(b) that any omission or mis-statement of the name, residence or description of any person be rectified by the insertion in the register of his true name, residence or description,
must be made by affidavit ex parte to a master of the Queen's Bench Division.

(2) The affidavit must set out particulars of the deed of arrangement and of the omission or mis-statement in question and must state the ground on which the application is made.

**Ord 94, r 5 Exercise of jurisdiction under Representation of the People Acts**

5.—(1) Proceedings in the High Court under the Representation of the People Acts shall be assigned to the Queen's Bench Division.

(2) Subject to paragraphs (3) and (4) the jurisdiction of the High Court under the said Acts in matters relating to parliamentary and local government elections shall be exercised by a Divisional Court.

(3) Paragraph (2) shall not be construed as taking away from a single judge or a master any jurisdiction under the said Acts which, but for that paragraph, would be exercisable by a single judge or, as the case may be, by a master.

(4) Where the jurisdiction of the High Court under the said Acts is by a provision of any of those Acts made exercisable in matters relating to parliamentary elections by a single judge, that jurisdiction in matters relating to local government elections shall also be exercisable by a single judge.

(5) An originating summons by which any application relating to parliamentary or local government elections is made shall be in Form No 10 in Appendix A.

**Ord 94, r 6 Appeal to High Court where Court's decision is final**

6.—(1) This rule applies to an appeal to the High Court under any of the following enactments, namely—
(a) section 9 of the Architects (Registration) Act 1931;
(b) section 82(3) and 83(2) of the Medicines Act 1968;
(c) section 12(3) of the Legal Aid Act 1974;
(d) section 13 of the Nurses, Midwives and Health Visitors Act 1979;
(e) section 10 of the Pharmacy Act 1954;
(f) [*Revoked*];
(g) [*Revoked*];
(h) section 38(3) of the Legal Aid Act 1974.

(2) Every appeal to which this rule applies must be supported by affidavit and, if the Court so directs, by evidence given orally.

(3) [*Revoked.*]

(4) Order 55, rule 4(2) shall apply in relation to an appeal under the enactments mentioned in paragraph (1)(c) and (h) as if for the period of 28 days therein specified there were substituted a period of 21 days.

(5) In the case of an appeal under an enactment specified in column (1) of the following Table, the persons to be made respondents are the persons specified in relation to that enactment in column (2) of that Table and the person to be served with notice of the originating motion by which the appeal is brought is the person so specified in column (3) thereof:

| (1) *Enactment* | (2) *Respondents* | (3) *Person to be served* |
|---|---|---|
| Architects (Registration) Act 1931, s 9 | The Architects' Registration Council of the United Kingdom | The registrar of the Council |
| Medicines Act 1968, s 82(3) and s 83(2) | The Pharmaceutical Society of Great Britain | The registrar of the Society |
| Legal Aid Act, 1974, s 12 | The appropriate Panel (Complaints) Tribunal set up under para 29 of the Legal Aid Scheme, 1950 | The clerk of the appropriate tribunal |
| Nurses, Midwives and Health Visitors Act, 1979, s 13 | The United Kingdom Council for Nursing, Midwifery and Health Visiting | The registrar of the Council |
| Pharmacy Act, 1954, s 10 | The Pharmaceutical Society of Great Britain | The registrar of the Society |
| Legal Aid 1974, s 38(2) | The appropriate tribunal set up under rule 2 of the Legal Aid in Criminal Cases (Complaints Tribunal) Rules 1968 | The clerk of the appropriate tribunal |

**Ord 94, r 7 Reference of question of law by Agricultural Land Tribunal**

7.—(1) Any question of law referred to the High Court by an Agricultural Land Tribunal under section 6 of the Agriculture (Miscellaneous Provisions) Act 1954, shall be referred by way of case stated by the Tribunal.

(2) The notice of the originating motion by which an application is made to the Court for an order under the said section 6 directing such a Tribunal to refer a question of law to the Court, and the notice of the originating motion by which an application is made to the Court to determine a question of law so referred, must, where the proceedings before the Tribunal arose on an application under section 4 of the Agriculture Act, 1958, be served on the authority having power to enforce the statutory requirement specified in the application as well as on every other party to those proceedings and on the secretary of the Tribunal.

(3) Where in accordance with the provisions of this rules notice of an originating motion is served on the authority mentioned in paragraph (2) that authority shall be entitled to appear and be heard in the proceedings on the motion.

**Ord 94, r 8 Tribunals and Inquiries Act 1971: appeal from tribunal**

8.—(1) A person who was a party to proceedings before any such tribunal as is mentioned in section 13(1) of the Tribunals and Inquiries Act 1971, and is dissatisfied in point of law with the decision of the tribunal may appeal to the High Court.

(2) Order 55, rule 4(1)(b) shall apply in relation to such an appeal as if for the reference to the chairman of a tribunal there were substituted—

(a) in the case of a tribunal which has no chairman or member who acts as a chairman, a reference to the member or members of the tribunal, and

(b) in the case of any such tribunal as is specified in paragraph 10 of Schedule 1 to the said Act of 1971, a reference to the secretary of the tribunal.

(3) Where such an appeal is against the decision of—

(a) the tribunal constituted under section 46 of the National Health Service Act 1977, or

(b) a tribunal established under section 128 of the Employment Protection (Consolidation) Act 1978,

Order 55, rule 4(2) shall apply in relation to the appeal as if for the period of 28 days therein specified there were substituted, in the case of the tribunal mentioned in sub-paragraph (a) a period of 14 days and, in the case of a tribunal mentioned in sub-paragraph (b) a period of 42 days.

### Ord 94, r 9 Tribunals and Inquiries Act 1971: case stated by tribunal

9.—(1) Any such tribunal as is mentioned in section 13(1) of the Tribunal and Inquiries Act 1971, may, of its own motion or at the request of any party to proceedings before it, state in the course of proceedings before it in the form of a special case for the decision of the High Court any question of law arising in the proceedings.

(2) Any party to proceedings before any such tribunal who is aggrieved by the tribunal's refusal to state such a case may apply to the High Court for an order directing the tribunal to do so.

(3) A case stated by any such tribunal which has no chairman or member who acts as a chairman must be signed by the member or members of the tribunal.

### Ord 94, r 9A Appeal from and case stated by industrial tribunal

9A. [*Revoked by RSC (Amendment No 3) 1977 (SI 1977 No 1995).*]

### Ord 94, r 10 Tribunals and Inquiries Act 1971: appeal from Minister of Transport

10.—(1) A person who is dissatisfied in point of law with a decision of the Secretary of State on such an appeal as is mentioned in section 13(5) of the Tribunals and Inquiries Act 1971, and had, or if aggrieved would have had, a right to appeal to that Secretary of State, whether or not he exercised that right, may appeal to the High Court.

(2) The persons to be served with notice of the originating motion by which such an appeal is brought are the Secretary of State and every person who had, or if aggrieved would have had, a right to appeal to the Secretary of State.

(3) The Court hearing the appeal may remit the matter to the Secretary of State to the extent necessary to enable him to provide the Court with such further information in connection with the matter as the Court may direct.

(4) If the Court is of opinion that the decision appealed against was erroneous in point of law, it shall not set aside or vary that decision but shall remit the matter to the Minister with the opinion of the Court for rehearing and determination by him.

(5) Order 55, rule 7(5) shall not apply in relation to the appeal.

### Ord 94, r 10A Consumer Credit Act 1974: appeal from Secretary of State

10A.—(1) A person who is dissatisfied in point of law with a decision of the Secretary of State on an appeal under section 41 of the Consumer Credit Act 1974 from a determination of the Director General of Fair Trading and had a right to appeal to the Secretary of State, whether or not he exercised that right, may appeal to the High Court.

(2) The persons to be served with notice of the originating motion by which such an appeal is brought are the Secretary of State and, where the appeal is by a licensee under a group licence against compulsory variation, suspension or revocation of that licence, the original applicant, if any; but the Court may in any case direct that the notice be served on any other person.

(3) The Court hearing the appeal may remit the matter to the Secretary of State to the extent necessary to enable him to provide the Court with such further information in connection with the matter as the Court may direct.

(4) If the Court is of the opinion that the decision appealed against was erroneous in point of law, it shall not set aside or vary that decision but shall remit the matter to the Secretary of State with the opinion of the Court for hearing and determination by him.

(5) Order 55, rule 7(5) shall not apply in relation to the appeal.

### Ord 94, r 11 Case stated by Mental Health Review Tribunal

11.—(1) In this rule 'the Act' means the Mental Health Act 1983.

(2) The reference in paragraph (3) to a party to proceedings before a Mental Health

Review Tribunal, and the references in Order 56, rules 8(1), 9(2) and 10 to a party to proceedings shall be construed as references to—

(a) the person who initiated the proceedings; and

(b) any person to whom, in accordance with rules made under section 78 of the Act, the Tribunal sent notice of the application or reference or a request instead of notice of reference.

(3) A party to proceedings before a Mental Health Review Tribunal shall not be entitled to apply to the High Court for an order under section 78(8) of the Act directing the Tribunal to state a case for determination by the Court unless—

(a) within 21 days after the decision of the Tribunal was communicated to him in accordance with rules made under section 78 of the Act he made a written request to the Tribunal to state a case, and

(b) either the Tribunal failed to comply with the last-mentioned request within 21 days after it was made or the Tribunal refused to comply with it.

(4) The period for entry of the originating motion by which an application to the Court for such an order as is mentioned in paragraph (3) is made, and for service of notice thereof, shall be—

(a) where the Tribunal refused the applicant's request to state a case, 14 days after receipt by the applicant of notice of the refusal of his request;

(b) where the Tribunal failed to comply with that request within the period mentioned in paragraph (3)(b) 14 days after the expiration of that period.

(5) A Mental Health Review Tribunal by whom a case is stated shall be entitled to appear and be heard in the proceedings for the determination of the case.

(6) If the Court is of opinion that any decision of such a Tribunal on the question of law raised by the case was erroneous, the Court may give any direction which the Tribunal ought to have given under Part V of the Act.

## Ord 94, r 12 Applications for leave under section 289(6) of the Town and Country Planning Act 1990 and section 65(5) of the Planning (Listed Buildings and Conservation Areas) Act 1990

12.—(1) An application for leave to appeal to the High Court under section 289 of the Town and Country Planning Act 1990 or section 65 of the Planning (Listed Buildings and Conservation Areas) Act 1990 shall be made within 28 days after the date on which notice of the decision was given to the applicant.

(2) An application shall—

(a) include, where necessary, any application to extend the time for applying,

(b) be in writing setting out the reasons why leave should be granted, and if the time for applying has expired, the reasons why the application was not made within that time,

(c) be made by filing it in the Crown Office together with the decision, a draft originating notice of motion, and an affidavit verifying any facts relied on,

(d) before being filed under sub-paragraph (c), be served together with the draft originating notice of motion and a copy of the affidavit to be filed with the application, upon the persons who are referred to in rule 13(5), and

(e) be accompanied by an affidavit giving the names and addresses of, and the places and dates of service on, all persons who have been served with the application and, if any person who ought to be served has not been served, the affidavit must state that fact and the reason for it.

(3) An application shall be heard—

(a) by a single judge sitting in open court;

(b) unless the Court otherwise orders, not less than 21 days after it was filed at the Crown Office.

Any person served with the application shall be entitled to appear and be heard.

(4) If on the hearing of an application the Court is of opinion that any person who ought to have been served has not been served, the Court may adjourn the hearing on such terms (if any) as it may direct in order that the application may be served on that person.

(5) If the Court grants leave—

(a) it may impose such terms as to costs and as to giving security as it thinks fit;

(b) it may give directions; and

(c) the originating notice of motion by which the appeal is to be brought shall be served and entered within 7 days of the grant.

(6) Any respondent who intends to use an affidavit at the hearing shall file it in the Crown Office and serve a copy thereof on the applicant as soon as is practicable and in any event, unless the Court otherwise allows, at least 2 days before the hearing.

The Court may allow the applicant to use a further affidavit.

## Ord 94, r 13 Proceedings under sections 289 and 290 of the Town and Country Planning Act 1990 and under section 65 of the Planning (Listed Buildings and Conservation Areas) Act 1990

13.—(1) In this rule a reference to 'section 65' is a reference to section 65 of the Planning (Listed Buildings and Conservation Areas) Act 1990, but, save as aforesaid, a reference to a section by number is a reference to the section so numbered in the Town and Country Planning Act 1990.

(2) An appeal shall lie to the High Court on a point of law against a decision of the Secretary of State under subsection (1) or (2) of section 289 or under subsection (1) of section 65 at the instance of any person or authority entitled to appeal under any of those subsections respectively.

(3) In the case of a decision to which section 290 applies, the person who made the application to which the decision relates, or the local planning authority, if dissatisfied with the decision in point of law, may appeal against the decision to the High Court.

(4) Any appeal under section 289(1) or (2), section 65(1) or section 290, and any case stated under section 289(3) or section 65(2), shall be heard and determined by a single judge unless the Court directs that the matter shall be heard and determined by a Divisional Court.

(5) The persons to be served with notice of the originating motion by which an appeal to the High Court is brought by virtue of section 289(1) or (2), section 65(1) or section 290 are—

(a) the Secretary of State;

(b) the local planning authority who served the notice or gave the decision, as the case may be, or, where the appeal is brought by that authority, the appellant or applicant in the proceedings in which the decision appealed against was given;

(c) in the case of an appeal brought by virtue of section 289(1) or section 65(1), any other person having an interest in the land to which the notice relates, and;

(d) in the case of an appeal brought by virtue of section 289(2), any other person on whom the notice to which those proceedings related was served.

(6) The Court hearing any such appeal may remit the matter to the Secretary of State to the extent necessary to enable him to provide the Court with such further information in connection with the matter as the Court may direct.

(7) Where the Court is of opinion that the decision appealed against was erroneous in point of law, it shall not set aside or vary that decision but shall remit the matter to the Secretary of State with the opinion of the Court for re-hearing and determination by him.

(8) Order 55, rule 7(5) shall not apply in relation to any such appeal.

(9) The Court may give directions as to the exercise, until an appeal brought by virtue of section 289(1) is finally concluded and any re-hearing and determination by the Secretary of State has taken place, of the power to serve, and institute proceedings (including criminal proceedings) concerning—

(a) a stop notice under section 183, and;

(b) a breach of condition notice under section 187A.

**Ord 94, r 14 Applications under section 13, Coroners Act 1988**

14.—(1) Any application under section 13 of the Coroners Act 1988 shall be heard and determined by a Divisional Court.

(2) The application must be made by originating motion and, without prejudice to Order 8, rule 3(2), the notice of such motion must state the grounds of the application and, unless the application is made by the Attorney General, shall be accompanied by his fiat.

(3) Notice of the motion must be entered in the Crown Office and served upon all persons directly affected by the application within six weeks after the grant of the fiat.

**Ord 94, r 15 Applications under section 42, Supreme Court Act 1981**

15.—(1) Every application to the High Court by the Attorney General under section 42 of the Supreme Court Act 1981 shall be heard and determined by a Divisional Court.

(2) The application must be made by originating motion, notice of which, together with an affidavit in support, shall be filed in the Crown Office and served on the person against whom the order is sought.

## 3 Procedural table for judicial review

| *Procedure* | *RSC and/or Statute* | *Page no.* |
|---|---|---|
| A. APPLICATION FOR LEAVE | | |
| *(i) Time limits*<br>Applications must be made promptly and in any event within *three months* from the date when grounds for the application first arose. | Ord 53, r 4 | 133 |
| The Court may extend time if it considers that there is good reason to do so. The grounds for such an extension should be set out in the supporting affidavit. | | |
| Where there has been *undue delay* in making the application the Court may refuse to grant leave if it considers that the granting of the relief sought would be likely to cause substantial hardship to, or substantially prejudice the rights of, any person or would be detrimental to good administration. | Supreme Court Act 1981, s 31(6) | 209 |
| *(ii) Locus standi*<br>The Court must not grant leave unless it considers that the applicant has *sufficient interest* in the matter to which the application relates. | Ord 53, r 3(7) | 97 |
| *(iii) Civil cases*<br>Notice of application in Form 86A, Affidavit(s) in support, Index of documents } filed in Crown Office | Ord 53, r 3(2) | 140 |
| If no request for hearing in notice of application then:<br>High Court judge considers the application by reading the papers in private.<br>The result is notified by service on the applicant of the judge's order by the Crown Office. | Ord 53, r 3(3) | |
| If refused or granted on terms to which objection is taken:<br>Application may be renewed ex parte to a single judge in open court (the usual method) or, if the Court directs, to a Divisional Court of the Queen's Bench Division by lodging notice of renewal in Form 86B in the Crown Office within ten days of service of the judge's order. | Ord 53, r 3(5) | |
| If refused or granted on terms to which objection is taken:<br>Appeal lies to Court of Appeal without leave | Ord 59 | 176 |
| If hearing is requested in notice of application then:<br>High Court judge considers the application at a hearing ex parte which may be in chambers or in open court.<br>Judge's order is served by Crown Office on applicant. | Ord 53, r 3(3) | 142 |
| If refused:<br>Appeal lies to Court of Appeal without leave. | Ord 59 | 176 |

| *Procedure* | *RSC and/or Statute* | *Page no.* |
|---|---|---|
| Notice of application in Form 86A<br>Affidavit(s) in support<br>Index of documents } *(iv) Criminal cases* filed in Crown Office | Ord 63, r 3(2) | 140 |
| If no request for hearing in notice of application then:<br>High Court judge considers the application by reading the papers in private.<br>Result is notified by service on the applicant of the judge's order by the Crown Office. | Ord 53, r 3(3) | |
| If refused or granted on terms to which objection is taken:<br>Application may be renewed ex parte to a Divisional Court of the Queen's Bench Division in open court by lodging a notice of renewal in Form 86B in the Crown Office within ten days of service of the judge's order. | Ord 53, r 3(4) | |
| If request for hearing in notice of application then:<br>High Court judge considers the application at a hearing which may be in chambers or open court.<br>Judge's order is served by Crown Office on applicant. | Ord 53, r 3(3) | |
| If refused or granted on terms to which objection is taken:<br>Application may be renewed to a Divisional Court of the Queen's Bench Division in open court by lodging notice of intention to renew in Form 86B in the Crown Office within ten days of service of judge's order. | Ord 53, r 3(4) | |
| If refused or granted on terms to which objection is taken:<br>Appeal lies to House of Lords with leave. | Supreme Court Act 1981, s 18(1)(a) and Administration of Justice Act 1960, s 1 | 177 |
| If leave is granted: | | |
| B. SETTING ASIDE OF LEAVE | | |
| If leave has been granted ex parte:<br>Application to set aside may be made to the Court which granted leave ie to the Divisional Court or to a single judge of the High Court as appropriate. | | 177 |
| If leave granted inter partes:<br>Appeal is to the Court of Appeal without leave. | Ord 59 | 177 |
| C. IF LEAVE IS GRANTED | | |
| *(i) Criminal matters*<br>Application to Divisional Court of Queen's Bench Division by originating motion | Ord 53, r 5(1) | 151 |

| *Procedure* | *RSC and/or Statute* | *Page no.* |
|---|---|---|
| *(ii) Civil matters* | | |
| Application to single judge in open court by originating motion (the usual method); | Ord 53, r 5(1) | 152 |
| Unless the Court directs that the application is to be by (i) originating summons to judge in chambers or (ii) originating motion to Divisional Court of Queen's Bench Division. | | |
| **D. SERVICE** | | |
| *(i) Service of proceedings* | | |
| The motion or summons together with copies of the statement in support of the application for leave contained in the notice of application for leave must be served on all persons directly affected and on the clerk or registrar of any lower court concerned and on any lower judge to whose conduct object is to be made. | Ord 53, r 5(2)<br>Ord 53, r 6(1) | 152 |
| The notice of motion or summons must be served at least ten days before the hearing date. The Court may abridge or extend this time. | Ord 53, r 5(4) | |
| An affidavit of service must be filed in the Crown Office before the motion or summons is entered for hearing. | Ord 53, r 5(6) | 154 |
| A motion must be entered for hearing within 14 days after the granting of leave—service must therefore have been effected within that time also. | Ord 53, r 5(5) | |
| *(ii) Service of affidavits* | | |
| Any respondent who intends to use an affidavit at the hearing must file it in the Crown Office as soon as practicable and in any event within 56 days after service of the notice of motion or summons and the accompanying copy of the applicant's statement. The Court may abridge or extend time. | Ord 53, r 6(4)+ Practice Note 1989 | 155 |
| Each party to an application must supply to every other party on demand and on payment of the proper charges copies of every affidavit which he proposes to use at the hearing, including, in the case of an applicant, the affidavit in support of application for leave. As a matter of practice all affidavits are normally served on other parties as a matter of course. | Ord 53, r 6(5) | |
| If an applicant intends to ask to be allowed to use further affidavits he must give notice of his intention to every other party. The application to use further affidavits may be made at the hearing of the application. | Ord 53, r 6(3) | |
| **E. AMENDMENTS** | | |
| If an applicant intends to ask at the hearing to be allowed to amend his statement he must give notice of his intention and of any proposed amendment to any other party. | Ord 53, r 6(3) | 155 |

| *Procedure* | *RSC and/or Statute* | *Page no.* |
|---|---|---|
| F. LODGING OF ORDERS | | |
| A copy of any order, warrant, commitment, conviction, inquisition or record the validity of which is to be questioned in an application for certiorari must be lodged in the Crown Office before the hearing of the motion or summons. It must be verified by an affidavit lodged with it in the Crown Office. | Ord 53, r 9(2) | 156 |
| G. INTERLOCUTORY APPLICATIONS | | |
| *(i) Applications* incl: Applications for interim relief, discovery, interrogatories, cross-examination of deponents and dismissals by consent. | Ord 53, r 8 | 147, 170, 204 |
| To a judge of Queen's Bench Division or to a master of Queen's Bench Division (the Master of the Crown Office). | | |
| *(ii) Interlocutory appeals from masters* To Divisional Court of Queen's Bench Division if the substantive hearing will be before that court otherwise to a single judge in chambers and in either case by notice of appeal issued within five days after the order of the master and served not less than two clear days before the day fixed for hearing the appeal. | Ord 58, r 1<br>Ord 53, r 8(2) | |
| H. MODE OF TRIAL | | |
| Applications may be made at the application for leave or afterwards for:<br>(i) in civil cases, a direction that the matter be heard by a Divisional Court rather than a single judge<br>(ii) in criminal cases, a direction that the matter be heard by a court comprising three rather than two judges<br>(iii) a hearing in chambers<br>(iv) a hearing before a judge specialised in family matters<br>(v) a direction that the matter be placed in the expedited hearing list. | | 145 |
| J. THE HEARING | | |
| Parties attend for trial on date fixed by Crown Office. Hearing before Divisional Court of Queen's Bench Division or single judge of Queen's Bench Division assigned to Crown Office List. | | |

# 4 Notice of application for leave to apply for judicial review: Form 86A

IN THE HIGH COURT OF JUSTICE QUEENS BENCH DIVISION CROWN OFFICE LIST — Crown Office Ref

NOTICE OF APPLICATION FOR LEAVE TO APPLY FOR JUDICIAL REVIEW (ORDER 53, RULE 3(2))

This form must be read together with Notes for Guidance obtainable from the Crown Office

To the Master of the Crown Office, Royal Courts of Justice, Strand, London WC2A 2LL

**The Applicant:**
Name
Address

Description

**Judgment, order, decision or other proceeding** in respect of which relief is sought, and the date thereof.

Relief Sought

Signed — Dated

Name and address of the applicant's solicitors, or, if no solicitors acting, the address for service of the applicant.

Applicant's Ref.

Telephone No.

Fax No.

GROUNDS ON WHICH RELIEF IS SOUGHT

(Include an outline of any propositions of law, supported by any authorities.)

(If there has been any delay, include the reasons here)

NOTE:
Grounds must be supported by an affidavit which verifies the facts relied on. Where grounds have been settled by Counsel they must be signed by Counsel.

## 5 Notice of renewal: Form 86B

**IN THE HIGH COURT OF JUSTICE**

| Applicant's Ref No | Note of RENEWAL of application for leave to apply for Judicial Review | Crown Office Ref No |
|---|---|---|

To the Master of the Crown Office, Royal Courts of Justice, Strand, London WC2A 2LL

The applicant intends to renew his application for leave to apply for Judicial Review.

[*Insert here any additional grounds. If only part of an application is to be renewed, state which part*]

Signed: Date:

| Received in the Crown Office | NOTE: This notice must be lodged in the Crown Office within 21 days* of the service on the applicant or his solicitor of notice that the original application for leave has been refused. |
|---|---|

* AUTHOR'S NOTE

This form is prescribed by Rules of the Supreme Court (Amendment No 4) Order 1980 (SI 1980/2000). The form contained in the Statutory Instrument refers to 21 days for lodging Form 86B even though Ord 53, r 3(5) as amended by the same SI provides for a time limit of ten days. The Form 86B issued by the Crown Office for the use of litigants in person has been changed to refer to ten days.

## 6 Notice of motion for judicial review

In the High Court of Justice
Queen's Bench Division

In the matter of an application by [ ]
for judicial review

and

In the matter of
[*insert*: the judgment, order, decision or other matter in respect of which relief is sought together with any relevant statute]

Take Notice that pursuant to the leave of a Divisional Court of the Queen's Bench Division [*or* the Honourable Mr Justice ] given on the Court will be moved as soon as counsel can be heard on the applicant's behalf for an order for relief in the terms, and on the grounds, set out in Form 86A, herewith.

And that the costs of and occasioned by this motion be* [paid by the Respondent to the Applicant to be taxed if not agreed].

And take notice that on the hearing of this motion the applicant will use the affidavit and exhibits copies of which accompany this notice.

*[And also take notice that the Divisional Court of the Queen's Bench Division [*or* the Honourable Mr Justice ] by order dated directed that all proceedings in* [*or* on] the said be stayed until after the hearing of this motion or further order.]

Dated the day of 19 .

To
solicitor for

(Signed)
of
solicitor for

---

IMPORTANT

Any respondent who intends to use an affidavit at the hearing should inform the Crown Office of his intention within 10 days of the service of this notice. Any such affidavit must be filed in the Crown Office as soon as practicable and in any event within 21 days of service.

*as applicable.

NOTE:
This form is prescribed by Rules of the Supreme Court (Amendment No 4) Order 1980 (SI 1980/2000).

Although cases are reported in the form eg *'R v Newtown District Council, ex p Smith'* and may be listed as such by the Court, this form is not used in pleadings.

# 7 Originating summons to judge in chambers for judicial review

In the High Court of Justice
Queen's Bench Division

In the matter of an application by [ ] for judicial review

and

In the matter of
[*insert*: the judgment, order, decision or other matter in respect of which relief is sought together with any relevant statute]

And pursuant to the leave of a Divisional Court of the Queen's Bench Division* [*or* the Honourable Mr Justice ] given on the day of and the further directions given.

Let all parties concerned attend the Judge in Chambers at the Royal Courts of Justice, London, on the day of , 19 , at o'clock in the noon, upon the hearing of an application on the part of [ ] for an order for relief in the terms, and on the grounds, set out in Form 86A, herewith.

And that the costs of and occasioned by this summons be* [paid by the Respondent to the Applicant to be taxed if not agreed].

And take notice that on the hearing of this summons the Applicant will use the affidavit and exhibits copies of which accompany this summons.

*[And also take notice that the Divisional Court of the Queen's Bench Division [*or* the Honourable Mr Justice ] by order dated directed that all proceedings in [*or* on] the said be stayed until after the hearing of this summons or further order.]

Dated the day of 19 .

To
solicitor for

(Signed)
of
solicitor for

---

IMPORTANT

Any respondent who intends to use an affidavit at the hearing should inform the Crown Office of his intention within 10 days of the service of this summons. Any such affidavit must be filed in the Crown Office as soon as practicable and in any event within 21 days of service.

*as applicable.

N.B. This form is rarely used since directions are rarely given for judicial review applications to be made by originating summons to a judge in chambers and so they proceed by way of notice of motion.

## 8 Notice of entry into Part B of the Crown Office List

Crown Office
Royal Courts of Justice
Strand
London WC2A 2LL

Telephone: 071–936 6013 or 6297
Fax: 071–936 6802 DX: 44450 STRAND

Messrs
Solicitors

Your reference:

Our reference:

Date:

Dear Sirs,

Re: ________________________________________________________________

The above matter entered Part B of the Crown Office List on

I write to inform you that the matter is likely to be listed as from . It may not be possible to give more than a day's notice of the hearing date.

It is your responsibility to notify all respondents of the likelihood of this matter being listed at short notice.

You are reminded of the need to comply with the Practice Note issued by the Lord Chief Justice on 21 July 1983 and reported at [1983] 3 All ER 33 in relation to the composition and pagination of bundles of documents. One/two paginated bundle(s) together with copies of the following documents must be lodged for the use of the Court no later than :

(a) a list of issues;
(b) a list of propositions of law to be advanced, together with the authorities relied on in support of each, with page references to passages relied on;
(c) a chronology of events, with reference to a properly paginated and indexed bundle of documents.

All copy documents in this case will be destroyed (as confidential waste) two working days after the final decision of the High Court unless a written request for the documents is received by the Crown Office within that period.

Should it be your client's intention not to proceed with this matter, you should obtain the consent of all parties to the matter being withdrawn. Such consent should indicate the terms of any agreed order that the parties would wish the Court to make and in any event should deal with the question of costs.

If there is a possibility that the case will settle, but no final agreement has been reached, you should apply by summons, forthwith, to the Master of the Crown Office to have the case stood out into Part C of the Crown Office List, see the Practice Direction issued by the Lord Chief Justice on 3 February 1987 and reported at [1987] 1 WLR 232 and [1987] 1 All ER 368.

The matter will only be taken out of the list when a notice of withdrawal/consent order with a provision for costs signed by all parties has been received in this office.

Yours faithfully,

for Head Clerk

N.B. It is the duty of the parties to notify the Crown Office of any problems that may affect the listing of the above-mentioned case (eg whether special facilities for disabled access are required).

## 9 'Active Case' letter from the Crown Office List

Crown Office
Royal Courts of Justice
Strand
London WC2A 2LL

Telephone: 071–936 6013 or 6297
Fax: 071–936 6802 DX: 44450 STRAND

Messrs
Solicitors

Your reference:

Our reference:

Date:

Dear Sirs,

I write to inform you that the case mentioned overleaf has now moved towards the top of part B of the Crown Office List and, *if you confirm that it is still active*, will be listed for hearing shortly.

IF YOU DO NOT CONFIRM THAT THIS CASE IS STILL ACTIVE, BY COMPLETING AND RETURNING THE FORM OVERLEAF *WITHIN TWO WEEKS OF THE DATE OF THIS LETTER*, THIS CASE WILL BE LISTED BEFORE THE COURT TO SHOW CAUSE AS TO WHY THIS MATTER SHOULD NOT BE STRUCK OUT FOR WANT OF PROSECUTION.

If there is a possibility that the case will settle, but no final agreement has been reached, you should apply by summons to the Master of the Crown Office to have the case stood out into part C of the Crown Office List, see the Practice Direction issued by the Lord Chief Justice on 3 February 1987 and reported at [1987] 1 WLR 232 and [1987] 1 All ER 368.

Where a case is to proceed you should ensure that there is lodged in the Crown Office, preferably at least two weeks before the date fixed for hearing, but in any event at least 3 clear working days, a document containing:

(a) a list of issues;
(b) a list of propositions of law to be advanced, together with the authorities relied on in support of each, with page references to passages relied on;
(c) a chronology of events, with reference to a properly paginated and indexed bundle of documents;
(d) a list of dramatis personae, where the number of people who feature in the documents warrants it.

The production of such a document does *not* remove the obligation to furnish the usher with a list of authorities before the morning of the day fixed for hearing.

Yours faithfully,

for Head Clerk

---

To the Master of the Crown Office
Crown Office
Royal Courts of Justice
Strand
London WC2A 2LL

CO ref: / /

Applicants ref:

Date:

---

I confirm that this matter is to proceed to hearing.
Counsel's time estimate for the hearing is ___________
Counsel's name:
Counsel's telephone number:

Signed:

## 10 Notice of entry into Part D of the Crown Office List

Crown Office
Royal Courts of Justice
Strand
London WC2A 2LL

Telephone: 071–936 6013 or 6297
Fax: 071–936 6802 DX: 44450 STRAND

Messrs
Solicitors

Your reference:

Our reference:

Date:

Dear Sirs,

THE CROWN OFFICE LIST: PART D—EXPEDITED LIST

Re: ________________________________________

Further to the Practice Direction issued by the Lord Chief Justice on 3 February 1987 and reported at [1987] 1 WLR 232, [1987] 1 All ER 368 and the Supreme Court Practice 53/1–14/41, I write to inform you that this matter has now been entered in Part D of the Crown Office List to be heard as soon as practicable by a single Judge/Divisional Court.

A hearing date will be fixed shortly. Given that this will be the first open date available, no undertaking can be given that the wishes of applicants, respondents, their solicitors or counsel will be accommodated. It may mean that parties are unable to be represented by counsel of their first choice. It should be remembered that cases listed in the Crown Office List take precedence, so far as the attendance of counsel is concerned, over cases listed for hearing in the Crown Court unless the Divisional Court or a Judge hearing cases in the Crown Office List otherwise directs.

You are reminded of the need to comply with the Practice Note issued by the Lord Chief Justice on 21 July 1983 and reported at [1983] 3 All ER 33 in relation to the composition and pagination of bundles of documents. If the case is to be listed before a Divisional Court two paginated bundles will be required.

It is the responsibility of an applicant or his solicitors to forward a copy of this letter to (1) the clerk to counsel instructed by the applicant and (2) any respondent or interested party or his solicitor who should in turn inform the clerk to counsel instructed by him. It is the responsibility of counsel's clerks to inform the Crown Office, in writing, of counsel's time estimates for the whole case, including any immediate delivery of judgment. This must be done as soon as possible on receipt of a copy of this letter. Any alteration in time estimate must be notified promptly, in writing.

Finally, you should ensure that there is lodged in the Crown Office, preferably at least two weeks before the hearing date, but in any event at least three clear working days, a document containing:

(a) a list of issues;
(b) a list of propositions of law to be advanced, together with the authorities relied on in support of each, with page references to passages relied on;
(c) a chronology of events, with reference to a properly paginated and indexed bundle of documents;
(d) a list of dramatis personae, where the number of people who feature in the documents warrants it.

The production of such a document does *not* remove the obligation to furnish the usher with a list of authorities before the morning of the day fixed for hearing.

Two copies of this document will be required where the matter is to be heard by a Divisional Court.

Yours faithfully,

for Head Clerk

## 11 Notice of hearing letter

Crown Office
Royal Courts of Justice
Strand
London WC2A 2LL

Telephone: 071–936 6013 or 6297
Fax: 071–936 6802 DX: 44450 STRAND

Messrs
Solicitors

Your reference:

Our reference:

Date:

Dear Sirs,

Re:

I write to inform you that the above matter has been listed for hearing on

You must notify the respondents and all interested parties of this date and instruct counsel to attend accordingly.

You are reminded of the need to comply with the Practice Note issued by the Lord Chief Justice on 21 July 1983 and reported at [1983] 3 All ER 33 in relation to the composition and pagination of bundles of documents. The case stated has already been lodged, however, two copies of the following documents must be lodged no later than

(a) a list of issues;
(b) a list of propositions of law to be advanced, together with the authorities relied on in support of each, with page references to passages relied on;
(c) a chronology of events, with reference to a properly paginated and indexed bundle of documents;
(d) a list of dramatis personae, where the number of people who feature in the documents warrants it.

All copy documents in this case will be destroyed (as confidential waste) two working days after the final decision of the High Court unless a written request for the documents is received by the Crown Office within that period.

Should it be your client's intention not to proceed with this matter, you should obtain the consent of all parties to the matter being withdrawn. Such consent should indicate the terms of any agreed order that the parties would wish the Court to make and in any event should deal with the question of costs.

If there is a possibility that the case will settle, but no final agreement has been reached, you should apply by summons, forthwith, to the Master of the Crown Office to have the case stood out into Part C of the Crown Office List, see the Practice Direction issued by the Lord Chief Justice on 3 February 1987 and reported at [1987] 1 WLR 232 and [1987] 1 All ER 368.

The matter will only be taken out of the list when a notice of withdrawal/consent order with a provision for costs signed by all parties has been received in this office.

Yours faithfully,

Listing Officer

NB: It is the duty of the parties to notify the Crown Office of any problems that may affect the listing of the above-mentioned case (eg whether special facilities for disabled access are required).

## 12 Illustration: application by L. J. Silver for judicial review of decisions by the Meadows District Council

### (i) Details of application for leave to be provided in statement in the form of Form 86A

Judgment, order, decision or other proceeding in respect of which relief is sought:

(i) The decision of Meadows District Council by or pursuant to the decision of its Social Services Committee on the 14th day of March 1992:

(a) that the Applicant is not in priority need within the meaning of section 11(1) of the Invalid Support Act 1981; and

(b) to levy a charge of £100 per annum of the Applicant for the use of a crutch supplied pursuant to section 2 of the said Act.

(ii) The decision of Meadows District Council by or pursuant to the decision of its Social Services Committee on the 3rd day of July 1992 to enforce the charge referred to above.

Relief sought:

(i) An Order of Certiorari quashing the decisions of the Meadows District Council set out above.

(ii) A Declaration that the Applicant is in priority need within the meaning of section 11(1) of the Invalid Support Act 1981.

(iii) An Order of Mandamus directed to the Meadows District Council requiring it to discharge its statutory duty under section 2 of the Invalid Support Act 1981 by supplying and/or continuing to supply to the applicant a crutch without charge.

(iv) An Order restraining the Meadows District Council from removing or attempting to remove from the Applicant the crutch supplied by it to the Applicant.

(v) An order restraining the Meadows District Council from taking any steps to enforce or attempt to enforce any charge, levy or debt against the Applicant in respect of any crutch supplied by it to the Applicant.

Grounds:

(i) The Meadows District Council ('the MDC') is under a mandatory statutory duty by virtue of section 2 of the Invalid Support Act 1981 ('the 1981 Act') to provide crutches to any persons who apply in the prescribed form and who satisfy the MDC that they require a crutch on medical grounds.

(ii) By section 11 of the 1981 Act the MDC are empowered to impose a reasonable charge for the supply of crutches otherwise than to applicants who the MDC are satisfied are in priority need.

(iii) By section 11(5) of the 1981 Act persons in priority need are defined as including persons who have lost one or more lower limbs and have retired from full-time employment.

(iv) In June of 1990 the Applicant, who was born on 20 January 1930, was involved in a motor accident as a result of which his left leg was amputated above the knee. As a result of his injury the Applicant was unable to continue his previous employment as a boilermaker and, therefore, retired from his job in November of 1990. He was then aged 60. The Applicant has not worked since his retirement and receives a weekly pension under an early retirement scheme set up by his former employers.

(v) In December of 1990 the Applicant applied to the MDC for the provision of a crutch under section 2 of the 1981 Act. In January of 1991 the MDC supplied the Applicant with a crutch without charge. It has never been disputed that the Applicant requires a crutch on medical grounds.

(vi) By virtue of his injury and his retirement the Applicant is a person in priority need within the meaning of section 11(5) of the 1981 Act.

(vii) By a letter dated 16 March 1992 the MDC wrote to the Applicant stating that the Council's Social Services Committee had undertaken a review of the provision of crutches by the Council under section 2 of the 1981 Act and at the Committee Meeting of 14 March 1992 had decided that since the Applicant was under the normal retirement age of 65 he could still be expected to undertake full-time work and would, therefore, not be treated as having retired from full-time employment within the meaning of section 11 of the 1981 Act. The letter further stated that the Council were imposing a charge for the use of the crutch of £100 per year.

(viii) The Applicant has not paid the charge of £100 per year to the MDC.

(ix) By a letter dated 3 July 1992 the MDC wrote to the Applicant stating that if the charge of £100 was not paid within 14 days the MDC would take steps to repossess the crutch or would commence proceedings for enforcement of the charge as a civil debt in the Meadows Magistrates' Court.

(x) The MDC has at all times since the Applicant's application for a crutch in December of 1990 had full knowledge of the Applicant's injury and employment position and cannot properly have been other than satisfied that he is a person in priority need. In these circumstances the MDC has no power to impose a charge for the supply of a crutch to the Applicant and the threats to repossess the crutch and/or to enforce the charge are wrongful and in derogation of the performance of the duties of the MDC under section 2 of the 1981 Act.

(xi) Since May of 1992 the Applicant has been in correspondence with the MDC through the Meadows Citizens Advice Bureau and his solicitors in an effort to reach agreement but the MDC has refused to alter its decision. It was only by a letter dated 6 September 1992 that the MDC confirmed that they would not alter their decision and thus that the Applicant needed to commence this Application. The Applicant immediately applied for Legal Aid and once that application was granted on 24 October 1992 this Application was commenced without delay.

Dated 31 October 1992

**(ii) Notice of motion**

In the High Court of Justice
Queen's Bench Division

In the Matter of
an application by Lionel James Silver for judicial review

and

In the matter of decisions of the Meadows District Council dated the 14th day of March 1984 and 3rd day of July 1992

and

In the Matter of the Invalid Support Act 1981

Take Notice that pursuant to the leave of the Honourable Mr Justice Wigg given on the 7th day of November 1992 the Court will be moved as soon as Counsel can be heard on the Applicant's behalf for an order for relief in the terms, and on the Grounds set out in Form 86A, herewith.

And that the costs of and occasioned by this Motion be paid by the Respondent to the Applicant to be taxed if not agreed.

And take notice that on the hearing of this Motion the Applicant will use the affidavit and exhibits copies of which accompany this notice.

Dated the 9th day of November 1992

To Mr J. R. Brown
Solicitor to the Meadows District Council

Faith, Hope, Charity & Co
of 21 The High Street
Meadows-under-Thumb
Loamshire.
Solicitors for the Applicant

---

**IMPORTANT**

Any respondent who intends to use an affidavit at the hearing should inform the Crown Office of his intention within 10 days of the service of this notice. Any such affidavit must be filed in the Crown Office as soon as practicable and in any event within 21 days of service.

# Index